Place Matters

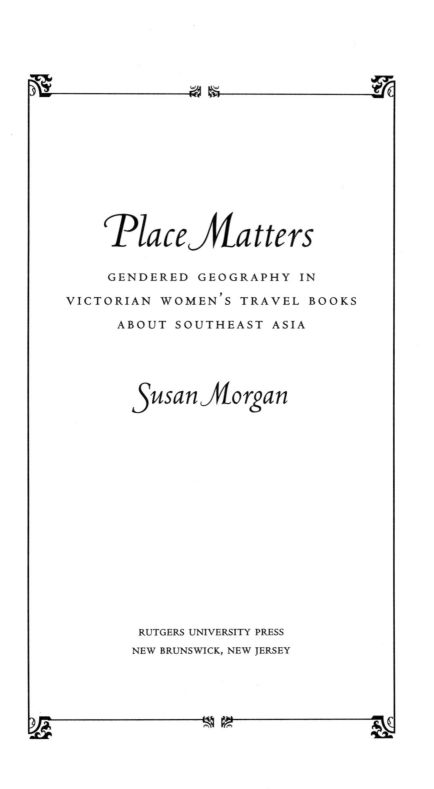

Place Matters

GENDERED GEOGRAPHY IN
VICTORIAN WOMEN'S TRAVEL BOOKS
ABOUT SOUTHEAST ASIA

Susan Morgan

RUTGERS UNIVERSITY PRESS
NEW BRUNSWICK, NEW JERSEY

LIBRARY OF CONGRESS CATALOGING-IN-PUBLICATION DATA

Morgan, Susan, 1943–

    Place matters : gendered geography in Victorian women's travel books about Southeast Asia / Susan Morgan.

    p.   cm.

    Includes bibliographical references and index.

    ISBN 0-8135-2248-x (cloth : alk. paper). —ISBN 0-8135-2249-8 (pbk. : alk. paper)

    1. Travelers' writings, English—History and criticism.   2. English prose literature—Women authors—History and criticism.   3. Women travelers—Asia, Southeastern—History— 19th century—Historiography.   4. British—Travel—Asia, Southeastern—History—19th century—Historiography.   5. Feminism and literature—Asia, Southeastern—History—19th century.   6. English prose literature—19th century—History and criticism.   7. Women and literature—Great Britain—History—19th century.   I. Title.

PR788.T72M67 1996   95-21408

820.9'355—dc20   CIP

BRITISH CATALOGING-IN-PUBLICATION INFORMATION AVAILABLE

Interior design and composition by Martin-Waterman Associates

Published by Rutgers University Press, New Brunswick, New Jersey

To Suzanne Faulds and Frederic Stewart,
for the joy in their smiles as they stood in the woods and as they sat
on the deck of a boat.

To Seneca Suzanne and Ethan Camber Sky,
for the joy in their smiles as they stood in the woods and as they sat
on the deck of a boat.

ᴤ Contents ᴥ

ACKNOWLEDGMENTS   ix

PART ONE. *Relocating*

Chapter 1. Place Matters   1
Chapter 2. Port of Entry: Colonial Singapore   31

PART TWO. *Non-British Colonies and the Naturalists*

Chapter 3. The Holy Land of Victorian Science: 51
     Anna Forbes, with Henry Forbes and
     Alfred Russel Wallace in the Eastern
     Archipelago
Chapter 4. Botany and Marianne North: Painting   91
     "A Garland about the Earth"

PART THREE. *British Colonies: A Crown Property and a*
Private Property

Chapter 5. The Company as the Country: On the   135
     Malay Peninsula with Isabella Bird and
     Emily Innes
Chapter 6. "One's Own State": Margaret Brooke,   177
     Harriette McDougall, and Sarawak

PART FOUR. *An Uncolonized State: Women in*
"The Kingdom of the Free"

Chapter 7. Anna Leonowens: Women Talking in the   221
     Royal Harem of Siam

PART FIVE. *Transit Lounge*

Chapter 8. Looking Behind and Ahead   269

NOTES   279
SELECTED BIBLIOGRAPHY   307
INDEX   333

﷽ *Acknowledgments* ﷽

T he sources of help I have received in writing this book are legion. There is Vassar College, which granted me the sabbatical leave during which I first went to Southeast Asia, and Barbara Page at Vassar, who reminded me before I went about the original writings of the woman featured in *Anna and the King of Siam*. There is the Huntington Library, which helped to fund my reading of the letters between Annie Fields and Anna Leonowens. At the Huntington I found a group of generous scholars, including Grace Ioppolo, Karen Langlois, Luther Luedtke, Karen Lystra, Barry Menikoff, Joseph Prabhu, and Betsy Truax, all of whom offered encouragement and information. At the University of Southern California, Peter Manning and Tim Gustafson helped me to continue my research at the Huntington. I found another group of warm and informative scholars, including Teresa Mangum, Deborah Morse, Richard Stein, Christine Thompson, Anca Vlasopolos, and Joyce Zonana, at the Interdisciplinary Nineteenth-Century Studies meetings. My title owes a debt both to Richard Stein and to the work of Cornel West.

Nancy Armstrong and Thaïs Morgan were early supporters of the project. Nancy published my first piece on the topic when she was a guest editor at *Genre*. Thaïs requested an essay for a critical book she edited. I was able to bring out editions of two of the travel books through the commitment and enduring enthusiasm of Jerome McGann, general editor of the Victorian Literature and Culture Series at the University of Virginia and old friend, as well as through the knowledge and patience of Nancy Essig, director of the through the knowledge and patience of Nancy Essig, director of the University Press of Virginia. At Cornell University, David Wyatt proved a generous source for checking my information on nine-teenth-century Siam. Usana Lelanuja has been a constant friend to me and in the process helped me to understand some of the cultural issues for women in Thailand. Geraldine Heng and Janadas Devan also offered friendship, along with a notable patience in introducing me to a range of perspectives on Singapore. Lucy and Larry Fisher, also friends made in the long course of thinking about this book, have done what they could to help me become more knowledgeable about Indonesia. My work has been continually supported by Rob Polhemus, who also gave me the great gift of believing in it. Leslie Mitchner, my editor, has been enthusiastic, understanding, and wittily patient for years. The NEH has also supported the project, providing a one-year fellowship which gave me the time to finish writing the manuscript.

In recent years I have received crucial support for the project from Miami University of Ohio, in the form of a summer research grant and grants for travel. The support at Miami has been much more pervasive than money. Barry Chabot has been continually encouraging in his confidence in the project. Encountering me in one of my disheartened moments in the xerox room, Paul Anderson offered an apt suggestion. Bill Wortman solved many research problems. Jackie Hearns and Leta Carmichael have been consistently agreeable in helping me get materials. Brit Harwood has offered real interest in the historical and theoretical problematics of the book. Susan Jarrett has given me many thoughtful hours discussing postcolonial and gender topics. Kate McCullough and Laura Mandell have read several parts of the manuscript and provided invaluable comments. So too have Fran Dolan and Mary Jean Corbett. Among many occasions, I think particularly of one evening when they offered me superb suggestions about the introductory chapter. Mary Jean, herself working with Victorian and colonial materials, has been an extraordinarily generous source of many ideas that have notably improved the book. As the reader of the manu-script, Nancy Paxton contributed suggestions with such perceptiveness and care that her advice greatly improved the work. My gratitude to those I have mentioned and to so many more.

Then there is the taxi driver in Penang who, when I told him I was going to see some old colonial photographs, offered me through his own family history an analysis of the relations between the British and the various kinds of Chinese in colonial Penang. This account is still an inspiration to me. Khoo Su Nin, another friendly stranger in Penang, made me at home on Armenian Street. Last I mention Eric Goodman, who, along with Ethan and Seneca Goodman, is in many ways the origin and illumination of the project. All three are bound together with me in sharing the memories and affections of brief times living in Thailand and Indonesia and visiting Singapore.

—MECKLENBURG, NEW YORK

1995

PART ONE
 *Relocating*

"*All profound changes in consciousness, by their very nature, bring with them characteristic amnesias. Out of such oblivions, in specific historical circumstances, spring narratives.*"
—BENEDICT ANDERSON, *IMAGINED COMMUNITIES*

"*One law for the lion and the ox is oppression.*"
—WILLIAM BLAKE, *THE MARRIAGE OF HEAVEN AND HELL*

CHAPTER I

Place Matters

*"England. I don't believe in it anyway. . . . Just a
conspiracy of cartographers."*
—TOM STOPPARD

At least one of the many beginnings of this book was in 1984,
when I went for the first time to Southeast Asia, spending
some months in Thailand and in Bali. It seemed to me that I was
somewhat changed in those places from the identities I experience in
North America. I realized, with a joy and an unease which have
continued, that I felt comfortable in parts of Southeast Asia as I
never have in the United States. This is not to say that anyone
besides myself could easily imagine my being comfortable in Thailand or Indonesia or Singapore, a point which does not simplify my
felt sense of connection to these places. Given the constructed
nature of any personal sense of "comfort," I could plausibly, if
artificially, choose to locate the origin of these feelings (including a
startling sense of physical ease in temperatures above one hundred
degrees Farenheit) in some of the hidden ways they may repeat my
forgotten early childhood. An earlier beginning of this book may be
that I was born and lived until five years old in South Africa, a quite
literal colonial origin.

But colonial origins have their own pasts and complexities. My
first-generation Canadian parents had children and were raising
them in South Africa reluctantly, because they had been literally
trapped there by World War II. In the summer of what would turn
out to be the extremely ill-chosen year of 1939, my father left his wife
and children to run off with the uneducated daughter of a widowed

1

waitress who had emigrated to Canada trying unsuccessfully to
escape poverty in Scotland. The illicit couple got on a boat to South
Africa for what they thought would be only a few months, imagining they could escape through sheer distance what would prove to be
permanently inescapable: the storm of anger from my father's rich,
merchant-class family. The outbreak of the war bound the couple in
South Africa for the next seven years.

My being born an imperialist in one of the most visibly imperialistic countries in the twentieth-century world had everything to do
with having parents who were themselves born to colonists, but of
vastly different classes, in a particular part of the British Commonwealth. Their presence in South Africa was a result first of challenging the ideological apparatuses which in the 1930s in Vancouver,
British Columbia dictated people's familial and class relations and
then of the Second World War. That presence also reflects directly
back to some of the early twentieth-century legal history of what
was called the "British Commonwealth of Nations," specifically the
shared struggles for greater independence by two of its most politically visible members during the twenties and thirties, the Dominion
of Canada and the Union of South Africa. The 1926 and 1930
Imperial Conferences on the subject of British relinquishment of
control and the celebrated 1931 Statute of Westminster ratifying
virtual independence for most Commonwealth member nations
functioned as highly visible and recent reasons for Canadians in the
1930s to feel significant ties to South Africa.

For myself and my older sister, our natal identities as colonizers
were inseparable from issues of gender and of class, and inseparable
also from the imperial history and European politics which shaped
the international history of those places and times. The lesson of my
own history, of the complexities of the "national" origins and
"imagined community" which composed my "family," is for me
precisely the unfixed quality of identity.[1] This book is infused with,
and critically driven by, my sense of the problematic relations
between identity and location, which directed my responses to
places in and writings about Southeast Asia. This sense comes from
a lifelong awareness of the slipperiness, the dangers, and the sheer

deceit of situating, culturally and geographically, where or whom I am "from."

Much as in so many people's life histories and daily experiences, in discourse the various intersections of region, nationality, and gender compose an unsettled subject location. This premise informs the following discussion of materials and regions so far neglected in contemporary postcolonial studies: Victorian women's writings about visits in Southeast Asia. In discussing travel writings, I assume that place matters. By place I mean subjectivity as much as physical location, for both are forms of political geography. I assume that critical concepts derived from considering writings about one area of the world cannot simply be transposed to writings about another area, in some sort of global theoretical move. Nor can concepts derived from male-authored travel accounts with male narrators simply be transposed to female-authored accounts with female narrators. I assume that gender matters, that the materials with which I approach colonial cultures are discursive and that those discourses are marked by gender, not simply in terms of the gender of their authors but in terms of the narrative voices these rhetorics construct. And I assume that narrative location, in terms of reading the cultural meanings of both subject voices and geographic places, is a specific, conventionalized, and yet changing affair.

In nineteenth-century England, particularly during the second half of the century and on into the early decades of the twentieth, distinctive and quite specific imperial discourses were being written, carrying specific conventions and about specific places. Further, these conventions were gender marked. Thus I approach texts through emphasizing the formative importance and some of the complexities of place, specifically in terms of gender and of geography. Interpreting past travel literature depends on taking up the difficult hermeneutic issues of who the writer was in Europe and where he or she wrote about in Southeast Asia, as represented in their writings and also outside their writings in other available historical documents. I will be focusing primarily, though not only, on works by Anna Forbes and Marianne North on the Indian Archipelago, by Margaret Brooke and Harriette McDougall on Sarawak, by Isabella Bird and Emily Innes on British Malaya, and by Anna Leonowens on Siam. In each case I attempt to sketch an imperial history and a rhetorical framework of some other writings within which to read the strategies and representations of these texts. My emphasis throughout is that, in the politics of culture, "where" is as complex and incoherent a category as "who." As Edward Said has noted, "geography and literary history" are linked, and what links them is first of all an "elaboration of power."[2] The specifics of this commonality need to be explored. In nineteenth-century British travel narratives there was no monolithic imperialist or imperialized location and no solidly bounded identity, authorial, narrative, or geographic.

I begin, then, this discussion of some Victorian women's writings about Southeast Asia with the question of what, or where, is Southeast Asia? Southeast Asia exists in the minds and words and pictures of people.[3] Twentieth-century scholars who use the phrase tend to locate World War II as the official time Southeast Asia was named as a region, and then by Europeans and Americans.[4] As Mary Turnbull points out, "at the Quebec Conference in August 1943, the Western Allies decided to establish a separate South East Asia Command (SEAC) [under Lord Mountbatten], embracing Burma, Malaya, Sumatra and Thailand. The Potsdam Conference in July 1945 extended SEAC's responsibility to cover the rest of the Netherlands East Indies and Indochina south of the sixteenth parallel, excluding [though no longer] only northern Vietnam, the Philippines and Laos."[5] Another way to describe Southeast Asia is as the area "south of China and east of India." The name for the region long used by the Chinese and Japanese is Nanyang (the South Seas).[6] The term Southeast Asia became particularly well known to Americans during the Vietnam War. Thus it is a name conceived and spread during the twentieth century by the international policies and wars of Europeans and Americans with each other and with the countries of Japan and Vietnam.

On the other hand, there were a great many connections between the countries "south of China and east of India" well before World War II and the Quebec Conference. These connections have to do with relations among the countries themselves and between them and other nearby states, as well as states located far away. Yet even this apparent observation carries its inventions about Southeast Asia. Just "to think in terms of national histories" is to offer "a distortion of the past."[7] These geographic areas were not "nations" as we now use the word and had no "national" identifying histories until twentieth-century historians began making them by grouping analyses and events under one heading instead of another. Rather than bounded territories, the states of the nineteenth century are better demarcated as having been "political centres, with power radiating out."[8] Nineteenth-century European aggressions helped to change the notion of what a state is in Southeast Asia and to draw some of what would become the literal boundaries of nations territorially defined. In the 1940s and late 1960s those nations became defined for Europeans and Americans as "Southeast Asia." Yet it is also true that the nations were themselves making moves to define themselves regionally, specifically in economic terms. First there was ASA (Association of Southeast Asia) in 1961, and, then, more successfully and extensively, ASEAN (Association of South-East Asian Nations) was formed in 1967. That the notion of which actual countries "belong" in Southeast Asia is itself a matter of change and conflict can be read from the debates about which countries may be members of the various organizations which have been formed in the region. Economics still drives geography, since ASEAN is now a powerful force in the global economy.

One clear limit of this book is that, taking as its materials some writings by nineteenth-century British authors, it remains a study of these writings and not of the geographic areas the narratives describe. Moreover, it is consciously anachronistic to use the term Southeast Asia when speaking of places which were the literal and discursive destinations of nineteenth-century British writers. I have projected the term into the past, just as I have projected the modern notion of what constitutes a country, by applying them both to the specific hermeneutic framework of nineteenth-century British imperial expansion. I would ask readers to keep these two projections in mind during the following discussions. By Southeast Asia and its "countries" I refer to Siam (now Thailand); south of Siam, the Malay Peninsula (now Malaysia); east of Siam, what were called Cochin-China, Laos, Vietnam, and Cambodia; and south of the large land mass of the mainland, hundreds of islands stretching east and composing the Eastern Archipelago (Indonesia) and then the Philippines.

The complex meanings of this region (even though not then named as the region of Southeast Asia) in Victorian Britain were shaped by two primary factors, which turn out to be substantially the same. First, the area lay between British India and China. It was through the routes of Southeast Asia that Britain would ply the China trade. Second, Southeast Asia was a region where other European nations were actively present and struggling for control, much as they were struggling in Europe. Their activities mattered because what they could gain control of was not only lands and people and resources—all of which Britain had plenty of opportunities to take from other places—but seas, which brings the point back to the perceived importance of Britain's trade routes to China.

In other words, in marked distinction to India, Britain did not love the area now making up what we Americans call Southeast Asia for itself alone but for the places, from a British governmental and commercial perspective, it lay between. "Location, location," as the realtors say. So also said many of the British travelers who went to Southeast Asia and wrote back to persuade a repeatedly recalcitrant (but never too recalcitrant) British Colonial Office to commit itself to taking over various parts of the region. The written British imperial history of Southeast Asia through most of the nineteenth century needs to be read not so much in terms of the economic values of the region's land resources but rather of its waters as highways of trade and also in terms of British responses to the moves of other governments in Europe. Spain took the Philippines and kept it until the United States took it away at the end of the nineteenth century in the Spanish-American war. France took what is now Vietnam and stayed until the mid-twentieth century. My geographic focus in this book is not on those two geographic regions. I focus on the places in Southeast Asia that the British wrote about, which were usually, but, I would stress, not always, places where British economic and political influences dominated. These include Singapore from the Straits Settlements, the islands of the East Indies, the Malay Peninsula, Sarawak, and Siam. The actual books British women wrote, more than any presumed "logic" of political geography, shaped the contents of this study.

In considering British writings about Southeast Asia, the complexities of location, of what constitutes a place, of how geographic and political boundaries are constructed and reconstructed, mean more than an historicized attention to changing conceptions of what we understand by nation and region. In the field of postcolonial studies the vexed question of a distinction between "colonial" and "imperial" needs to be seen in relation to the point that the very notion of what constitutes a colony is historically and also geographically problematic. It may be fairly easy to define a British colony when India is the touchstone. Though the territories which the British controlled on the Indian subcontinent expanded greatly during the nineteenth century, the colony of "British India" was already a well-established concept by the eighteenth century in the rhetorics of British imperialism. This confident power to define the colony, in spite of ongoing arguments about the content of that definition, was not true of the rhetorics I will be discussing. One of the distinctive characteristics of the discourses of British imperial presences in Southeast Asia in the nineteenth century is that what would constitute a British colony or even a British imperial presence was explicitly represented as both hard to define and a matter of debate. Did "colony" mean territorial control or legal status in England or both? Was a "Straits Settlement" a colony when under the control of the British colonial government in India? Was a "nation" privately owned by a British family a colony? Perhaps at least as knotty a question was, Who were the colonizers and who were the colonized? Were they to be defined by place of birth, official "citizenship" (where there was often no such thing), "race," or professional function?

As Ann Stoler eloquently argues in relation to a colonial community in Dutch Java, "colonizers themselves . . . were neither by nature unified nor did they inevitably share common interests and fears; their boundaries—always marked by whom those in power considered legitimate progeny and whom they did not—were never clear."9 Stoler's insistence that the task of anthropologists is to take the "politically constructed dichotomy of colonizer and colonized

[not] as a given, rather . . . as a historically shifting pair of social categories" needs to be attended to by literary critics as well. The very notion of a "colony" or of an "imperial presence" in Southeast Asia in the nineteenth century is problematic. The point is true in part because the very notion of the "colonized" or the "indigenous" people was often itself problematic. The variety of kinds of British presences and/or forms of British territorial control, the sheer range of imperial meanings being constructed in the region, along with the instability of those meanings and the ongoing public debate concerning them, the impossibility of drawing clear boundaries not only between colonizer and colonized but between imperial and colonial—these make up some of the distinctive qualities of the range of British imperialism in Southeast Asia.

As a final introductory point, I suggest that for a critic to take up some Victorian women's discourses about places in Southeast Asia, location needs to be a not only a conscious critical project, but a self-conscious one. Many writers and readers have recognized a continuing political and rhetorical problem: any critique we offer about the limitations of other cultures in other places and times can be a way of exempting or approving ourselves (as "postcolonialist," for example, another dubious and undefinable term). Moreover, contemporary studies of the literature of British colonialism from perspectives of critique have too often been read as delineating, at least implicitly, "typical" qualities of Victorian imperialist attitudes. One critical activity I see as particularly dangerous is to simplify by generalizing from a powerful critical study. Such generalizing makes the claim, however inadvertently, that nineteenth-century writings about other countries ideologically mapped as "east" of Europe, whether they be Egypt ("middle east") or India ("South Asia") or Japan ("far east") or Borneo ("Southeast Asia"), reflect a British mentality which in its basic outlines was pretty much the same everywhere. "East" is a way to invent the "west."

Gauri Viswanathan has articulated what should have long been treated in English studies as a central point, that English culture was (and is) not self-generated, any more than were the cultures of the countries now comprising Southeast Asia.[10] Looking at even a few of the complexities and specificities of the role of "empire" in the formation of Victorian British culture means rewriting literary history as cultural history, given that we understand and continue trying to compensate for the totalizing lie which defines "history" as some past we can "recover" if we are just thorough and objective enough. The specifics of this recreation, or rewriting, through the lens of the drives of empires have everything to do with who is doing the recreating.[11]

I have tried with the partial success attendant on any efforts of self-consciousness to abandon my well-taught and well-learned urge to "unify" through an underlying critical emphasis on an underlying pattern or structure "in" the material. Instead, I have made an effort to attend as much as possible to the details, the particular and the peculiar as I see them, the representations of self and locale in a few Victorian travel books, considering each as an imperialist text. The "underlying pattern" to the argument is that there is no bare-bones British Victorian imperialist, no bare-bones British Victorian imperialism. Late twentieth-century critics approaching these travel books need to resist not only traditional truisms about Victorian culture but also more recent critiques which generalize about the nineteenth-century imperialist project. If one of the continuing villainies of imperialism has been located in an inherited European rhetoric which racially essentializes and reduces the colonized ("the Malay"), I cannot fight it or partly distance myself from it, in myself and others, through a rhetoric which essentializes and reduces the would-be colonizers ("British imperialism" or "the British colonial/imperial perspective").

Just as the past is always in the present, readings of discourses about another place are always offered from a place as well, with its own hermeneutic framework. Abandoning the tired and dangerous dichotomy of objective and subjective, the point for me is not at all that writing from a place is undesirable and that we should instead choose evasion or flight. Such apparent choices, after all, don't work anyway (we will always have that appointment in Samarra). Rather, the point is to insist that neither there nor here, neither the places I write about nor the place I write from, carries a fixed, which is to say, definitively locatable, identity. On the other hand, to write about place is not to write about some unknowable, ever-moving flux, a

1990s critical version of "on the road." Nor is it to offer generalities or theoretical paradigms. In this study, one key meaning of looking at place is looking at the conventions of a range of particular historical discourses, considering both that place entails history and that place is always framed by the points of view of other places.

Gender in Imperial Narratives

The beginnings of this study lay in a suspicion which emerged from my own perspective that the experience of going to various countries in Asia was different, importantly different, for women than for men, probably in the nineteenth century as much as now. This is a plausible suspicion but hardly a demonstrable one, and full of pitfalls anyway. The next step, both more problematic and more interesting, forms the argument of this book. It is similar to the perspective of Sara Mills, that "theoretical models of colonial discourse should be reformulated to account for the differences of women's texts"[12] (though I find the notion of "theoretical models" troublingly close to the notion of abstract and generally applicable concepts). Victorian women's travel books about their experiences in Southeast Asia offer a range of rhetorics informed in traceable ways by the imperial policies toward the places they wrote about and also by the restraints and the opportunities afforded their authors by some Victorian ideologies of gender. As inscribed by women, representations of British imperialism in various imperial "contact zones" have some distinctive qualities, both limitations and liberations.[13]

From where I look and I write, one of the most significant and complex topics emerging from the issue of imperialism in Victorian culture is the question of the relations of imperialism to discursive constructions of subjectivities, inevitably marked as masculine or feminine, and how these are entwined with constructions of national or ethnic identities. There was a distinctive and quite specific British imperial discourse in nineteenth-century England about each individual region marked for a variety of reasons as being encompassed in the imperial enterprise. The specifics of each discourse were intertwined with the "facts" of the history of British relations to a particular region. Women's books were rhetorically positioned in relation to the dominant and masculine discourse about the particular places they visited. In the discourse of the British colonial enterprise, gender, always itself a racialized category, is inseparable from geography.

Recent studies of imperial writings which do distinguish books by the gender of the author, particularly two published in the United States which I am particularly indebted to, *Discourses of Difference* by Sara Mills and *Imperial Eyes* by Mary Louise Pratt, are also impressive in considering imperial travel books in terms of historical particulars.[14] Both avoid suggesting a critical pattern of a dualism between Britain and the rest of the non-European world, and both look at specific locations of imperialism. Yet their differences from this study are perhaps easiest seen in the fact that neither book focuses only on writings about a particular region or attends specifically to Victorian writings about Southeast Asia. One book that does focus on women's works about a particular region, though in a wide span of time, is Billie Melman's fine study, *Women's Orients: English Women and the Middle East, 1718–1918*.[15]

In British Victorian travel narratives the rhetoric of a particular text and the gendered self or, more accurately, selves (masculine or feminine) constructed in that text need to be read within very specific frameworks of public British discourse about the actual place in which the book is set. Interpreting a specific public discourse requires attentiveness to constructing a political history of Britain's relations with the place functioning as the geographic locus of that discourse, the "where" it purports to be "about." As Sara Mills has pointed out, "texts written within the colonial situation cannot be analyzed without an examination of the effect that context has on the way the text is structured."[16] Part of the effort of this study is to read "that context" as a specific political geography and at the same time as a framework of masculine gendered discourse. This initial step may be what it means to read the "absent text of history in the margins of literature," as what is unsaid.[17] It does mean to see that Isabella Bird's *The Golden Chersonese and the Way Thither* cannot be approached without first knowing something of the history, as it was rhetorically constructed by British men, about their own presence and activities on (and visions about) the Malay Peninsula.

Much as Sara Suleri appropriately speaks about a nineteenth-century British rhetoric of English India, we need also to speak of a
nineteenth-century Engish rhetoric of British Malaya or of the
Netherlands Indies or of Singapore and, I would emphasize, to
speak of that rhetoric as gendered.[18]

Some declaration of the dominance/superiority of England and
what are offered as "western" culture and masculine values reappears
in various forms in these female-authored imperial narratives, both
explicitly and also implicitly, at the very least in the sense that
representations of gender are encompassed in representations of
"whiteness." But if that were the place there is to go as well as the
place from which to start, I would not have written this book. We
might notice first that among Victorian travel writings about Southeast Asia, the few voices critical of aspects of the British presence are
mostly women's (Margaret Brooke on Sarawak, Emily Innes on
British Malaya, Anna Leonowens on Siam). It is not that these
women were anti-imperial or even opposed to territorial colonization. They just did not mouth (and sometimes offered alternatives
to) the party lines. These rhetorical alternatives sometimes opened
up through narrative distancing, implied or explicit, from the narrative conventions according to which British male imperialists were
represented. In some women's travel accounts about places in Southeast Asia, it was possible through gender to see past particular
imperial ideologies.

This study takes up a few of the questions of the relations of
imperialism to Victorian constructions of female subjectivity. It
offers analyses of the discursive production of what would be
culturally labeled "white" femininity in women's imperial writings
about a specific region, the boundaries of which were marked by
influences rather than by nationality. I am particularly interested in
how the intersections of imperial and local events in some of the
places in Southeast Asia and the intersection of creations of gender
and creations of nationality or ethnicity in the books make possible
moments when British women's liberation is not business as usual.

Within the still-familiar hegemonic framework of British superiority (be it "racial," sociopolitical, evolutionary, or economic), in
some women's writings here and there are confluences of various

factors which suddenly allow for other kinds of perspectives and construct other narrative identities than those familiar conventions of feminine imperialism typically offered in the narratives. I have been interested in locating such moments of outbreak and in attempting to retrace how they might rhetorically have come about. The following chapters offer a continuing interest in the discursive shaping of female subjectivities in relation to the shaping of some regional histories. They also offer an interest in the ways occasional breaks out of an imperial mentality are linked in the narratives to femininity and/or to represented qualities of the places—and sometimes of the indigenous women—the narrators write about.

I argue that there are some rhetorical moments in these travel narratives which do not dramatize the "selves" of the narrative voice in terms of the familiar constructions of personal female liberation through imperial concepts of "racial" and national superiority.[19] I read these occasional outbursts as happening in different ways in different narratives. Moreover, they sometimes appear to me to offer transformations of domestic ideology. These moments are discursive freedoms and not complete narratives. Nor can they be read as oppositional narratives. Yet they are moments when imperial and patriarchal conventions, though seldom disappearing, lose their hermeneutic force.

The particular interests of this study mean abandoning many of the more generalized conventions that contemporary postcolonial theory as practiced in the United States has presented as characteristic of imperial texts. The superb insights of Edward Said's *Orientalism* or Patrick Brantlinger's *Rule of Darkness*, as well as the insights of several other postcolonial theorists, although not explicitly glossed by their authors as pertaining to masculinity, perhaps should be by their readers.[20] These insights often look less insightful when applied to women writers. Moreover, their received status as general insights about nineteenth-century European imperialism looks less far-reaching once we begin to pay attention even to how many visible and audible women writers on topics related to empire there were. Many received insights about imperial texts may positively shrink when critics attend to the often quite distinctive tropes appearing in some women's travel narratives.

Given that Victorian writings about distinct geographic constructions in Southeast Asia have distinct masculine imperial rhetorics, it is within the context of those distinctions that the lineaments
of women's imperial rhetorics, including their moments of critique,
can be discerned. This temporal, political, and cultural specificity
implies that what the Victorian and "white" feminine meant in
travel books about places in Southeast Asia varied depending upon
where and when the travels were rhetorically situated. Set within
such highly localized hermeneutic frameworks, gender in Victorian
travel narratives is represented in a range of illuminating ways.
Marianne North as a scientist/artist is a "new" woman, but in quite
special and particularized terms which can only be sustained by very
old conventions of class, not to mention old money. Margaret
Brooke writes of herself as outside the British colonial community
in Sarawak and feels so strongly that she shares the gendered
location of her Malay women friends as to imagine she can share
their "racial"/national identity as well and become virtually Malay
herself.

Yet this rhetorical identification shifts moral and imaginative
shape when read in relation to the common trope in Victorian
writings about Sarawak by European men, who argued that successful rule by the "White Rajahs" required precisely the power of
empathy to the point of merging identities with the natives and their
cultures. In the light of such expressed opinions by colonial administrators and male visitors in Sarawak and also in the Malay States, I
argue that Emily Innes's unsympathetic style and frequent expressions of hostility toward the Chinese and Malays in her writing
about British Malaya read less like racism and more like an anti-
imperialism linked to her gendered self-placement as a wife without
public power. Thus Brooke's and Innes's differing readings of their
gendered positions are not a matter of good or bad, nonracist or
racist. Both of these are historically impoverished categories. Interpreting these writers' differing representations of their relations to
indigenous peoples emerges from reading their works within the
contexts of the specific tradition of British colonial rhetoric each
was writing within.

I find the transformative quality of so-called imperial narratives particularly acute in the writings of Anna Leonowens. When, at certain points in her narratives, Leonowens represents King Mongkut of Siam as implicitly a "barbarian," this representation occasionally, though not always, has a dimension other than the obvious one of mimicking masculine British views of European civilization and Siamese backwardness. Leonowens's construction of the king at certain moments has to do with her narrative construction of herself first as a woman, a mother, and a "sister," and secondarily as British or "western." I argue that it is gender as much as, and sometimes even more than, orientalism which drives such moments. Fanon continually attempted to remind his readers that "colonialism cannot be understood without the possibility of torturing, of violating, or of massacring."[21] The locations from which Leonowens's books are narrated serve to offer a different reminder: that sexual slavery of women also cannot be understood without the same possibilities of torturing, of violating, and of massacring. Leonowens's version of the king stands as a lone, if conflicted, voice against the European conglomerate, and orientalist, portrait of him as a force of "modernization." The king's portrait has been constructed in the discourses of European men who have read him as "modern" precisely to the extent that they have read as male and natural, which is to say, desirable, the political and domestic oppression of women in Siam.

If eighteenth-century and nineteenth-century British fiction frequently played out the colonial encounter as a romance, those conventions are not much replicated in the Victorian nonfiction genre of women's narratives set in the regions of Southeast Asia.[22] The language of sexual aggression, the erotic possibility of sexual experience, the rhetoric of virile masculine conquest of a supine and mysterious but finally penetrable and controllable feminine land, form the lineaments of an utterly familiar metaphor in Victorian men's travel accounts about the "near" and "far" east and Africa. In his classic study of "Orientalism" as a "western" phenomenon, Said has commented that "virtually no European writer who wrote on or travelled to the Orient in the period after 1800 exempted himself or herself from this quest."[23] Mary Louise Pratt has extended Said's insight by exploring examples of a variation on this theme, one which takes the form of the masculine quest for sexual experience as homoerotic as well as heterosexual romance.[24] What both these forms share is the given of a masculine voice and the positioning which masculine gender implies. The superiority of that position operates for both private and public encounters. The miserable parallels, indeed the traditional and mutually rewarding relationship, ideological and economic, between national and sexual politics, between the dominations of the imperial powers and of the men and masculine-labeled values in nineteenth-century England, are all too clear.[25]

I suggest that once the gendered qualities of travel discourses are critically pursued, it becomes less convincing to claim that representations of colonial conquest have been, either conceptually or historically, primarily imaged as entwined with a masculinized sexual conquest. However imaginatively powerful and culturally destructive to women and to colonized peoples that entwining has been— and certainly it has been one dominant trope—I am not persuaded to give it primary place as a dominant pattern in a range of imperial relations in contact zones. To do so seems to me to continue, though now in the name of radical critique, the erasure of the crucial specificities of place and the extensive presence of Victorian women's writings about particular foreign locations. Moreover, postcolonial critics need to start seriously taking into account that not everybody was colonized and that this fact mattered a great deal, both to them and to the British traveling in and writing about their states. Victorian women's travel books frequently offer patterns of relations, either between colonial authority and indigenous peoples (itself a problematic category given the scattered presence of just the "Chinese" in Southeast Asia) or between foreign visitor from an imperial nation and local resident, which do not fit the model of a basic entwining of masculinity and imperial presence.

I should say here that the imperial voices which were imaging the ties between European and male hegemony were not always male. The language of masculine domination certainly does appear sometimes in accounts written by women, just as it sometimes does not occur in male-authored accounts.[26] Nonetheless, the international language of heterosexuality, of national as sexual dominance, is not that frequent in the female-authored accounts I consider.[27] For example, very seldom do metaphors which position the landscape as a supine femininity and the speaker/author as a standing-tall masculinity appear. This is hardly to say that British women's writings about visiting places in Southeast Asia are somehow more innocent or less imperializing than men's. They offer plenty of tropes of imperial conquest, but not cast as sexual domination. Said's insight here is finally about a masculine rhetoric. In spite of his general claim, many a European writer who wrote on the Orient "in the period after 1800" (whether, like Innes, Brooke, McDougall, and Leonowens, she "lived" for a while in a region or, like North, Forbes, and Bird, she was a traveler) did exempt herself, explicitly and in the rhetorical tropes of her accounts, from the quest for sexual experience.

The frequent absence of the culturally defined rhetoric for expressing sexual desire and dominance is not the only characteristic of many Victorian women's accounts of travel in Southeast Asia. Just as significant, British imperial rhetorics of feminine domination are by cultural definition "unnatural," which is to say, "uncultural," precisely because they contain not the tried and true parallel between masculine and European superiority but the contradiction between feminine inferiority and European superiority. In other words, ideologically they make up an unstable category, one I view as particularly conducive to narrative moments where the dominant imperial position of the feminine narrative subject is not smoothly or consistently sustained.

One critical attempt to establish stability, to model how gender functions rhetorically, is what I think of as the sidekick explanation/interpretation of female-authored travel narratives. The feminine rhetoric of imperial domination is understood to repeat, copy, imitate, mimic the masculine rhetoric its function is to serve. Their cultural aims are similar—in fact, his defines hers—but their specific positions and content are different. He writes of the stupidity of Indian rajahs; she writes of the stupidity of servants. He critiques the Malay system of justice; she critiques their marriage customs. He writes of the problems of establishing an efficient bureaucracy; she writes of the difficulties of preserving butter. Both, in his and her separate spheres, replicate the appropriate masculine and feminine values of their culture and the superiority of that culture. The hierarchies of gender entwine satisfyingly with those of class as, say, the superiority of the British woman in Africa to the indigenous peoples parallels the superiority of upper-class to lower-class British woman in England.

This interpretation of feminine imperial rhetorics may well offer a useful paradigm for approaching a great deal of the work written by European and American women about their experiences in imperial contact zones. One important qualification is that the usefulness of the paradigm depends on which geographic location is being described. Feminine rhetoric which is fairly straightforwardly at the service of masculine imperial rhetoric and in a dependent relation to it tends to carry with it some representation of the notion of separate spheres, of the appropriateness of limiting the feminine to the interior or domestic world. Perhaps this sense of clearly distinguished dominions does operate frequently in books about women's experiences in some colonies. Perhaps not. But I suggest that it is not a particularly relevant critical tool for reading Victorian women's books about Southeast Asia. A different critical approach, one which does not mark as hermeneutically central the question of which women writers actually "lived," which is to signify, set up housekeeping or enacted domesticity, in a particular region, as opposed to which writers journeyed through, seems to me useful for women's travel books about some regions of Southeast Asia.

Anna Leonowens, Marianne North, Isabella Bird—the writings of these women show no interest in enacting domesticity, though Leonowens is interested in motherhood. Neither do the works of Harriette McDougall and Margaret Brooke, both of whom "lived" in Sarawak. Emily Innes's book is the only one considered here which represents its narrator as existing, and in extraordinary detail, in a domestic colonial space. Yet that pose is exaggeratedly rhetorical, often to the point of being notably not "domestic." Innes's *The Chersonese with the Gilding Off* is the one directly polemical work I take up, the only one explicitly aimed at juxtaposing its "truths" of actual colonial experience with the lies of the Colonial Office. It is hardly a "women's" book in the sense of being aimed at a women's audience. Anna Forbes, who actually claims to be writing a book for women, represents what can frequently be characterized as a narrative of a botanical expedition rather than a narrative of domesticity. Explicitly, implicitly, or simply by silence, the writings of all these authors challenge as inappropriate that dubious hierarchical division between private/domestic and public spheres. Related to these challenges are the ways the writings of these women and several others bring into focus the self-contradictory and finally unstable quality of any critical category of feminine imperial rhetorics.

When Isabella Bird writes about the Malay justice system, does not that discussion, even where it seems to express the position of male British colonialism and simply to mimic or appropriate masculine rhetoric, still do something different? To argue otherwise is to ignore the inequalities of Victorian gender, to ignore precisely the different places in Victorian Britain from which men and women spoke. I take as culturally insightful Samuel Johnson's grotesque remark, made from his perspective of superior masculinity, that the surprise when a woman speaks rationally, like that of seeing a dog walk on its hind legs, lies not in what she says or how well she says it but that she does it at all. Rhetoric cannot be distinguished from the gender of the speaker. As Homi Bhabha has suggested, from a rather different political position from Johnson's, mimicry can carry its own critiques of the colonial position it purports to occupy.[28]

A truism of Victorian studies before the last ten years in the United States (and one still ideologically vital) had been that the Victorian period, though a time of great change and development, was fundamentally less advanced and less liberated than the modern age. The staid Victorian male, the oppressed female confined to being the angel in the house, the separation of public and private spheres, these linger as familiar twentieth-century images of nineteenth-century England. The sheer number of books by Victorian women about their stays in various parts of Southeast Asia is one example of increasingly visible evidence which casts doubt on the traditional twentieth-century images of Victorian culture and the role of women in it.

In both their quantity and their public agendas, these books do not reflect the familiar clichés, but rather challenge the often hidden assumptions about historical progress in traditional Victorian studies. The hope that Ada Pryer expressed in her account of her ten years working on coffee and hemp plantations in North Borneo, that "this little book may at least have the effect of attracting greater interest and attention to the unrivalled agricultural advantages of this fertile land," is not unusual in its self-definition as a practical political work, offered to influence British government policies.[29] The popularity of many such travel memoirs in their own time, along with their frequently explicit claims to be politically aimed, suggest that women's voices were frequently raised not simply in dutiful articulations of the ideology of the domestic sphere but as contibutions to the public debates of the Victorian age to an extent many later readers continue to be reluctant to recognize. Their very invisibility now seems politically telling as one indicator of how conventional views of Victorian women as confined are to a great extent a favored twentieth-century American and European project, enacted to demonstrate our own cultural "advances" (and thereby draw a curtain over our constraints).

Place and Expertise

In looking primarily at Victorian travel books by women, but also occasionally by men, about some places in Southeast Asia, I have borrowed ideas and approaches from a great many twentieth-century critics. Many of their works were not published in Europe or the United States. It is one of the odd elements of recent colonial studies and postcolonial theory as practiced in the last two decades in the United States (at conferences, in book lists and footnotes and bibliographies) that there is quite a short list of visible practitioners. This list seems typically composed of European men and non–American-born academics who come from regions which were or are colonized and who therefore, by unspoken presumption, have some sort of "authentic" voices. Whatever their ethnic or national origin, this second group is primarily working at universities in the United States. They speak and write of other places, but most of the time, with the exception of occasional visiting professorships, leaves, etcetera, they speak from here. This relocation process has led to crucial illuminations in academic writings and also provided rich sources of critique. These sources have enabled some indigenous United States critics to become alert to their own cultural blindnesses and partialities as well as to some of the inherited ideological biases of their culture.[30]

It is also true that it has become far too easy to round up the usual suspects whose theoretical works on imperialism are typically referred to, put on reading lists, and footnoted in the American academy. A canon is being formed with what I consider frightening rapidity and rigidity. Some of the names now de rigueur are Sara Suleri, Homi Bhabha, Gayatri Spivak, Chandra and Satya Mohanty, Abdul JanMohamed, Gauri Viswanathan, Edward Said, and Kwame Appiah, with an earlier generation inevitably being represented by Frantz Fanon, Albert Memmi, and Aime Cesaire (check my own, quite typical, first footnotes).[31] In the field of postcolonial studies, this short list of authors, with a few variations and additions, forms, in a phrase borrowed from Laurie Langbauer, what is in practice "a celebrity economy," and that practice remains "largely unquestioned within it."[32]

These are all authors whose works are particularly helpful in thinking about and discussing issues of imperialism. I by no means suggest that we stop reading their writings. On the contrary, I would like everyone to read them. However, I do suggest that there are limitations in attending only or primarily to such a narrow band of voices, themselves tending to take their insights from so few geographical sites. Christopher Miller has argued compellingly that "there is no way to break down intellectual imperialism if Western disciplines are not reconceived as 'local knowledge.'"[33] There is a dangerous geographical insularity and, just as important, an appropriating conservatism involved in taking primarily the insights and positionings of a small group of theorists, no matter how compelling their work, to define the field of colonial studies and postcolonial theory. This reductive practice saves us the effort of listening to the rest of the world. This reductive practice claims, implicitly, that academic writers working in the United States and Europe "operate in a meritocracy" and are the intellectual avant garde.[34] Behind and sustaining that claim, and even more disguised, is a hidden commitment to that most basic of ideas in imperial historiography: "western" progress.

Looking even briefly at the variety of nations in Southeast Asia challenges to the point of destroying many of the working terms—long acknowledged to be inadequate but still in use—of postcolonial theory today. I am particularly concerned that insights about the colonial experience in British India not be taken up, in ways their authors have themselves eloquently warned against, as global insights about imperialism. For example, even with Gramsci's creative expansion of the meaning of "subaltern," whether subalterns can speak seems to me a tricky concept to apply to British Malaya, where, unlike in British India, the colonized peoples, the Malays and Chinese, were not in the British army. A "subaltern" is not just a mobile metaphor. Quite unlike in India, the British had very little military presence on the Malay Peninsula.[35] The major military British presence in Malay waters was the Royal Navy. What kind of aggression is being performed on the insights of the Subaltern Studies group or on Spivak's somewhat different insights when we eliminate the historically located context of meaning for "subaltern" and read it as an ahistoric category, signifying a generic subordinate or colonized person?

Similarly, Bhabha's idea of mimicry as a concept representing in some ways the colonized response to the colonizers in British India carries difficulties in, say, colonial Singapore, precisely because the lines between colonizer and colonized were so much more multifarious than in British India. In Singapore virtually the entire population were immigrants, and the Chinese, themselves foreigners who frequently went back to China, provided most of that population, including a politically powerful elite which functioned in many ways as the colonizers as well as the colonized. Moreover, many familiar locutions such as the language of metropolitan center and periphery don't fit, however self-consciously they are used. I would argue that these terms are more dangerous than useful to postcolonial critics. What can "metropolis," that fancy critical word carrying a usually unmentioned connotation of an important or central city/urban area, signify when the "periphery" contains in its discursive borders such major metropolitan centers in Southeast Asia alone as Singapore, Kuala Lumpur and Jakarta? "East" and "west" erase place, as well as naturalizing a certain form of political raphy. Then there is that total fantasy land, the Third World could locate this lowly world, it might be worthwhile to talk about it. Until then, we need not.

Among the seemingly endless ways a postcolonial critique can become coopted into neocolonialism is on the subject of technology. While it is generally acknowledged among readers interested in postcolonial studies that technology does not equal progress, it is perhaps less acknowledged that technology does not equal Europe and the United States, a point which in no way lessons the significance of technology as a crucial element in European imperial enterprises.[36] A connected point is the relative neglect so far by postcolonial theorists in the United States and Britain of considerations of European imperial history in many of the places lumped as the "east," specifically many of the nations in Southeast and East Asia. Japan haunts the United States for many reasons, not least of which is the likelihood that "they" are more technologically developed then "we." Currently visible academic writings in the United States on nineteenth and twentieth-century imperial activities tend to focus on places conceived as less technological than Europe and the United States, places such as the West Indies or India or states in Africa. But certainly technologies have many definitions and ties to other kinds of historically and geographically specific systems and are not some general and independent box. Their practical and political uses should not give them the status of barometers of national "progress" or cultural superiority.[37]

In the growing field of colonial studies, it may well be useful to associate concepts with specific histories, theory with place, instead of hungering for "models" or metaconcepts and metahistories. I argue that ideas, terms, concepts, critical theories, all emerge from and take their illuminating power from particular locations. Moreover, we might look in other places than the usual presently fashionable journals or even Zed Press for writings offering terms useful to specific critical and theoretical contexts. The currently popular concepts in theoretical discussions about colonialism published in the United States and Europe cannot, and should not, offer a global fit. But there are many other writings published in other places which focus on colonial and postcolonial issues. Among many authors of helpful works, I only mention here Syed Alatas and Eng Lai Ah on Malaya, Carl Trocki on Singapore, Pasuk Phongpaichit and Thongchai Winichakul on Siam, Lucile Brockway on botany in Britain, Daniel Chew and Paul Yong on Sarawak, and Jean Taylor on Batavia.[38]

A great deal of the problem of repeatedly referring to the same short list of theorists must be located in the economics of publishing practices (without even taking up the question of who gets published). Publishers have their territories, their regions of distribution, and are not eager to see other publishers move in. Thus many books published by Oxford University Press in Singapore and Kuala Lumpur are not available in the United States, because the United States distributor of Oxford University Press does not stock them. With some exceptions, it stocks the New York and London publications. There is an extensive field of writings on colonial issues which are coming not from academics working in the United States, or even in Britain or France, but from people living and working in Southeast Asia, as well as from people in what used to be called the commonwealth countries. Academics in Canada, that ex-colony right next door which American intellectuals, replicating the prejudices of our national politics, tend to ignore, have been writing about colonialism for quite some time.[39]

My point here is not that we need to turn to a wider range of authorities in discussing colonial issues, rummaging around for more authenticity. Looking at regional writers from many continents, getting away from our all-too-rapidly canonized short list of postcolonial authors at United States universities, I hope could be an opposite effort to going looking for other experts "out there." There are no experts, not from India or Pakistan, not from Indonesia, not at Columbia University or the University of Sydney or the National University of Singapore. But there are local academics in regions of Southeast Asia and other places writing about colonialism from the vantage of the complexities of familiarity. Expertise is itself a commodifying move, a form of imperial takeover. That may be the most useful insight Said's *Orientalism* gave us, and the one academic critics are most in danger of burying in the hurry at United States and British universities to create new and authentic (i.e., not "white," not "western") experts with, as they say in the movie business, "high concept" theories.

The whole question of who is speaking, of the imperial narrative voice and postimperial critical voice, is complex and often irresolvably ambiguous, though I would also argue, critically accessible in its particularities. To "locate" writers, to "put them in their place," is itself a dominating act when it makes the assumption of the fixity or static nature of place. The various familiar labels of British Victorian imperialism are not of use in critiques of that imperialism. To label the female voice as metropolitan or as marginal is to invoke a false category. Which box would Emily Innes fit in? What of Leonowens, who spent most of her life in either India, Southeast Asia, or North America and about whom we can be sure of neither ethnic origins nor birthplace nor class, yet who represented herself as upper-class, British, and "white"? My own voice has a complex of inventions and limits, which includes not only the problematics of where I am from but also of where I have been, the journeys and sojourns which have provided me with a superficial sense of the regions which are the subjects of the travel books I discuss. This is an expression not of feminine humility but of celebration that I'm no expert (the academic world of Southeast Asian studies has been filled with experts, each with his marked-off territory), and a form of insisting on the piecemeal quality of what I write.

Arrangements

The earth is very big, and this study is very small, hardly touching the European writings about even the places it does focus on. There probably is no large justification for why I have selected certain places and writers. Geographic proximity was a factor. Starting at the north with Siam and sweeping south on the Malay Peninsula to Singapore and then east through the islands of the East Indies, I found places with often interlocking histories and with many political and economic connections. There were also some British women's travel books about these places. With the exception of Margaret Brooke's work, which was about experiences from the late Victorian period but was published in the twentieth century, I have limited discussion to writings from the second half of the nineteenth century (and certainly not all of those). I have grouped particular regions not by literal geography but by what I might call political location: territorial status in the nineteenth century in relation to England. By this arrangement I mean to emphasize that there were very different kinds of imperial definitions, a range of rhetorics, involved in "mapping," which is to say, giving "coherent" and therefore usable (by Europeans) identities to, the lands of Southeast Asia.

Chapter 2 takes up the traditional port of entry for Victorian travelers: colonial Singapore. My discussion of that island city offers a reconstruction of the economics of its imperial history during the nineteenth century in order to explore how cruel economic practices are rewritten through a gendered rhetoric which "draws a veil" over the ugliness of colonial exploitation. The readily available version of Singapore in travelers' writings as a delightful destination is juxtaposed with a more hidden version as a location of acute colonial violence, primarily through opium addiction.

Following the discussion of Singapore, I have grouped the central chapters of the book into three parts, each loosely representing one type of British imperial mapping of the territories it aggressively encountered in Southeast Asia. The first part deals with writings about colonies which were territorially controlled not by England but by other European countries. The second part includes discussions of travel writings about what I very problematically refer to as British colonies. I take up in this section two very different colonizations and some of the discourse about them. The third part addresses writings about states in Southeast Asia which did not experience territorial takeover by any European nation and thus could be viewed as not colonized. This last is a somewhat bare category. With the exception of the innumerable islands which in the twentieth century have been gathered up in the net of nationalism as parts of Indonesia and the Philippines, it consisted only of Siam.

I begin in chapters 3 and 4 with the discussion of particular texts about non-British colonies, looking at European presences in some portions of what is now Indonesia. In the nineteenth century many of the islands were governed by the Dutch, with the Portuguese also occupying territory. British male-authored travel accounts had to locate themselves within an already in place colonial framework, but one in which they could not locate themselves as the colonizers. I suggest that one way British subjects were constructed in these particular narratives was by locating themselves as scientists, typically amateur botanists, collectors, and anthropologists. They could thus represent themselves as bringing back to England something of higher value than the usual colonial material gains: proofs about the order of the earth and the origins of man. As disinterested participants in the great march of science, their business in the islands of the East Indies was to find the facts which justified the Victorian ideology of progress and European, particularly British, superiority. Within such a hermeneutic framework, the writings of Anna Forbes and Marianne North each offer versions of feminine "selves" in relation to the amateur science of botanical collecting.

Of the British "colonies," I take up only two. Chapter 5 looks at what was rhetorically constructed in many accounts as a typical British colony as it evolved specifically in British Malaya. Part of my point is precisely that there was no such thing as a typical colony. If some of the islands of Indonesia contributed to those dimensions of British imperial rhetoric which would argue for a kind of irrefutable scientific hierarchy, in which Europeans in general were superior to other peoples and the British to other Europeans, the role of Malaya in British imperial discourses was quite different. Since the British were the European colonizers in Malaya, there was no impetus to denigrate other colonizers or to offer an arguably superior alternative to the traditionally supplied motive for having colonies, that is, to provide an orderly context for carrying on the business of trade, which is to say, to make money. Within a continuing political framework of government reluctance (both parliamentary and Colonial Office) to take territory during the late nineteenth century, the British took control of the states which would become by 1909 British Malaya. Through tin and then through rubber, Malaya brought enormous wealth to Britain, just as the islands which would become Indonesia had to Holland.

The self-presentation of the colonizers in the Malay Peninsula focused on the argument that Britain needed to keep order there so as to protect its investments and expand its profits. In the imperial writings about the regions, the indigenous populations were frequently glossed as too ignorant and lazy to know how to make money, while the British were glossed as efficient, as good managers and astute businessmen. Two feminine locations within this rhetorical framework were, first, Isabella Bird's in *The Golden Chersonese and the Way Thither*, which upheld the colonial administration by domesticating it as a good example of bourgeois family values doing public work, and then later Emily Innes's *The Golden Chersonese with the Gilding Off*, which attacked the colonial administration and, by implication, Bird's book by switching the terms of representing that administration from family to class. The woman as company whistle blower argues for the masculine as a matter of business corruption, poor economic practices, upper-class exploitation of the workers, and racist aggression against the true owners of the land and minerals.

Chapter 6 considers a unique version of a British colony, held through private "ownership." It takes up the small state of Sarawak (on the northwest coast of Borneo), where, unlike Malaya, the state was owned by the British but not by the British government. Sarawak became the territory of a single British family, the Brookes. Commercial profits were distinctly not priorities for the Brooke family, but their own stature as rulers and whether what they ruled was a "sovereign" state were. For the British public, the ideological function of Sarawak, which is to say, of the rule of what were known as the White Rajahs in Sarawak, was to justify on the level of fantasy an imperial policy which in Malaya was being justified on the level of practicality, as providing the public order necessary for good business. If the male-authored discourse on British Malaya functioned within the ideology of imperialism to persuade the British reading public of the great material gains for England in having an empire, the discourse on Sarawak functioned to persuade them of the higher possibilities involved. Dreams could come true, one could become a king; one could still make one's mark on history, like the great knights of old. And unlike the knights of the Crusades, one could win. The discourse on Sarawak enforced the notion of British imperialism as a great adventure. In a virtual reversal of the discourse about Malaya, the indigenous peoples were cast either as the upper-class leaders who did care about profits and therefore were evil or the masses who just needed a hero to lead them. In this particular imperial discourse, with its emphasis on boyish adventure and sexual innocence (in tandem with an unusual argument for the value of miscegenation, of producing "mixed-race" children with Malay women), the European feminine was not only absent but had no right to a place. To claim a place, as did Margaret Brooke and Harriette McDougall in their books, was, to a greater and lesser extent, to critique the dominant masculine narrative about Sarawak in British accounts.

The third major section (part four), considering a region which had some political shape that could define it as a nation but which was not colonized, consists of Siam, which I discuss in chapter 7. Siam is the only country in Southeast Asia which has not been colonized, which, with the exception of occasional invasions by the Burmese before the modern period, has never had its territories in the control of a foreign government. Even though a great many qualifications need to be made to that statement, it is hard to overestimate its significance both for the peoples of nineteenth-century Siam, now twentieth-century Thailand, and for the representation of Siam in British imperial discourse. The most famous of those "British" representations, though famous because of twentieth-century American and highly romanticized and orientalized recreations of them, were the books written by Anna Leonowens. She worked as a governess for over five years to the women and children in the Siamese royal harem and wrote the only known account in any language of the daily lives of the women inside that place. Even now there are conflicting versions of who Leonowens was and where she came from.

Approaching Siam and specifically *The Romance of the Harem* in terms of both national and personal identities points up some of the continuing ambiguities and the resilient problems one encounters in attempting to discuss any of the multiple and gendered rhetorics of nineteenth-century British imperialism. The voices in that imperial text offer moments of what Nicholas Thomas has called "practically mediated relation " rather than a "global and transhistorical logic of denigration."[40] In a brief, and temporalizing, concluding chapter I turn again to the matter of difficulties and mediated relations and offer a few partial, which is to say, insistently incomplete and avidly partisan, opinions about feminist critical perspectives.

CHAPTER 2

Port of Entry

Colonial Singapore

"No man is an island."
—JOHN DONNE

"No island is an island."
—SUSAN MORGAN

T he politics of postcolonial theory becomes murkier, and the number of articles and books written and read by academics working in the United States and Britain much, much fewer, when the so-called imperialized area or "periphery" is located in that ex-colonial city-state, Singapore. The vast enthusiasm in the United States media, led by such distinguished newspapers as the *New York Times,* for avidly horrified coverage of how an American teenager resident in Singapore in 1994 was sentenced to caning for vandalism points to the tremendous ideological usefulness of this event to American conservative culture. The sentence was endlessly offered both in startlingly selective "reports" and in explicit editorials as proof of "barbarism," thus working to erase the threat of Singapore as a social and technological model which in many ways can presently be read as in "advance" of the United States.[1] The Soviet Union during much of the twentieth century took an alternate political route to that of "the American way" of democracy and, with its recent dissolution and resultant spate of localized wars, had the grace to look like a failure. From the perspective of United States jingoism, Singapore in the 1990s remains, according to our own national economic values, a mortifying and enviable success. What may be most galling to conservatives is precisely that

Singapore's economic growth was accomplished according to the imperial tenets of international capitalism. The tiny nineteenth-century colony has become, in the twentieth century, arguably the most technological state, with the most extensive infrastructure and service system for its citizens, on earth.

What would it mean, except yet another disturbing instance of the cooption of the categories of the political left by the political right, to culturally map Singapore as "third world" or less civilized, while locating a civilized metropolitan "center" in such urban landscapes as Chicago or London or Berlin? Which is not at all to imply that I would read Singapore as politically liberated. In the midst of all its economic "success," Singapore has major and special problems of political repression and can in certain ways accurately be called a police state. These problems affect all its residents but are perhaps most easily read in terms of the social manipulation of women of various classes and of those considered minority "races," as well as of exploitation of foreign workers.[2] The same problems affect residents of the United States, though often in less openly legislated ways. But Singapore's controlling brand of national socialism mixed with capitalism, along with its dual identity as a city and a nation, defy simple political labels.

The complexities of reading late twentieth-century Singapore as a gendered and racialized political space are reflected in the conflicting present images of it in the United States as technological and economic wonder and/or barbaric "eastern" locale. Reconstructing the imperial history of that ideological conflict is beyond the scope of this chapter. Yet the qualities of instability and change which compose present productions of the meaning of Singapore reflect, and in part emerged from, nineteenth-century depictions of colonial Singapore. Some of the elements of those complex colonial depictions are clearly marked in current United States representations. Then as now, what constituted imperial history could only be read through a double viewing: of what was not being written along with what was.

Mapping the Mappings of Singapore

There were some places on the globe during the nineteenth and early twentieth century which British travelers were particularly frequent in representing as convenient and appealing destinations. One such place in what would come to be known as Southeast Asia, and the place through which most nineteenth-century British imperial travellers entered the regions of the South Seas and began their books, was the portal of Singapore. A short section on passing through Singapore is so commonplace in European accounts in the second half of the nineteenth century and the early decades of the twentieth that to take up the range of specific representations of Singapore would require its own book-length study.[3]

This island city/Straits Settlement/Crown Colony/Federated Malaysian State/independent nation was during the nineteenth century a central geographic and rhetorical location for European visits and interests in the Southeast Asia. I too enter the "foreign field" through the port of Singapore. My use of it here differs from those imperial uses, but also from my own practice in the rest of this book, in that I do not focus here on one or two Victorian writings about visiting Singapore. Instead, as an opening move in arguing for a critical practice of place, I offer a portrait here of precisely that urban landscape which was left out of the many travelers' sketches which constituted the semiofficial imperial history of Singapore. Through re-creating this picture behind the picture, as it were, I hope to suggest not the "real story" of Singapore but the double, and reciprocal, quality of imperial narratives about this place, as what was said was shaped by what was not. One fascination for me of the peculiar combinations of silence and declaration which composed British travelers' rhetorics about nineteenth-century Singapore was that the imperial space they created was decidedly feminine, in the sense of being marked by conventions about gender as a woman's space.

Paul Carter begins his study of what he calls "spacial history" by suggesting that the kind of history "which reduces space to a stage, that pays attention to events unfolding in time alone, might be called imperial history."[4] To attend to issues of space not as the stage but as itself the action characterizes a history that "discovers and explores the lacuna left by imperial history."[5]

Mentioning the unmentionable, pointing to the economic and political dimensions of nineteenth-century Singapore which Victorian writings spoke nothing of, images rather vividly how the discursive conventions of what was written were shaped by what was not. I hope through discussing this special "city" to emphasize both the centrality of geographical and gendered space in reading British imperialism in Southeast Asia and the hermeneutic value of viewing as unique the imperial lineaments of a particular place.[6] My point is precisely not to fix Singapore's "true" identity but to chart its instabilities, changes, and negotiations as a continually constructed and contested location. I also hope to emphasize the extent to which its changes and gendered constructs need to be interpreted within the context of international politics and how Singapore functioned as a key location for the nineteenth-century upsurge in global capitalism.

Among many, three presently visible and huge metropolitan spaces in Southeast Asia are Kuala Lumpur, Jakarta, and Singapore. Except for Jakarta, they came into existence as cities during the nineteenth century, and all three developed from villages to cities because of a European colonial presence in the region. Kuala Lumpur, now the capital of Malaysia, was developed from a tiny village because the British Civil Service in Malaya wanted a regional head-quarters. Kuala Lumpur was inland and thus not a starting point for European travelers. Jakarta, then Batavia, was the major Dutch port in the East Indies, a possible landing-place for the Victorian British but not the main one. Singapore was the major British port and thus usually the first destination for British travelers to the region. At the end of the nineteenth century an American missionary, Elizabeth Scidmore, summed up with memorable eloquence the spacial experience of arriving in Southeast Asia as a matter of uncomfortable proximity, of "landing in small boats among the screaming heathen." This description, an image of both aggression and fright, is offered in the text precisely as a contrast to arriving in Singapore. There the female imperial traveler, able to maintain a comfortable distance, "walks down a gang-plank in civilized fashion."[7] The critical question I want to take up is of what the "civilized" quality of the colonial presence in Singapore was composed of.

There are two primary phases to the nineteenth-century imperial history of Singapore, one building on the other. The presumed civilization of Singapore must first be placed within the conventions of the familiar narrative of its colonial origins, what is commonly referred to as the "founding" of Singapore. That founding, I will suggest, is represented as a masculine heroic event. What follows that founding, the second phase of the imperial historiography of nineteenth-century Singapore, is not only no longer represented in terms of the masculine imperial heroic but, on the contrary, may well be read as a feminine event.

The Founding of Singapore

The narrative of Singapore's virtual creation from nothingness was possible, first, because of the precolonial historical situation of Singapore. During the nineteenth century, the mainland region of what is now the nation of Malaysia was called by Europeans the Malay Peninsula, and throughout the latter half of the century was gradually taken over, state by state, by the British. The Peninsula, somewhat like Italy's boot but much larger, drops almost straight south from continental Southeast Asia. At its southern tip, a just barely separate little island, is Singapore. In the fourteenth century, and perhaps later, there had been some settlement of Singapore. But by the beginning of the nineteenth century the island was mostly unused, having a population of perhaps five hundred, mostly Malays but from a range of locations and more than a third not even actually resident on the island but living in their boats. Apart from these various wandering Malays, there were some Johore Malays (Johore was the Malay state on the mainland immediately to the north) in a fishing village and, inland, a few scattered groups of Chinese farmers.[8]

The story of Singapore's "founding" is a particularly visible one in British imperial historiography, and the "facts" of that founding are easily accessible and well known.[9] At the center of that story are the heroic narratives about Sir Stamford Raffles. With a very limited mandate from the governor general of India (itself still the territory of the East India Company) to set up a British port somewhere in the Eastern Archipelago before the Dutch controlled the whole Indies, yet with unlimited visionary zeal, Stamford Raffles landed on the little island on January 29, 1819. He sailed away again on

February 7. He had arranged, first with the local Malay prince and then with the rightful heir to the sultanate of Johore (Singapore belonging to the territories of the Malay state of Johore, directly to the north of it), to lease a part of the island. Raffles left Colonel Farquhar, his second-in-command, to function as Resident (the representative of British authority) and to establish a trading settlement and port. Raffles's repeatedly declared motive was to foil the Dutch. That same month he wrote that "with this single station alone would I undertake to counteract all plans of the Mynheer; it breaks the spell; and they are no longer the exclusive sovereigns of the Eastern Seas."[10]

Raffles returned briefly in May 1819 and apparently found a town of close to five thousand people (or perhaps less), Malay with Chinese a close second, but also including two hundred Indian sepoys Farquhar had brought in from India. Later many Indian convicts would be sent to Singapore to do some of the hard work of building docks and buildings and roads. During this 1819 return Raffles composed an architectural "plan" of the city, organizing it into sections or neighborhoods according to "race" and business or profession, and moved several hundred people to make sure the city would develop according to the layout in his "plan." It did. Rich British and Chinese merchants had established companies in Singapore by 1820. In August 1824, with Singapore having eleven thousand inhabitants, only a little over one hundred of which could be classed as European, the British were granted official ownership of the entire island from the sultan of Johore rather than just the section originally allotted to them for their outpost. The trading settlement had expanded into a city and a major port, and the Malay rajahs had officially ceded the island "in full sovereignty and property to the East India Company, its heirs and successors."[11] Then in 1867 control of the island moved from India to London, and from the India Office to the Colonial Office, when Singapore officially gained the status of a Crown Colony.[12]

Quite unlike the nineteenth-century colonial history of the Malay Peninsula just to its north, Singapore became British very quickly, very dramatically, and very early in the nineteenth century. Its conceived functions were to provide, first, a popular trading port for

British interests in the region so that, apart from the small settlement of Malacca part way up the coast, there would be no need to
land anywhere on the peninsula; and, second, to provide a safe
stopping place for British shipping rounding the southern point of
land between India and China.[13] It is also clear that, as with so many
of the events which make up the colonial histories of much of
Southeast Asia, what happened there had everything to do with what
was happening in Europe. Singapore's colonial takeover had to do
specifically with the power struggles between the Dutch and the
British, struggles which to a great extent took place far away from
Europe.

The smooth "founding" of Singapore has an almost mythologi-
cal significance in imperial lore, with Raffles playing the part of the
visionary individual hero, almost a god. There are clear echoes of
the Christian creation narrative in the repeated detail that Raffles
arranged to create this world in a mere seven days. There are many
explanations for the glorification of Raffles, the most generous of
which may be what Alatas has called a "naive and docile attitude to
colonial historiography."[14] The writing of Raffles as a hero parallels
the glorification of Frank Swettenham in the stories of colonial
Malaya. Yet Raffles has arguably the grandest reputation of a British
colonial in the nineteenth century, a placement, I suggest, which is
geographic rather than personal, having less to do with any actual
claims to "greatness" in the narrative or Raffles's actions and
more to do with the central imperial significance of the island of
Singapore.[15]

One factor in that significance was, quite simply, Singapore's
economic success, measured as making huge profits for British
businesses.[16] Such success was not sustained in India apart from
enormous cultural and political and military problems and did not
come in Malaya until the late nineteenth and early twentieth century, with the demand for tin and then for rubber for the automo-
bile. But in Singapore it came easily, almost immediately (certainly
by the 1830s) and, at least from perspectives in England, with
apparently very little social, political, or economic cost.[17]

The narrative of the "founding" of Singapore in imperial historiography functioned as a way of marking an extraordinary colonial

success. Singapore could be written as a case of "civilizing," of making a civilized place, because its history was originary, a matter of making what was glossed as an always already British city from the raw materials of a tropical island. Before the British, what existed on that island was only, in Wallace Stevens's words, "the nothing that is." There had been no prior civilization, no culture needing to be rewritten as too primitive or too decadent. Raffles literally "founded" a city where there was none. He created a place. Singapore could be read as civilized, indeed, it had to be read as civilized, because it was British. And as a result of the Raffles creation narrative, Singapore was represented as always having been British.

Singaporeans

From its 1819 beginnings Singapore had a special identity as a British colony.[18] It is difficult even to know what is signified by calling it a "colony" and distortingly reductive to try to discuss it in the simple dualistic frame of colonizer and colonized. First there is the matter of the composition of its population. Singapore was an imperially constructed place which in the first half of the nineteenth century was peopled virtually entirely by migrants. By mid-century the Chinese made up 50 percent of the population, and by around 1900 they were 75 percent. The composition of Singapore is now 76 percent Chinese, 15 percent Malays, 7 percent Indian and 2 percent everything else. But the term "Chinese" is itself dangerously reductive, for it was, and is, a useful tool in erasing the actual workings of imperialism in nineteenth-century Singapore. The Chinese, much as the Malays, are certainly not a "race" and probably never were. It is a "common error" (and a convenient one in imperial historiography) to regard "the Chinese as a homogeneous ethnic group."[19]

Originally in Singapore the Chinese immigrants were understood as two main loose groupings.[20] The first, often known by themselves as well as by the British as the Straits-born Chinese, or Babas (men) and Nonyas (women), did not come from mainland China at all. They came primarily from the two earlier British settlements along the Straits of Malacca, Penang and Malacca.

These "Chinese" were typically considered multiracial, with "Chinese" as a kind of umbrella grouping for many combinations of peoples. A great many of them were what was often called Eurasian, meaning that either they themselves or their ancestors had intermarried with the Portuguese and/or Dutch (who were in Malacca and Penang well before the British). Others had intermarried with Indians or Malays or Arabs.[21] Intermarriages as well as births within Singapore meant that over the decades the multiracial Straits-born Chinese were to become the largest grouping of Chinese in Singapore. The second main group, known as the overseas Chinese, did come (or their parents or grandparents had) from mainland China, usually from two maritime provinces.[22] The overseas Chinese were subdivided into six major competing groups, with different customs and dialect languages.[23] There are also, of course, small numbers of many other groups, more than can be listed, including the British and other Europeans, Jews and various peoples from the "middle east," and the Armenians.[24]

Considering some of the characteristics of the population of nineteenth-century Singapore is one way to discern the fluid and changing quality of its spatial history. That population was difficult to locate in terms of ethnic constructions; moreover, it was neither indigenous nor stable. The instability of Singapore's colonial identity in its first few decades is not marked only by the fact that it was almost entirely a state of immigrants. The absence of a substantial indigenous population along with the particulars of why people came to Singapore helps to explain the phenomenon that great numbers of these immigrants did not settle permanently once they arrived. The Europeans themselves, particularly the British colonial administrators, the vast numbers of poor overseas Chinese men who had to agree to leave their families at home in order to come to Singapore to make a living, some of the Straits-born Chinese with relatives in Malacca or Penang, the Arabs with their strong sense of a religious center somewhere else—many of the members of these nominal groups settled only temporarily in Singapore.

As well as Singapore having a fluid international population almost as engaged in leaving as in arriving, another complicating aspect of Singapore's colonial identity is how to group the colonizers as well as the colonized. Along with the two other Straits Settlements up the Malay Peninsula along the sea route to India, Singapore was a "colony" in which the British colonizers actually present were themselves governed until 1867 by other British colonizers not present whose first priority was the economic and political success of British interests in India rather than in Singapore. This "Straits Settlement" was for the first half of the nineteenth century directly under the control of the governor general of India. When the East India Company lost its monopoly of the China trade in 1833, it also lost much of its financial incentive for attending to the Straits Settlements which, after all, it had acquired precisely to support and supply that trade.

The dissatisfactions with an arrangement whereby Singapore was governed by a distant commercial bureaucracy which by 1833 no longer saw it as worth an investment of either time or money fueled much of the political history of early Singapore. Sharing those dissatisfactions were many of the "colonized," themselves not even from the place, nor even, for part of the century, primarily composed of permanent immigrants. In the case of the overseas Chinese, themselves simultaneously colonized and colonizers, their various cultures were transported in, and were continually being revitalized by, new arrivals from particular provinces in China. Thus many of the people in Singapore, colonizers and colonized, had come to that location for similar reasons and were brought together by shared interests that were not fully supported by their governors in India, or in England when at last the government took over Singapore.

Singapore's special history continually complicates the identities of its colonizers, its colonized, and its own designation as a colony, highlighting the critical inadequacy of these terms. Along with Malacca and Penang, the actual colonial title of Singapore for much of the century was "Straits Settlement," and the center for the early decades was Penang. Singapore's founding concept not as a colony but simply as a facilitating entrepôt (with emphasis on the "entre"), conveniently located between what were considered the important imperial interests; its sparsity of inhabitants with any historic connection to the island before 1819—and therefore its lack of an established indigenous culture which the British would have had simultaneously to "appreciate" and destroy; its inundation by all different kinds of Chinese workers and investors, themselves with differing cultures, most of whom considered themselves temporary and many of whom until late in the century did not settle in Singapore but returned home to their families after a few years; its international character both in its settled population of a vast range of non-Europeans and as a free port full of briefly disembarked visitors; its role as the center or headquarters for many of the companies from all over the world doing business in the "east": all these reasons and more map Singapore as a unique imperial location.[25]

Government by Opium

Most of the various immigrants to Singapore, whatever their differing colonial labels, found their similarities in the shared goal of making money.[26] Taking up the representations of Singapore which followed the Raffles narratives, which is to say from about the 1830s on into the twentieth century, means turning first to a consideration of the historic situation in Singapore during the times the many travelers' tales offered their representations of it. It is within the context of activities and events in Singapore that colonial descriptions of visiting there can be read.

Talking about Singapore from the 1830s as a British colonial city means talking about business. There are two factors of primary economic importance about nineteenth-century Singapore. First, it functioned for the East India Company as a stopover port for ships engaged in the China trade. Second, it was a free port. But what was "the China trade"? What was so important about the sea routes between India and China as to put not only the tiny island of Singapore but most of what we now call Southeast Asia on colonial maps? And what was so important about Singapore being a free port? The major part of the answer is opium.

The history of the opium trade is the major narrative hidden by the imperial songs of praise about the development of Singapore. By the end of the eighteenth century, the East India Company had a solid system for its opium trade, a system which lacked only a desirable port in the South Seas. The Company grew and packaged

large quantities of opium in India. After it lost the China monopoly
in 1833, the Company sold the opium at auction in Calcutta to
traders.[27] These private traders sailed the opium through Nanyang
(the South Seas) and on to China (where it was illegal), selling it to
smugglers there, much as people bring cocaine and heroin into the
United States now. The traders, first those working for the Company and then the independents, wanted a stopover in the South
Seas, and the Dutch port of Batavia in Java had heavy customs duties
and port charges. Raffles had established Singapore as a free port not
only for Company ships but precisely to draw the shipping business
from the Dutch ports, none of which were free. The opium was
often landed and often resold in Singapore, stored in the large
warehouses that framed the docks. Ships would carry it eastward,
while the ships which had brought it from India would return
westward with goods from China.[28]

Two decades after Singapore was established as a key port in the
opium trade to China there began what was to be a crucial shift in
the port's relations to opium, a shift which would transform the
imperial identity of Singapore. After the "Opium Wars" at the
beginning of the 1840s, when China tried to stop the British from
the illegal trade of smuggling opium into their country and lost
badly (British naval ships were apparently unbeatable), the British
got the island of Hong Kong in the 1842 Treaty of Nanking. The
founding of Hong Kong as a British free port was to draw much of
the China trade from Singapore.[29] One result was that what used to
be the entrepôt became itself the destination. The way to get some
of the opium to stop in Singapore rather than Hong Kong was for
Singapore to provide the buyers. Through the century more and
more of the opium which stopped over in the waterfront warehouses
of Singapore no longer found its destination in China but in various
areas around Singapore, in what came to be known as the "native
trade." A large portion of that local market became Singapore itself,
which takes this discussion back to the central point of Singapore
being a free port. With no customs duties, dock charges, or sales
taxes, the city had no governmental or administrative income. The
solution was local opium licenses to sell the drug, which during the
century accounted for 50 to 70 percent of government revenues.

Opium use in nineteenth-century Singapore cannot be read in simple terms as a matter of the British colonizers exploiting the colonized population of "Chinese." The local business of opium was totally in the hands of the wealthy class of Chinese businessmen. The British, in literal terms, had nothing at all to do with the opium. They would sell licenses/leases to these local Chinese, usually large syndicates of investors, to sell opium at a certain number of shops for a certain time (usually three years).[30] The first opium licenses were sold by Farquhar as early as 1820, to raise revenues, since the Company from the very beginning was not interested in having Singapore cost them anything.[31] Licenses for opium farms (an interesting euphemism for monopolies, and having nothing to do with actual farming) were still the major source of revenue for financing the business of government in the Settlement in 1907, when the then governor, Sir John Anderson, announced that "to protect the farmer was to protect the revenue."[32]

Opium shops required customers. The buyers, like the sellers, were racially labeled "Chinese," but these were poor working-class men in the mines and farms of Singapore, usually from the two provinces of China. Their long separations from their families, lack of women and thus enforced heterosexual celibacy, health problems, and hard working conditions made opium the weekly easement in getting by.[33] This system had evolved by mid-century into a tidy and hugely profitable cycle. The Chinese agricultural farm and mine owners could tolerate fairly low profits on the mines and agricultural farms because they were pretty much the same people who had invested in purchasing the opium licenses.[34] The big profits were in opium, but the other kinds of investments were crucial for drawing working Chinese from China to Singapore to experience the terrible working situations and thus to become the customers. The more agricultural and other sorts of poor workers there were in Singapore, and the drearier their living and working conditions, the more opium the shops would sell. Thus the higher the profits for their Chinese owners and the more the British administrators could charge those owners for the licenses.

"Government by opium" meant, in the first place, that the fees from opium licenses accounted for about half of the total revenue of the city (there were also licenses for tobacco, spirits, and, for a while, gambling), literally paying the costs of governing and administering Singapore, first as an East India Company settlement and then as a Crown Colony.[35] In Trocki's words, "Raffles's liberal capitalist Singapore not only created the opium-smoking Chinese coolie; it literally lived on his back. He paid for free trade."[36] Government by opium also meant that an extraordinarily small number of Europeans, along with another extraordinarily small number of Chinese businessmen, controlled a large population of men whose living conditions were horrific.[37] That control was crucial, because the "Chinese were the real power in nineteenth-century Singapore."[38] But that statement needs amplification. The workers were numerically the power, but the businessmen were economically the power. Since government revenues depended on the value of licenses, which in turn depended on how many workers were buying how much opium, the "Chinese" businessmen, very often "Straits-born," shared virtually identical financial and political interests with European businessmen and the British colonial authorities.

Even with opium the control could slip, as is attested by the 1854 and 1871 coolie riots.[39] The British expressed continual concern throughout the second half of the century about the danger from all those Chinese, particularly from the secret societies which controlled and directed the coolies. These were the very societies which the British also counted on to control thousands of Chinese through their procolonial leaders.[40] In fact, the occasional Chinese outbursts of rebellion were not sustained. One of the persistent rumors in Iran during the early 1970s was that a fate the shah's police reserved for special political enemies was to jail them, addict them to opium, and let them go free. Whatever the facts, the rumor was based on the simple assumption that an addicted population is a malleable population. The colonial history of Singapore supports that assumption. Estimates are that nearly two-thirds of the Chinese workers in Singapore throughout the nineteenth century regularly used opium.[41] In Singapore the "contradiction involving prosperity and poverty remained hidden, deliberately buried in the illusion of an economic miracle."[42] Moreover, there was no center for resistance to British colonial government. Two possible reasons there were no "scream-

ing heathens" to greet Scidmore in Singapore were that the "heathens" were busy working—having, among other things, built all
those docks and gangplanks—and, when not working, were under-
nourished, ill, and lost in the prone and silent pleasures of opium.

Consuming Singapore

The economic history of Singapore as represented in imperial historiography, usually in the form of travelers' tales, was hardly a history
of grand avenues built on opium revenues. The discourses certainly
were about economic success, but represented not in terms of the
cruel realities of profit through terrible working conditions and high
fees for addiction. Instead, the imperial rhetoric about Singapore
and its huge profitability focused on commerce, on the innocent
world of trade.

From the 1830s on Singapore was the center not only of the
opium trade and then of opium usage in the "South Seas" but also
of the trade in British travelers. These apparently parallel functions
intersect. An entrepôt for goods east from India to China and west
to India and England, Singapore was also an entrepôt for Europeans
moving back and forth between Europe and the United States and
the regions of Southeast Asia. During much of the nineteenth
century it was the gateway, the door, the hub, the jumping-off place,
and all those other tired metaphors which indicate that Singapore
was usually the first and the last destination for foreigners in Southeast Asia.[43]

By the second half of the nineteenth century Singapore was
continually pictured as a world of cricket and lawn tennis, of
newspapers published in English and visiting cards. Glossed as
neither elegant nor tidy, it was nonetheless to be defined as cosmo-
politan and worldly and, best of all, invented to meet the demands
of British commerce. Many nineteenth-century European and American narratives offered vivid portraits of Singapore, stressing its
liveliness as a testimonial to the imperial enterprise.[44] As P. J. Begbie
aptly phrased it in 1834, Singapore "inspires the spectator with an
idea that he is gazing upon a settlement which is naturally rising in
importance under the united influences of English capital and

industry and an advantageous locality."[45] Accounts by visitors offered recurrent images of the "strange motley crowd," the "Babel of languages," the range of unfamiliar foods and unfamiliar peoples, all serving to construct a landscape of apparent chaos revealed to be that "glorious profusion" indicative of a commercial paradise.[46] In such accounts Singapore represents the lushness and prodigality, the sheer energy and variety of the "east." But it is variety in a package, prodigality harnessed at the service of the British consumer. And that consumer, as a consumer, is represented in Victorian and early twentieth-century accounts as female.

One implication of the centrality of Singapore in terms of travel routes from Europe was that it was a frequent and favorite place to visit for British women. It was from Singapore that British living in British Malaya or Sarawak or Siam would order their household goods. It was to Singapore that Emily Innes reported going to recover when she became too ill in British Malaya, and from Singapore that she returned home. It was at Singapore that Margaret Brooke, as a young bride, dined with Governor Ord and his wife and spent the day at the country home of the chief justice. It was in Singapore that Isabella Bird attended services at St. Andrew's Cathedral and received her invitation to visit the Malay States. And it was in Singapore that Anna Leonowens, having moved there with her children after burying her husband in Penang, was hired as a governess by an agent of the king of Siam.

Almost whatever the Europeans, men and women, wanted while in Southeast Asia they could acquire in Singapore, particularly European customs and ways. Throughout the Victorian period and the early twentieth century it had a virtually worldwide reputation as a shopper's paradise, where you could buy almost anything and at a good price, This reputation is still being avidly reproduced in the late twentieth century, in many travel articles touting the virtues of visiting Singapore and in the city's own self-promotion.[47] It is startling how much Singapore's contemporary image for foreigners continues and sustains its Victorian image, regardless of such realities as that Americans can get the same range of goods and prices in New York. The discourse of the past reaches its still-warm hand into the present to shape the very substance of many of the streets and shops of Singapore.

The unspoken history of Singapore as a city created and built by multiracial foreigners and financed by opium addiction is hidden by its visible colonial identity as the city literally mapped out and developed by the needs of British trade. Singapore was written and read as the empire at its best, a place where the appetites of European consumers had metamorphosed what might have been read as a frightening "otherness" into a reassuring usefulness. In nineteenth-century Singapore, place signified marketplace. Singapore's dangerous potential for difference could be mediated, and controlled, by turning it into something to buy. Singapore's variety of peoples, its bustling activities, all contained within the geographic and cultural and political boundaries of British authority, rendered it the perfect icon for the rightness, which was to say, the commercial and social success, of the British imperial enterprise.

Creating that icon required at best an insistent ignorance, and certainly a stunning reversal, of the truths of oppression and cruelty which were the actual economic foundations on which Singapore's growth and its riches were built. The opium, the very basis of the Straits Settlement government's budget and thus its ability to function, had to be erased. We can read this erasure and its orientalizing replacement in Isabella Bird's description of the charms of Singapore. Her words conveniently render invisible the opium shops and transfer responsibility for their debilitating effects to "Chinese" culture and away from their actual source in British economic practices as the enabling basis for this British free port. Bird locates the charm of Singapore in her view that "here is none of the indolence and apathy which one associates with Oriental life."[48]

Inseparable from its lucrative policy of addicting Chinese coolies to opium and from the terrible conditions of their lives as workers was the bustle, the continuing city growth in revenues and construction, the big municipal buildings and wide avenues, and the availability of most European goods and luxuries. These were the elements which made Singapore so attractive to Europeans, and, cloaking its economic base in the cruelties of men's business practices in opium, glossed it instead as an apt destination for European women. Singapore was narratively represented as that best of all imperial places. It was where the desirable prodigality of the "east" had been separated from its undesirable local "life" and regrouped or reordered within the controlled boundaries of the island city, thus taking on its greater purpose of fulfilling European commercial appetites. The ruthless violence of those appetites was erased by a rhetoric which conveniently labeled them as feminine. Singapore was a shop. What British women could browse for among its safe and civilized isles was the entire world.

PART TWO

 Non-British Colonies and the Naturalists

CHAPTER 3

The Holy Land of Victorian Science

Anna Forbes, with Henry Forbes and Alfred Russel Wallace in the Eastern Archipelago

"Above all, never wear a sarong."
—ROLAND BRADDELL

Imperial Geography in the Eastern Archipelago

What was known in the countries of Europe and America during the second half of the nineteenth century as Malaya is actually the bottom part of a long peninsula. It drops almost straight south from the main continental area of Southeast Asia. The top part of the peninsula was part of Siam. Until late in the century, when, with the influx of the Europeans, boundaries of land began to define the boundaries of a nation, Siam influenced and, to some degree, controlled, the northern Malay States. To the west of Siam and Malaya, across the Bay of Bengal, there were British-controlled Burma and India. Directly to the east of Siam, and with no body of water to mark the boundary, there was French-controlled Cochin-China, now the countries of Vietnam and Cambodia. At the very southern tip of the Malay Peninsula is the tiny island of Singapore. Just south and sweeping eastward from the Malay Peninsula are some scattered lines of islands, over three thousand of them, a few large and many small. The first and biggest islands, Java, Sumatra, and Borneo, are clumped on either side of Singapore. Directly below Singapore and stretching away eastward into the

51

Pacific virtually to Australia are a myriad of other islands. Because of the particular geographic context of the islands in relation to Malaya, nineteenth-century Europeans lumped all these very different islands under a single name, the Malay Archipelago or, more commonly, the Eastern Archipelago.

The British were the dominant foreign power in the Malay Peninsula by the mid-nineteenth century. By the late nineteenth century they controlled the Malay States up to what they defined as the Siamese border in the north and down to include Singapore, the island city at the southern tip of Malaya. But their domination did not extend south of Singapore.[1] The numerous islands of the Malay Archipelago were of interest to several European countries. Yet the geography of the islands, cultural as well as physical, made colonizing them a difficult, an erratic, even a random affair.[2] Islands would occasionally be partitioned, with various groups controlling various pieces. The Portuguese were there, in East Timor. The British had a range of small presences, including direct government control, a commercial charter which amounted to rule, and government by a private family. Major settlements of Chinese were located throughout the islands, sometimes controlling their areas economically if not governmentally.[3] Some Chinese formed a particularly large and economically powerful community of miners and farmers in Borneo. A great many of the islands and parts of islands remained independent of European imperial designs. These were under the control of various indigenous peoples, many of whom were themselves of differing cultures and languages. Some of them occasionally made their own successful efforts at taking control of another group's land and/or people. But undoubtedly the most extensive European presence in the Malay Archipelago was the Dutch.

The Dutch foothold in the Eastern Archipelago had been well established in the seventeenth century. In 1702 all the various small Dutch businesses trying to get rich in the Archipelago (sometimes called the Indies) agreed to merge to form the Dutch East India Company. Through business networks set up by the employees of the Dutch East India Company (known as the voc), by the eighteenth century Holland had in place an extensive system of revenue collection and land management, including compulsory coffee cultivation in areas it controlled. In a pattern that was similar to the history of the British East India Company, the fortunes of the voc rose and fell as it moved from a merchant company to an official colonial administration.[4] At the end of the eighteenth century the voc was operating under such an enormous deficit that its debts had to be assumed by the state, and the crown of Holland formally took over the voc holdings in the Malay Archipelago. The one major city in the islands, Batavia (now Jakarta, the capital of Indonesia) on the island of Java, was the headquarters of Dutch control. And the Dutch had given their own name to their Southeast Asian island empire: Insulinde.

By the nineteenth century English and Dutch interests coexisted fairly smoothly throughout the Archipelago. This dual colonial presence is geographically represented by the two Europeanized metropolitan centers in the region: British Singapore and Dutch Batavia. Virtually everyone (and everyone meant every European or American) who went to the Malay Archipelago in the second half of the nineteenth century began or ended the journey in one or the other of these major ports. By that period these were the two main "civilized" cities in Southeast Asia, offering the familiarity of European comforts and the security of European rule.

As I discussed in the previous chapter, Singapore's domination of Southeast Asian waters had everything to do with its being a free port (no port taxes, no duty), its central location as the place for shipping materials between China, India, Malaya, and Europe, and the safety and protection it could provide as a city governed by the British and thus backed by the empire's naval might. Batavia was a different matter. It did have the similar charm of being a well-located port, governed by a European power. But it was not a free port. In the nineteenth century Batavia never quite became the bustling international hub which Singapore became. It was a convenient jumping-off place to more interesting locales or a place to get hot baths and sheets and see people in European clothes—even if those people were, from a British perspective, not true Europeans at all—while waiting for the boat back to real civilization after thrilling but grueling adventures.[5] Batavia functioned as an important and reliable base for colonial enterprise and may accurately be described as the secondary center of European culture and goods in Southeast Asia during the nineteenth century.

The lesser stature of Batavia both in port usage and in its cultural image for Europeans had several explanations. Perhaps the most fundamental was that the Netherlands did not have the financial reach or the government commitment or the navy of England. The connections between the home country and this colonial city were less frequent and less influential than those between England and Singapore. Because of Holland's sometimes minimal connections to her colony (particularly in the late eighteenth and early nineteenth century, when Holland was suffering its own economic and political problems) and for many other reasons as well, the European and Asian peoples in Batavia formed a highly blended culture.[6]

British travelers to the region often responded to Batavia with a mix of contempt, condescension, and easy familiarity. Batavia was not British and was not even inhabited by Europeans who were pure Dutch.[7] "Europeans" in Batavia were to a great extent the offspring of a generation or more of intermarriages and thus, from a conservative English perspective, of degraded lineage.[8] Even by 1820 John Crawfurd was commenting critically that "most of the white women, who are seen at Batavia, are born in the Indies."[9] For the British, Batavia had the crucial hermeneutic function of a bad example, an image of what happens when Europeans "go native" by mingling on intimate terms with local peoples. There were, of course, highly visible intermarriages and plenty of less formalized mingling in the British colony of Penang. Yet because Batavia was Dutch, it, and not Penang, was imaged as the negative exemplar in British accounts. Though the British were not literally in power in Insulinde, they often wrote as if in the ways that mattered they were.

Holland and England certainly had squabbles about which of these two civilized nations should be the major influence on—which is to say, who should control the most of—Insulinde.[10] During the confusion which followed the change in Dutch administrative procedures in their colony at the beginning of the nineteenth century, and before the founding of colonial Singapore, Stamford Raffles moved into Dutch Java.[11] The Netherlands, invaded by France, found their Southeast Asian colonies also being invaded by their "ally," England, officially to keep the French from claiming them. From 1811 to 1816, Java, and thus Batavia, was governed by the British. By the Treaty of London in 1814 the Dutch settlement and the other Dutch parts of Java reverted to Holland's control in 1816. Yet that brief period of English control had a profound cultural and political effect on the colony. The British had committed themselves to firming up what they saw to their horror as the relaxed maintenance by the Dutch—many of whom had already been there for a few generations—of the crucial separation between their European ways and those of the indigenous Malays.[12] Six years after the next treaty between England and the Netherlands, according to which the English agreed to leave everything south of Singapore to the Dutch, John Crawfurd was arguing to a British audience for the economic desirability, indeed, the "moral duty," of England establishing colonies in the Indies.[13]

During the nineteenth century the Dutch established a system of economic and political control in the Archipelago that was a huge success, at least in the sense of providing the enormous profits which allowed the faltering Netherlands to flourish for a while during the Victorian period. This notable success of the Dutch colonial system in the Archipelago after the Napoleonic Wars was widely discussed in Europe during the nineteenth century. Discussions focused on a method in Java which the Dutch began around 1830 and ended during the 1870s, of forcing the Javanese to grow cash crops for the world markets and then tithing them. Each region was governed by two parallel bureaucracies, one indigenous (headed by a regent) and one Dutch (headed by an Assistant Resident), with a Dutch Resident in charge of both. Called variously the "Cultivation System" or the "Culture System," "it meant compulsory labor and the exploitation of the entire island as if it were a feudal estate."[14] The system functioned as a possible model for other colonial powers, particularly for England as Holland's main competitor in the region. "In 1861, an admiring Englishman, called [unbelievably] James W. B. Money, summed it up in a book entitled *Java, or How to Manage a Colony*."[15] Money's subtitle, *A Practical Solution to the Questions Now Affecting British India*, is one indication of how much the issue of successful colonial approaches was linked in the minds of British audiences to post-"Mutiny" anxieties about what had gone wrong in India.

Precisely because the "Culture System" was so visibly profitable for Holland, literally rescuing the colonial homeland in the mid-nineteenth century from its political and economic abyss of debt and insignificance, and also because more and more the economic success of the British program in India was being debated at home, it would have been difficult for a British commentator to dismiss the Dutch achievement in Insulinde out of hand.[16] After the "Indian Mutiny," or the Rebellion of 1857, British writers could not, as they had done in so many other colonial situations, argue with easy certainty about Insulinde that they could run Insulinde better than the Dutch did. It was widely accepted opinion in Europe during the mid-nineteenth century that the Dutch were running the place very well indeed, and Holland's fast-growing wealth seemed to prove it.[17]

British writers frequently did not join in the chorus of praise. These shows of reluctance had many reasons, probably including a general sense that Britain was superior to the Netherlands, an awareness that the British in their colonies were not using the "Culture System," and an acceptance—gained through contemplating England's own past history—of the cultural truism that a feudal system was a backward rather than up-to-date structure for managing colonial affairs. The delicate rhetorical problem for many British travelers writing about the East Indies was how to attack a specific colonial system internationally recognized in Europe and America as highly successful while avoiding also attacking, at least by implication, colonialism itself.

This rhetorical dilemma in writing about the Netherlands East Indies is, I suggest, of central importance in any critical approach to British travel writings about the Malay Archipelago in the nineteenth century. These are the works of imperialists writing about an imperial encounter, but in the case of Insulinde it was not their own national colonialism they were encountering but rather that of one of their European neighbors. Moreover, that neighbor wasn't France or Germany, both nations that Britain in the mid-to-late nineteenth century had some respect for, but only Holland.[18] Not only had Raffles, who was openly contemptuous of the Dutch, briefly taken

Java from them in 1811, but in Africa as well the British knew themselves well able to beat out this particular European competitor for desirable territory. They took the Cape Colony away from the Dutch in 1795, they returned it in 1803, but took it back again, and finally made it a British colony in 1815. As imperialists go, by the beginning of the nineteenth century the British had historical reasons to feel their superiority to the Dutch.

In other words, since the colonial position in the Archipelago was already occupied by another European nation, and since Holland had, in the opinion of many British in the nineteenth century, considerably less cultural cachet and less power in Europe than England, British travelers in the Archipelago were both displaced from the colonial role and culturally already in the position of being critical of the occupiers of that role. To borrow Pratt's wonderful phrase, British "imperial eyes" were looking at a disparaged competitor's imperialism at work.[19] This displacement allowed for and even encouraged various critiques of the colonial enterprise, at least insofar as it was manifested in the Archipelago. British travel accounts which express that critique often employ complex rhetorical strategies, often contradict themselves, in the process of criticizing—but not too much—the Dutch colonial system in place.

Reading these texts while distinguishing between whose imperial eyes are looking and whose literal colony is being looked at makes it possible to be much more precise in distinguishing among various representations of the imperial encounter in British Victorian travel books. To put it in the useful anthropological terms creatively borrowed by Pratt, we can read nineteenth-century British travel writing about Southeast Asia as literature about one of the "contact zones." The next step is to attempt a greater historical specificity through describing that contact zone in other than simple bipolar terms. In the islands loosely comprising the East Indies there were, even by the most reductive accounting, a minimum of three groups in the contact zone and actually many more, depending on which island was the setting of the discourse. The indigenous peoples were precisely not one group but a great many, some different Malay tribes, some not, with some locals colonizing others. Besides the Dutch and British there were other foreign groups as well, both

Chinese and European, including the French and, in particularly large numbers, the Portuguese.

There is another important implication of the effects of place on British imperial discourse about the East Indies. Along with the question of the complexity of British representations of their views of Dutch rule in Insulinde is the related question of the ways British discourses about the region created alternative placements for themselves. If, for example, when the subjects of British narratives stand on Dutch Java or Portuguese Timor and thus do not stand on British-controlled land, where do they stand? Or, more precisely, how do they stand? Why are they standing there? On what grounds, as it were, do they stand there? What right do they have to stand there at all? That this last question far from automatically implies a critique of imperialism is clear from that fact that it was virtually never raised in travel books of the second half of the century about standing in British-controlled places—the very places where it should most often have been raised.[20] Precisely because the familiar official colonial position was closed to the British in the East Indies, something much more subtle was opened: the possibility of articulating the imperial encounter in a variety of political ways.

One primary choice was simply to define domination in other than the conventional way of territorial control by a foreign government. The repeated presumption of both the greater importance of their own particular business and the general cultural superiority of British to Dutch ways in the rhetoric of British travelers to the area was connected to a pattern of placing themselves in a relation to the Archipelago which was seen to be more significant, more central, than anything another group might be doing there. The Dutch might officially be running the place, but the major European/local relationship in the Archipelago was frequently described in British travel accounts as being between the islands and the British. That's where history was being made.

This notion implied, of course, that "history" would have to be defined in other than the traditional political or governmental terms and, perhaps more radically, that there was more than one "history" to be told. Moreover, "histories" could compete with one another, could bury other possible histories in the act of narrating any particular history. What kind of history did British travel writers narrate themselves as making in the Archipelago? If they were not governing the place, what, according to their own accounts, were they doing there? And what, if anything, made their doings nationally significant? There were, certainly, many individual if unarticulated answers to these questions. I want to stress that there was no monolithic British "purpose" in the Archipelago. I do want to look at a specific memoir of travel in the Archipelago by Annabella Keith Forbes, in order to suggest at least one important way Victorian culture read—and wrote—the unofficial British presence in the Archipelago as a matter of important history being made.

Book Titles and Indonesia

In March of 1882 a Scottish woman in her twenties arrived by boat in Batavia. Annabella Keith had made the long trip from home to be married. The wedding took place on April 5 in Batavia, and Anna's new husband was Henry Ogg Forbes, then just thirty-one years old, an adventurous Scottish biologist from Aberdeen and then the University of Edinburgh. Since sailing from Southampton three and a half years earlier (in October 1878), Henry had been traveling around in the islands of the Eastern Archipelago. His adventures included spending all of 1881 collecting bird and plant specimens in the interior of many remote islands, living for part of that time on a raft. He had only returned to the sophistication of city life in Batavia on December 27, 1881.

Henry passed the first three months of 1882 in Batavia, waiting for his fiancée and, as he termed it, setting about his "preparations for an extended journey to the less civilized islands in the Far East of the Archipelago."[21] That "extended journey" began on April 15, 1882, ten days after the couple's marriage and less then three weeks after Anna's first arrival in the East. It was Anna's honeymoon. The honeymoon continued for fourteen months, then had to be cut short because of the young bride's near death from bouts of malarial fever and malnutrition. The couple landed back at the comforts of Batavia on June 28, 1883, and on July 9th they sailed to England, reaching London on August 14.

Out of the trip came two books. Henry published *A Naturalist's Wanderings in the Eastern Archipelago* in 1885. It was very successful and became a minor classic in the genre of travel memoirs by Victorian naturalists. In 1887 Anna offered her version, entitled *Insulinde: Experiences of a Naturalist's Wife in the Eastern Archipelago*.[22] She borrowed her name for the islands from the Dutch, though it was certainly a common enough usage among all Europeans when referring to the Dutch colony. What was not common is that in the opening chapter Anna introduced her title in a quotation from a then internationally known 1860 Dutch novel by Eduard Douwes Dekker called *Max Havelaar; or, The Coffee Auctions of the Dutch Trading-Company*.[23] Published under the pseudonym of Multatuli and immediately available in various translations throughout Europe, *Max Havelaar* had become instantly famous as "a crushing exposure of the iniquities of the Dutch" colonial administration for putting Dutch interests ahead of those of the indigenous peoples of the islands.[24] Even though, when the first edition sold out virtually overnight, the second edition was suppressed, *Max Havelaar* caused a "sensation" throughout Europe that was "unequalled by anything of the sort ever printed in the Netherlands."[25] In using the Dekker reference as the context for introducing the name Insulinde, Anna implicitly but unmistakably invoked the extensive public critique circulating in Europe of the colonial enterprise in the Dutch-held islands.

The Singapore branch of Oxford University Press published a paperback edition of Forbes's *Insulinde* in 1987, exactly a century after it first appeared. The paperback is a straightforward reprinting of the original, but with one significant change: a new and naturalized, or depoliticized, title. The references both to the Dutch name for the area and to the nineteenth-century name in English have been removed and replaced with a virtually generic description of the narrative's locale. The new paperback is titled *Unbeaten Tracks in Islands of the Far East: Experiences of a Naturalist's Wife in the 1880s*. The change erases the colonial invocation in Anna's title. In yet the latest variation of the ways several histories, including those of the indigenous peoples, have been unmade, this sanitized title is able to erase colonial history only by erasing the entire region as well.[26] There is no place known to anyone as "Islands of the Far East."

This recent awkward resolution of an editorial dilemma in reprinting colonial texts, particularly when the publisher is located in a former colony, graphically dramatizes the politics of geography, the oppressions of maps, the imperialism of names. For the European powers encountering and moving into areas outside Europe, naming a place was an act of possession which was often indistinguishable from an act of creation. For the English to name the Malay Archipelago was to give it being, to bring it into cognitive and quite material existence. But perhaps even more fascinating, to deny the European names, Insulinde and Eastern Archipelago, even if in the spirit of rejecting colonialism, is to deny the very existence of the place as well. This became hauntingly true of the region I am discussing, particularly during its struggles to achieve support for an independence movement during the first decades of the twentieth century, struggles which Benedict Anderson has so eloquently discussed.[27] Before the Europeans came there was no such region as Insulinde. They made it up.

To put the issue of reading present-day Indonesia's political geography more precisely, between what would be Singapore at the northern extreme and what would be Australia to the south and east, there are a great number of islands. Many of these islands had quite differing peoples, cultures, languages, and beliefs. The Europeans, when they arrived, grouped these lands and peoples together as much as they could under an umbrella name or, in fact, a few umbrella names. This was partly because there were different groups of Europeans, often with different times of arrival, and partly because the imperially designated boundaries of this newly invented grouping were unusually flexible (given the sheer quantity of islands) and imaginary, though also of course political and real. Thus European invaders used a range of imperial names: the Malay Archipelago or the Eastern Archipelago or Insulinde or the Dutch Indies or the Netherlands East Indies or simply the East Indies. All these names, by their undulating inclusiveness, erased the fact that there simply had not been any such coherent place when the Europeans got there.

But there was by World War II, when most of the Europeans left. One of the bizarre elements in the uneasy relations between what Bhabha and others have aptly named nation and narration, or in this case between the colonial language of possession and the process of making a nation in those land masses between Singapore and Australia, was the need to accept the colonizer's labels.[28] For the widely disparate peoples inhabiting those land masses, one key step in the enormous effort to get rid of their oppressors was the particularly difficult one of relinquishing their struggles to keep precisely that most precious quality which their oppressors would take from them: their distinctive social identities. In one of those eery reversals so often characterizing the experiences of the "colonized," the erasure of independent group existences in the Archipelago, which had been gradually taking place in spite of their resistance during the almost four centuries of the colonial encounter, had to be quickly if partially embraced in order for the many disparate groups in what is now Indonesia to throw off colonial control.[29]

The exercise of colonial control in the East Indies had operated in part through control of language. The disparate peoples in these land masses had to cease trying to be what they had been, cease trying to retain their precolonial identities. Only when they abandoned their various claims to the right to name and thus create themselves; only when they imaginatively and discursively let themselves in their precolonial identities go and accepted the monolithic and essentializing colonial identity invented by their oppressors— even in the early twentieth century deliberately abandoning their own languages—only then was their struggle for independence a success. "The idea of Indonesia required the denial of the political meaning of the societies into which the first Indonesians had been born. It required also the acceptance of the new reality of the Dutch Indies, and then the transmuting of that into 'Indonesia.'"[30] That transmutation was greatly aided by the actions of another imperial aggressor besides the Dutch and Portuguese, the Japanese in World War II.[31] The anti-"western" racial policies of the Japanese during their occupation, followed by their own subsequent defeats and departures, were a boon in forging the imaginary boundaries of the nation of Indonesia.[32]

The difficulties of creating an Indonesian identity might be measured by the fact that even in the 1990s there are still over 250 local languages in Indonesia. Ironically, an important step leading to the beginning of independence movements was inadvertently arranged and paid for by the Dutch colonizers themselves, when they decided as part of their famous "Ethical Policy" to take the responsibility of educating the indigenous peoples by providing them with a common language: Dutch. That the problems of liberation were, in fact, often impossibly complex is clear from the history of Portuguese Timor, an island as far to the east in the Archipelago as Java is far to the west. The Timor people, radically different from the larger group struggling for independence in Java and other islands, had no wish to be rid of the Portuguese only to be colonized by a new group of foreigners, admittedly living closer by, calling themselves Indonesians. The recent history of East Timor is one of continuing war up through the 1990s, as it resisted annexation first by the Portuguese and then by the Indonesians, having been officially colonized by them in 1975.[33] Benedict Anderson's stress on the distinction between imperialism and nationalism, also taken up in important ways by Gauri Viswanathan, is certainly crucial here for understanding the Indonesian struggle for independence.[34] Keeping the distinction clear helps us to see how the history of that struggle consists in some fundamental way of a troubled intertwining of the two terms. In the case of present-day Indonesia, nationalism was the centerpiece both of imperialism and of the rebellion which after four centuries drove out the imperialists. The colonial encounter, the colonizers' invention and naming of various lands as one region and the colonized peoples' acceptance of that name and all that it implied—including, as it turned out, the colonizing activity itself—was the prerequisite for the creation in the 1920s of the political movement which would come to power in the 1940s as the force creating the nation of Indonesia.

Beaten Tracks in the Archipelago

If the new title of Anna Forbes's book, with its reference to "Islands of the Far East," effectively denies both the colonial history and the national present of "Insulinde," situating the narrative in some kind of never-never land, its reference to "Unbeaten Tracks" is equally fictional—and perhaps equally evocative of the opposing meaning it appears to repress. *Insulinde* was discursively located in a very real colonial territory. By virtue of that fact, it was but the latest in a series of European discourses about the region, discourses which were products of what was by the time of the book's writing already a four century colonial encounter. And to make that point, of course, is only to take up the question of the geographic tracks of the European foreigners in the regions. The islanders and many kinds of foreigners had certainly been beating their own tracks throughout the islands for many centuries.

In *Insulinde* the European discursive tracks most immediately in front of Anna's are those of her husband. Her written account of their journey was strongly influenced by Henry's and often paraphrases whole paragraphs from his work. The first sentence of her preface called attention to the "certain resemblance in these pages to the latter part of the work issued by my husband last year."[35] Anna justified what she referred to as "my simpler account" on the grounds that she and Henry "shared for the most part the same experiences; but we looked upon them from an entirely different standpoint." Her book is therefore of interest to a different audience, described as "many of my own sex."

In other words, *A Naturalist's Wanderings* and *Insulinde* offer "his" and "hers" accounts of the same journey. These are clearly not independent perspectives. Henry wrote his account from the fulsome journals he kept during the journey. Working from a much shorter journal, Anna's book is a reconstruction, partly, as she says, from letters sent home, partly from journal entries, and partly from "recollections that can never be dimmed" (viii). Also, in ways that cannot now be measured, *Insulinde* is a reconstruction from Henry's journals and Henry's recollections.

But *A Naturalist's Wanderings*, itself a classic in the genre of British naturalist writings in the nineteenth century, is not the only British account which shadows, and directs, Anna's work. For both Henry and Anna Forbes, another book looms large as the major influence on their perceptions of and writings about their experiences: Alfred Russel Wallace's then-famous *The Malay Archipelago, the Land of the*

Orang-Utan and the Bird of Paradise, first published in 1869 (and translated into Dutch as *Insulinde*). Frequently considered to be the greatest travel book on the region and "one of the most important natural history books of the nineteenth century," *The Malay Archipelago* is Wallace's narrative of an extraordinary eight years—from 1854 to 1862—of wandering around the Archipelago.[36] Through his work in the Archipelago and also in the Amazon, Wallace earned one of the most distinguished reputations in the history of European botanical discovery.

Wallace's monumental book was written to a great extent from the field journal he kept throughout the eight years. But Wallace too had his literary sources.[37] Standing behind *The Malay Archipelago* are many other books. Among them were two older Dutch accounts, translated into English: Linschoten's *His Discours of Voyages into ye Easte & West Indies* (London, 1598) and Bruyn's *Travels into Muscovy . . . and Part of the East-Indies* (London, 1737). Of British travelers' accounts there were some general classics: Francis Drake's *The World Encompassed* (1628), William Funnell's *A Voyage Round the World* (1707), and William Dampier's *A Collection of Voyages* (1729). These three were required reading, perhaps even required quoting, but not of great relevance to Wallace's particular project. More specific, and of limited yet essential use as the hermeneutic frames within which to write about the region, were Stamford Raffles's *The History of Java* (1817), published just after Raffles relinquished his control of the colony and returned it to the Dutch, and John Crawfurd's *History of the Indian Archipelago* (1820).

What distinguishes Wallace's book within the established rhetorical tradition of these fairly well-known previous accounts is that its declared subject matter is natural history. As Pratt has discussed, the system invented by Linnaeus was, effectively, a "global classificatory project" which established natural history as a "global secular labor."[38] Its content consists of nothing less than a complete mapping of the earth, here in terms of plants and animals rather than lands and water. European natural science, as a form of mapping, "produced an order" to the world.[39] It also gave a purpose which could be defined as benign and disinterested, nonimperial as it were, to the British traveler.[40] The British traveler could go anywhere and have a right to be there, the transcendentally apolitical right of disinterestedness, of innocence, of being the true student in quest of knowledge. As a nonpartisan observer, the natural scientist simply described the world. Thus *The Malay Archipelago* consists primarily of geological and botanical descriptions of what Wallace encountered during his journey. The purpose of that journey, in Wallace's words, is "to fill up this great gap in the past history of the earth."[41]

One measure of A. R. Wallace's achievement as a naturalist in the Dutch East Indies is that he collected an "astonishing 125,660 specimens," mainly beetles, butterflies, and birds, many previously unknown.[42] That collection filled a lot of gaps, material as well as scientific, since Wallace derived his income from selling what he collected. He was a professional collector and had been long before he came to the Archipelago, having spent some years in South America as well. His London agent worked for him from 1848 to 1862, selling, often at auction, the specimens he shipped home.

Another measure of Wallace's achievement is that during his Indonesian journey, in the spring of 1858, Wallace had his famous "flash of insight."[43] He mailed to his friend, Charles Darwin, a paper which significantly anticipated Darwin's yet-unpublished theory of the evolution of species through natural selection. It was that paper, entitled "On the Tendency of Varieties to Depart Indefinitely from the Original Type," itself based on an 1855 paper also written in the Archipelago and entitled "On the Law Which Has Regulated the Introduction of New Species," which provoked Darwin to hurry up to publish *The Origin of Species*. Wallace shares with Darwin the credit—if not the glory—for developing the theory of evolution through natural selection. An indication of the kind of scientific reputation Wallace enjoyed is given by the review of *The Malay Archipelago* in the *Anthropological Review*. Eleven out of fourteen pages are devoted to a detailed discussion on the single topic of Wallace's claims about the differences between and respective origins of the "Malayan and Papuan races."[44]

Wallace's book has remained the touchstone for a whole line of famous and not-so-famous naturalist studies about the Malay Archipelago, often focusing on the island of Borneo. I mention only a few of these works extensive enough to constitute virtually their

own genre. European travel literature on Borneo alone would require at least a book-length study. Published the same year as Henry
Forbes's book was one by an American who was to become the first
director of the New York (Bronx) Zoo: William Hornaday's *Two
Years in the Jungle: The Experiences of a Hunter and Naturalist in India, Ceylon,
the Malay Peninsula and Borneo* (1885).[45] Its extended discussion of the
orangutan was surely inspired by Wallace's. Encouraged by Margaret Brooke, the ranee of Sarawak, the botanist Odoardo Beccari
published at the beginning of this century one of the best-known
naturalist memoirs on the region, *Wanderings in the Great Forests of
Borneo*.[46] Traveling after Beccari and to some extent in his footsteps
but publishing before him was Carl Bock, the Norwegian naturalist
whose 1881 book, with the sensational title *The Headhunters of Borneo*,
was a great success.[47] In 1929 Charles Hose, the British collector,
came out with *The Field-Book of a Jungle-Wallah*.[48] Just one year later
Hose published *A Natural Man: A Record from Borneo*, informed by
Victorian primitivist views of "eastern" peoples as in a state of
nature.[49] As recently as 1984 Redmond O'Hanlon, a British reviewer
of natural history books, inspired by this impressive tradition of
naturalist works, made his own pilgrimage and published *Into the
Heart of Borneo*, a seriously funny account with occasional loving
references to *The Malay Archipelago*.[50]

The working assumption in the travel accounts of both Henry
and Anna Forbes, as well as the many other European books about
what was considered the East Indies, was that they were writing
within one of the most important, perhaps the most important,
scientific tradition of the nineteenth century. These "scientific"
narratives erased explicitly colonial narratives by placing the meaning of the East Indies within a different hermeneutic framework,
outside the colonial debate. The theory of evolution had been
scientifically documented by Wallace in his voyages of discovery
among the islands of Indonesia. Behind *Insulinde*, then, as behind so
many accounts of travel in this special region, stands not only Anna
Forbes's husband's more detailed book, as well as his notes and
journals, but also the major opus of that region's greatest British
explorer, a scientist whose name and work would permanently be
associated with the ideas of natural selection. *The Malay Archipelago*,

along with the reputation of its author, endowed that particular region for other Europeans and Americans with a tremendously important and evocative significance. For a scientifically literate British person in the 1880s (and on into the 1980s) the Dutch East Indies was not an unmapped region, not an "Unbeaten Track," and not just some other country's colony. In the great march of civilization, it was hallowed ground.

Déjà Vu

In the Malay Archipelago Henry and Anna Forbes found the paradise that British natural science in the nineteenth century was promising, just where they had been told it would be. Henry, "urged by enthusiasm," and Anna, "voluntary companion of an ardent lover of Nature" (305), were there, they had the right and even the obligation to be there, as pilgrims at the shrine. Nor was their presence a merely passive matter. Writing their books, both of their books, was part of the requirement that they testify to the truths they, to paraphrase Wordsworth, half discovered and half knew. As pilgrims of the new religion called evolution, they were there to see and to record, to locate and to testify, not only about the development of the birds and insects but about the development of the human species. Their mission in Insulinde, like Wallace's and Darwin's before them, was far more historically significant than the Dutch goal of growing coffee and spices efficiently and for profit. Their right to be there was a function of the scientific importance of their mission. Much as British archaeologists and amateur collectors had the right to be in Egypt to trace and preserve the record of mankind's cultural history, so scientists had the right to be in the East Indies to trace the record of natural history. And both groups had the obligation to preserve those records by acquiring specimens to ship to museums and collectors back home.

The very opening of Henry's book establishes the sacred quality for him, as a fresh worshiper in the church of science, of the colonial encounter in the Malay Archipelago. In 1878 he finally succeeds in getting his first passage out of Batavia and arrives at the Cocos-Keeling Islands, "made famous by Mr. Darwin's visit in 1836." "The slowly passing shores and isles" amply fulfill Henry's expectations, being "of surpassing beauty to my novitiate eyes."[51] His first view of New Guinea is of a "land over which there lies such a halo of romance and mystery."[52] *A Naturalist's Wanderings* continually celebrates "the nomadic joyous life of a field naturalist," among these holy lands of the natural sciences. Traveling in the Archipelago is a kind of endless holy communion, a matter of swallowing the wafer of truth, of feeling "that constant flash of delighted surprise, . . . the throb of pleasure experienced, as each new morsel of knowledge amalgamates with one's self."[53]

Like Henry's, Anna's discourse also narrates the pleasures of accumulation and consumption, of feeling the delights of Insulinde amalgamating "with oneself." She gazes at the Orient and finds there the Occident she sought, the Occident she had come to see. In a narrative rhetorically more committed to invoking authority directly than was Henry's, *Insulinde* offers frequent quotations from *The Malay Archipelago*, because of what we are assured is Wallace's "absolute fidelity" (127) to what he saw. Anna's experience is explicitly represented as a "a repetition of the scene depicted by Mr. Wallace"(127). Thus she need only quote him, for "I could not tell it better." The quotations she selects are presumably objective observations, such as those describing the first view of the Ke islanders: "black, naked, mop-headed savages," whose "eyes glisten" and whose behavior is a matter of "exuberant animal enjoyment" (127–128).

Insulinde offers a particularly rich example of what I want to stress is one of the most common tropes of British imperial discourse. That is the moment when what is seen is represented as, and takes its meaning from being, *déjà vu*. The lived experience of the narrator is cast as a repetition—directly quoted, alluded to, or simply imagined—of what previous European imperial eyes have (or might have) seen. This repetition can be written by a range of narrators, including Keats as he reimagined "stout Cortez" gazing at the Pacific, thus making clear that it doesn't matter much, is often insignificant to the experience, which actual European was previously there. The trope is particularly common in "scientific" travel narratives. There the previous gazer usually is important. For part of what renders this moment of repetition virtually sacred is precisely its power to reaffirm the authority of the original gaze (Wallace was right—I see what he saw) and, at the same time, participate in the authority of that original (I'm right too—I see what he saw).

Visual repetition-as-confirmation often functions as a form of imperial control over a foreign landscape. It is imperial in that the viewer, by nationality, by culture, by "racial" ability, sees clearly and objectively in a way that those peoples who belong in the scene being observed cannot. But this form of visual repetition is also something else of key importance in the writings of Victorian naturalists. The trope of vision as revision functions to assert human and botanical and geographical continuity, with the emphasis not on spatial control (of the "west" over the "east," for example) but on temporal stability. The past and the present are recognizably linked as a shared, in the sense of repeated, experience of origins. To recognize those connections, to experience the joy of familiarity amongst apparent difference, is to participate in the great task of tracing the already long existing order of the universe. The seer is precisely not the monarch of the scene. In a role which arguably may have conveyed even more nobility in Victorian discourse, the seer takes on the Shelleyan form of that unacknowledged legislator which was the heritage of romanticism: the scene's poet, its visionary and revisionary scribe.[54]

Tied to the commitment to continuity and stability, to ideas of order, is an idea of progress. Anna Forbes does not rely solely on Wallace's authoritative account. She can find her own words for what she repeatedly and variously calls this "rude savage life" (123), these "untutored races" (163), or for "black, the lowest in the scale of civilized life" (138). What she finds in Insulinde is an originary primitivism which provided the key scientific requirement—verification in the realm of natural law—of what Frederic Harrison, lecturing in 1879, had called "the onward march of the human race, and its continual rising to a better mode of life."[55]

The racism which pervades Insulinde is inseparable from its ideas of temporal continuity and cultural progress. This link in the book is common enough in British Victorian writing, one of a wealth of examples reinforcing one of the primary tenets of the cultural ideology of Victorian Britain. Like most other men and women of her presumed "race" and class, Annabelle Keith had been carefully taught. There have been many recent studies of the cultural sources of the interdependence of racism with notions of progress in Victorian England, all of which would apply to Anna Forbes as much as to any other Victorian of similar background. But I want to focus here on a quite specific form of this general belief: the ties between Victorian ideologies of "race" and progress and the British presence in the Malay Archipelago. The fields of knowledge which directly link this particular ideology with this particular place are the Victorian natural sciences. For Henry Forbes and Anna Forbes, the Dutch East Indies embodied the proof, the living scientific verification, of European advancement and superiority.

But *Insulinde* is also much more of an explicitly social text than was *A Naturalist's Wanderings* or *The Malay Archipelago*. Indeed, Anna Forbes's book imputes to Wallace's book a commitment to European imperialism and social Darwinism which is only intermittently there and sometimes quite vividly denied.[56] If Anna's "simpler account" tells us less about species and the habitats of birds, it tells us more about the category Anna so grotesquely and self-consciously names "the savage at home" (144). James Boon has discussed how Wallace's narrative proceeds as "a continual tension between desired orderly divisions, and their enticing chinks."[57] Anna Forbes's narrative offers more obviously consistent and extended sections devoted to imperial orderliness than did Wallace's longer and more detailed book. But, as I will be discussing later in this chapter, Anna's feminine imperial rhetoric is not the whole story her narrative tells. It also offers, at least once, perhaps as significant a moment of dissolution, as "enticing" a chink, as the famous conclusion of *The Malay Archipelago*.

The explicitly social and domestic cast to the discourse of *Insulinde* is related to Anna's initial claim that the book was written to interest an audience of "many of my own sex" (vi). In this sense the feminine imperial rhetoric of her account is represented as an "exact complement" of the masculine imperial rhetoric of Henry's "Narrative of Travel and Exploration."[58] Like the women's section of the newspaper, *Insulinde* is the version of the journey which, unlike

Henry's narrative, includes within it all those little particulars which are presumed to belong to the women's sphere. We hear the details of the Dutch rice table and how Tenimber women weave their sarongs and of their marriage customs (these generally get a small paragraph) or how the Portuguese nuns at Lahany care for some "very intractable" (239) Malay girls. A great deal of the discourse of *Insulinde* consists of representations of this feminine or domestic perspective.

The almost continuous focus on recounting foreign domesticity in *Insulinde* is inseparable from its claims that the Dutch East Indies embodied the proof not only of European intellectual advancement but also of something even more significant. It embodied the proof of human progress, of the ongoing *moral* improvement of mankind. The link between scientific and moral progress is by no means automatic in these books which mine the Malay Archipelago for the gold of British cultural and racial superiority. The virtual absence of the subject of moral progress from *A Naturalist's Wanderings* and its frequent presence in *Insulinde* have the effect of placing the question of moral progress within the discourse of Victorian natural science outside the masculine but within the feminine rhetorical sphere. Certainly, in *Insulinde* the measure of moral development is made in the realm of feelings, the ability to be selfless or merciful or generous or honest.

Moreover, the claims in *Insulinde* that the natives of the Archipelago are morally as well as technologically backward depart significantly from the startling and eloquent conclusion of *The Malay Archipelago*. After hundreds of pages of categorizing the various peoples of the islands in terms of their inherent racial limitations in comparison to civilized Europeans, Wallace's narrative suddenly distinguishes precisely between technological and moral improvements. In an impressively sweeping critique, the narrator contrasts "our wondrous progress in physical science and its practical applications" with the "barbarism" of "our system of government, of administering justice, of national education, and our whole social and moral organization."[59]

Using language which echos Percy Shelley's own indictment of science in his *Defence of Poetry*, that we lack the moral development to imagine what we know, Wallace is suddenly the narrator who directly and explicitly challenges the Victorian belief "that we, the higher races, have progressed and are progressing."[60] Wallace draws on his presumably objective and scientific observations in the Archipelago to assert that, unlike the English, some "communities of savages" in the "east" and South America live in ways that approach "a perfect state."[61] In other words, not only does the book's conclusion challenge the idea of European progress but it also explicitly suggests that somewhere else, that is to say, outside Europe, Wallace has actually observed people who have in their community relations progressed beyond the communities of Europe. *The Malay Archipelago* ends with a single-page clarifying "Note." It offers the resounding assertion that it is we (the British) who "are in a state of social barbarism," and then repeats, as its very last words, that "we are still in a state of barbarism."[62]

Wallace's concluding rejection of the notions of what would later be referred to as social Darwinism must certainly have been known to Anna Forbes, who could quote with such alacrity other passages in *The Malay Archipelago*. The unconventionality of the concluding pages are among the most famous sections of the book. Yet *Insulinde* does not at all acknowledge Wallace's special distinction between practical or technological and moral progress. The morals of Eastern peoples, as defined by Anna in the Malay and Tenimber islanders, were "such as might be expected from a rude people" (178). They were "savagely cruel, . . . essentially selfish," and "devoid of all feelings of gratitude or pity" (178). In her work, technological and scientific advances in Europe and England did include advances in what the previous century had considered the realm of religion: such virtues as honesty, kindness, pity, and gratitude. In other words, a trip to Insulinde, much like a trip down Alice's rabbit hole, could prove to Anna that she, and the British world awaiting her back home, were brave and sensible and good and, in the words of the Beatles, getting better all the time.

In *Insulinde*, as well as in the two major British works that stand behind it, *A Naturalist's Wanderings* and *The Malay Archipelago*, at least one major cultural meaning of the East Indies in nineteenth-century Britain is clear. In the debates between Victorian science and

Victorian Christianity, each laid claim to its own sacred territory. The Malay Archipelago was the holy land of British Victorian natural science, as the "middle east" was the holy land of Victorian religion. In the religion of natural science, space substituted for the more traditional medium of progress; time, as "long ago" was translated into "far away." To the natural scientists paradise, or that present version of the eden of our human origins, could only be found by traveling a great distance from the advanced civilizations of Europe. In that eden, the rational observer could read the past, could locate origins still practiced by savage tribes in the Indies. This effort was necessary, even invaluable, because traces of origins had long since been erased by cultural development among the civilized tribes of Europe.

The science of evolution, insofar as it became social Darwinism in late nineteenth-century England, required an actual place where it could point to "real," meaning actually existing, evidence of less evolved species. One place where the findings could seem to be "objective," that is to say, presumably untainted by the politics and economics of an official British colonial presence, and where there appeared to British imperial eyes to be no developed cultural history but just a lush nature with a few primitives living in it, was the islands of Insulinde. In the narratives of Henry and Anna Forbes the business the British had there, the scientific business which was so much more historically important than the mere territorial and economic interests of the Dutch government, was nothing less than to trace and to record the evolution of the earth, including most especially the history of the human race.

A Gendered Narrative

In *The Rule of Darkness* Patrick Brantlinger has suggested how much of the late Victorian insistence on progress tended to mask its opposite: an increasing anxiety about Britain degenerating into barbarism.[63] This fear of reversing the march of progress which had placed Europeans, and particularly the British, at the head of the line appears not only in the cultural critique with which Wallace closes *The Malay Archipelago*, but also in Anna Forbes's disturbed report on first reaching Batavia of seeing European and even British women in the Dutch East Indies "going native" by wearing sarongs.

But the specific differences between these two examples point to another critical issue. When we learn to trace Anna's cultural anxiety in her cultural complacency, we are still reading *Insulinde* as if it has a masculine subject, which just happens in this case to have a feminine substitute, who just happens in the above example to be discussing what women are wearing. It is no longer possible, I hope, to subsume issues of gender so easily. Anna's own explanation, if I can call it that, of writing for a female audience about the feminine side of the couple's journey, finally is too limited, too reductive. Upper-class men and women were not in parallel or equivalent situations in relation to Victorian cultural ideologies. "His" and "hers" as a polarity through which to read feminine imperial discourse won't do.

The many parts of *Insulinde* which seem to represent the declared intentions of the discourse—to offer the feminine perspective— certainly do repeat conventional Victorian ideologies about the advancements of British culture and of European, particularly British, people. Gender functions as an eager servant of imperialism as the Victorian clichés of feminine delicacy are put to use to represent the indigenous peoples of the islands Anna visits as ugly and dirty and cruel and subhuman, without those finer feelings which mark the Europeans. An obvious moment is when Anna is walking alone and meets a Timor man. We are first reminded that "I am only a small and feminine woman, and no masculine female with top-boots and a fowling piece." But Anna has culture, has history, on her side. Faced with "one of these dusky gentlemen" with a "fatuous leer, and an expression of hideous cunning," she remembers that "bulls, and even mad people, may be quelled by the power of the eye" (281–283). And thus, in a scene as preposterous as it is evil in its feminine representation of the imperial eye, the two walk for almost two hours along the path to Dilly, while Anna fixes the Timor man with her "unflinching stare." What the Timor man thought must have been amazing.

On the vexing nineteenth-century question of whether the moral advancement of the British kept pace with their technological progress, *Insulinde* is in most of its chapters even more culturally normative in its chauvinism and consistent racism than the books immediately preceding it which represented the masculine point of view. Its rabid social Darwinism, its representations of the higher virtues of moral and emotional refinement exhibited by the more human Europeans, allow it positively to lead the way.

But gender in Anna's narrative is complex and even self-contradictory in ways that are merely smoothed away by describing it generally as voicing the domestic or feminine side of the imperial enterprise. In *Insulinde* the problematic relations between colonial and gender questions have no easy solutions, offer no critical maps we can follow with security. For there is more than one kind of discourse and more than one constructed female subject in *Insulinde*. What the feminine means, or how representations of the feminine function to enable certain kinds of representations of experiences in the contact zone, changes in certain places in the narrative. The narrative voice, and with it the narrator it creates, are not monolithic. There are various Annas in *Insulinde*, at least one of which is a self quite different from the ones culturally prescribed for her. Without privileging one version over another, I want to consider some of the forms the subject takes in this memoir.

As Gayatri Spivak pointed out in a now-classic essay, imperialism in nineteenth-century British fiction is often encoded as the process of gaining an identity at the expense of the "native" subject, precisely what Jane Eyre does to Bertha Mason and what, Spivak reminded us, feminist critics, in their hunger for a feminine subject, often have done as well.[64] One critical approach to the question of gender in *Insulinde*, now so well marked that I need only mention it here, would have been to read this woman's text as participating in the patriarchal ideologies of colonialism that preceded it and shaped it in both Henry Forbes's and Alfred Wallace's work. I could then address the question of agency and writing by a woman by going on to reveal how the book offers at moments a hidden but authentic rebellious voice, or, in a more Althusserian key, a rebellious voice compounded from conflicting ideologies (for example, in such details as the subversive way the narrative introduces the meaning of its title).

Yet I am suspicious of readings of Victorian literature which discuss writings by women in metaphors of oppression, victimization, and/or rebellion. Not only are such readings self-serving; they are also self-destructive. I do not mean that in Victorian culture women were not oppressed, victimized, and rebellious. Although perhaps they weren't in the sense that these very terms seem to fix patriarchal values more than erode them. Many twentieth-century evaluations of the oppression of white upper-class nineteenth-century women provide an important ideological service to twentieth-century American, and I would say, European, patriarchal culture. The comparative claim implicit in such evaluations—that women now are more liberated—is neither beneficial nor liberating to women. "You've come a long way, baby," said the cigarette ad. We might ponder the fellowship between literary criticism, colonialism, women's lungs, and the Reynolds Tobacco Company. In the United States, inside the academy as well as out, progress has always been one of our most important ideological products. Moreover, the ideology of progress remains one of the most useful tools in the workshop of male and American "supremacy."

My critical question is whether, having abandoned as of limited use the familiar critical approach of reading a dualism of patriarchal surface and somehow rebellious feminine voice, I will be left with an occidental subject created by objectifying an oriental subject, and for whom gender does not matter. I share Laura Donaldson's position in "The Miranda Complex: Colonialism and the Question of Feminist Reading," that women's participation in the colonial enterprise must be considered differently from men's and their writings read differently from men's. At the very least, in their sexual oppression these Mirandas had at least a double relation with the Calibans.[65]

Thinking about Anna Forbes's travel memoir recollecting those months in the eastern islands of Indonesia leads fairly quickly to the large critical problem of the intersection of questions of gender with questions of color and nationality. As Donaldson puts it, there are "grave questions about any politics of reading which privileges one oppression over another."[66] How then do we insist on the significance of gender without reinforcing our own complicity in some form of nationalist or racist or temporal chauvinism? I am not sure anyone can. There is no way back to a presumed eden of innocence for those of us who live in history, just as there is no such thing as a moral theoretical position. There are just pieces. One specific way to begin to account for gender in *Insulinde* is to consider the various methods by which the narrative voice, the "I," of the memoir, establishes its subjectivity, its identity, and the forms that subjectivity takes.

Feminine Subjectivities

Again and again the narrative voice in *Insulinde* establishes its own superiority through contrasts with the inferior peoples Anna and Henry meet, specifically from the perspective of the domestic sphere. What distinguishes this voice, or, more accurately, these voices, from many travel accounts about the "East" by British men and women or, even more significantly, from its self-proclaimed identity as the feminine half of a "his and hers" discourse, is its intense and compelling final section. Chapters 20 and 21 recount Anna's solitary ordeal during April and May of 1883 in an isolated bamboo hut far up on a hill above the town of Dilly on the island of Timor. The special quality of this section was noted even at the time of the book's publication, at least by its reviewer in the *Spectator*. The reviewer does "not remember to have read anywhere of such sufferings so pluckily borne as Mrs. Forbes's four attacks when she was all alone in a hut far up the country, and her husband away."[67] The admiring review concludes with the claim that "this story alone would make this thoroughly interesting book worth reading."

Anna reports that she and Henry had the hut built in January and moved into it on January 6, to escape from the disease in the town below. In chapter 18 "our little homestead" (246) is represented in idyllic terms, offering a verandah with a beautiful sea view and a stream reached by a path through "luxuriantly healthy coffee trees" and "coming out on a small cascade of clear cold water under a canopy of the tallest trees I have ever seen" (247). The narrative devotes a few pages to a description of the hut and its environs. Then, in a sudden turn away from this beautiful and romantic image, the narrative voice, in a direct address to her presumably female reader, rejects the "little homestead." She tells her/me/us in an unusually cruel and violent sentence: "I hope I do not mislead you by this language; the thing is only a miserable shanty, fit for the last days of a worn-out negro" (248).

The power of language to mislead is contrasted with another version and another view of the scene, looked at through quite different eyes and described with a quite different kind of language, as the narrative for a moment breaks out of one rhetorical convention and into another. Those two rhetorical conventions prescribe two radically different identities for the narrative voice. We can get a clearer sense of those conventions and the conflicting options they offer for defining the subject by turning back to chapters 18 and 19.

The couple spent most of January and all of February and March in the hut on the hilltop, and Anna's account of that pleasant time forms the bulk of these two chapters. The language is repeatedly joyous, describing work and practical difficulties, yet making an explicit claim that the narrator is "as delighted as ever with the beautiful situation" (255). In its reference to "enjoyment of the serenest kind," its lists of "our pleasures" (269), the account clearly invokes the conventional picture of a romantic getaway. With its verandah with an ocean view; its exotic orchids and pineapples, so rare in civilization but here so plentiful; and its somewhat newly married lovers wandering alone in this luxurious landscape, taking moonlit walks when "the cool night wind came laden with the scent of wild thyme" (272), the narrative could form the text for the front page of the travel section of the Sunday *New York Times* or a television commercial for Bermuda. Anna's role is the gay young bride, ignorant but playful, charming her groom by coyly trying her hand at science: "I am serving my apprenticeship as a naturalist, and have made such progress that I can net a bee without getting stung" (269). This is the very stuff consumers will now pay thousands of dollars for. The conventions of the "romantic" vacation and the roles it offers its upper-middle-class or professional participants are at least as popular and as familiar today as when Forbes wrote *Insulinde*.

But *Insulinde* soon adopts yet another discursive voice and another set of hermeneutic conventions. In the midst of the idyll, the narrative is suddenly explicit that science, rather than an idyllic vacation, informs their journey and their narratives: "to live this Arcadian life was not the object of our visit to Timor" (270). After what is cast in retrospect as a narrative interlude, fitting for a book for leisured tourists, we are firmly told that for Henry duty called. Although the couple were already gathering specimens daily from the areas around the hut, Henry chose to press on into the interior of the island to collect yet more. Following that announcement, the idyllic chapter 19 ends on a gothic note. After the moonlit walk back to their "little homestead," Henry, by an accident which was, of course, their servant's fault, gave Anna a draught of "wine and arsenic, which had formed the death-potion of our collection of beetles." The chapter ends with Anna recovering, though experiencing a few days of the "terrible retching and strong fever" (273) which accompanied being "nearly poisoned."

Chapters 18 and 19, recalling the story of Anna's and Henry's three-month interlude in their hillside home, each contain at least one particularly startling moment when the discourse changes and the identity being created collapses. Certainly, the narrative offers many other moments which are critical of aspects of the couple's life on the hill, most often expressed in terms of Anna's disgust for the indigenous people they encounter. But that disgust pervades the book. It is hardly startling, rather quite expected, this late in the narrative. On the other hand, the two incidents I have noted— abruptly calling the hill a miserable shanty after having extolled the beauties of the place, and ending chapter 19 with the story of how her husband gave her poison—are rhetorically startling, both generally in this book and given their specific contexts. The very next line in the book, the opening sentence of chapter 20, is "I have already been one week alone" (274). This follows directly upon the "terrible retching and strong fever," even though there must have been at least two and probably three weeks between that literal moment and the time of the poisoning. But, indeed, the poisoning is the last narrative moment we have of the couple together on that idyllic hill. Rhetorically, Anna's isolation seems to follow from it.

The two incidents I have noted have some common qualities. Both are about dying, and about dying in service to the imperial enterprise. The negro in his last days has been "worn-out" from working the plantations. Joseph Conrad a few years later would direct his full narrative gaze on this image and bring into focus the horror of it, in his account of the dark shapes that line the river banks in *Heart of Darkness*. And the beetle, of course, takes the death-potion in the name of European science, for Linnaeus, for Wallace, for filling "up this great gap in the past history of the earth." Both incidents involve the transformation of the narrating subject from her conventional feminine identity as the charming and playful "companion" of a man with a higher purpose to a sudden revelatory vision of herself as actually in the position not of subject but of object of that purpose.

The narrative is a memoir in the sense of a recollection, written when Anna is back in Aberdeen. The language of the earlier chapters is informed by the memory of what is not recounted until the later chapters. In the two narrative incidents I have singled out, the female voice invokes the affinity of her cultural position as a naturalist's companion (wife) with the position of a slave or a specimen. All are at the service of, and can be sacrificed for, her nation's presumably progressive and scientific aims. I would suggest, a good deal because of what follows in chapters 20 and 21, that in both these moments the narrative voice does not merely turn an imperial gaze upon these two objects being killed by the imperial enterprise. That narrative voice, at least for these moments, takes the object position, takes on the identity of that subject who is being killed.

Anna Forbes, of course, is neither a worn-out negro nor a beetle. As a white woman, her cultural value is a great deal higher. Henry will force an antidote upon her, and she will recover, taking up again in the narrative the culturally prescribed voice of dear companion or beloved wife. But before she does, before she can conclude that "the remembrance of my sufferings will grow dimmer . . . and I shall be able to say what I now only faintly realize, that they are not worthy of mention beside the value of my experience" (305), Anna will suffer. She will know something of what it feels like to be left dying alone in that hut, like the negro and the beetle. And she will find it most "worthy of mention."

Henry left on a collecting trip into the interior on March 30,

1883. He would reappear, summoned by their Portuguese friends in Dilly, in late May. Though recovered, we assume, from being poisoned, Anna still had recurrent bouts of malarial fever in March and could not go with him. When it became clear that the person Henry referred to throughout his narrative as "the companion of my travels" would not be accompanying him, the question was what to do with her.[68] Anna preferred to be left in the higher air of the hut, even though it did not have a door, to the heavy atmosphere down in Dilly, deemed at that time the most unhealthful town in the East Indies, so unhealthful that Europeans on ships stopping there overnight were advised to stay on board. The town was almost a day's hike from the hut, including a five-hour scramble down a steep and rocky stream bed through the jungle. Anna, who was already suffering from malaria, would not only be alone, with the exception of a single old woman occupying a hut farther along the hillside, but also quite remote from any town or source of supplies.

Henry's discourse is properly concerned. As he records in *A Naturalist's Wanderings*:

> I feel quite anxious at leaving A. here alone. Female servants are impossible to be found in Dilly; but the old woman who looks after the coffee-gardens near us, has agreed to sleep in the hut within her call, and to assist her in her few domestic duties. She herself will not hear of anyone else, and scouts the idea of danger from the natives, and is quite brave over it. (426)

During those weeks alone the "quite brave" Anna, who had no choice but to be brave, ran out of lamp oil, cooking oil, and food. The old woman stopped sleeping there fairly soon: she had to go back to her job of watching the coffee plants and, plausibly enough, it was against her custom to sleep in a place of disease. Anna would not have been able, in Henry's conveniently deceptive language, to "hear of anyone else" because, as Henry knew as well as she, "women do not serve in Timor" (275), and there was no one else.

Henry's narrative tells us that at the actual moment of his departure Henry's guide, a Hindu officer, "expressed the greatest astonishment at all absence of timidity on A's part on being left alone." Henry's narrative recounts how when he reminded the Hindu that she was an "'English Senhora,' he appeared satisfied that the fact was sufficient to explain the phenomena."[69] Anna's being left, Anna's allowing herself to be left, is a straightforward representation of the subjectivity prescribed for the colonial woman by Victorian imperial ideology. It is recorded in Henry's book precisely as a representative moment, a moment when Anna rises to the occasion, embraces her role, becomes who she should be, and thus fulfills, before the eyes of the colonized, his and his British readers' expectations about her.

As I mentioned earlier, Anna's narrative notably does not record anything about herself and Henry at the moment of his departure, when this Scottish woman, by her husband's account, presumably rose to the occasion as an English senhora. Less familiarly but more interestingly, her discourse buries the good-bye scene, and its ideological potential, through a direct leap from being poisoned to being alone. Only a little later in chapter 20 does she refer to the departure scene, and then in order to recount an incident which through its choice of words gives her a regal or dominating position, claiming that Henry's Hindu guide behaved to her like "a courtier" (277).

If the narrative of *Insulinde* rejects the opportunity the departure scene offered to represent its female subject as a brave colonial senhora, it does construct a role for her which is also familiar in the imperial female's discursive repertoire, but perhaps more fun. In chapter 18, Anna had described the "hot, draggled, and dusty" walk down to Dilly from the hut, in order to "bring home to you the nature of the discomforts attendant on such a life as mine" (262). The very next sentence makes explicit what sort of life and what sort of subject are being represented at this point in the narrative. Her Portuguese friend in Dilly responds to the details of Anna's discomforts. "Mdle Isabel tells me it was a girlish dream of hers to be a *femme d'explorateur* . . . , but she now sees that the life is not all romance and perpetual picnicking" (262–263). The "English Senhora" and the "femme d'explorateur" are closely related, both named in a foreign or foreign-sounding phrase, both invoking the imperial discursive category of the intrepid Victorian female traveler. The "Senhora" of Henry's narrative implies a Senhor, indeed only exists in relation to a Senhor, while the "femme" of Anna's narrative implies un homme. Both serve the empire.

The Hindu and the Portuguese are alike in their amazement at and admiration for this phenomenon. The two gazes here, that of the successfully colonized Indian "race" which has adopted, though with imperfect mimicry, the values of its British masters, and that of the competing colonizing "race" which the British have beaten because of their superiority in what Kipling, in *Kim* called the Great Game, share a similar position in the way the two narratives represent these men's relations to Anna Forbes. Both are inferior and, just as important, both are presented as being able to appreciate, at least to some extent, the British superiority they see.

Subjectivity and Pain

The sentimentalized version of Anna's imperial experiences as "romance and perpetual picnicking" in a vacation idyll, along with the two more versions in French and Spanish of the female imperial role of struggle, dust, and important discoveries as a female explorer and as the senhora of a naturalist, are all exploded in chapters 20 and 21. These chapters offer a different kind of rhetoric, and also a different kind of feminine-gendered identity, one which, I suggest, does not fulfil the requirements of British imperial purposes (scientific, cultural, or economic). Here is a version of experience and of selfhood having more in common with the worn-out negro and the poisoned beetle than with the available clichés of British mem sahibs or Spanish senhoras or French femmes d'explorateurs. Intertwined with this different kind of gendered identity—and, perhaps, inseparable from it—is another special quality of that rhetoric. It expresses what Elaine Scarry has compellingly argued is a rarity in literature, a rarity *Insulinde*'s contemporary reviewer in the *Spectator* took note of as well, a discourse which represents the body in pain.[70] The reviewer was struck by the pain "so pluckily borne." But that reading, doing the hermeneutic work of its culture by locating the subject as another instance of British courage, merely takes a rarity and metamorphoses it back into the ideological usefulness of a familiarity.

What follows is a consideration of what it might mean to leave this narrated subject as a rarity.

Chapters 20 and 21 recount the story of Anna's long bout of malaria in the hut in Timor, of her increasing weakness and of her near-death. Early in this section the narrator asks the reader a direct and frightening question, "Have you any distinct idea what this fever is of which I so often speak?"(287). Invoking what Scarry has argued is a basic quality of pain, its presence for the one suffering it and its absence, its virtual unknowability, to those not suffering it, Anna immediately says that "before I suffered it myself, I used to account these malarial attacks a trifling matter." At least one function of this section then, a function offered as the single explanation for including the section, is to convince the reader that malaria is far from a "trifling matter."

The answer to the question of what the fever is continues, explicitly and in detail, for the next five pages. Here are some pieces of it: "The fever is never done. . . . The slightest effort is a burden, life is a weariness, and the future looks overwhelmingly black" (288). There is often a stage of "mental exhilaration." But then, "A sensation as if cold water were trickling down the spine arrests you. There is no mistaking this symptom. You may feel rebellious, you may weep for very chagrin; but get into bed, and heap every garment you possess upon you" (289). Then "the real suffering begins. Every pore of the body becomes a needle-point, and million simultaneous prickings cause you to actually leap into the air. Every joint becomes a centre of acute agony, and each limb a vehicle for shooting pains, which in passing from the fingers and toes seem to tear the nails off with them. I have often been surprised on looking to find my nails in their place, for I was positive they were gone" (291).

The subject in *Insulinde*, that created identity who is both narrator and character at the center of the narrative, is in many parts of the book the conventional female gendered subject of British imperialism. Anna is self-described as delicate, as "only a small and very feminine woman" (281). Yet for brief moments in other parts, and extensively in the long section about being ill in the hut, the narrative concentrates on crumbling that identity, transforming that advanced British self into a semi-undifferentiated person, specifically insofar as a particular culture shapes individual identity. Anna was often delirious, and when she was not, would watch the rats tearing birds apart on the floor and gnawing at the mosquito netting on the bed. British tastes in food become a longing for a little rice-water to drink. The pain of isolation competes with the pangs of starvation as Anna reaches the point of making a necessary, and notably evocative, sacrifice. She finally wrings the neck of a pet chicken who roosts in her bed, her "one little companion" (297), as she had been Henry's little companion. Anna throws it across the room, lies for hours in feverish misery, and at last gets up to find the body and make some soup. The chicken, like the negro and the beetle and, as a fear pervading the narrative, like Anna herself, is sacrificed, here literally consumed, for the cause. But the cause is not British imperialism. The cause, on a culturally nonspecific level, is simple physical survival. On the other hand, it is Anna who has taken on the role of sacrificer of "the trusting little thing," in order to save herself.

The Anna of this section is not the subject as a self-conscious and emotionally developed member of a culturally superior civilization or a female variation of Robinson Crusoe mastering the island. Nor had she, as the British might call it, "gone native," replacing one culture with another. Anna was dying, not because the East Indian world of Insulinde would not nourish her British appetites but because in the European hierarchy of male and female, specimens take precedence over wives, men are hunters not nurses, and she had been left to have malaria alone. The injustice toward women in Victorian culture, the insignificance of the role assigned to her because of the meaning of her gender to the colonial enterprise, is the precondition for the rhetoric of pain in *Insulinde*.

I know of no British travel book with a male subject which offers anything comparable to Anna's intimate and elaborately, even lovingly, detailed description of the disabling physical symptoms of her own malaria. Moreover, this narrative of a female subject is made possible in the book because the experiences of husband and wife were not the same. The British man is an important adventurer and the British wife is a stay-at-home, even when home is a hut in Timor. The account offers lingering descriptions of pain, fear, and loneliness and elaborate acknowledgments of bodily and emotional vulnerability. It is that vulnerability, made possible precisely because the subject carries the weight of the cultural definitions of being female, which opens the narrative space to re-create herself as a subject carrying cultural values which do not participate in the British imperialist enterprise.

Scarry has persuasively argued that the articulation of pain, like its silencing, is a political act. Anna's sick consciousness unites her with all people: in her need to eat, to drink, and to feel a connection with any living being—even a worn-out negro, even a beetle, even a scrawny little chicken. In that hut Anna's appropriate community is not the British. It is the human community, the living community. Her bodily vulnerability is the necessary prerequisite for her experience that identity is not found in the false dualisms of self and other, white and black, "western" and "eastern," but in the basic, and specific, fact of being conscious of life in the face of death. To articulate her pain is to reject the female roles of romantic tourist or stoic British wife or daring female adventurer. To tell of her pain, to confess it in all its graphic bodily detail, and still to grieve for that chicken, is to speak not only of weakness and vulnerability but of the failure of the British enterprise of scientific imperialism.

In the march of progress, the supposedly civilized man has done that most barbaric of things, left his sick woman behind. As a result of that leaving, the narrative voice of this section of *Insulinde*, a voice which would never have been heard had Henry not abandoned her, is a voice that speaks aloud the language of pain. That language is the language of the oppressed. Its theme is not only pain but pain in isolation, "so ill, with no human being to tend me" (295). The connections so scorned by the hegemonic impulses which drive the rest of the narrative are longed for here. The imperialist message of *Insulinde* is difference. At least one feminine message is sameness.

Insulinde almost continuously represents human difference, and thus argues implicitly as well as explicitly for European imperialism. It also, at certain narrative moments, uses the cultural devaluation combined with the bodily fragility of its female subject to represent the possibility of some kind of identification with those who are sacrificed in the colonial march of progress. That such an identification is not sustainable, indeed, is only experienced through articulating moments of intense pain, an articulation and a pain associated with the inferior position of the feminine in British culture, is at once the horror and the fascination of *Insulinde*.

Reconstructions of Subjectivities

Insulinde ended by distinguishing Anna's journey to the Archipelago from the visits of those "who must dwell in it at the call of duty, or who travel through it urged by enthusiasm" (305). Having neither business nor pleasure in the East Indies, the familiar feminine subject constructed by the narrative has primarily only one position: that of "a Naturalist's companion in his roamings." In the language of her own text, Anna has been self-defined as the tag along, the sidekick, the wife, and even the feminine adventurer—all within the range of conventional female slots. In the familiar hegemony of gender relations, the discourse of *Insulinde* almost continuously insists on its function as a representation of the feminine position, explicitly offering as its raison d'être that it sees with the female imperial eye. Only when the position changes is the rhetoric of the narrative radically transformed. That is the moment when the subject is reconstructed through the language of her own pain.

But if the subject creates the rhetoric, and is in turn created by it, she has not initiated her change in position. Anna's insights are not represented as emerging from her own agency, itself a concept too problematic to be of much critical use. Anna does not break out of the role of female dependency, of wifely accompaniment. It has been temporarily taken away from her, implicitly against her own desires. The man gallops out of the text, and thus the woman finds herself out of the role of companion. Anna's temporary freedom, made possible by malaria and abandonment, engenders a physical suffering which simultaneously almost kills her and provides her with a verbal rebirth, a liberation, at least until her husband returns, from the culturally conformist language of the rest of *Insulinde*.

Anna has already been rescued by the Portuguese and is in Dilly when Henry, at this moment no longer imaged as the daring naturalist but now "the sorriest sight imaginable—burnt and travel-stained to a ludicrous degree" (300), rides back, presumably to take up his masculine narrative role as leader and rescuer and to save her. Instead, at this moment the narrative gaze turns on him from a different perspective, one which, still infused with the recollection of how he abandoned her, refuses Henry his usual efficacious role. But then, almost immediately, the moment is over, the perspective vanishes, the rebellious vision fades. The couple returns to the hut to wait for Henry's collection of plants to arrive. The narrative voice, under cultural control once again, makes the amazing claim that "we are again enjoying the old tranquil life," back both rhetorically and literally in the same old place. That claim is an attempt to silence the vibrant language of pain, to get back to "the way we were." But readers have now seen more than one vision of what life in the hut is like. These familiar rhetorics of romance, of the happy young couple in their simple paradise, of the brave wife, or of the damsel in distress have all been undercut. And at least for a time, so too have British claims to progress and the use of the language of the natural sciences as a justification for racism and colonialism.

Anna Forbes and Henry went back to Scotland and wrote their books. But Henry quickly returned to the East Indies, in 1885, this time to New Guinea, and not as a private collector but with an actual appointment from the British Association for the Advancement of Science and the Royal Geographical Society. He led an exploratory expedition. It was a disaster. Boats sank; members of the group died; guides quit; promised funds never arrived. In 1886 Henry went back to New Guinea for a few months, as acting government agent at Dinner Island. Anna, having just finished her own manuscript, joined him once more in the islands of her sufferings. There is no record of her experiences on this occasion. Her stay must have been fairly short, because in 1887 Henry made his third attempt to explore and map some of the mountains of New Guinea, and failed again. Henry and Anna did return together to spend a few years in the Pacific, when Henry served from 1890–1893 as director of the Canterbury Museum in New Zealand. His career had shifted from botanist and explorer/collector to maintainer of collections. Most of the rest of their lives were spent back home, with Henry becoming consulting director of museums in Liverpool.

Anna only published one other piece, a novel called *Helena* in 1905. It was set in New Zealand, no doubt inspired by her three years' sojourn there. *Helena* is notable because, though almost utterly predictable in telling the story of the romance of a lovely and cultured young Englishwoman, it offers a special twist. Its heroine is half-Maori.[71] Helena's dilemma, discussed throughout the book, is that she is torn between two "races," wanting both to save the culture of the Maoris from disappearing and also to embrace the forces of the future in the form of the British settlers.[72] *Helena* is implicitly an argument for miscegenation, for a New Zealand future which, while certainly dominated by the whites, includes the customs, the insights, and the very blood of the original inhabitants. The novel is explicitly an impassioned argument for better treatment of the Maoris and, startlingly, for the intellectual and political connections between the need to reform racial policies and the right of women to have the vote.

The terms of the narrative's argument are quite clear. The land "had been wrested from its true owners," and Helena must fight for "my own people."[73] The novel's happy romantic ending, a kind of model village for the Maoris and a noble politician husband for Helena, writes against the novel's own critique of the British treatment of indigenous peoples and of women. Nonetheless, this second work, published almost twenty years after Forbes's first, stands at a distance from *Insulinde* in more than just years. The "mixed race" of the heroine speaks perhaps not only of the possibility of a changed political positioning on the part of its author but, more interestingly, of the extent to which literary history has elided literature not purely in the English tradition. *Helena*, and its leading character, may not have been so unique, or so daring, after all.[74] *Helena* opens up the possibility that there was a literature of the British colonies in the early decades of the twentieth century which addressed radical political concerns—such as "mixed-race" children as the product of the imperial encounter. The virtual invisibility of such literature now also suggests the possibility that many readers, publishers, and critics in the 1990s who read themselves as "advanced" still would have the theme of miscegenation conveniently erased.

CHAPTER 4

Botany and Marianne North

Painting "A Garland about the Earth"

*"What a drab world it will be when our great grand-
children come to it! The levelling of education will have
killed the beauty of rustic language and weakened original
thought, the levelling of class will have killed individuality
and wilted the life of art. The westernizing of the world
will have withered the picturesque, the great wild animals
will have been killed out, the naked will be clothed in
ugliness."*

—VIOLET CLIFTON, *ISLANDS OF INDONESIA*

*"An hour or two every day spent after business hours in
botany, geology, entomology, at the telescope or the
microscope, is so much refreshment fained for the mind for
tomorrow's labour."*

—CHARLES KINGSLEY

In writing the history of European and American science, it has
become a twentieth-century truism that the nineteenth century
was the time when great scientific discoveries were made and when
science as a field of endeavor left the shadow of philosophy and took
its own rightful place. Less emphasized in this construction of
history has been what Suzanne Zeller has referred to as "the symbiotic relationship between science and imperialism in Victorian culture."[1] Attending to this symbiosis suggests not only that in examining
Victorian science we need to look at its aspect as imperialism but
also that in approaching Victorian imperialism we need to include
some analyses of Victorian science.

My discussion will focus specifically on Victorian botany and on

91

the travel books of Marianne North. Unlike the writings of Anna Forbes, self-defined by their author not as scientific but as written for women and from the perspective of a female "voluntary companion" of a male naturalist, North's writings are self defined as those of a female naturalist, or, perhaps more precisely, an amateur botanist. In a way that is not appropriate to Forbes's work, North's work can best be initially approached by placing it within the context of the various discourses of the natural sciences in late nineteenth-century England. Part of what distinguished these several discourses was specific rhetorical conventions. These in turn were intertwined with specific places.

Peter Morton opens his detailed study of the "impact of certain selected topics within post-Darwinian biology on the late-Victorian literary imagination" by stressing that for the Victorians "the life sciences were much more loosely organized than they are today."[2] Botany often merged with biology. The resulting blend had much to do with the practices of the natural sciences in the nineteenth century, including the cultural associations of particular sciences with particular geographic locations. Place mattered a great deal in the practice of the Victorian natural sciences, a point which can help to explain the emphasis in North's writings on her travels in the East Indies and Brazil and the rather short shrift she gives to her travels to such culturally looming locales as Africa or even India. It is within the specific rhetorical conventions associated with particular sciences and places that North's writings need to be read.

Locating Victorian Natural Sciences

Scientific research in nineteenth-century England required money, primarily government money. In twentieth-century America this embarrassingly direct relationship, challenging so visibly the claims of the research sciences to objectivity, is often shaded, and even sometimes conveniently obscured, by the umbrella of the university. There was virtually no such umbrella in Victorian England. There were two major visible possibilities: government money, including royal patronage, and private funding. Not only did "scientists" typically belong to the wealthy and leisured class. It was also true that for large projects many a scientist's time was spent trying to raise money, often directly from the Colonial Office. The intertwining of political and national goals with scientific interests and discoveries is a matter of vivid record, in the usually shared background and class of the scientists and the politicians, as well as in the plethora of letters, reports of meetings, and accounts of plans and directions which constitute the writings of scientific societies and government.

Through many activities, including the medium of literature, the natural sciences in British culture earned their political keep and funded their growth by providing key justifications for the European imperial enterprise. One of the most central representations of the intersection of Victorian science and imperialism, along with records of meetings of scientific societies and government correspondence, is located in travel books. In terms of travel accounts, science was understood to mean the natural sciences, focused on analyses of particular locales. The scientist examined the particular plants and animals, including human ones, in a particular area and reported what he saw. In practice, the medium of literature, particularly autobiography, provided "objective" or factual proof of the superiority of the British to other peoples.

The interdependence of imperialist goals, nineteenth-century British travel narratives, and the natural sciences becomes quite clear when we realize that publishing accounts of their expeditions was de rigueur for those travelers who hoped to be funded for further journeys. Scientific funding for trips was closely linked to the matter of national and racial hegemony. British superiority was actually established in two fairly broad media, both of which influenced where scientific travelers would go and what they would write about. First, there were the personal testimonials of the travel books. Anthropological analyses of other peoples and cultures were routinely offered by the travelers themselves in their published narratives of their journeys. The writers had a direct financial stake in representing themselves as having been scientifically successful and the peoples they met as being inferior and yet culturally significant (needing more observation).

There was also a second important source testifying to British hegemony and the need for more funding of these scientific journeys so central to sustaining an imperial ideology. British superiority was established in newspaper accounts about these scientific "expeditions," particularly from the 1860s on. Newspapers tended to glorify, or sensationalize, the travelers themselves.[3] Why the papers did so was increasing circulation but also a "glorification of the role of the explorer-hero in Britain's imperial mission." That function resonates clearly in the 1864 obituary in the *Times* for John Hanning Speke, who had traveled to Africa with Richard Burton in 1857 and been the European discoverer (and namer) of Lake Victoria. For the *Times,* Speke was one of those "pioneers who have gone before our merchants, our missionaries, and our colonists, and have pointed out to us new regions where we may make homes for the overflow of our populations, new provinces for our great Empire, new countries adapted to the conditions required for the spread of our language, our institutions, and our spirit of Anglo-Saxon freedom."[4]

In terms of travel literature to faraway places which could reinforce the images of British superiority being promulgated as eagerly in newspapers as in books, Victorian favorites were probably Africa and also the Arctic and Antarctic.[5] Livingstone's 1857 *Missionary Travels,* Stanley's 1872 *In Darkest Africa,* and a host of other books narrating African expeditions were eloquent on the inferiority of the African races. Recent critics have begun to examine some of the rhetorical conventions of English discourse on Africa (south of Egypt) in travel books. In "Narrating the Anti-Conquest," Pratt looks at how late eighteenth-century books by William Paterson, a Scot, John Barrow, an Englishman, and Anders Sparrman, a Swede, represent the new Linnaean form of narratives of travel, in which "the encounter with nature, and its conversion into natural history, form the narrative scaffolding."[6] Brantlinger's chapter on "The Genealogy of the 'Dark Continent'" examines the interrelations between imperialism, Darwinism, and racism in some nineteenth-century British narratives.[7] Brantlinger points out that the dominant format of these English travel books about Africa is that they are narratives of expeditions, "nonfictional quest romances in which the hero-authors struggle through enchanted, bedeviled lands toward an ostensible goal," moving "from adventure to adventure against a dark, infernal backdrop where there are no characters of equal stature, only bewitched or demonic savages."[8]

The rhetoric of quest romance in many narratives about Africa in the mid- to late nineteenth century is notably different from the rhetorical conventions of many Victorian books about places in Southeast Asia. There are various subject roles possible for nineteenth-century British imperial narrators, though all require, in Said's terms, a "flexible *positional* superiority."[9] The strong current of masculine adventurism in Victorian accounts of visiting Africa tends to be absent or present in a different way in accounts of journeys to Southeast Asia. This difference is to some extent one of emphasis. Alfred Wallace and Henry Forbes did see themselves as explorers and one could describe their work as accounts of their adventures. They did write of danger, of such possibilities as dying from malarial fever or from being attacked by a tiger or a head hunter or a Borneo cannibal. But their texts do not express pervasive or even frequent concerns about the threat from the indigenous peoples, from roaming animals, or from unknown plants. The heightened feeling of danger which Brantlinger points out in his account of books about Africa, the awareness that the places they were traveling in were wild, in the sense of darkly or threateningly dangerous, is not much there.

Rhetorical differences between books about traveling in Africa and in Southeast Asia can be explained in part by the different functions of these two regions in the history of Victorian natural sciences. The botanists had their center at the Royal Botanic Gardens at Kew. Their most visible leaders were probably William Jackson Hooker and Joseph Hooker, father and son, who as first and second directors of the Royal Botanic Gardens were the effective leaders of British botany throughout most of the reign of Queen Victoria. Two other dominant natural sciences in Victorian England which I mention briefly here are geology and geography, with their centers also in institutions, the Geological Society and the Royal Geographical Society, and their leadership perhaps best represented by Sir Roderick Murchison. As Robert Stafford pointed out in his study of scientific exploration and Victorian imperialism, "Murchison and his colleagues at RSG filtered an awareness of the resources, geography, natural history, and ethnology of the non-European world into the British consciousness for the first time on a large scale."[10]

According to the conventions operating in the travel literature of many Victorian amateur scientists, the "explorer" is a rational observer and the universe, when properly understood, is revealed as well organized. The value of the expedition is judged in terms of the extent to which it uncovers (i.e., discovers) the order of the region it explores, by such means as the accuracy of the map that it can produce or the rarity of the specimens it has found. The major male adventure narrations about Africa were primarily geological and geographical, rather than botanical, expeditions. The adventurer as geographer and geologist is concerned with ordering the very earth itself, and thus controlling it. This is, of course, another variation on the colonial enterprise as aggression and accumulation and in this sense is the same activity as the botanist's focus on collecting. But there are discernible differences in rhetorical tone. Finding the source of the White Nile was a great adventure in a violent universe, requiring a brave adventurer. The emphasis on violence, and by implication on the world as dangerous and dark rather than benign, is often characteristic of narratives of geographical expeditions in a way that it is not of botanical expeditions.

The representation of Africa as a violent universe, and thus the European and American naturalists in Africa as great heroes, was from the 1850s on a narrative created to a great extent by British and American newspapers.[11] There was a symbiotic relation between newspaper accounts, travel books, and actual journeys, as the adventure myths promulgated by the newspapers more and more controlled even where people went. A newspaper's sensational coverage was to a great extent the basis for a public and government interest which led to funding particular expeditions. A key moment in this symbiosis came in 1874, when the *Herald* in New York and *Daily Telegraph* in London combined to fund Henry Morton Stanley's search for the source of the Nile. This represented "the first major British press-sponsored expedition of exploration."[12] It also represents a highly visible moment when newspapers selected and paid for the actual site, the particular heroes, and the specific kind of adventures they wanted, so as to shape all three into an imperial narrative of daring and dangerous enterprise.

Complicating the distinction between a geographical and geological interest more focused on Africa and a botanical and zoological interest more focused on Southeast Asia, with the changes in style of presentation these different "scientific" activities produced, is the distinction in narratives about Africa between science and religion. Again, the differences are hardly absolute. The dominant Victorian metaphor of Africa as a dark continent (particularly in its vast, "unknown" interior) in need of British light, while frequently linked to Christian themes, also often appeared as a version of the scientific process of charting the order of a region and thus dissipating its apparent "chaotic" threat. There was plenty of European and American scientific interest in Africa throughout the nineteenth century. There was hardly a travel book that did not offer as part of its justification for narrating a journey to Africa that it could contribute new knowledge to the ever accumulating insights in the march of European science. Victorian ideology about the "black races" was as crucial to Victorian social Darwinism as to Victorian Christianity. Still, by late in the nineteenth century, in part for geographic reasons (given "darkest Africa's" proximity to the "holy land" of the "middle east"), in part through the processes of colonial history (including England's relations to other colonial powers also present in Southeast Asia), and in part through England's historical acquaintance with the Southeast Asian religions of Hinduism, Buddhism, and Islam, Africa seemed a particularly suitable venue for British missionaries to an extent that Southeast Asia did not.

The "black" world of Africa created by British and American travel books and British and American newspapers cast the British traveler in a particularly heroic masculine role, one which was tied to the casting of Africa as dangerous and evil. It was not until most of the geographic exploration was complete near the end of the century that, in Mary Kingsley's 1897 *Travels in West Africa*, a woman's writing about Africa could attain public visibility in England. It is hardly surprising that transforming the masculine hero into a feminine one also required a rhetoric which would transform Africa into a fine place. Before Kingsley's admiring book on the charms of West

Africa I know of none offering arguments similar to Wallace's about the East Indies, that some cultures there were socially in advance of, actually more civilized than, the British. Even Conrad's eloquent critique of the evils of colonialism is ambiguous about whether the heart of darkness is entirely a cultural product of imperialism or in some way also a natural product of Africa itself.

The natural sciences, particularly geography and botany, had an almost talismanic power over British travelers to certain regions and over their travel memoirs in the 1870s and 1880s.[13] They served a social function in terms of defining acceptable activities for bourgeois and upper-class leisure. Not only did geography and botany "baptize fresh-air fun." These two sciences for "amateurs" also served the ideological function of providing orderly categories for apparent lushness and disorder. To practice natural science was to participate in the great Victorian effort "to stabilize the world."[14] Yet even in their shared functions, these two natural sciences highlighted different places and had different rhetorical requirements. Unlike in geographical narratives about Africa, Conrad's "the horror" seems notably lacking in nineteenth-century natural history books about Southeast Asia.

Botanical narrators were particularly sure of tone and purpose when rummaging around for underlying order in the Malay Archipelago and also along the Brazilian Amazon. I would claim that these were two particularly sacred sites for Victorian imperial botany. Amateur botanical collectors tended to like what they saw, whatever meaning they made of it. Lynn Merrill has convincingly traced "the stupendous popularity of natural history in the nineteenth century." She offers as one explanation for this social phenomenon that "the discourse of natural history was, and still remains, a powerful imaginative expression of the pleasures of the concrete world."[15] An additional explanation is surely that natural history appealed to many British because anybody could declare himself or herself an amateur scientist without undergoing a socially controlled screening process or rite of passage. The appeal of the role was simple: "the tradition of the wealthy amateur pursuing scientific research at his leisure was an ideal because of its association with the aristocracy."[16]

The activity was glossed as a pleasure rather than a danger, and that "wealthy amateur" could be a woman.

Given that different places carried associations with different kinds of natural history, it needs also to be said that these hermeneutic boundaries were hardly fixed. Whether in Victorian British travel memoirs the narrative represented the subject position as that of a botanist, a geologist, or a geographer, the hermeneutic path could be open to going wherever one liked. All these subject locations provided the possibility of viewing virtually any geographic location as a potential source of positive information, as potentially consumable, and potentially benign. Indeed, the scientific narrator could posit a veritable obligation to go to many regions, if possible to go everywhere. The promise of natural history, though made with special fervor in regard to botany, was that almost anyone, not just a masculinized adventurer/hero, could be that narrator. As useful tools of imperialism, the conventions of natural history, like the conventions of a proselytizing Christianity, opened the ideological way for more British people, and more different kinds of British people, to go to a lot more places.

But these scientific conventions, particularly in the discourse of botany, opened up another, quite special, possibility as well. They allowed Victorian writers to represent those places as much more enjoyable than did the conventions of either Christianity or the heroic quest romance of geographic expeditions.[17] The journey was typically described in the language of enjoyment, Henry Forbes's "delighted surprise" and "pleasure experienced" in leading "the joyous life of a field naturalist." One of those Victorian field naturalists was Marianne North. The tone of celebration informing her discourse places it as the direct inheritance of the rhetoric of the great male botanical naturalists, singing their songs of love for what Henry Walter Bates called "this free and wild life on the rivers."[18] In approaching North's work I want to look more specifically at the science of botany, to suggest some of the particulars of its intersection with imperialism, and also to suggest some of the ways the conventions of nineteenth-century British botany intersected with issues of gender.

Locating Marianne North

In spite of her lack of reputation in the United States, Marianne North has been publicly enshrined in England for over a century as one of the significant artifacts of nineteenth-century English culture. One of the key cultural qualities of North is that she was a confirmed spinster, a woman whose life and discourse had nothing to do with those conventional female subjectivities in Victorian culture of heterosexual romance and motherhood. As North herself commented, "I prefer vegetables."[19] Another key quality of North is that she spent five decades traveling. The last fourteen years of that time she went to all the continents outside Europe, painting pictures everywhere she went. Her declaredly impartial desire literally to cover the territory led her in the early 1880s to Africa, because she had no paintings of plants from that continent. She set out for Australia because Charles Darwin told her it should not be missed. North did not stop traveling until she was almost fifty-five and too ill to be active in the tropics any more.

North's status as a Victorian cultural icon began during her own lifetime and in part through her own efforts. Her fame rested primarily on her paintings, which were explicitly described—and admired—as copies, not of other paintings but of exotic natural objects in faraway places. North was a collector and a botanic artist, a plant illustrator, a woman who "put a garland about the earth."[20] She enjoyed the role and did what she could to arrange for her temporal fame to acquire a kind of permanence. In 1879, in the *Pall Mall Gazette*'s admiring review of North's private exhibition in London of her paintings, the reviewer suggested that North find a permanent place to house her collection. On August 11, 1879, North wrote to the director of the Royal Botanic Gardens at Kew, Sir Joseph Hooker, to offer her paintings.[21] She paid for building a small museum in which to house them, hired the architect, and supervised the gallery's construction and interior decoration, herself painting the interior frieze and the decorations around the doors. Between 1882 and 1885 North took charge of the hanging of 832 paintings, primarily but not entirely of plants, which she had done during her travels. In a master stroke of symbolic consumerism, she had the lower walls lined with boards made of the 246 different types of wood which she had collected on her travels. Finally, she paid for two thousand copies of a catalog, compiled at her request by the distinguished and well-known Kew botanist, W. Botting Hemsley. The collection was arranged geographically and designated in Hemsley's catalog under the title of paintings of "plants and their homes." North's venue as an amateur naturalist was the entire world. She did what she could to bring it all back to England and put it on display.[22]

The terms of North's cultural status were laid out in 1882 when the North Gallery opened to the public and the Director of Kew wrote the first official guide. Hooker stressed that North's paintings represent objects already disappearing in the march of progress. "Such scenes can never be renewed . . . except by means of such records as this lady has presented to us." Hooker predicted that a grateful posterity would particularly praise "her fortitude as a traveler, her talent and industry as an artist, and her liberality and public spirit."[23] To a great extent he was right. The enshrinement of North carries on into the 1990s. In 1990, on the centennial of her death, Laura Ponsonby's *Marianne North at Kew Gardens* offered a fascinating narrative of North's life and artistic achievement, including superb color reproductions of many of the paintings. Dea Birkett, in a 1992 *New York Times* article on the newly restored North Gallery, points out that it is still "the only permanent solo exhibition by a female artist in Britain."[24] Birkett goes on to suggest that North's vibrant style, in its "strong female imagery, suggests a 19th-century Georgia O'Keeffe," and to call the gallery "our only record of a lost botanical world" (30). In the preface to Ponsonby's *Marianne North at Kew Gardens* the then Director of Kew asked, "Who was this extraordinary woman?" The answer will "elevate Marianne North to her rightful position among the great plant explorers of the Victorian age."[25]

Who Marianne North was, her public location through her paintings and writings as "among the great plant explorers of the Victorian age," had everything to do with whom she came from. North was one of the rare Victorians writing about journeys to Southeast Asia who was upper-class. The North family had been particularly distinguished for centuries among English country gentry.[26] Born in 1830, Marianne spent her childhood on three large family estates, moving from one to the next depending on the season of the year. Also, like many other wealthy English gentry, the Norths spent part of the year in London and traveled with impressive frequency to Europe. "Extended visits coincided with the periods when Mr. North had failed to get into Parliament."[27] What was unusual about the family was that they chose all the options: living on not one but three country estates, spending the season in London, and taking trips to the Continent. One of these, when Marianne was sixteen, lasted almost three years, only the first eight months of which were spent in one place.

Marianne was twenty-four when her mother died in 1855. Frederick North lived with his two daughters in London, and the three often went to Europe, taking sketchbooks and also keeping little travel journals. Marianne North had been collecting and painting flowers and plants since she was a child. After her mother's death she became even more serious about plant illustration, developing her scientific knowledge of some of the characteristics and varieties of plants. When Catherine North married John Addington Symonds in 1864, the nine years of life shared by the sisters and their father was over. Marianne North was now thirty-four, and the North household had dwindled to two. Over the next five years Marianne and her father took many trips, including a particularly memorable one to Turkey, Egypt, and Syria. These trips form the first part of her memoirs (published last). Then, in 1869, Frederick North died, when Marianne had just turned thirty-nine. The traveling North family had dwindled to one. Yet that one would carry on the meandering family tradition alone, keeping a flat in London and traveling on by herself for the next fourteen years.

Marianne North was well connected in more than being of impressive descent and rich. Her intellectual and artistic achievements were made possible by the intellectual interests, emotional and financial support, and social connections of her father. It is a situation common enough with sons, much less so with daughters.[28] Frederick North traveled with his elder daughter not only on his literal journeys but also on his intellectual ones. They studied plants together. He built three glass greenhouses at Hastings, and Marianne describes living "in those houses all the spring, my father smoking and reading in the temperate regions. . . . while I washed and doctored all the sick plants, and potted off the young seedlings."[29] He also introduced his daughter to a whole circle of publicly powerful scientific men. Sir Edward Sabine, president of the Royal Society, was a North houseguest, as had been Sir Davie Gilbert, another Royal Society president a few decades before. The Norths took holidays with Francis Galton, one of the originators of eugenics. Sir William Hooker was not only the most famous botanist in England but also virtually the creator, and the first director, of the Royal Botanic Gardens at Kew. His son, Sir Joseph Hooker, second director of Kew, was Marianne's friend for many years. During the time the Norths were living in London after Mrs. North died, they would often ride over to Kew to admire the gardens and to take home rare plants to paint. Their host was, of course, Mr. North's friend, Sir William. It was Sir William's gift one day to Marianne, then in her twenties, of a hanging bunch of *Amherstia nobilis,* the first ever to bloom in England, that made her "long more and more to see the tropics" (*Recollections* 1:31).

Unlike many privileged Victorian women, Marianne North consistently represented herself as a woman who had done what she wanted with her life. She followed her own advice to Amelia Edwards, to "do exactly what you think best for yourself."[30] North not only remained single but also appears never to have indicated, either in personal letters or the three volumes of her *Recollections,* anything besides amused contempt for the roles of wife and mother. A central element of her social and personal location was that she had no economic or familial incentives to marry. Moreover, she did have a long-term domestic relationship with her father, the man of whom she said, "He was from first to last the one idol and friend of my life" (*Recollections* 1:5), the man who said of her, "She is the main link that binds me to life."[31] She spent the almost fifteen years before 1870 being the female head of his impressive household. Whatever twentieth-century readers locked into a post-Freudian culture may want to make of her living with her father until she was thirty-nine, North wrote of the situation as emotionally and intellectually liberating. She frequently remarked on having escaped her sister's fate of wife and mother. She recalls that in the early weeks of 1855 her dying mother "made me promise never to leave my father"(*Recollections* 1:30). It could have been a heavy weight to put on a young woman of twenty-four. But there is no evidence that Marianne North felt it as a burden. Almost ten years after her father's death she was still exorcising her sense of being alone by invoking his companionship, writing to Dr. Burnell that "sometimes as I sit and paint, he seems to come and watch me, and the very thought of him keeps me from harm."[32]

While the unusual specifics of North's not only upper-class but highly privileged background made her career possible, they did not make it happen. The first, and perhaps the most, significant difference between North's life with her father and life for the next fifteen years alone after his death is simply where she went. When North traveled with her father, her range was fairly typical of the travel patterns of the Victorian upper class. Frederick North was a cultural product of the early nineteenth century, before the multiplying discoveries in science, the insatiable colonial appetites, and increased ease of travel had expanded the British imperial view. For most Englishmen raised in the early part of the century the world—which meant, of course, the inhabitable, civilized, and culturally interesting world—lay directly to the east. It included the countries of the Continent, particularly France, what would become Germany, Italy, Switzerland, and Spain. And it was bounded on the far reaches of the cultural universe by what was thought of then as the exotic East and is now called the "middle east": the wild Greece and lurid Turkey of Byron's poetry, or the holy lands of the Christian bible.

At her father's death, Marianne North stepped into the kind of traveling career British imperial aggressions had made possible by the late Victorian age. The differences between British imperial attitudes, at least as exhibited by the English upper class, in the first and second halves of the nineteenth century are clearly marked in the different careers of Frederick North and Marianne North. Her traveling range suddenly exploded. She took one decorous journey in the old mode, to Italy in the spring of 1870, immediately follow- ing her loss. But never again. Instead of Europe and the "Middle

East," North's destinations by herself were the entire rest of the world. Her first trip in the new mode began in the summer of 1871. In fact she headed west, for the cultural wilderness of the Americas, beginning in the north with the United States and Canada and, as winter arrived, continuing on south to Jamaica. On Christmas Eve, 1871, Marianne North, full of joy, had reached the longed-for tropics at last.

A second change from traveling with her father was that now North traveled alone. This is not to say that she was always or even most of the time by herself. She often had companions for parts of her trips, and she almost always stayed with old or new friends. But after her father's death she would never again take the role of companion. With the exception of that first trip to the United States, which she began with Mrs. Skinner (though the two gladly parted by the time they got to Canada), North did not travel with another person. She preferred the control, the freedom, of life on her own. How she used that freedom, where she chose to go, was no longer to "the Continent" but to all the continents, with particular emphasis on the tropics. When North's travel style and range changed, so did the cultural category she inhabited. North went from living what may be described as just an unusually ambulatory version of what was, nonetheless, a familiar lifestyle for an upper-class Englishwoman to living what can well be represented as the distinctly unusual life of the Victorian woman wanderer.

The period of North's travels was followed by establishing the cultural meaning of those travels for the English public through creating the gallery for her paintings and writing her memoirs. At fifty-five, with what had become serious health problems, at last North settled in England. She saw through to its finish the enormous project of creating the North Gallery at Kew for her paintings. She also finished an immensely long manuscript recounting her travels. North occasionally wrote to friends of writing about her travels, but no one is quite sure when she began the manuscript.[33] As early as January 17, 1880, before her trip to Australia, she wrote to Dr. Burnell that "I am passing a very pleasant winter at home by the fire, . . . when it is dark and yellow fog, I scribble—I am writing 'recollections of a happy life' and putting all my journals and odds and ends of letters together."[34] It is likely that some of her friends and family who had saved her letters over the years sent them back to her to help her reconstruct her experiences. This is certainly true of Amelia Edwards, since the many letters Marianne wrote to this friend contain several passages reproduced in her manuscript. But as to "what the journals were, and what has become of them," that "remains a mystery."[35]

North's major period of writing her manuscript was from 1886 to 1888, after she had given up traveling itself. But she could not get it published. John Murray felt the "recollections" had drawbacks, particularly "their very great extent & 2ndly their very peculiar character."[36] Macmillan thought the memoir was worth publishing because of "the unusual interest of the work" but also complained of its "immense bulk."[37] The subject of publication was closed for Marianne North's lifetime. She died August 30, 1890. That December, Catherine Symonds, Marianne's younger sister, began to edit the memoirs for publication. Catherine was not terribly in tune with Marianne's wandering habits, feeling "it was impossible not to wish sometimes, as the years went on, that she might be content to live this pleasant life among her friends, and leave the ends of the earth unvisited—a remnant of them, at least."[38] Catherine made many changes, such as deleting Marianne's unkind remarks about her family, including remarks about the dullness of the married state as she observed it in her sister. Until someone publishes a comparison of the manuscript and the books, we cannot assess how much Catherine domesticated the memoirs by removing the obstacle of "their very peculiar character."

In 1892 Macmillan published two volumes of *Recollections of a Happy Life: Being the Autobiography of Marianne North*. They sold an impressive 4000 copies.[39] The positive reviews suggest the extent to which North's writing, particularly this edited version, supported rather than challenged public assumptions both about the role of England in relation to the rest of the world and the role of English women in supporting the imperial enterprise. The reviewer in the *Athenaeum* assured his readers that "Nature revealed itself to her as Nature only does reveal itself to lofty souls dowered with gentleness, courage, reverence, and love" (Feb. 27, 1892, 270). Of the

American reviews, the one in the *Dial* called the *Recollections* "a work of the same nature as Charles Darwin's 'Naturalist's Voyage Round the World'"(May 1892, 15). The one negative note came from the *Nation,* in an otherwise typically sweet American review, and the sticking point was race. The reviewer commented that North was "very decidedly of the opinion that, except in unfavorable climates, the white man must inevitably drive out the colored—a view which it would be difficult to maintain successfully" (June 2, 1892, 418). No such doubt entered the English reviews, at least about the superiority of this "white," and English, woman. The *Athenaeum* suggested that North's constitutional fearlessness not only gave her "a wonderful power over animals, but it instinctively attracted something like worship from rough or semi-civilized men and women"(Feb. 27, 1892, 269). The image is of Marianne as the great "white" lady, gracefully traveling the globe, astride the backs of the beasts, human and otherwise.

The *Athenaeum* review does the cultural work of domesticating North, of fitting her unusual activities into a culturally familiar and colonially useful feminine norm (as her sister had perhaps done earlier in the editing of the manuscript). Sketching had long been a socially approved enterprise for British women. The image of Marianne and Catherine sitting beside their father and making sketches of the Italian Alps could not be more decorous, in part because it was such a marginal task. Sara Suleri, discussing Anglo-Indian women, has pointed out that "outside the confines of domesticity, one of the few socially responsible positions available to them was the role of female as amateur ethnographer."[40] She argues that British women were "required to remain on the peripheries of colonization" on the subcontinent. The Anglo-Indian woman is a "symbolic casualty," who "could, however, sketch." Sketching, then, had the double colonial function of keeping British women marginalized and at the same time turning "subcontinental threats" into watercolors and thereby domesticating them as well. Like Dracula's female victims, the domesticated were put to the work of domesticating those not yet tamed. The sketches could, of course, be written as well as painted.

This pervasive process of what Suleri calls the feminine picturesque used to define the role of Anglo-Indian women living for a time in British India offers a useful comparison with reading the work of Marianne North. It certainly fits the narrative image of the two daughters with their father. North's later activities, both her paintings and her memoirs, offer an important variation on the imperial category of "feminine picturesque." In an age when many of the great discoverers in the physical sciences, like Darwin and Wallace, were amateurs, when many scientific fields were themselves just being developed, Marianne North developed herself as an amateur scientist. Through the acceptably feminine aesthetic genres of travel writing and painting, North to some extent moved out of the feminine imperial role of a person who could not actively be an imperialist but "could, however, sketch." Her botanical discoveries, if not her travel writings themselves, successfully lay claim to the masculine world of objectivity and discovery. Moreover, her visual subjects were generally neither people nor buildings nor even landscapes. In her paintings North did not so much "sketch" as delineate. As illustrations, her work focused on the kind of close-up detail of plants and their flowers which later would become the province of photography.

North drew presumably accurate botanic illustrations of plants in all the places she traveled and wrote her memoirs as an accompaniment to her exhibited work in the North Gallery. She also collected thousands of specimens to take back to Kew and discovered four species of plants, the *Nepenthes northiana*, *Crinum northianum*, *Areca northiana*, and *Kniphofia northiana*. Sir Joseph Hooker was able to distinguish a new genus of tree, in part from her drawing of it while in the Seychelles, and named it *Northea seychellana* in her honor. Marianne North was that virtual anomaly in Victorian culture, an English woman naturalist respected by eminent scientific men. It is clear that, as a woman, North was not culturally victimized in the same way or to the same degree as the many British women residing for a time in India whom Suleri described as "required to remain on the peripheries of colonization." North's work does not exhibit the rhetoric of dependency. Nor can we grant it the degree of exoneration from imperial responsibility that such a victimization implies.

When people in the nineteenth century and the twentieth conjure up that convenient and familiar convention from imperial discourse, the British woman traveler, adventurous, unflappable, full-skirted and well bred, a central example working to define this supposedly independent category is Marianne North.[41] It is important to challenge both this representation of North and the category itself. Instead of being put at the service of some sort of ideology of female independence from Victorian social convention, North's writings need to be read within the frames of Victorian botany, gender, and place.

British Botany and Kew

Residing in the cultural heavens constructed in North's writing were many eminent Victorians. A place there was not granted by fiat to those Victorians who were wellborn or even those in positions of public power, but only to those who really *did* something, who worked hard, and at certain kinds of work. The heroes of North's discourse were the natural scientists, the great Darwin, Alfred Russel Wallace, and on a lesser scale the botanists she knew well: the Hookers of Kew (both Sir William and his son, Sir Joseph), Hemsley, and even an amateur like her father. As we might expect, North made particularly long trips, virtually pilgrimages, to those favored places for Victorian naturalists: the Malay Archipelago and Brazil. In language we have come to expect from these proponents of a new religion, she found Wallace's book "a bible to me in Java" (*Recollections* 1:282). She corresponded with Wallace in the late eighties, and he sent her his book on the Amazon.[42]

For the self-proclaimed "heathen" with the "belief in next to nothing," rejecting the next life meant attending to this one.[43] The great and sacred adventure of life was a matter of looking around at the beautiful world. That looking around, that aesthetic contemplation, was not a static event. It was not to be accomplished with a passive or spontaneous gaze. *Recollections of a Happy Life* is a narrative of unceasing activity, of self-education and self-discipline, of traveling on an ox for eight hours to get on a twenty-foot boat for another day and a night in order to paint for sixteen hours a day at almost 100 percent humidity. And that painting would be "accurate," precise, "objective," a matter of correct illustration rather than creative art. Margaret Brooke described Miss North in Sarawak as "hurtlingly energetic" and "ready for any emergency."[44] Looking at the beautiful world was a matter of rigorous effort, a matter of working to develop a trained eye. It was a matter of science.

During the nineteenth century different sciences—biology, geology, botany, entomology—developed in different ways and in different relations to various other European countries. The science of botany in England was in some important senses an amateur activity. This does not mean that nineteenth-century botany, in England or elsewhere, was an amateur science. But the development of botany as a science was to a great extent a national affair, with different countries dominating at different periods. During the eighteenth century in Europe, an idea had emerged that living organisms "had not reproduced themselves unchanged since some moment of divine creation, but had undergone a development in time."[45] The problem of classifying plants in the light of their historical development was the major focus of most botanists, and much of the work, both theoretical and practical, was done in France, at the Jardin du Roi. Founded in the seventeenth century and funded by the government, the Jardin (renamed the Musée d'histoire naturelle in 1793) was the "first, and for over a hundred and fifty years, the only national biological research institute in Europe."[46] The Jardin's facilities, and its permanent staff of salaried scientists, gave France the edge in many fields of natural history.

But in terms of quantitative research the nineteenth century was led by the Germans, largely because of the explosion of new universities in many of the separate states, universities that jostled for power in what had not yet become a united Germany. In botany the dominant question was plant anatomy. How do plants work? Specific problems, often explored in university laboratories, focused on such matters as cell theory and plant reproduction. With M. J. Schleiden's 1842 *Principles of Scientific Botany* (translated into English in 1851), Wilhelm Hofmeister's 1851 *Comparative Researches* on plant reproduction, and Hugo von Mohl's and Carl W. Nageli's work on cell theory, modern botany came into its own as a specialized science.

This is not to say that most of the great nineteenth-century scientists were German. Among many others there was Robert Brown, a Scot in London, who described the nucleus of a cell; R.-J.-H. Dutrochet in France, who discovered osmosis; and Count Leszozyc-Suminski, a Pole who made the amazing discovery of the female organs in ferns. And, of course, there was Charles Darwin. But the topics and directions of botanical research were being set primarily in Germany. Interested young botanists from other European countries, including Darwin's son, Francis, went to Germany to learn the field.

Britain did have its centers of botanical research, primarily in Dublin, Edinburgh, and Kew. The Royal Botanic Gardens at Kew were comparable to the French Jardin du Roi. When the Dowager Princess of Wales died in 1772, her son, George III, inherited her property, including the gardens at Kew, at that point mostly devoted to producing medicinal herbs. King George then made a decision which would shape the direction of British botany, and British colonial life, for the next two hundred years. He chose Sir Joseph Banks, a leading gentleman scientist and benefactor of the Linnaean Society who had traveled with Captain Cook, to direct the Royal Botanic Gardens. It was Banks, with his particular understanding of scientific activity as literally exploration and discovery, who envisioned Kew as a place to display plants from all over the world. Banks sent trained collectors across the globe to do the gathering.

After the death of both George III and Sir Joseph Banks in 1820, nothing much happened until 1840, when ownership of Kew was transferred from the Crown, which is to say, the royal family, to the nation, which is to say, the British government. Then, in 1841, the legacy of Sir Joseph Banks was assured. The Lindley Report urged founding a national garden, not for aesthetic reasons but with the declared purpose of "aiding the Mother Country in everything that is useful in the vegetable kingdom."[47] William Jackson Hooker, professor of botany at Glasgow University, was appointed the first director of this new national research center. Just four years after Victoria had become queen, a new and major era of British botany had begun.

Of the three major botanical research centers in Britain, major because they were government-funded, Kew was arguably the most important. Certainly, botanists in the labs at Kew studied plant anatomy. But a notable part of Kew's function was to display plants from all over the world, as well as to map their local habitats. There was a strong emphasis on what I call geographic botany. This was botany understood as a matter of plant collection and classification, the effort to determine in some complete way what plants exist in the world, where they grow, and what their uses are.

A similar emphasis was occurring in American botany as well, but with some key differences. The strong sense in America of living in the New World, in a land which itself needed exploring, meant that for many American botanists the commitment to geographical botany was a commitment to studying indigenous plants. American botanists, also often amateurs, also included quite a few women. The pioneering women in American botany in the nineteenth century were for the most part backyard botanists, collecting, studying, and classifying the plants in their particular area.[48] In the second half of the century, Kate Brandegee collected plants in California; Alice Eastwood collected flowers in California and Colorado; Ellen Quillin studied the wildflowers of Texas; and Kate Furbish aimed to collect, classify, and paint the flora of Maine. Those who did leave the continent, such as Annie Montague Alexander, who went to Hawaii; Ynes Mexia, who collected in South America; or Elizabeth Britton, who collected in the West Indies, all stayed in the Americas. Nineteenth-century American botany, while sharing with British botany an emphasis on plant collection and classification, tended to be regional rather than global, while British botany was both. Amateur British botanists certainly collected and classified plants in their own backyards. But they also, in significant numbers, collected plants throughout the rest of the world.

The difference in emphasis between botanical practices in England and Germany in the nineteenth century also reflects differences in these countries' historical status as nations. While Britain was actively engaged in sustaining, and even extending, the empire on which the sun never set, Germany's imperialistic designs were limited, partly by its internal struggles and concomitant focus on the drive toward nationalism.[49] There was no united Germany until 1871. The interesting result was that there was a great deal more government money for academic botany in what we call Germany because there were a great many more governments, each independent state having the option to fund its own university research. There was only one British government, for all its various departments or offices, and a great deal of its attention in international matters was taken up by issues of competitive trade and empire. The international geographic emphasis of nineteenth-century English botany is inseparable from English imperialism.

The complicity of Kew with the imperialist enterprise is no mere metaphor. Since Britain's imperialist designs, economically speaking, were directed toward attaining control of lands which could supply the raw materials for the industrial revolution going on in the little isle, and since Britain's power in the world had to do with its ability to manufacture finished products from raw materials, it is clear that the science most closely linked to those designs and that power was botany. The subject of botany was precisely those raw materials. And, of course, the center of British botany was Kew.

Sir William Hooker had been a professor at Glasgow University because in the first half of the nineteenth century the two great British universities, Oxford and Cambridge, simply did not consistently offer scientific courses of study and would not begin to do so until the 1850s. Part of what this meant is that Hooker's social milieu was composed of people of professional status rather than of members of the traditional British aristocracy (although to a great extent the two groups overlapped). Sir William's friendship with Frederick North reflects both men's commitment, a commitment North's daughter would inherit, to the kind of aristocracy which developed in England when class privilege was put to the service of practical intellectual work and personal achievement. Sir William Hooker's appointment as first director of the new Kew represented the transformation of Kew "from royal garden to state institution."[50] A large part of what the government explicitly wanted from the research it would fund at Kew was "to obtain authentic and official information on points connected with the founding of new colonies."[51] The economics of colonial expansion was a key reason for government funding of Kew.

Sir William Hooker reestablished an elaborate system of plant collectors for Kew, a practice first set up by Sir Joseph Banks. Hooker's collections, dried, mounted, and classified, formed the basis of what would become the world's largest herbarium. Selling samples to Kew to expand that herbarium was a major part of what both Alfred Russel Wallace in the 1850s and early 1860s and Henry Ogg Forbes in the 1880s were doing in the Malay Archipelago. There were satellite gardens in most English colonies, to a great extent controlled by Kew, because the director of Kew had the right to nominate, and de facto appoint, the directors of those gardens. In other words, one of the main roads of advancement for botanists training at Kew, in Sir William Hooker's tenure as director and even more so during his son's, was to be sent to oversee colonial botanical gardens. "By the end of the century, there were 700 Kew-trained botanists and gardeners" running colonial gardens and botanical stations around the globe.[52] One reason Marianne North's travel memoirs include frequent accounts of her visits to colonial gardens was that part of her social obligation was to bring greetings from Kew to many of the director's colleagues.

If British botany was a fairly small community, for the most part a men's club with the main clubhouse being Kew, it is important to recognize what visibly stellar practitioners made up this particular scientific group. Joseph Hooker, who was director of Kew for thirty years, "was at the center of the world of botany, his reputation unequalled by any other botanist."[53] Kew's control, and thus its director's influence, extended over the entire British empire. Hooker's leadership in the British scientific community extended well beyond botany. His close friend was Charles Darwin. And it was Hooker, along with Charles Lyell and Thomas Huxley (the three called "the greatest botanist, the greatest geologist, and the greatest zoologist, respectively, in Britain then"), who led the defense of Darwin's *Origin of Species* after its publication in 1859.[54]

The imperialistic aspect of British botany should not be taken to mean that the British simply gathered up raw materials from the countries they were indigenous to and brought those materials to English factories. The process was much more active, creative, and interventionist than that. Kew's work of plant collection and classification also extended to plant distribution. Kew was, effectively, the depot, through which were funneled enormous numbers of species of plants in the nineteenth century. At Kew they were classified and their uses determined and described, and from Kew they were often sent on to satellite gardens all over the world, but particularly in the tropics and subtropics. Joseph Hooker brought, among thousands of other plants, forty-three species of rhododendrons from the Himalayas. Their hybrid descendants pervade the suburban gardens of the United States.

More ominously, particularly in terms of the costs to indigenous peoples of planting, growing, and harvesting it on extensive plantations, is rubber, the tree the British took from Brazil in 1876 and cultivated in the huge plantations of Southeast Asia. Joseph Hooker planned and initiated that transfer. It was carried out by the man he trained: Henry Ridley, superintendent of the Botanic Garden in Singapore, who started the Malaya rubber industry. The importance of that industry to the British economy in the late nineteenth and early twentieth century was immense. W. T. Thiselton-Dyer, the third director of Kew (and Joseph Hooker's son-in-law), writing in 1905 on the subject of Kew's achievements, invoked the memorable British saying that the rubber business produced "wealth beyond the dreams of avarice."[55]

Kew botanists were also responsible for beginning the tea industry in India, with plants they took from China. But perhaps the most subtle and far-reaching example of Kew's key role in the work of British imperialism, traced in detail by Lucile Brockway, began in 1859 and 1860 and was overseen by Sir William Hooker himself.[56] One measure of the family's long-term personal interest in this project is that Sir William's son (William Dawson), who died young, had written a doctoral dissertation at Edinburgh in 1839 entitled "On Cinchona."[57] Almost twenty years later, partly in response to the poor health, and thus lack of fighting fitness, of British soldiers during the 1857 rebellion in India, the government funded a project whereby British botanists shipped cinchona seeds and seedlings from Peru, Bolivia, and Ecuador to Kew. There they were cultivated and shipped to the satellite gardens in India, where cinchona was successfully cultivated as a plantation crop.

The cinchona seeds were collected by means of threats, bribes, tricks, and secrecy, over the strong opposition of the indigenous peoples and their governments. Exporting the seed was explicitly against the law in Bolivia and Peru and became illegal in May of 1861 in Ecuador, but the British continued to do it. The British attitude to violating national borders and laws is perhaps captured in a 1962 evaluation of Clements Markham's expedition, that "the extraction of the cinchona tree from under the nose of the ramshackle administration of Peru is in the best tradition of nineteenth century adventurism."[58] Visiting the Dutch Netherlands Government's cinchona plantations in the 1880s, Henry Forbes found the story of how one particularly good variety of this "priceless tree" reached "the Old World . . . so interesting" (*A Naturalist's Wanderings*, 109). The Dutch, who also saw the value of having cinchona plantations, bought the original seeds from Charles Ledger, an Englishman. Then one of their own botanists, working in concert with a Kew-trained botanist, developed this variety into a new species. With evident admiration, Forbes included in *A Naturalist's Wanderings* several pages (109–112) of Ledger's narrative of how he exploited his supposed friendship with a particular family of Bolivian workers, lying to and then bullying them from the late 1850s to the 1870s, so they would give him some of the seeds the English later named *Cinchona Ledgeriana*.

Indigenous to South America, cinchona became one of the most important crops in Asia. The Dutch plantations in Java proved more productive than did the English ones in India, with the Dutch later capturing most of the world market. But both countries made huge profits from their trees. The bark of the cinchona contains the alkaloid which produces quinine, the wonder drug that cured the symptoms of malaria, with different varieties having a higher amount of the alkaloid.[59] Once the English could produce quinine in quantity, they could not only go anywhere in the world but, much more importantly in terms of imperial enterprise, they could remain there.[60] Before the cultivation of cinchona, the English, and not only English men but more particularly English women and English children, wore away and died of fever in the unfamiliar tropical climates. It was mass-produced quinine which enabled the English to bring their families along and thereby to create lasting settlements in the countries of their empire. It was mass-produced quinine which opened up for Marianne North, along with many other Victorian men and women, the sheer physical possibility of touring the world.

Built into the geographic side of British botany is a cultural placement of the scientist as an explorer, as probably of independent means (in order to meet the expenses of travel), and as gracefully an amateur. This particular image of scientific activity opened the possibility of North being a botanist. The traditional ways for British women to enter botany were through drawing and writing about gardening, as Jane Webb Loudon did, herself the wife of a well-known writer of books on botany. There were certainly women botanists who focused on the plants of Britain, writers such as Elizabeth Twining and Anne Pratt. There was even an early nature photographer, Anna Atkins. What makes Marianne North's place in botany so unusual, even unique, is both the quality and extent of her paintings and the fact that the plants she collected and illustrated were not British, not even European, but from what were from Britain the far corners of the world.

When the subject matter to be studied was plants outside Britain, the conventions for a successful naturalist were clearly marked. The amateur botanist must travel afar, must observe in an objective and detached fashion, must represent the objects of that observation with accuracy and precision, and must gather up whatever can be gathered and sent home. It is no accident that the North Gallery at Kew displays paintings of the plants of every continent; that because when North first set up the display she had not been to Africa, she felt she had to gather specimens, both actual and on canvas, from that continent for her collection to be complete; and, finally, that the North Gallery is lined with wood from 246 countries. The North Gallery is an amazing experience. It is an extraordinary monument to one woman's talent and almost superhuman achievement. It is an equally extraordinary monument to a nation's almost worldwide crimes of conquest and occupation.

North's Recollections

In her discussion of eighteenth-century European travel books, Pratt suggests that "in the literature of the imperial frontier, the conspicuous innocence of the naturalist . . . acquires meaning in relation to an assumed guilt of conquest, a guilt the naturalist figure eternally tries to escape, and eternally invokes." Pratt's conclusion is that "the *discourse* of travel turns on a great longing: for a way of taking possession without subjugation and violence." The sexual language of Pratt's interpretation, the naturalist's discursive desire for conquest or consumption without rape in a kind of pre-experiential world, is linked to her other point that "the naturalist-heroes are not, however, women—no world is more androcentric than that of natural history (which is not, of course, to say there were no women naturalists)."[61] The travel discourse Pratt describes is entirely masculine.

These categories need to be reshaped in important ways when the materials under discussion are the travel discourses of later nineteenth-century, and specifically British, naturalists about the Malay Archipelago. I have suggested that by the nineteenth century, in British discourse the Archipelago was precisely not the "frontier" but rather the déjà vu, the place always already known. It is hard to find more than traces of the rhetorical conventions of guilt and longing Pratt discusses when we turn to the 1820 travel volumes of John Crawfurd or the later writings of Alfred Wallace or Charles Darwin or Henry Forbes. Moreover, the British naturalist heroes represented themselves more and more in the nineteenth century as practitioners of a well-established and an ever-advancing scientific discipline. In many regions European conquest was understood as receding into history, and colonialism was increasingly represented as already in place, a given condition of travel to distant lands. One implication of this sense of completed conquest is that, to borrow Pratt's metaphor, in the nineteenth century the imperial Adam could travel with an Eve. The self located as the feminine subject of *Insulinde* is certainly neither naturalist nor hero. But in the discourses of both Henry and Anna Forbes, the masculine for the most part does take the feminine along. It is precisely when he doesn't, when Eve finds herself alone, that her discourse takes on an unusual, even startling, dimension.

The travel books of Marianne North offer their own significant modifications of the rhetoric of nineteenth-century British women's travel discourse. To begin with, they express a quite different relation to Victorian natural science and cultural ideology, to the Malay Archipelago, and to gender from that represented in Anna Forbes's *Insulinde*. The full-time daughter, until she was almost forty, of an accomplished man who "was all in all to me," North nonetheless wrote a book which does not participate in the kind of gender role playing which informs the rhetoric of *Insulinde*.[62] There is no self-placement as the voice of a "companion." Nor does this nonparticipation in the conventions of feminine dependency imply that North, as a collector and naturalist in her own right, took on the role of Henry Forbes, the independent masculine leader. Her writing breaks out of both these familiar gender prescriptions.

The special, even unique, quality of *Recollections of a Happy Life* may well be located in the ways it represents its subject as both a naturalist-hero and a woman. One result is that the narrative does not use the language of sexual desire to represent North's experiences in the contact zone. Indeed, I would argue that precisely because the naturalist-hero is here a woman, even traces of the rhetorical tension between the guilt of conquest and the longing for innocence are absent. The question in approaching *Recollections of a Happy Life* is how scientific imperialism is being represented when the leading imperialist role is filled by a female subject. If not the eighteenth-century masculine conquest language of guilt and desire, if not the nineteenth-century masculine scientific language of discovery as a rediscovery, carrying not guilt and longing but confirmation and reassurance, what then is the gendered rhetoric which animates these memoirs?

One pervasive quality of the three volumes of *Recollections* and various letters is their continuing rhetoric of emancipation. Starting a new trip, North writes that "I am such an old vagabond that I own to being delighted to be perfectly free again."[63] Indeed, North's writings, both her books and her letters, are full of positively gleeful remarks expressing joy in what she continually represented as a liberated self, including a strong awareness of the relative distinctiveness, the special quality, of her situation as an upper-class Victorian woman. This distinctiveness shows up both in the narrator's frequently declared pleasure in her work as a naturalist and in her contempt for the ties of domesticity binding and deadening the lives of so many other European women. One way North establishes herself as occupying a different cultural location from other European women is through her characterizations of them when she encounters them in foreign places. A constant character in the *Recollections* is the colonial wife, be she Dutch or English or Portuguese. She appears in doorway after doorway to greet her ambulatory houseguest and is usually wan, often feverish, frequently with a baby on her arm, and almost always with a desperate need for adult female company on her face. She often appears for a second time, at the moment of being left behind at North's departure, waving a tearful goodbye.

The liberated feminine subject of *Recollections* is continually presented as indifferent to dress and fairly indifferent even to basic physical comfort, traveling for days on horseback during monsoon season, often eating anything and sleeping anywhere, sometimes neither eating nor sleeping at all. She is in rebellion against the very comforts of Victorian culture, explicitly identifying herself in opposition to many of the forms and basic shibboleths of Victorian "civilization," especially those of her own class. A similar self-positioning runs through North's letters. North wrote to W. B. Hemsley that "I rather like to keep my own individuality, not having any respect for any of the North name except my dear old father, some of the time of Old Roger."[64] At her niece's wedding she abhorred the other guests as "strangers of the powdered footman class, with whom I have no two ideas in common."[65] While a houseguest at Government House in Bombay, she "could not stand all the red servants and magnificence and left the next day."[66] North's writings abound with comic and contemptuous sketches of the British upper class abroad, "the great people in the usual state of amiable limpness," lolling on their verandahs and never looking around at the beautiful world.[67] As she wrote to Dr. Burnell, "when summer comes, and country house dressed up parties, are put as counter temptations to wandering away quietly with my easel and old portmanteau to unseen wonders the other side of the world, I think both you and I can guess which will carry the day."[68] And on a more serious level, North represented herself as an atheist, seeing herself as culturally advanced, a "Bohemian . . . with thoughts on the most serious things which would perfectly dumbfound most of one's best friends."[69]

It would require an ideological blindness indistinguishable from complicity to try to separate issues of gender from those of class in North's writings. The self fashioned in the *Recollections* was enabled to be free from the conventions of femininity and the conventions of being upper-class precisely because of the privileges attached to being an upper-class, and rich, woman. Moreover, this was not a freedom which enabled her to define herself outside her culture but rather a freedom from living older cultural roles and thus a freedom to live, to some extent even to invent, new ones. Like many a supposed free spirit, the North of the book is as trapped in the ideology of her culture as the Victorian women the narrative represents as being so trapped in their domestic and social obligations. The *Recollections* embodies Blake's great insight in *Milton* about cooption through the interdependence of conformity and rebellion: "Satan! My Spectre! I know my power thee to annihilate/and be a greater in thy place, and be thy Tabernacle."

The autobiographic portrait sketched in North's letters and posthumously published travel books is not that of an outsider at all but of a specific type in Victorian ideology, a representative of the new kind of ruling class which can lead Britain into its dominant future. Created in keeping with the conventions of the serious naturalist, the subject in the North's writings is independent, physically intrepid, with great stamina; indifferent to creature comforts and traditional social customs; the objective collector and detached observer with the well-trained eye. She would be, in terms of the cultural significance of such attributes, in the role of a man. Here is North writing to Dr. Burnell on marriage: "it is a terrible experiment matrimony for a man especially; as a woman is something like your cat and gets to like the person who feeds her and the house she lives in—but men if they have brains have a romantic idea of companionship in their wife and they discover they have no two ideas in common."[70] Where is the self-location of the subject gaze of this speaker: with the cat or the "they" who have brains?

Far from being a discourse outside the semantic field of the society from which North depicted herself as having escaped, the

Recollections and the available letters replicate the imperialistic values of the upper-class botanical community of North's culture. Those values may be glossed individually as independence and collectively as science. The book's opinions on religion, on natural selection, and from there to cultural and racial selection, reflected the writings of many of the most visible scientists of her day. If in some sense Victorian intellectual writing contained a debate between science and Christianity, North's work lined up with the scientists. But I suggest that it lined up not as masculine or even male-identified discourse but as a version of the new kind of feminine discourse.

I cannot distinguish between the imperial cast of North's work and its female narrator's discursive liberations from some powerful Victorian ideologies about the domestic place of true womanhood. North could be an amateur botanist because the Royal Botanic Gardens had impressive garden outposts in many tropical countries whose functions were in large part to cultivate plants in order to service and further British imperial policies. North could be an independent woman traveler because upper-class English people lived in elaborate bungalows all around the world, governing local laborers and gathering local goods, and were delighted to put up a woman from such a distinguished family. They were equally delighted to have their servants do her bidding as part of their function of disseminating British culture and supporting the expansion of British knowledge.

North traveled, painted, and wrote very much by the grace of, and in the service of, the men in power in her country. This point may well explain the notable lack of criticism, indeed, the explicitly voiced approval, of her travels on the part of those men. No one seems to have expressed the view (often written about Mary Kingsley, for example) that North was behaving too independently for a woman. The point must be that she wasn't. Independence for Victorian women was, to an extent we too often fail to acknowledge, a matter of class, family, and money. The specific hermeneutic link between North's representation of her economic and class privileges and her culturally accepted self-representation as a nondomestic woman can be located within the enabling ideological practices of late Victorian British botany. The very vision of per-

sonal female liberation her books present offers an argument for the
Victorian imperial enterprise.

Natural Science, the Indian Archipelago, and Brazil

One indication of the location of North's self-construction within a
specifically imperialistic naturalist tradition is how much of her
narrative is set in the Malay Archipelago and Brazil. I have been
arguing that the hegemonic principles extracted—which is to say,
invented—from the discoveries in the natural sciences were especially useful to the English for rationalizing the imperial encounter
in those places where the English themselves were not the official
imperial presence. At the very least, botany often provided English
travelers with an ironclad reason for being there, wherever "there"
might be. Attending to what were some of the most publicly visible
research projects in the natural sciences (a visibility typically attained through popular books and newspaper accounts) can help to
account for why different "theres" had different values in the cur-
rency of Victorian imperialism. Specific places tended to have specific
significance and to contribute specific pieces of meaning in writing a
"history" of British hegemony.

One crucial "there," a place particularly blessed by the English
naturalists' reverent association of it with the past of mankind, an
association nourished by English contempt for the Dutch as brother
members of the advanced species, was the Malay Archipelago. The
peoples of the Eastern Archipelago met the requirement of primitivism. Their cultural geography could easily be represented as less
urban, less given to written records of their cultural history, and less
committed to obviously visible cultural artifacts, such as buildings
or statues or paintings, than, for example, many of the peoples of
India, the place I suggest the Victorians were most acutely and
anxiously aware of when they looked to the "East."

In representing the island peoples in the Malay Archipelago,
British writings frequently offered an imperial narrative of lack of
development rather than of that common rhetorical alternative:
decadence. Because these peoples were written as not having developed the qualities of a sophisticated culture, they could also be

represented as providing an unusually clear window on the past, as offering a special opportunity for advanced "western" scientists to study the great subject of human origins. Thus a key effort of *The Malay Archipelago*, one to which the narrator devotes a great deal of space and earnest and careful analysis, is to demonstrate the original separateness of the lighter (and more socially admirable) Malay from the darker, more apelike Papuan races. In the words of the reviewer of his book in the *Anthropological Review*, Wallace could rely on "the diversity of moral features to prove difference of race."[71]

There were other places besides the islands of the East Indies which were not under the control of the English and also carried a special meaning in the cosmology sustained by the blend of the British government's imperial pursuits and the projects of Victorian natural scientists. For Victorians knowledgeable in the natural sciences the other region geographically distant from yet ideologically close to the Malay Archipelago was Brazil.[72] The reasons why this South American country colonized in the sixteenth century by the Portuguese should be significant to British botanical imperialism in the nineteenth century had first to do with England's warm relations with Portugal, then with Portugal's complex colonial relations with Brazil, and finally with British economic interests in Brazil.[73] In 1807 France invaded Portugal, and the Portuguese royal family escaped, moving their court to their richest colony. That escape was made possible by their escort of British warships, England being an old enemy of France and therefore a powerful friend to and protector of Portugal. The French threat to the crown was soon over, and the king returned to Portugal. But a branch of the Portuguese royal family was permanently ensconced in Brazil, as were their ubiquitous British allies. In 1815 Portugal declared Brazil no longer to be a colony but rather a kingdom and, even more surprisingly, of equal stature with Portugal. In 1822 the king's son, Dom Pedro, who had been left to rule Brazil, rejected Portuguese control entirely and declared independence. In 1825 Portugal officially accepted that declaration. Brazil was free of external imperial control, perhaps because the enemy had so literally moved within.[74]

By the mid-nineteenth century, upper-class Brazilians, many of whom were of Portuguese descent, and many of the British, in a country especially welcoming to British business interests, were getting rich from the gold mines and sugar and coffee plantations, worked by vast numbers of Africans imported as slave labor and also by indigenous peoples who, while not legally slaves, in fact were so. British business interests, and the slavery that led to the profits, extended throughout the Americas.[75] The possibilities for huge profits in the Americas led to a spate of "anti-aesthetic" travel accounts, arguing the need for commercial development, by writers Pratt has called the "capitalist vanguard."[76] Within this economic push Brazil's odd colonial history gave it a special relation to nineteenth-century England, as both exempt from the usual coloniz-ing drive which followed economic opportunity and yet as specially welcoming to British economic opportunities.

Brazil also, both politically and geographically, had another important ideological function in the nineteenth century. It was specially welcoming to British scientific interests. Brazil was the location of one of the world's great tropical rivers and some of its largest jungles. Like the Malay Archipelago, it was regarded as a natural scientist's paradise. This view, at least in terms of the educated Victorian reader, was advanced through popular travel books. There are two important Victorian works of natural science that are based on research in Brazil. The first was Alfred Russel Wallace's own *A Narrative of Travels on the Amazon and Rio Negro, with an Account of the Native Tribes, and Observations on the Climate, Geography, and Natural History of the Amazon Valley* (1853). Wallace had spent only two years in South America, and the book was not immediately success-ful. But his next stop would be the East Indies and his next book, sixteen years after *A Narrative of Travels,* was the hugely successful *Malay Archipelago.* This chronology, and Wallace's increasingly exten-sive reputation by the 1870s, was at least part of what linked Brazil with the Archipelago, and all it came to signify, in the minds of scientifically knowledgeable Victorians. When Thomas Hardy's 1891 novel, *Tess of the d'Urbervilles,* represented Brazil as the place Angel Clare took off to, it would immediately signal to his Victorian readership Angel's pretensions to being not only intellectual but somehow scientific.

By far the most famous Victorian book on the Amazon region

was written by the man Wallace had gone to the Amazon with, Henry Walter Bates, who stayed there much longer. Bates's *The Naturalist on the River Amazons: A Record of Adventures, Habits of Animals, Sketches of Brazilian and Indian Life, and Aspects of Nature under the Equator, during Eleven Years of Travel* came out in 1863 and, unlike Wallace's account a decade earlier, was a sellout. The book "enthralled readers with accounts of how different, how various, how *other* nature could be. The world's multitudinousness, as Arnold would say, was precisely what appealed."[77] In 1862 Bates had published a still famous paper outlining what would become one of the key concepts in modern scientific explanations of natural selection: mimicry.[78] Darwin found it "one of the most beautiful and remarkable papers I have ever read in my whole life."[79]

As is clear from their fulsome titles, both Bates's and Wallace's books turned the European scientific gaze on a vast range of objects, including beetles, flowers, mountains, and people. All were "natural"; all by implication existed at the same level of consciousness, or lack of it; all were appropriate raw material for a naturalist to study. This presumption, though contradicted explicitly in the final sections of *The Malay Archipelago*, was the familiar stuff of late Victorian primitivism and social Darwinism. Primitivism provided an important rationale not only for investing in English imperial designs but also for investing in technology. In parts of Brazil, the region Bates called "under the equator," very much as in the tropical islands of the Indian Archipelago on the other side of the globe, people could be described as living in an undeveloped or precivilized state.

Wallace and particularly Bates promulgated the widely accepted "scientific" significance of Brazil which provided the justification for British investments that would, presumably "develop" these crude peoples. That scientific significance was to provide a hermeneutic framework for the discourse of many later Victorian travel writers. The very "multitudinousness" which Bates celebrated was a sign of a primitive fecundity which required human, which is to say, imperial, order, what Wallace Stevens a century later was to call placing "a jar in Tennessee." I am suggesting that, through the practices of Victorian natural historians, the Amazon and the Eastern Archipelago had a relationship with each other in Victorian discourses. They were the particularly favored hunting grounds for the nineteenth-century sport of finding "scientific" evidence for British evolutionary superiority and thus justification for both imperial economic enterprises and domestic technological research.

On the other hand, the rest of the globe often could do almost as well. The ideology of English, and European, cultural advance and racial superiority, in contrast to the wilderness of other places, was in general such a pleasing and useful concept in Victorian England that it appeared in various forms in English discourses about almost any country outside Europe and often enough in discourses about countries other than England in Europe. One did not even have to travel very far, as is clear from the assumptions which drove many accounts of travel to Ireland, Wales, or the highlands of Scotland.[80]

The Gendered Subject and a Happy Life

Relations between the imperial enterprise and gender at play in the representations of the subject in North's work have to do both with its special version of place and with its definition of the natural sciences as a matter of visual representation. The North of the *Recollections* was not masculine, but neither was she a version of what in traditional Victorian studies has been known as "the New Woman." That phrase has gathered a fairly familiar meaning, in the sense that twentieth-century readers have tended to associate it with Victorians who challenged the ideologies of their culture by struggling for women's rights in ways that North did not. The question of gender North's writings illuminate is this: What is Victorian femininity if it does not fit the conventional dualism of old-fashioned domesticity and new-fashioned, culturally threatening professionalism? There was, I suggest, another alternative, another "new" kind of female, indifferent to the private sphere, yet contributing her feminine vision to the great work of sustaining and extending British power in the public sphere. This new kind of woman is particularly present in North's representation of herself within the late Victorian hermeneutic framework provided in scientific discourses on Brazil as well as on the East Indies.

In the first volume of *Recollections* (1892), there is a particularly long section on traveling in Brazil in 1872. That section offers opinions which, even in Victorian England, were conservative and reactionary, particularly on the subject of race. It had been 1772 when Lord Chief Justice Mansfield had ruled in the James Somerset case that slaves could not be forcibly returned from England to the Caribbean, a ruling that was taken to mean the legal end of slavery in England. Certainly, slavery continued to be legal outside England in many European, including British, colonies up through much of the nineteenth century. But by 1872, a full century after the Somerset case, it was also an indisputable, if hardly universal, aspect of liberal Victorian culture to be opposed to, and often repelled by, literal slavery. Near the end of 1872 the practice was in the midst of being slowly phased out in Brazil. But English people owning and managing mines and farms in Brazil did use, which meant they effectively owned, slaves.

North's narrative offers slavery as an admirable, even an enjoyable, institution, certainly better than freedom for the originally African peoples of Brazil. In language that echos the claims of apologists for slavery in pre–Civil War America, the narrator assures the reader that "If they have abundant food, gay clothing, and little work, they are very tolerably happy." In March of 1873, by which time children eleven years old and under could no longer be gathered up to be enslaved in Brazil, North saw a room full of what she cheerfully described as "remarkably clean little black boys" (*Recollections* 1:148) who had been gathered up by a slave dealer because they were at least twelve years old. Again, the narrator offers assurances "these boys looked very happy, and as if they enjoyed the process of being fatted up" (*Recollections* 1:156). Clearly, the subject here being constructed in North's narrative belongs to the reactionary camp. These views on slavery in Brazil are located within an imperial rhetorical tradition which locates Brazil as a site of the human primitive. The claim of this cheerful woman traveler is that slavery, as the ownership and maintenance of the primitive by the evolved, unlike an egalitarianism dismissable as that "absurd idea of 'a man and a brother'" (*Recollections* 1:120), is an excellent system.

Yet the complexities of gender in *Recollections* go beyond the nondomestic female narrator who forwards the business of empire by the absence of any sadness at the spectacle of children taken from their families. I turn to another passage, this time with the narrator offering her "observations" on the new antislavery laws in Brazil. "All babies were born free, the consequence of which was that the mothers took no more care of them, as they said they were now worth nothing! In the 'good old days,' when black babies were saleable articles, the masters used to have them properly cared for; and the mothers didn't see why they should be bothered with them now" (*Recollections* 1:148).

These remarks offer a familiar Victorian imperialist vision cast in the dualistic terms of the developmental primitivism of the Other. The rhetoric of this passage supports the belief that evolution provided some kind of "objective" evidence for the widespread conviction of the British that they had a right to take over other people's countries, and even other people's very lives, because certain races had evolved further than others. In 1878 North, worried about the health of Dr. Burnell, wrote to him urging that he stop his relief work among the poor in India: "I would have you do good to those who are nearer yourself—& farther from monkeys."[81] Yet her comments about black mothers in Brazil offer an even more extreme version of Victorian social Darwinism. The passage represents these darker foreign peoples not only as subhuman but as even lower on the evolutionary scale than monkeys. After all, many scientific observers would have acknowledged that monkey mothers did care for, and possibly care about, their young without economic inducement.

Yet the rhetorical shock created by such a grotesque defense of the humanizing qualities of slavery—with its twisted argument for the dehumanizing effect on a mother of her child being born free—depends in part on its being narrated by a woman's voice, albeit one self-identified as belonging among the scientists. That voice challenges conventional cultural expectations about sympathy being a feminized trait by exhibiting not the slightest sympathetic feeling for the children of another "race," even as she defines that other "race" as inferior according to precisely the cultural assumption of the feminine as a realm of feeling. What is wrong with these women, lower and more primitive about them, is their lack of feeling for their children. We are drawn to notice the narrative's own lack of sympathy in part because ideological expectations about female self-representation are both pointed to and, in terms of the narrator herself, confounded, as I suggest they are again and again throughout the narrative.

The passage also offers another important dimension. It undermines its own implicit claims for the superiority of the narrator's "race." The European "masters" cared for the babies not from a more highly evolved European humanity, which the voice is showing to be lacking, but precisely because those "babies were saleable articles." Indeed, valuing human life on the basis of economics is the fundamental principle of the institution of slavery—the very institution which European men introduced to indigenous peoples in the Americas through importing black slaves. Slavery is the major cultural gift from the European foreigners. It is slavery, the traffic in human life, which the passage presents as the cause of these black women's present inhumanity. By the logic of the passage, it was their British and Portuguese masters in Brazil who taught them to view babies monetarily, in terms of an infant's material value or lack of it.

While North's own expressed lack of maternal or nurturing feelings links her voice with those voices (also, of course, her voice) of the black mothers she criticizes for not bothering with their children, her implied critique of the economic basis of human value separates the narrator's imperial position from that of the British and Portuguese masters. Insofar as these mothers are dehumanized, what has deprived them of their humanity is not far to seek. They, or more probably their grandmothers or great-great-grandmothers, were stolen from their places in Africa and turned into commodities in order to be brought to Brazil to work the colonial plantations and mines. It might have been relatives of these very women North critiques who did the physical labor which made possible the gathering of cinchona in the Andes to send to the satellite gardens in India.

North's narrative voice speaks of apparently unbridgeable distances from these African/Brazilian mothers. Yet it also tells of deep connections, and not in some subcultural biological sense, "as a woman." North's links to these supposedly primitive or unevolved darker women need to be located in the ways they are all, herself included, quite evolved products of the imperial enterprise. For

North, through her own family ancestors, her own ties to British botany and British colonialism, has surely been dehumanized even as she claims the African/Brazilian women have. Indeed, I would argue that it has not been the slave mothers who have been educated by the history of colonial slavery into a hardness of heart, but rather North herself. Even as the narrator points to the drawbacks of phasing out slavery in Brazil, her critique founders on the self-contradictions in her argument, invoking a principle of humane and specifically maternal concern tellingly absent from her own rhetoric.

That lack of feeling pervades North's memoirs and provides the very basis for their special, and highly appealing, rhetorical tone. These are memoirs full of cheerfulness, of wit, of a successfully conveyed sense of pleasure and delight in the wonders of the beautiful world. There is plenty of certain kinds of feeling in these narratives, with their focus on the disinterested joys of the visual and their scorn for those who "persist in seeing Nature everywhere alike" (*Recollections* 1:298). North's narrative does not erase indigenous peoples; it merely celebrates the pleasure of looking at them—which is, of course, erasure.

Yet, though racial and national hierarchies are continuously sustained in North's narratives, it is also notable that even the Europeans usually function in the narratives as aesthetic figures on a ground. People of all nationalities are located as participants in a panorama of "gorgeousness," a much homier and thus more domesticated and feminine version of Wallace's or Henry Forbes's enthusiasm or Darwin's famous "tangled bank." In North's discourse this naturalized cultural universe overflows with the delight of man-made as much as botanical details, of delicate temple walls, "saddle-bags well filled with cakes and oranges" (1:168), "nice invalid officers and their wives" (1:289), "popped corn and cream for breakfast" (1:206), "silvery banana leaves flapping against the shutters" (1:93), bored monkeys and "Stag's-horn ferns" (1:297).

The narrator's lush appreciation of the little things, her feminine gendered affection for homey detail and spontaneous tableaux vivants achieved precisely by the erasure of the deeper sympathy of a critique of imperialism, defines North's discourse as composed of memories which can exist only within a certain kind of forgetfulness, as "recollections of a happy life." While located solidly within the rhetorical framework of Victorian natural history, the *Recollections* is also a supreme moment in the nineteenth-century imperial practice of travel rhetoric as a gesture of aesthetic consumerism, of locating and dispensing upper-class good taste. North's narrator enjoys her trips immensely. The writings, like the paintings, offer pictures from the outside. The voices of the *Recollections* move delightedly from caterpillars to a lady who shades her windows with creeping plants instead of blinds to a Jesuit aqueduct to the 'common snail of Brazil, ... as large as a French roll" (1:125). Nature and culture intersperse in a style which expresses the joy of the male naturalist rhetoric yet ignores the boundaries limiting the appropriate objects of the naturalist's gaze.

North's writings bring together in one constitutive discourse the apparently opposite visions of a feminized appreciation of, and even joyous love for, the multitudinous details of the human as well as the natural world with a masculinized "objectivity" and indifference toward so many of the living beings populating that world. This combination forms an eloquent testament to the powerful, and humanly ominous, union of imperialism, women's emancipation, and the natural sciences in nineteenth-century Britain.

PART THREE

British Colonies

A Crown Property and a Private Property

CHAPTER 5

The Company as the Country
On the Malay Peninsula with Isabella Bird and Emily Innes

"The Malay has been a fearful enemy for months. I have been every night, through his means, transported into Asiatic scenes."
—DEQUINCEY, *THE PAINS OF OPIUM*

There was no typical or paradigmatic British colony in the regions of Southeast Asia. On the other hand, I suggest that there was a colony, or what would by the beginning of the twentieth century become completely a colony, whose role in British imperial historiography during the late nineteenth century was very much to represent what a paradigmatic British colony might be. The reputation of British Malaya in England until the First World War was built of many complex factors, a few of which I want to discuss. Central to the rhetorical construction of British Malaya for home consumption was the work of two well-known late century writers, Frank Swettenham and Isabella Bird. Not central at all, in fact positively dismissed, was the work on British Malaya of another writer, Emily Innes. The discussion here will focus primarily on Bird and Innes and the radically differing representations of the Malay Peninsula in their works.

Why British Malaya

England's struggle during the seventeenth, eighteenth, and nineteenth centuries to control the waterway from her Indian empire to the China Sea was continually challenged by the expansionist drives

135

of other European nations also eager to establish and maintain their own trade routes to the "east."[1] Germany, Portugal, and Spain all maneuvered for footholds in Southeast Asia. Germany, itself struggling with the question of national borders, was a limited presence for most of the nineteenth century. The Portuguese controlled some small holdings. Spain did exceptionally well, between the sixteenth and the mid-nineteenth centuries gaining sole control of the Philippines. But the two nations most competitive with England were France and Holland. The French were firmly in Indochina and were not directly pursuing territories outside that sphere (though indirectly, through private traders, priests, and diplomacy, of course they were).[2] That left Holland. Without question the Dutch were the direct competitive threat to England in the seventeenth and eighteenth centuries in pushing to control trade in the lands surrounding the Straits of Malacca. That crucial waterway between British India and the Malay Peninsula is bounded to the north by the Indian Ocean and the Bay of Bengal, on the west side of which lie what were the key shipping ports of Madras and Calcutta. The Straits of Malacca forms the main link between the ports of eastern India and the China Sea.

Again and again the lesson of the past two centuries of the European presence in Southeast Asia is that European aggressive actions there were, to an appalling extent, shaped by relations between countries in Europe. At the beginning of the nineteenth century the Napoleonic Wars easily reached all the way to Southeast Asia. Those wars, and their consequences, would be a major factor in shaping the nineteenth-century history of the region. The British had determined that, as Canning put it in a famous phrase, "if France had Spain, it should not be Spain 'with the Indies'."[3] That this was a real worry was clear from French attacks on East India Company ships in the Indian Ocean.[4] Aiming to block French colonial expansion, the English invaded Dutch colonial possessions and occupied them for the duration of the war, to ensure that France would not get them even if France kept its hold on Holland. Some possessions, like Ceylon, the British kept, while others, like Java, they returned to Dutch control after the end of the war.

Nine years after the Treaty of Vienna the successful British and

Dutch allies agreed that the best, which was to say, the most efficiently profitable, way for each to develop a stable trading presence in Southeast Asia was to stop trying to outwit each other for the spoils and instead to divide up the region by mutual consent before the actual fact. Looking at a region that, with small exceptions, belonged to neither of them, they simply decided which part each could have. The Dutch had already spent two centuries unsuccessfully competing with the Bugis people from Sumatra to control trade along the coasts of the Malay Peninsula. They were loathe to spend the next century competing with the English, who were rather better armed than the Bugis. And the English could clearly see that Dutch business in the Malay Archipelago (south of the Peninsula) was so extensive that before long Holland might well control all of Java and Sumatra.

The Anglo-Dutch Treaty of 1824 established by mutual agreement that England would officially get Malacca, keep Singapore, and have the right to develop British economic interests in the region from Singapore on north up to Siam, while the Netherlands could control trade in everything south of Singapore. This treaty closed two centuries of Dutch interests on the Malay Peninsula. Effectively, these two European competitors-turned-allies drew an imaginary line and split in two for themselves the general Malay region of the globe. The Netherlands then concentrated its trade efforts in the Malay Archipelago, a concentration which can fairly be described as one of the originary factors in evolving a sense of group identity which would result in the twentieth-century nation of Indonesia. As for the Malay Peninsula, the British invented Malaya.[5]

For the first several decades of the nineteenth century the official British policy was solidly against territorial expansion into the Malay States. The crucial requirement for safe ports for British ships, both commercial and naval, was to be satisfied by English control of one or two of the small islands that ringed the Malay Peninsula. Lord Castlereagh's instructions to his ambassador for negotiating the Anglo-Dutch Treaty were explicit that the issue was trading rights and no more, that "territorial dominion is to be confined to India, an exception to prove the rule."[6] It had been only thirty-five years earlier that the historic India Act of 1784 had declared British territorial expansion in India to be "repugnant to the wish, the honour and policy of this nation."[7] As with the history of colonial India, the British policy of nonintervention in the affairs of the Peninsula dated from the earliest years of the British presence, originating in both regions from the stated rules of the East India Company.

The explicit and often repeated British commitment to influence rather than to actual occupation in this region, to what Eunice Thio has called "the Victorian preference for informal rather than formal rule," continued throughout the nineteenth century.[8] This preference reflected not so much any squeamishness about controlling other countries as a prevailing, though continually contested, British concept of empire as ideally a matter of economic primacy. The goal of empire, as members of Parliament and various Colonial Office administrators frequently defined it during the nineteenth century, was not land but money or, rather, economic opportunity for the little island with the big ships. "Intervention, though often urged and sometimes undertaken, was regrettable or temporary."[9] The very existence of the Straits Settlements was a reflection of the British commitment to not having a physical, which is to say, a territorial, presence in peninsular Malaya.

But by the 1870s the space between policy and events was to become at least as marked in British relations to the Malay States as it had become by the 1850s in their relations to India.[10] The Malay Peninsula at the beginning of the century was a loose aggregate of more than nine independent states, with flexible boundaries marked by influence and loyalty rather than by land, and with peoples of a range of races and cultures, though frequently Muslim. In the fifty years from 1824 to 1874, unevenly but relentlessly, the British extended their influence into what were, by late in the century, clearly defined by number and territory as the nine Malay States. Tin production exploded with expanded European demand for tin plate. But Malays would not work in the mines. The important result was that by far the greatest number of people in the States were not Malays at all, and certainly not Europeans, but Chinese immigrants, come to mine the tin. During the 1850s and 1860s there was a

veritable "tin rush" of Chinese immigrants to the west coast of the
Malay Peninsula.[11] The tens of thousands of miners were laborers,
partly paid in opium. But the owners were usually rich Chinese who
also owned the franchises for the opium farms. Almost all these
businessmen lived in Singapore, though there was also a large and
influential group of Chinese businessmen in the Straits Settlement
of Penang. The revenues of the free port of British Singapore were
more than half composed of the fees from the farming and sale of
opium.

Even by the late 1850s neither the Chinese nor the English
businessmen believed they could afford to have anything damage tin
production. By 1869, with the opening of the Suez Canal, many
people, Europeans and Chinese, who were getting rich from tin,
believed that there was a need to protect the growing trade possibilities in and around the Malay Peninsula from the threat of "instability" among the peoples of the Peninsula, including wars among
Chinese miners. The threat of "intervention from the other major
powers along the route to China" was then interpreted, with a great
deal of vocal support from Singapore businessmen, Chinese as well
as European, to require some sort of expanded British role in the
region.[12] The Peninsula, a region where virtually all settlements, and
thus all traffic in goods, were along rivers, was particularly vulnerable to British naval power.

In 1874 the new British governor of the Straits Settlements, Sir
Andrew Clarke, arrived with a new mandate from the Colonial
Office authorizing him to intervene with advice, but only with
advice, in the affairs of the Malay States. He immediately exceeded
his mandate by forcing one of the Malay contenders for power in
the western state of Perak to sign the Pangkor Engagement, the
famous treaty whereby, in exchange for British backing and a size-
able salary, the new sultan would accept the presence of a British
Resident, with powers to advise on all except matters of Malay
custom and religion. Just fifty years after the Anglo-Dutch Treaty,
the British Resident system, "that extraordinary device for running
another people's affairs by tendering 'advice which must be acted
upon,'" had established its first hold on the Malay Peninsula.[13]

By the end of 1874, after less than a year as governor of the

Straits Settlements, Clarke had established Residents and/or Assistant Residents in three large states: Perak, Selangor, and Sungei Ujong. Again and again the colonial secretary in London articulated what would be the consistently repeated policy of the Colonial Office through the last quarter of the nineteenth century: that the role of the Residents must be to advise and only to advise, not to govern. In Lord Carnarvon's telegrammed orders in 1875 the governor who followed Clarke was directly warned that "neither annexation nor government of country by British officials in name of Sultan can be allowed."[4] But that, of course, was exactly what the Residents were proceeding, quite deliberately, and without being recalled by their Colonial Office superiors or having their policies reversed, to do.

In 1896 the British created a category which they named the Federated States, composed of those four Malay states which were already being ruled by a British Resident. The government also appointed a Resident General, headquartered in Kuala Lumpur, as the centralized head of the Residents of the Federated States. The Resident General was still subordinate to the governor of the Straits Settlements in Singapore. Even for the sultans of those particular states, who received generous annual allowances from the British in exchange for allowing the Resident to set state policy and collect state income, the tattered fiction of British advising rather than governing was really at an end. By 1909 four out of five of what had come to be known as the Unfederated States had been taken over too, under the control of a Federal Council. In 1914 British control was extended to Johor, and Malaya was entirely ruled by the British.

The rhetoric of official nonintervention which shaped the process of British intervention in the Malay Peninsula had many functions. Generally, it allowed the takeover of the Peninsula by a government in England composed of participants with widely conflicting ideas about the methods and moral justifications of the British empire. During the second half of the century many people, inside the government and out, questioned what was often represented as the steep price of intervention in India. In other words, the space between Colonial Office rhetoric and actual practice in the Malay Peninsula was to some extent the space which enabled colonial enterprise in an ambivalent, contested, and occasionally antico-lonial public atmosphere.

Even with the opening of the Suez Canal in 1869 and the introduction of the telegraph to Singapore in 1871, it took long enough to communicate with London. Residents could still argue the practical necessity of making their own decisions and the neces-sity of Colonial Office support for what was already a fait accompli, because Residents were not living in Singapore anyway. They could quite easily make their own judgments about events on the spot in ways that violated their general orders. Such irregularities were tolerated, in part because the Colonial Office accepted the argument that it would be at best undignified and at worst chaos to function by reversing decisions of presumably knowledgeable men in the field. Those men were seldom removed from their positions because of their expansionist decisions, in spite of belated Colonial Office statements of disapproval. The space between the government's stated aims and accepted practice was obvious to all.

The New Breed of Expert

The Colonial Office rhetoric of nonintervention also provided the hermeneutic context within which late nineteenth-century British accounts of travel in the Malay States could be articulated. Frank Swettenham arrived in the Straits colony as a Civil Service Cadet in 1871 to begin a thirty-year career. The highlights of that career included being at age twenty-three one of the translators into Malay of the Pangkor Engagement, also the Assistant Resident and later the Resident of Selangor, the Resident of Perak, the first Resident General of the Federated States, and finally being governor of the Straits Settlements, the highest British office in the region. Swettenham's nineteenth-century reputation was enormous. Of men in the Malayan Civil Service, Swettenham was "the best of them all," and "would scale the heights of fame" as "the giant among builders of British Malaya."[15]

Swettenham was the great hero of British imperial historiogra-phy about nineteenth-century British intervention in the Peninsula, one of the great heroes of Victorian imperialism. Swettenham is the epitome of the empire builder. His image happily combined dashing adventurer and dedicated and highly professional civil servant. His own understanding of the doublespeak in the Colonial Office's descriptions of the Resident system was quite clear. "It is one thing to write in Downing Street—or even in Singapore—such contradictory and impossible instructions, . . . quite a different thing . . . to carry them out."[16] Swettenham's own articulated position epitomizes the transformation of imperial transgression into national heroism which the British Resident system on the Peninsula seemed to facilitate. In his account the Residents simply violated their orders to respect local Malay authority and then "accepted the responsibility" that "they would be held answerable."[17]

Swettenham was probably the most famous British writer on the region in the last decades of the century. In England, Swettenham's Malay activities and his books, along with the British public reception of them, represented, and were a major public relations factor in creating and justifying, the English imperial stance on the importance of keeping order in Malaya. Swettenham was represented by himself and many others as handsome, vigorous, larger than the region he embraced, a jungle explorer and a man of action rather than contemplation. On the other hand, he was a sensitive preserver of the indigenous culture, fair judge, sweet-tongued persuader and clear-minded administrator; altogether, someone who got things done. His career and his writings were arguments for the professionalization of the empire and the Malayan Civil Service and for the reliability of career empire builders. Swettenham was a proselytizer for the future economic importance of British Malaya, if the job of administration were done right. His writings were frequently the forum for explanations of his method. As he put it in his address to the Royal Colonial Institute in 1895 on "British Rule in Malaya," knowing well the language and the people leads one to the "sympathy" which is absolutely necessary "for the successful government of natives."[18]

Swettenham's career and writings created a cultural image which melded together and sustained in one figure ideological positions which might otherwise have been perceived as canceling each other out. Swettenham's public personae covered basic contradictions

both in the expressed British government position on Malaya and in
the premises of the Resident system. On the one hand, the British
were committed to respecting and preserving Malay people, Malay
customs, and Malay control. On the other hand, the British goal was
effectively to eradicate those customs and, if necessary, even those
people, in the process of taking control away from the Malays for
the sake of British trade interests.

Reading Frank Swettenham as the defining public icon for the
British presence in Malaya opens the way for understanding what
Malaya itself signified during the last decade of the nineteenth
century in the cosmology of British imperialism. Swettenham's *Malay
Sketches* was reviewed in the *Saturday Review* in 1895. As much concerned with reproducing the author as the book, the reviewer assures
us that "these sketches are written by a man of action who holds his
pen in a way which a master of literary penmanship would be
justified in reprehending."[19] Yet this critique of Swettenham's rhetorical abilities has an important function. We are assured that these
"rough descriptions" and the "very literary incapacity of the man"
enable the book to create "powerful sensations of reality." In other
words, this book, by its very crudeness and lack of rhetorical
control, records rather than invents. We see the "real" Peninsula in
Swettenham's sketches. He was no mere tourist.[20] In our twentieth-
century neocolonial rhetoric, he would be known as a real "Asia
hand." In his own words, Swettenham can "reveal the secrets of this
remote corner of the earth," can show us things "still hidden from
the ken of Cook and the race of Globe trotters."[21] Those secrets, in
the Victorian imperial rhetoric of his reviewer, are of "the leering
crocodile," the "unfathomable jungle," and "a world separated from
ours by a gulf as mysteriously wide as that which yawns between
antiquity and modernity." British Malaya was Frank Swettenham, a
melding of modern man and antique world.

In Swettenham's published writings and in his life as an icon of
Victorian colonial ideology, Malaya was "sketched" as a world
whose interior, like that of Africa, was unexplored and unknown. It
was a tropical jungle, in effect a vast, murky, mostly impassable
swamp, framed by coastal settlements of exotic people. The distinctive point is that these representations did not "naturally" lead to

describing Malaya in terms of some of the typical conventions of an ideology of primitivism, as "wild" or a "dark" jungle. The Malay States had a different function in writing the history of colonial enterprise.

British representations of the Malay States had more to do with British national and economic concerns and less to do with the region's actual geography, its climate, or the conventional glossing of jungles as primitive and untamed. What may be specific to the Malay case is that the British representations, though certainly ideologically driven, tend not to participate in the all-too-common rhetorical practice of establishing European superiority as urban through representing another people as precultural or closer to a state of nature (although, in the racism of British accounts of Southeast Asian peoples, some variation on this claim is always at least implicitly present). The particular form taken by the hegemonic practice of representing Malays and the British presence in Malaya had everything to do with European, and specifically British, colonial history, along with British economic hopes for the future.

British Malaya and British India

One important way to approach the rhetoric of British representations of the Malay States is in relation to the rhetoric of British India.[22] A crucial aspect of what Malaya, and the British presence there signified so powerfully in late Victorian imperial writings was a plausible continuation of, and answer to, India and the British presence there. Having, as many people suspected, done it wrong in India (though only in terms of methods, not in terms of the more fundamental question of being there at all), Malaya was the chance to do it right. Malaya would be India with a difference. But this perspective required a version of Malaya which saw it in terms of its similarities to India, which is to say, offered a political geography which was not based on the literal geography of the Malay Peninsula as a group of port towns and villages skirting a large and virtually uninhabited interior jungle. Thus the qualities of Malaya offered in British imperial discourse tend to stress the Peninsula's perceived similarities to, along with important but predictable differences from, British representations of India.

The already established connections between India and Malaya in British discourse before the second half of the nineteenth century have a fairly accessible history. To begin with, the Malay Peninsula became a place of significance for the English precisely in terms of its geographic proximity to India, as the land fronting the waterway from India to China. After leaving the eastern ports of India, the next stops for European ships were the ports of Penang and Malacca, off the western coast of the Malay Peninsula. The British had no independent economic interest in the Malay Peninsula until the middle of the nineteenth-century. They explicitly acquired Penang in 1786 because they wanted a base on the eastern side of the Indian Ocean, as part of a larger policy of protecting their hugely profitable imports of opium to, and exports of tea from, China. The economic geography of Penang and Malacca, and by extension the Malay Peninsula and surrounding islands, helps to explain why the government of the Straits Settlements, up until the late date of 1867, was officially in the hands of the governor general or viceroy in India. They existed as British colonies precisely in terms of their practical usefulness to British business concerns in India. The Straits Settlements, and by extension the Malay States, were considered the next step to China after Burma, which was itself frequently referred to as "further India."

The man honored in many British historical accounts as the first British settler in the Malay region is Francis Light, canonized as the "founder" of Penang and representative of the East India Company's interests in establishing a port there. Only three months after his landing in 1787, Light requested that the governor general in India send him some "coolies."[23] Some "artificers," or skilled workers, were sent to him, the beginning of what would be at least a century of substantial British-controlled immigration from India to the Straits Settlements and the Malay States. India was a major source of workers as the British struggled to find "reliable" labor for the mines, farms, and plantations of British Malaya and the laborers fled from the lack of work, and finally from the famines of the 1880s, in

India. Chinese businessmen developed local resources their own way, by importing many thousands of Chinese miners. The English, who no more than the Chinese could get the Malays to see the presumed advantages of working for the foreigners, created a work force by bringing in thousands of Indians. Beneath the administrator and officer level, many of the British police were Indian, usually Sikhs, brought in because of British convictions of their loyalty.

The business practices of the East India Company and its original presence in both India and Malaya, the organization of the Peninsula into small states ruled by sultans or rajas, the ancient and often elaborate religious traditions of Islam, the transformation of British staff from East India Company employees to advisors hired by the British government to oversee British economic interests, the British focus on the potential for "eastern" trade—all these factors tended to associate for many British writers the Malay Peninsula with the British experience in India. In spite of the physical geography of the region, those enormous and uninhabited tropical jungles which might have led the Malay Peninsula to be associated with Africa in the minds of many Victorians, its imaginative and rhetorical link was clearly with the heavily populated and frequently urban-dominated states of India.[24]

The initial control of the Straits Settlements by the governor general in India had been central to establishing the colonial perception of British interests in the Malay Peninsula as an extension of British interests in India and therefore of the Peninsula itself as an extension of India. But similarity gave way at least partially to difference as the East India Company lost its monopoly on the China trade in 1833, the British acquired Hong Kong in 1842, business affairs became extremely successful in the Straits Settlements, particularly in terms of local trade, and events in the 1850s in British India created debates back home about the success of previous British policies for governing India. The intense lobbying of the commercial men in Singapore (many of the most powerful of whom were Chinese) to be considered independently of British economic interests in India and to be allowed to focus more on local trade than on operating as a resting place and free port along the trade route between India and China were major reasons for removing control of the Straits Settlements from the British administrators in India. The argument of all the Singapore businessmen was precisely that they could do a better development job than the India Office had done in India. Surely it is not just a coincidence that their arguments finally carried the day in the decade after the Indian "Mutiny" of 1857.

From the 1870s what the Malay States offered in British colonial discourse was the crucial possibility of a second chance. The "Mutiny" had not shaken the British commitment to empire, but it had led to public debates about how this business of ruling colonies should best proceed. In its policies and activities in the Malay States, the British government could make up for, could rewrite, what in the 1860s many British had come to see as the significant mistakes, moral as well as practical and economic, in India. They could salvage the very notion of the glory of the British Empire, tarnished as it had been by recent events in India. John Thomson's 1864 account of working twenty years earlier in the Malay States and in Singapore, *Some Glimpses of Life in the Far East,* fits the mood of the postmutiny decade in its frank representations of the stupidities and prejudices of the East India Company's business practices in the region.[25] Thomson's work precedes Swettenham's in its message that control—and profits—will emerge from the gentler virtues of knowledge and sympathy. You can only take over and destroy a custom if you really appreciate it.

Many in England felt that the simple purpose of profit had gotten bogged down in the complex process of governing British India, in wars, in politics, in religion, in culture. Economics had lost out to politics. If there is a primary difference in the visions of Malaya and of India in British travel accounts after the 1850s, it may well be the insistence that Malaya is an easier place, easier to know and easier to control. These accounts stress that the British remember that their purpose is simply trade and profits and stay out of the unprofitable business of refashioning culture. The Malays are good, and British relations to them are sensitive, open, and kind. Frank Swettenham speaks fluent Malay and really cares about the culture. He does not command the native rulers but persuades them. The Well of Cawnpore will never be replayed in Kuala Lumpur.

The already well-established British trade interests in the Malay Peninsula in the mid-nineteenth century plausibly opened the possibility of turning toward what might be read as the next India and inscribing the British presence there in a less contested and more directly profitable way. For the British that meant less entwinement with the regional cultures, with all the dangers and expense that intervention represented, and more commitment to the business of business. Unlike upper-class Indians in India, who in very limited ways could serve in the Indian Civil Service, upper-class Malays were barred from serving in the administrative ranks of the Malay Civil Service. Sympathy was to be understood as a tool for change, a nonviolent method for slowly revising Malay customs and practices and finally replacing them with British ones. But the policy of sympathy was flexible enough so that it could easily be invoked as an argument for not interfering with those local customs, such as the extensive practice of debt slavery, which aided British productivity.

Profits, not "western" cultural principles, and certainly not internal cultural or political issues, should direct British rule in Malaya. The perceived success of this approach is expressed by one of its most visible proponents. Swettenham delightedly reported to the Royal Colonial Institute that "in the time British residents have controlled the finances of the Protected States they have succeeded in increasing the revenues at least twentyfold."[26] Another expression of the overflowing material as well as ideological value of this land of the second chance is the popular British saying, approvingly quoted by an early twentieth-century director of the Royal Botanic Gardens, that rubber in Malaya brought England "wealth beyond the dreams of avarice."[27]

Making Malaya and Making Isabella Bird

Many Englishmen grew to fame nurturing the enormous economic potential and the benign public image of British interests in Malaya. Their fame was consistently based on how well they increased the area's economical potential, usually measured in the nineteenth century by how much tin productivity increased in a particular state during a particular Resident's tenure. If Frank Swettenham stood the tallest of these Victorian empire builders, right next to him was Hugh Low, Resident of Perak. There were several others as well, all appearing as characters in the narratives of British travelers to the Peninsula. Standing a lot shorter than these many colonial officials and businessmen who played roles in the "making of Malaya," yet often compared through her diminutive height and looks to Queen Victoria, was another important imperial character in creating the colonial narrative of British Malaya. Isabella Bird wrote what might well be, along with Swettenham's *Malay Sketches,* the best-known nineteenth-century memoir of the region, *The Golden Chersonese and the Way Thither.*[28]

Isabella Bird, the daughter of a clergyman, grew up in Yorkshire and Birmingham. A serious and lifelong spinal problem led to the prescription of travel, beginning when she was twenty-three years old. After a long trip to Canada and the United States she wrote her first travel book, *An Englishwoman in America.* Bird's father died when she was twenty-nine, and the widow and her two daughters moved to Edinburgh. The rest of Bird's life combined years of following charitable causes in Edinburgh with years of ecstatic traveling, during which she wrote detailed letters home to her sister, Henrietta. After Henrietta died, Isabella had a five-year marriage to an Edinburgh doctor, who also died. She went back to traveling and writing travel books, these with less delighted immediacy than the earlier ones based on letters to Henrietta.

The Golden Chersonese (considered a literary name for the Malay Peninsula) was published in 1883. It is an account of a journey taken in 1879 which had lasted only five weeks. Henrietta died between the trip and the publication of the book. The narrative is based on letters to Henrietta, but the editing and revision took so long because of the heavy weight of Isabella's grief. The book, like Bird's actual trip to Malaya, was just the tag end of a much more extensive journey and of what she conceived of as a more important book. Bird had just spent two years traveling around Japan, in preparation for writing what would be the hugely successful *Unbeaten Tracks in Japan,* published in 1880.[29] She made some side trips from Hong

Kong, to Canton in China and to Saigon in French Cochin-China, then on to Singapore, where the colonial secretary unexpectedly offered to send her on a little tour of the Malay States.

It would be her book on Japan which significantly increased the reputation of her work and led in part to the avid reception of *The Golden Chersonese,* her next book. But even in 1879 Bird was already a well-established and well-known travel writer. She had written very successful books on the Rocky Mountains and on the Hawaiian Islands, both of which went into several editions. She would go on to write about Kashmir, Tibet, Korea, Persia, and China. Considering the places Bird went and wrote about, it is somewhat accurate, if overstated, to conclude that "she tended to avoid the [British] Empire altogether."[30] The major exception, of course, is that unplanned side trip from Singapore which is the basis of *The Golden Chersonese.*

The repeatedly published strictures of British administrators on the importance of deep familiarity with Malay language and customs are completely ignored in this book. Yet still Bird's account of her whirlwind tour (if it's Tuesday, it must be Perak) reached the stature of an icon of what it must "really" have been like in British Malaya. The glowing review in the *Spectator* assured the public that "she can see, and she can use the words that place what she sees before the reader" (52:1414). The reviewer in the *Nation* simply found *The Golden Chersonese* "for popular use, the best work in English on the Malay Peninsula" (36:516). The narrative has what Roy Lichtenstein, commenting in ways reminiscent of Althusser on what is artificial about "realistic" painting, called the gift of reproducing the two-dimensional as the three-dimensional.[31]

The Golden Chersonese offers what is virtually a hymn to British imperialism. To get some sense of how this rhetoric works involves considering the structure, characterizations, values, and style of Bird's popular little book on the Malay Peninsula. The order of Bird's narrative is a good representation of its ideological function. Why begin a book on British Malaya with chapters on Canton? The naturalistic answer would be that Bird was just narrating her trip in the order it actually happened, and that once she left Japan she needed somewhere to write about between Japan and Singapore. An answer which attends to the cultural function of *The Golden Chersonese* is that what the narrative order effectively does is to reiterate the British trade route from the China of its opening chapters to the "indolent roll of the Bay of Bengal" (368) which closes the book. The center of the book, the chapters on British Malaya, are framed within their primary imperial meaning, as stopovers between India and the "far east."

Moreover, *The Golden Chersonese* could not have been written before 1875. Not only the beginning and ending of the narrative but its center as an exploration of Malaya replicates the very specific situation and policies of the British colonial presence in the Peninsula in the late 1870s. The trip, and the chapters, are comprised of visits to a very small portion of the Malay Peninsula, in fact only to the Straits Settlements colonies and to those three Malay states in which Andrew Clarke had established the resident system by the end of 1874. Bird, in what was, after all, a semiofficial tour, visits the three western states of Sungei Ujong, Selangor, and Perak. She prefaces her letters "written on the spot" (xxiii) with a formal, introductory chapter of information on each of these states. The information is drawn from "sundry reports and other official papers, . . . those storehouses of accurate and valuable information" (xxii). These information chapters offer miniature histories which justify the British presence and predict a peaceful colonial future. Thus the narrator claims to explain directly to her audience why these "feeble protected States" (those with Residents) will never "seek to shake off" a British system which "gives them security and justice" (161).

Finally, the characters Bird introduces, the people she meets in her journey, also tend to be represented in ways that replicate the semiofficial ideology of the British presence in the Malay States. There are, to begin with, the Malays themselves, usually referred to, with the same singular, essentialized terminology Swettenham used, as "the Malay." The book is full of lists of attributes typical of British imperial writings about many other peoples. The Malay, female as well as male, is lazy, suspicious, ugly, bigoted, et cetera and does "not care for work" (138). As Syed Alatas points out, in Bird's narrative, as in most British writings describing the peoples of Southeast Asia, the definition of work is "that activity introduced by colonial capitalism. If the ladies became coolies or servants of British planters, she would then have considered them as working."[32]

Perhaps more significant in terms of the particular ways in which Bird's book is ideologically driven is the special quality of its representations of the indigenous people of Malaya. Replicating the position of Swettenham and the Colonial Office in terms of the particular imperial premises underlying the Resident system, *The Golden Chersonese* mentions several times that these people are "the rightful owners" (137) of their country and are emphatically not "savages" but "have an elaborate civilization, etiquette, and laws of their own" (171). They do not need to be overrun and ruled, to be educated in the "western" way and culturally remade, as so many British policies in India before 1857 had aimed at doing. But they definitely need to be guided and looked after, to be "advised" (which is to say, ruled), for their own good. For the narrator, the Malays are lazy, but the benign British response to these negative qualities of their culture must be to oversee the Malays and to improve them, as it were, by teaching them to work for the British.

The individuals Bird's narrative sketches are almost entirely British administrators, the empire builders engaged in the great work of creating British Malaya. They turn out to be people who were then in the process of developing extensive reputations in England and who would, in the three decades following the publication of Bird's book, reach enormous fame. What is particularly notable about the sketches of these British administrators in *The Golden Chersonese* is that their governing abilities are presented and evaluated in the language of what is traditionally categorized as a feminine domestic ideology. Thus Captain Shaw, lieutenant governor of Malacca, is "of an especially unselfish, loving, and tender nature, considerate to an unusual degree of the happiness and comfort of those about him." The link between the familial and the colonial does not long remain implicit: "among the Chinese he has won the name of 'Father,' and among the Malays English rule by him is 'the rule of the just'" (127).[33] As for the British Residents, Captain Murray in Sungei Ujong is open and honest, "a thoroughly honourable man, . . . both beloved and trusted" (187), while Mr. Bloomfield Douglas in Selangor is the wrong kind of father, authoritative and unsympathetic. He has a "plaintive" wife and an "afflicted daughter" and runs the residency like "an armed post amidst a hostile population" (218). Bird's comments to John Murray, her publisher, were even more graphic: "Mr. Douglas is the most *fiendish* human being that I have ever seen. After close study I failed to find a redeeming point in his character."[34]

These colonial administrators are judged in Bird's narrative according to a British domestic ideology which values sympathy and tenderness over a more aggressive representation of manliness (or fatherhood) as discipline and control by force. As with Swettenham's work, *The Golden Chersonese* argues for a future British Malaya built on the British ability to dominate and transform the Malays through kindness and understanding, not through distance and harshness. Imperialism in British Malaya was to be understood "as a kind of rescue-service," liberating the native peoples from the tyrannies and corrupt economic policies of bad native fathers.[35] According to these values the narrative represents Hugh Low, Resident in Perak, as the best father of them all and thus "a model administrator," having "not only a thoroughly idiomatic knowledge of the Malay language, but a sympathetic insight into the Malay character." Mr. Low combines thirty years of knowledge with a style which mixes friend-liness and firmness, and his "manner is as quiet and unpretending as can possibly be" (323).

As *The Golden Chersonese* is discursively framed at beginning and end by the China and India of British trade interests, so within the narrative are the individual places and people on the Malay Penin-sula and in the Straits Settlements framed by their colonial meaning. While the terms according to which the narrative presents the British colonial administrators may have been Bird's own, they were also the publicly expressed terms according to which service in British Malaya was to be evaluated. British profits in Perak increased enormously during Hugh Low's residency, and he was considered, along with Swettenham, as the finest administrator in British Ma-laya. Even the critique of Douglas reproduced the official line. Three years after Bird met him, and after many complaints about his autocratic and corrupt rule, the Colonial Office finally gave him the choice of facing an inquiry or resigning.

The narrative structure of *The Golden Chersonese* is ordered so as to reproduce the political structure of the British presence in Malaya. Its personal descriptions reproduce the lineaments of the imperial argument which officially justified that presence. The book can be read virtually as a textbook, made readable by personal anecdotes and color photos (in words, of course), of the geography, history, and government of British Malaya. The need for such a textbook, and its larger purpose, is made quite explicit in the preface. The book is "an honest attempt to make a popular contribution to the sum of knowledge of a beautiful and little-traveled region, . . . which is practically under British rule, and is probably destined to afford increasing employment to British capital and enterprise" (xxi–xxii). This "book of travels in this gorgeous tropical country" by "so enterprising a traveler as Miss Bird" explicitly offers to its British audience a way of reading Malaya designed to enlighten them as to its inevitably increasing significance as a site of British economic enterprise.[36] It offers them a hermeneutic path to the future, a way for the audience to read what the Malay Peninsula is and has been which will ensure their understanding and accepting as both practical and profitable the British colony that it is "probably destined," the readers are assured, to become.

A Feminine Colony

The ideological function of *The Golden Chersonese* as a mouthpiece of colonial policy, the thoroughness of its support of British interests in Malaya, its structure as virtual propaganda are informed by a narrative voice and style which continuously lay claim to the nonpolitical, or perhaps to the politically independent, content of the book. There are many disclaimers: this trip was a spontaneous accident; it was just a quick side excursion; these were simply familial letters to my "beloved and only sister" (xxi), now dead; "the opinions expressed are wholly my own" (xxii); these are "'Letters' which have not received any literary dress"; and, finally, these are direct personal observations, "first impressions in their original vividness" (xxiii).

Certainly, the many disclaimers, the method of writing on the spot, the sincere admission that there is a "risk of seeing things through official spectacles" (324), and, most of all, the very descriptive power of Bird's style, all function to compose a rhetorical strategy which effectively renders the two-dimensional as three-dimensional. The narrative functions to represent what was in fact a relentless colonialist reading of the Malay States as the way things really were. The supposedly nonpolitical qualities of the narrative, along with its self-placement as a descriptive record of just a private person's delightful and spontaneous visit, are key factors in its political strategy.

A crucial element in the political effectiveness of *The Golden Chersonese* is that its narrator is a woman. In gendered terms, *The Golden Chersonese* is a feminine imperial discourse, popularizing by means of what is represented in the narrative as a "woman's perspective" a spatially and temporally specific definition of British colonialism. I suggest that this perspective was more than just a feminine gendered variant of British colonial policy. Instead, British colonial policy in Malaya was itself to a great extent gendered as feminine. That feminine cast is what gave Swettenham's testimony such historic importance. No one could be in doubt as to the manliness of this most masculine hero. Thus it was quite effective when this larger-than-life man himself argued for the importance of sympathy and gentleness in ruling British Malaya.

Moreover, in the 1870s this was actually an argument about how to bring about a desired future, how to make a colony as opposed to how to remake or repair it. On the Malay Peninsula heroic adventure needed to be metamorphosed into successful administration. One way to mark this ideological change in public policy is that the masculine needed to be transformed into the feminine. The masculine adventure approach had already been done, and done successfully, in the founding of Penang and Singapore and in the many European explorations up the rivers of the Malay Peninsula. But its time was past. The murder in 1875 of Birch, the first Resident of Perak, whom the Malays hated and had futilely requested be replaced, was seen by many in the Straits Settlements as tragic, intolerable, yet in some sense also fortuitous in making clear at the very beginning of active British colonial intervention that the aggressive and unbending approach was not the path to a successful colonial future on the Malay Peninsula. The very premise of the Resident system in British Malaya, that one rules by suggesting and advising and not by commanding and forcing, presumes the effectiveness and power of what, in Victorian England were normatively considered the more feminine virtues, those used in raising a family and running a home: familiarity, understanding, kindness, and persuasion.

Near the end of Bird's stay in Perak, Mr. Low expressed his regret at her leaving: "You never speak at the wrong time. When men are visiting me they never know when to be quiet" (348). The point here is exactly not the predictable one that Bird, as a woman, knows her inferior place in relation to a man and that the man is praising her for it. The point, made repeatedly in the long descriptions of Low's habits and governing style which preceded this moment, is that Bird and Low are alike in their quietness. They both eschew what Mr. Maxwell, whom the narrative invokes as sharing their values, called the hothead "clatter" of the masculine style, preferring a quiet and perceptive effectiveness. In this shared style, both Bird and Low are glossed as feminine and as powerful.

This feminine quality of successful colonial government as a matter of knowing "when to be quiet" is invoked in the claim that "there are very few circumstances which Mr. Hayward is not prepared to meet," because "he has a reserve of quiet strength" (200). Incident after incident in the narrative points up that these are precisely the characteristics of Isabella Bird. This feminine quality is already evident in that early description of Captain Shaw. In his "unselfish, loving, and tender nature" and in his quality of being "considerate to an unusual degree of the happiness and comfort of those about him," the imperial father reads very much like a mother. *The Golden Chersonese* is hardly an argument for letting women into the colonial service. It does offer an argument for what constitutes an effective and productive colonial administrator. In Bird's account, British leadership in Malaya through the Resident system of advising requires those very qualities which in Victorian culture had so often been denigrated as weakness and cast into a negatively valued feminine sphere.

The kind of domesticated or feminine colonial qualities which

Bird's narrative casts as positive are clearly represented as qualities not to be confused with those negative ones associated with feminine weakness. This distinction informs many of the representations by the narrator about herself and about other female characters. The female subject which is constructed in *The Golden Chersonese* is similar to the best of the British administrators in Malaya. In the narrative not only Mr. Low but also Captain Shaw, Captain Murray, Captain Walker, Major Paul Swinburne (Charles Algernon's cousin), and Mr. Maxwell feel some sort of bond with the narrator, exhibiting on all sides the fine imperial qualities of understanding and sympathy. These are all people who work quietly, who are sensitive to what is going on around them, who do not talk too much and when they do talk, speak softly, who make it a principle to help others and "avoid being a bother" themselves (345).

Moreover, this shared feminized bond explicitly excludes certain kinds of qualities culturally labeled in Britain as feminine, particularly the dependent roles of wife and mother. Thus, in the long trip to the residency in Sungei Ujong, Bird and Mr. Hayward find themselves in charge of the two daughters of Captain Shaw. These two "fragile girls" lie around "limp and helpless" (172), get "a violent sick headache" (169), are "prey of many terrors" (179), insist on traveling with a trunk, and in general exhibit many of the conventional signs which mark feminine weakness. The narrator not only has no maternal feelings toward these girls but both she and Mr. Hayward, in often unspoken communication, find them "unfit" (165) and an "encumbrance" to the pleasures of the trip (169). This scene is replayed in a comic way when Bird, Major Swinburne, and Mr. Maxwell take a night boat and must share the cabin with "an English would-be lady" who wants to be looked after, her servants, and an infant who "screamed with a ferocious persistency" (367). The three humorists are clearly the ones with sensitivity toward others. The sympathetic ties between them had been previously established in Perak, when they worked quietly together "with no women to twitter," then "talked of things that are worth talking about" (291).

In *The Golden Chersonese* feminine helplessness and masculine assertiveness, "twitter" and "clatter," are both finally forms of bad taste. Good taste, if one is a man, looks much like the kind of attentive thoughtfulness and quiet usefulness of a true lady. The pretensions of the "would-be lady" on the night boat are a kind of false, which is to say, low-bred, femininity, which contrasts with the narrator's self-representation as a sensitive observer, as open to her environment, and as self-sufficient. The imperial feminine turns out to be a matter of being the right class, of being a true "lady." The insistence on being a lady pervades Bird's writings. It has nothing to do with such conventional indicators as being looked after, or having servants or public acknowledgments. It has everything to do with a certain social level, specifically with the upper-middle class Christian world from which Bird had come, where femininity means to be gentle but clear-minded, soft-spoken but active in helping others, selfless in not being an imposition but self-assertive in accomplishing good works. That Bird's social level was distinctly upper-middle-class rather than upper-class may be seen in Marianne North's dismissive account of her as a "substantial little person" who talked "as if she were reciting from one of her books."[37]

Bird the gentlewoman, like Mr. Hayward the gentleman, is "prepared to meet" almost any circumstances at the same time that she is extraordinarily responsive to the world about her. Thus, in Bird's narrative being a "lady" includes maintaining standards of decorum which have nothing to do with such material issues as eating at a table or sleeping on sheets or even on a bed. At one moment Bird reports the pleasures of taking to the "Malay custom of a sleeping mat" (325).

The importance of the concept of a gentlewoman to Bird's literary self-fashioning is evident just after her return from the Malay Peninsula, in her response to the *Times* review in 1879 of *A Lady's Life in the Rocky Mountains*. The reviewer's casual comment that Bird "donned masculine habiliments" for convenience in riding outraged her. She wrote to Murray protesting that her outfit was actually a riding "dress worn by *ladies* at Mountain Resorts in America." To be sure there would be no more confusion on the part of her readers, Bird included in the next seven editions of the book a sketch of the actual outfit, which she continued to wear throughout her travels after that Hawaiian trip, along with an explanatory note.[38] This famous "riding dress," in a sign so hermeneutically overdetermined that I think I will make no comment, was a skirt with attached pants under it.

Joy: The Rhetoric of Emotion

Bird's book on her tour of the Malay Peninsula continually blends feminine domestic with colonial ideology, defining and evaluating public achievement in familial terms. But again, this self-positioning should not be reduced to being described as merely the perspective of a woman who prefers ideological to literal parenthood, who has cast off her traditional role to move out to the public rather than the private sphere. *The Golden Chersonese* explicitly distinguishes between kinds of domesticity, arguing that "the peculiar form of domesticity which we still cultivate to some extent in England, and which is largely connected with the fireside, cannot exist in a tropical country" (171). In other words, it's just too hot in the tropics for women to be confined to the home. Nor should British homes in Malaya resemble those in England.

In its marvelous blend of the literal and the ideological, this argument partly explains why neither the female narrator nor the male British administrators in Malaya reject domestic values. They simply move them, as it were, out of doors—and thus into the public sphere. On the crucial subject in the 1870s and 1880s of how to intervene successfully in Malay affairs, projecting solutions to political problems in domestic terms, and reading that domesticity as public activity, was a basic element in men's analyses as well.

The hymn to quietness which pervades *The Golden Chersonese* is about talking, about what constitutes successful social and political relations, about how to take effective action in the world. It is emphatically not about repressing feelings, or silencing women. One of the reasons good colonial administrators and true ladies do not talk very much and actually prefer to remain silent a good part of the time is that they are busily at work articulating their positions, which is to say, writing. They are vocal on paper. Bird's representations of her stays at British residencies have to do with sitting quietly in a room with the Resident or Assistant Resident or governor, he at his work, she at hers, the two of them writing away. Writing, as I have been arguing in the previous pages, was Bird's form of political action, her entry into the public world of colonial debate.

The narrator's ability to meet almost any circumstance—or, in other words, to govern—is continually represented through her emotional power to describe the circumstances she meets. The British can control because they can inscribe, and the better the power to inscribe, the better the power to control. For its large British readership *The Golden Chersonese* literally writes British Malaya into being. It can do so in part because it offers a rhetoric so vivid, so intensely enthusiastic, that one reviewer likened it to traveling with a coachman who "marks the dizzy verge [of the precipice] with her tire half over."[39] Here is most, but not all, of a single sentence (one of many such):

> often, through rifts in the leafage aloft, there were glimpses of the sunny, heavenly blue sky, and now and then there were openings where trees had fallen, and the glorious tropical sunshine streamed in on gaudy blossoms of huge trees, and on pure white orchids, and canary-coloured clusters borne by lianas; on sun-birds, iridescent and gorgeous in the sunlight; and on butterflies, some all golden, others amber and black, and amber and blue, some with velvety bands of velvet and green, others altogether velvety black with spots of vermilion or emerald-green . . . ; the flash of sun-birds and the flutter of butterflies giving one an idea of the joy which possibly was intended to be the heritage of all animated existence. (311)

The Golden Chersonese is filled with such alluring passages, descriptions so lush as to invoke the sensuous language of Keats. Contemporary reviewers repeatedly praised this quality of Bird's style, admiring the "descriptions, which are like bits out of the *Arabian Nights*" and her "rare gift of pictorial description."[40]

The "joy" which may well be "the heritage of all" is, in some form, a frequent reference in a book written in the language of feeling. At one moment the narrator grandly claims that life is so wonderful that "there would have been nothing left to wish for" but for one thing. She would have liked to share her joy, to have had her sister, Henrietta, there to see Bird's ride on an elephant, "the elephant moving submerged along a tropical river . . . with people of three races on his back" (317). At another moment Bird comments that the trip has given her some of the few "days in my life in which I have felt mere living to be a luxury, and what it is to be akin to seas and breezes, and birds and insects, and to know why nature sings and smiles" (226).

The joyousness of Bird's discourse, its celebratory quality, even excess of expressiveness, is gendered as feminine in a way other writings about the British presence in the Peninsula are not. *The Golden Chersonese* replicates the values of other more or less contemporary writings about the Malay Peninsula by British men, but it does not replicate the style. Bird's book is a testimony to personal joy. Its feminine imperial rhetoric is the rhetoric of intense emotion. The book is filled with elaborate descriptions in which the narrator is no objective or detached observer but an enchanted participant. The subject, representing what she sees and also how she feels about what she sees, is explicit in discussing the happiness she experiences, how much her life is fulfilled, through the simple acts of being in and moving through this Malay world, of which "the loveliness is intoxicating" (310). The place makes Bird happy, sometimes even deliriously so, a point implicit in Swettenham's writings but distinctly not said expressly and repeatedly.

In *The Golden Chersonese* everything matters enormously. And not, as one might suspect, because Bird's imperial gaze gives this world meaning, but because this world gives meaning to her. The place creates the subject, as she becomes the English lady who is there. Writing British Malaya into being, she writes herself into being, painting a picture of the place and of herself in it.[41] And both are irresistible, in the land where mere living is a luxury. Bird's debt, therefore, to the British imperial presence in the Malay States is total, since it is the precondition for her creation, as a celebrated and respected professional woman traveler. It gives her herself—that intrepid woman who her biographers repeatedly note with amazement was so eerily the opposite of the timid invalid with the spinal

disease suffering at home in Edinburgh.[42] Thus the prose reads like
an extended celebration, a shout of happiness, a Victorian feminine
"song of myself," as step after step in her journey the Malay
Peninsula provides Bird with her ambulatory identity by providing
her with "everything that could rejoice the eye upon its shores"
(317).

The energy of this rhetoric of emotion, the piling up of lush
details, is not reserved for circumstances which are easy to meet: the
pretty places and the comfortable moments. The ugly and the
uncomfortable are also verbally caressed as offering their own felt
delights. We hear quite cheerily of Bird's shoes filling with blood
from leeches or of her hammock falling down and her being covered
by the ants which chewed away the ropes. Then there is the swampy
town in Selangor exuberantly, even rapturously, described: "slime
was everywhere oozing, bubbling, smelling putrid in the sun, all
glimmering, shining, and iridescent, breeding fever and horrible life;
while land-crabs boring holes, crabs of a brilliant turquoise-blue
colour, which fades at death, and reptiles like fish, with great bags
below their mouths, and innumerable armour-plated insects, were
rioting in it under the broiling sun" (243). Rapture, bounding
energy, excess of delight—these are the qualities which render the
feminine subjectivity of *The Golden Chersonese* a voice for the "right"
kind of imperial administrative policies in British Malaya and at the
same time indicate to the reader why Bird's colonial role is more
properly the recorder than the implementer of those policies.

Not everyone can find everything, including swamps, a rhetorical
delight. In Perak Bird takes a boat with some colonial officers. One
of them, "Mr. Innes, Superintendent of Lower Perak, whose wife so
nearly lost her life in the horrible affair at Pulo Pangkor, was in
dejected spirits, as if the swamps . . . had been too much for him"
(276). Both of those details, the first, Innes's being "in dejected
spirits," and the second, even more damning in its speculation, that
the swamps "had been too much for him," mark Innes as a poor
administrator according to the criteria of *The Golden Chersonese*. He is
not a man who is "prepared to meet" all circumstances. And his wife
is virtually an object of pity, a poor victim. When the Chinese
murdered Mr. Lloyd, British superintendent on the tiny island of

Pangkor, Mrs. Lloyd and her visitor, Mrs. Innes, were knocked unconscious but somehow were not killed.

Bird's comment on Mr. Innes is another of those moments in the book when presumably "on the spot" observations reflect with uncanny accuracy the official Colonial Office position. By the very end of 1881, when Bird was still writing *The Golden Chersonese*, James Innes had voluntarily resigned from his post in the colonial service.[43] He was denied not only his pension (even the "fiend," Douglas, got a pension) but close to six years of back pay and spent the next three years unsuccessfully campaigning for compensation. Mr. Innes's crime, in large part, was to blow the whistle on Douglas for holding back income due to the Malay sultan of Selangor. He also argued with that adored colonialist Hugh Low, publicly protesting Low's order forcing British magistrates in Perak to support the extensive Malay practice of debt slavery by writing warrants for the arrest of runaway slaves. The response of both the Colonial Office in London and the governor of Singapore, who was directly in charge of the Residents, was to deny these accusations (both of which, in later investigations, proved to be true) and to label Innes a spiteful malcontent.

The British Colonial Office position was to support the admittedly reprehensible practice of Malay debt slavery for the time being as part of a British policy of respecting Malay customs and not offending the sultans and rajas, those titular rulers who were the primary slaveholders and to whom the British Residents offered their "advice." In 1884 the British did ban debt slavery in Perak. But in the first years of the 1880s their position of support and Innes's objections were being argued out in British newspapers, while Bird was home writing her book. Mr. Innes was labeled a man who would not follow orders, a complainer, a whiner, and a poor worker, as if the demands of imperial responsibility in the Malay States "had been too much for him."

Mr. Innes's almost-murdered wife went on to garner herself a reputation more dreary, if possible, than her husband's. She published a book in two volumes in 1885 called *The Chersonese with the Gilding Off*, explicitly offering another version of the British colonial presence in the Malay Peninsula to counteract both the representations of the Colonial Office and the brilliantly sunny picture conjured up in *The Golden Chersonese*.[44]

Writing against Sympathy

The three British-advised States in 1876 were referred to at the time, with an imperial impulse which is obvious enough, as the Protected States. Each had a Resident who lived in one part of the state, and under him there could be a variety of subordinates: an Assistant Resident, income collectors, magistrates, superintendents, perhaps a captain of police. In the late 1870s, when the system had just been set up, a Protected State might have one or none or several of these officers. They constituted the Resident's staff, and all of them were subject to, and of much lower status than, the Resident. This hierarchy reflected "the great power the Residents exercised over careers," virtually controlling both promotions and dismissals.[45] The second-level civil servants almost always would live in some other part of the state from the Resident, often days from contact with him, and were forbidden to leave their station without his permission. In a region where travel was almost entirely by river, they often lived quite alone in isolated Malay villages, without the government providing them with a boat of their own. This policy would presumably allow not only British influence but also a Resident's control to be as widespread as possible.

In 1876 James Innes was appointed collector and magistrate in Selangor. Since there was no Assistant Resident in Selangor, he was directly under Mr. Bloomfield Douglas. Mr. Innes's colonial career consisted of one year in the privately owned British country of Sarawak (on the island of Borneo), then three years in the remote village of Langat in Selangor (Douglas lived in the more central town of Klang), then some months filling in for a colleague, sent home on sick leave, as acting superintendent in the village of Durian Sabatang in Perak (the Resident of Perak, Hugh Low, lived at some distance in the village of Kuala Kangsar), a few months at home on sick leave of his own (Durian Sabatang had a reputation at that time among Europeans of making everybody ill, usually from malaria), and a final two years back in his regular appointment in Langat, again under Douglas. Apart from the time in Sarawak, Mr. Innes spent over five and a half years in the Malay colonial service. Of that time the first two years and the last two were at Langat in Selangor, with that temporary stint in the middle in Perak.

Emily Innes was with him throughout, with a brief exception when she got sick before he did and went home a few months earlier than he during their stay at Durian Sabatang in Perak. After returning to England at the beginning of 1882 Mr. Innes started a new career as a tea importer, and Mrs. Innes wrote a book about their colonial years, published in 1885. Her motives must have been partly to get back some of the money they had used up in British Malaya. But she also very much wanted a chance to offer to the public her own version of the history of both Mr. Innes's relations to the Colonial Service and the British presence in the Malay States. *The Gilding Off* was a title consciously aimed at advertising the book as an exposé, borrowing some of the light from the brilliant reception of Bird's book and at the same time implicitly critiquing *The Golden Chersonese* by promising to tell the truth as Bird's book had not. If Bird's narrative represented itself as apolitical, an independent narrative of a private journey, Innes's positively trumpeted itself as a public, and political, testimony.

The imbalance between the reception of *The Golden Chersonese* and the reception of *The Chersonese with the Gilding Off* has been impressively consistent. If mentioned at all, Innes's book tends to be dismissed, often with some combination of contempt, disgust, and anger. Her criticisms of the British colonial system in British Malaya have conveniently been read as indications of a woman "too bitter to be a reliable witness."[46] The mildest responses were in contemporary reviews. In the *Athenaeum* the reviewer simply remarked that "'one story is good until another is told'; and the charges are so direct and circumstantial that the other story ought to be forthcoming."[47] The reviewer in the *Asiatic Quarterly Review* for 1886, though remaining neutral on the substance of Innes's charges, was willing to agree with her that "the individual, unlucky or indiscreet enough to come into collision with a government, generally gets the worst of it, and very little sympathy besides."[48]

In the twentieth century the dismissal has become more dramatic.

The most common tactic is omission. Even though *The Chersonese with the Gilding Off* is the only fairly independent account of the Resident system in Malaya in its first decade (other accounts being written by the people who were directly hired and promoted within that system), it is the memoirs of the Residents and governors, particularly Swettenham and Low, but also governors' reports and Colonial Office correspondence, which have been used to reconstruct the history of those times. Usually, the specifics of Innes's often conflicting and thoroughly detailed version are ignored. A kind of critique which was tolerated was Mrs. Douglas Cator's 1909 talk to the Royal Colonial Institute on "Some Experiences of Colonial Life," which reads like a recipe on how to be a better imperialist.[49] Even those with a special interest in women's travel books have abandoned Innes. Pat Barr, Bird's modern biographer, labeled *The Gilding Off* "a peevish, trivial, quaint little book" by a woman who complained a lot and, unlike Isabella Bird, "was not one to make the best of a bad job."[50]

The few "western" male "Malay experts" in the twentieth century do occasionally quote Bird. When they even mention Innes's book, they do not do so favorably. The standard modern history of that time and place in the colonial service, Robert Heussler's *British Rule in Malaya: The Malayan Civil Service and Its Predecessors, 1867–1942*, explicitly passes judgment on the critique of the colonial service in *The Gilding Off*. Heussler's own scholarly evaluation as late as 1981, over one hundred years after the British takeover of the Malay States, is breathtaking in its endorsement of British imperial positions. His writing of the history of the region so as to explain, which is to say, justify, what became the British takeover of Malay lands is virtually identical to the one the Colonial Office was disseminating in the mid-nineteenth century: the Malays, through fighting among themselves, "had lost the moral right to stand on their own traditions" and needed the British presence "to put starch into them."[51] For him, Mrs. Innes's book, suggesting as it does something dark, and perhaps limp, about how that British presence actually operated, "bears the mark of acute paranoia."[52] Heussler does not mention that the charges the Inneses brought against the colonial administration in general and Douglas in particular were later verified. Nor does he bring up the Colonial Office minute refusing partly on gender grounds, at the time to investigate the charges: "wouldn't it be unwise to commit ourselves to the keeping of a woman, and to embark with her on a private crusade against the manner in which our own commissioned officer has exercised his large and undoubted discretion and power in matters of local administration?"[53]

There is no point in arguing the "truth" of Innes's representations in comparison to Bird's. Not surprisingly, there seems to be a correlation between support for the British presence in Malaya and the differences in reception of Bird's and Innes's books. The ideological basis of literary and historical opinions is hardly news, at least for many critics. Within this particular discussion my interest in Innes's book lies not so much in the ways it may be read as an exposé—taking the gilding off and revealing the shoddy materials underneath—as in the peculiar combination of gender and imperialism its rhetorical strategies create.

Those strategies are particularly accessible in the self-fashioning of the narrator. Innes's voice in *The Gilding Off* addresses directly the compelling question of its relations to its famous and popular predecessor. The narrator asserts of *The Golden Chersonese* that "notwithstanding the brilliancy and attractiveness of her descriptions, and the dulness and gloom of mine, I can honestly say that her account is perfectly and literally true. So is mine. The explanation is that she and I saw the Malayan country under totally different circumstances" (242). Part of what marks the difference in Innes's version was that Bird was "a celebrated person" (242), and wherever she went, as Bird's own narrative confirms, "Government officers did their best to make themselves agreeable" (243). Their motives were simple: "knowing that she wielded in her right hand a little instrument that might chastise or reward them as they deserved of her" (243). By Innes's account, Bird's pen was a political instrument, and *The Golden Chersonese* played a crucial role in relation to the British reading audience as political propaganda for the British takeover of the Malay States.

Just as significant is Innes's suggestion that the propaganda potential of what Bird would write was clearly understood by the colonial administrators at the time of Bird's impromptu and presumably casual little excursion (with the implication that this understanding may have been a substantial motive in inviting her in the first place). Certainly, this puts the many compliments Bird reported and the charming familial picture she painted of sitting cozily in Hugh Low's bungalow, the brother and sister—and in some ways sister and sister—pair engaged in their writing, in a less spontaneously simpatico light. Not just any witness to the grand imperial adventure of these administrators, Bird would be testifying to a large and friendly audience back in England about what she saw. On the other hand, Innes's narrative represents itself as offering a portrait of a particular version of British colonialism in a particular place and time which specifically argues that this version is unjust and corrupt. Like the reports of some American war correspondents in Vietnam in the 1970s, Innes's narrative insists that it is an eyewitness account of a national activity that has been glossed at home as noble but that, when you are really there to experience it, is revealed as ignoble and immoral.

The self-positioning of *The Gilding Off* as a political document and, even more precisely, as one important colonial record of the British presence in Malaya takes place through the medium of gender. In the passage on Bird's work, the narrator of *The Gilding Off* is also, by the force of contrast, defining herself. Precisely what she is not is a "celebrated person." Her pen, unlike Bird's, has little or no power to "chastise or reward" the members of the Malayan Colonial Service. Innes does not count for much in the colonial or the European world, and her voice is little heard. And she sees from a perspective different from Bird's; she sees and writes "under totally different circumstances," because she is in a different position. That difference is glossed as a specific combination of gender and class, at least as understood in the realm of civil servants. The narrator is "just the wife of a junior government servant."[54] Mr. Innes is in an inferior position in the British colonial hierarchy, and his wife's position is lower than his. Indeed, the wife of a junior government servant is the lowest position in the imperial hierarchy, her husband occupying the second lowest.[55] Below Emily, as her narrative frequently claims, come the Eurasians.

Yet part of the inventiveness of *The Gilding Off* is that upon that very lowness rests the narrator's claims to authority. Like many politically and socially powerless female narrators in nineteenth-century fiction, including Jane Austen's Fanny Price in *Mansfield Park* and Charlotte Brontë's Lucy Snowe in *Villette*, Emily Innes displays in her narrative the intellectual freedom which comes of social and political insignificance, a visibility made possible because in the social world of the Malay Civil Service she was virtually invisible. No colonial administrator bothered to take account of her presence, certainly not to think about what kind of witness she would be. Yet as a wife she was included as well as excluded, frequently quite literally sitting at the table during discussions of British policy, but with no professional mandate to uphold it. Thus the narrator's claims to superior information, to having the "truth," are based on her claims to an access made possible by her gendered public insignificance.

Those claims are also based on the argument of personal experience. Unlike the fictional counterparts I have just mentioned, and also unlike Anna Forbes in her narrative about a natural history expedition, Emily Innes lays claim to a wealth of experience, which provides her with a notably wide range of narrative authority. She knows about many kinds of things. *The Gilding Off* continually acknowledges that its narrative of Emily and James Innes's life in Selangor and Perak is both a private and a public, a domestic and a political, event. One of the more frequent forms this acknowledgment takes is the sudden and rapid switches in subject, almost like quick cuts in film, from a voice whose range of interests testifies, at least implicitly, to its right to discuss virtually all the aspects of the British Resident system. The narrator moves from predictable topics like Innes's occupations of sewing and raising hens and figuring out how to order tinned food to less predictable ones, such as Mr. Innes's occupation of judging cases as magistrate, including details of the cases. She moves from detailing how the sultan of Selangor has had his dignity taken by the English to assertions that Malay women are "unintelligent" (1:82) and Malay and English marriage laws are similar in that both have been made "exclusively by the men and for the men's advantage" (1:85). We also hear contempt for "the red tapists in Singapore" (1:65) and an account of the scents of various flowers, along with a version of her arguing with Hugh Low about his helping slaveholders and several analyses of the undesirability of visits from the Resident. The book discusses in detail the problems of what to have for lunch and just as freely discusses what's wrong with the colonial system of "Protection," since "the only persons protected by it are H.B.M.'s Residents. Everyone else in the country—native or European—is practically at their mercy" (2:247). The book closes with a claim, backed up by arguments, that "Annexation" is a more effective and just colonial system for colonists, but not at all because it would be just for the Malays.

In this range of topics the narrative does not sustain a gendered separation of spheres. The narrator claims authority over issues conventionally glossed as masculine quite as much as those glossed as feminine. This is a rhetoric of authority, an authority based directly on the experience of not being one of those with public authority. As a woman, as someone not a member of the Colonial Service, not working for the government, and not directly engaged in making the decisions of government and carrying on the business of government; engaged instead in the less important domestic chores of sewing, raising chickens, finding enough food, keeping the rain out of the bungalow, and planting flowers, the author can look at everything. She, because she is a she and an insignificant she, can turn her colonizer's gaze on everything around her. She can look from the distance of subject to object on Malay sultans but also on colonial Residents and the British governor, with his free "horses, carriages, plate, linen, and servants" (2:147), and on herself, walking in the swamp "wearing the idiotic frilled skirts of Europe" (1:137).

The absence of any tacit recognition of a separation of intellectual spheres by gender is balanced in the text by powerful claims about the unjust separation of spheres by class, here measured by place in the colonial hierarchy in Malaya. Within the British hierarchy the Innes family are the workers, the lower-class underlings gazing with both a sense of envy and a sense of injustice at the doings of the upper class. For them, "mere living" is decidedly not a "luxury." Not only the narrative perspective but also the narrative content have explicitly to do with constraints of class. Thus *The*

Gilding Off exhibits no ladylike, upper-class delicacy in its attention to crass material details, particularly food and money. Much of the discussion about the Residents, Hugh Low and Bloomfield Douglas, focuses on what food they get to eat and where they get it, as opposed to what Innes has and how she has to get it. We hear frankly of salary differences, of which perks are denied to those below Resident rank, of how Douglas kept the government boat usually used by the magistrate, of how much he cheated the sultan out of, of what the Inneses lose each year by the devaluation of the pound, and how they got their passage home.

In *The Gilding Off* the Resident is most assuredly not a father. He is a boss, and, in the case of Douglas, a crooked one at that. For all its plethora of details about the minutiae of jungle housekeeping, for all that it recounts a middle-class colonial housewife's six-year struggle to make a home in the Malay States, the book does not represent the colonial through the framework of bourgeois familial ideology. Much of the content is domestic, but much of the content is not, and neither is the narrator's position. It is Bird who invokes the familial to justify the colonial, presuming that the two ideologies are in harmony. And it is Bird, not Innes, who finds Douglas a bad father. The hermeneutic framework of *The Gilding Off* is drawn not from the domestic but from the professional or working sphere. The Colonial Service is not a family, it is a career. The narrative continually presents both husband and wife as subject to the Colonial Service, he officially, and she unofficially, he underpaid, she unpaid, but both required to work nonetheless. Emily and James are in this together. They decide to go together, and they decide to resign together, even if only he signs the letter.

Once the key British administrators are no longer your relatives, elders to be respected, they become the other side. The Colonial Office is effectively glossed as a company, and the Residents are the bosses as opposed to the workers. The British government is a commercial enterprise, and the political is revealed as synonymous with the economic. For the narrative the relation between the worker and the company, represented by its management, is in some primary way adversarial. Innes, as a woman and therefore never actually on the payroll, as the wife of an underling and therefore treated as an inferior by the administrators of rank above her husband (and their wives), as insignificant and therefore free to look around and draw her own conclusions, and as the victim of company injustice through its denying her husband his back pay, has no company loyalty. *The Gilding Off* offers no ideological justification for the British moving into the Malay States. On the contrary, its discourse works to discredit the justifications that have been offered, specifically in *The Golden Chersonese*.

This is not to suggest that the book critiques colonialism in any general or fundamental way. *The Gilding Off* does employ, and pervasively, many of the tropes of colonialism, particularly those of European racial and cultural superiority. What is notable is the unconventional, even anticolonial, rhetorical use those all-too-conventional tropes are put to in this book. The narrator exhibits the usual British Victorian sense of superiority to Malay people and offers some familiar racist analyses of the lazy Malay, the ugly sarong, the inferior tropical fruit, et cetera. She continually reads the Malays in negative and essentialist ways. *The Gilding Off* is part of an extensive women's imperial discourse in Victorian England. Yet its notable and unusual argument is that the British colonial presence in the Malay States cannot be read as desirable or inevitable or good.

The special quality of the rhetoric of *The Gilding Off* is its deliberate absence of eloquence, of enthusiasm or empathy or delight. Innes does not love what she sees, does not express waves of joy in her experiences. There is no language of sweetness here, none of the lyrical consumerism which characterizes the sensitive and warm lady who narrates *The Golden Chersonese*. Also significantly absent is Swettenham's and Bird's language of sympathy, of friendly expressions of concern for, and willingness to come to the rescue of, those glossed as less fortunate and less capable in the family of man. The descriptive language is sparse and crude, the tone is frank and comic, often self-deprecating, and just as often nasty and critical of what she sees. Bird's work invokes the tropes of personal affection to justify domination: she loves the place and people, so the British should, in the famous remark of an American officer in Vietnam, "destroy the village to save it." Innes's book invokes the tropes of colonial racism to discredit colonialism. She does not like the place or the people, and we should all go home.

At one moment in what the British considered the model "Protected State," Perak, Innes describes herself watching some Chinese coolies, "almost all with repulsive skin diseases," who are in turn watching her and scowling while she and James take their evening walk. Having thus established what might seem an unbridgeable difference, her startling colonial response to these colonized eyes is suddenly to surmise that she is standing in their position, is looking from their location out at what she imagines they see about her. And what she imagines them as seeing is that she is in the wrong place. Her comment is that "probably they could not see—as, indeed, I never could myself—what business we English had there at all" (2:65). Her view of the coolies as repellent here cannot be glossed as an instance of the typical British assumptions of superiority. Her "recognition" of their ugly scowling faces is entwined with her recognition and sudden sharing of their subjectivity, through her idea that they are objectifying the Inneses even as she is objectifying them. This acknowledgment of mutual distance rather than of human connection, this recognition of there being two sides and of the simultaneous refusal of either side to view the other as some kind of relative in the human family, is precisely the lens through which Innes glimpses that the British colonial presence is wrong. What Innes and the coolies share is not a sense of how they are alike but a sense of how far they are apart. Racism, almost always the handmaiden of imperialism in Victorian travel books, at this moment in *The Gilding Off* functions as the central argument against imperialism.

If the British Colonial Service is not a family, with grandmother Queen Victoria, through her fatherly representatives, busy looking after her family, both British and native, in the Malay States, a major ideological justification for the British colonial presence there is lost. The marked absence of the domestic in *The Gilding Off*, the absence of the metaphors of the family of man and also of the language of sympathy for and appreciation of the landscape and people of the Malay Peninsula, effectively negates the major rhetorical justification for the British presence there.

Sympathy as the gilding of cultural erasure and formal nonintervention as the gilding of substantive intervention are both scraped
away to reveal the cold material basis for the British presence in
Malaya. The matter-of-fact tone of Innes's book, its explicit refusal
to appreciate, and its insistence that the Malay landscape and people
are repeatedly dirty and ugly and inexplicable, employ familiar
conventions of imperial rhetoric to reject imperialism, stripping
away British claims of their right to be on the Malay Peninsula. In
the place of Swettenham's and Bird's lyric sympathy and understanding, at the service of destroying what they purport to love,
Innes's unfeeling and businesslike language works primarily to lay
bare and discredit British economic motives under their gilding of
paternal concern for the peoples of the Peninsula.

Also, very occasionally, Innes's antisympathetic rhetoric functions to depict what a disinterested sympathy with the Malays might
mean. The most notable occasion for representing that sympathy in
the narrative emerges in a discussion of gender, in the narrator's long
account of the sultan of Selangor's daughter and the most important
woman in Selangor, Tunku Chi. The narrator frames the account by
drily observing that Malays "were not in all respects improved by
contact with Europeans" (88). Tunku's husband, the viceroy of
Selangor, had become partly Europeanized and drank brandy, so she
left him. She, on the other hand, remained completely Malay, would
never call on Mrs. Innes, and "hated the English, very naturally, with
all her heart" (89).

After introducing this Malay woman into the narrative, Innes
tells a crucial framing story about Tunku Chi's "ferocious temper"
in beating a servant. The story establishes this Malay's lack of a
feminized kindness or sympathetic heart and thereby closes off any
rhetorical possibility of a reader sympathizing with her because of
her own sympathetic feelings. It is not on such rhetorically familiar
imperial grounds that a British audience will be allowed to have a
positive response to this foreign character. Innes then concludes that
precisely in consequence of Tunku Chi's lack of sweetness or warmth,
her hatred of the English and "her unbending attitude of defiance
and conservative views, I could not but respect and admire her." For
Innes, had Tunku Chi been a man or had women had a real say in

the political fate of their state, "the British would never have been invited to 'protect' Selangor, and it is probable they would not have dared to come uninvited" (96–97). Instead, and clearly regrettably, the British have come, and Tunku Chi's "life at Langat must have been a very dull one" (97).

The values Tunku Chi's attitude and activities represent here are of independent thinking, refusal to glorify the familial, rejection of a romanticized sympathy, rejection of the terms of imperial representations of Malays, distance from the concerns of and even active dislike of the masculine political authorities because of being treated unjustly, a sense of being publicly insignificant yet personally highly competent, and confinement to a life which does not realize the possibilities of one's character and abilities or provide an outlet for one's intellectual energy. It is hard to miss the similarities between this sketch of Tunku Chi and the self-representation of Emily Innes, one presented as limited by race, the other by class, and both by gender. Tunku Chi's very negative qualities—the anger, the boredom, the closed-mindedness about another culture, the lack of exercise—all contributing to her growing "more and more ill-tempered every day" (97), are familiar in invoking some of the complaints, the self-definition, and the claims to see clearly offered through the rhetorical style of the narrator.

The implication of the narrative similarities between this Malay princess and the lowly wife of a junior administrator is that bourgeois domesticity, like colonialism, is a form of institutional injustice, and that the two work together to sustain economic inequality in many places in the world. If British women like Emily Innes ran the Colonial Service and Malay women like Tunku Chi ran the Malay States, there would be no British colonial presence on the Malay Peninsula. Without the comforts made available to her through colonialism in the relatively luxurious bungalow of the British Resident, Isabella Bird would not have the room of her own necessary to rhapsodize about the familial joys of life in the Malay Peninsula, while some "lazy" Malay was being culturally uplifted by having been taught to wash Bird's clothes and make her dinner. The British and the Malays could remain physically as well as culturally worlds apart. And that, in the unspoken conclusion of *The Gilding Off*, would be best.

CHAPTER 6

"One's Own State"

Margaret Brooke, Harriette McDougall, and Sarawak

*"Why not try to tell the almost legendary story of the rule of
the Brookes in Sarawak, and let others see and feel what it
was like to be sovereign rulers of one's own state."*
—SYLVIA BROOKE, *QUEEN OF THE HEAD-HUNTERS*

*"'We are not living in a boy's adventure tale,' I protested.
His scornful whispering took me up. 'We aren't indeed!
There's nothing of a boy's tale in this.'"*
—JOSEPH CONRAD, *THE SECRET SHARER*

Directly east of the Malay Peninsula and stretching far to the
northeast and southeast of Singapore lies Borneo, largest
island in the Indian Archipelago and third largest island in the
world. The island is now not part of any single country but is
divided between Malaysia at the top (the two states of Sarawak in
the northwest and Sabah at the northern tip—these two states
together being larger than all of peninsular Malaysia) and Indonesia
in all the rest of the island, now called Kalimantan. In the nineteenth
century, as a result of European and regional aggressions, Borneo
was much more divided, being at various times part Dutch
(Kalimantan), part Malayo-Muslim (Brunei), part non-Malay
tribes, part British protectorate (Sarawak, then also Brunei), part
British colony (the small island of Labuan, just off the mainland),
part British commercial property (then British North Borneo, now
Sabah), and part privately owned by an Englishman (Sarawak).

Making Sarawak

Borneo had a special place in nineteenth-century British imperial discourse. It was an unusually popular place for private travelers to visit and to write about, particularly for those self-styled as naturalists who were traveling through areas controlled by the Dutch or by the Malays, but also for many other travelers as well. Yet the official British attitude toward Borneo was deeply ambivalent at best. In the first half of the nineteenth century the British government was even less interested in Borneo than it was in the Malay Peninsula) and gave little thought to developing its commercial potential or establishing trade with it, even after antimony and large pockets of coal were discovered there.

What the British were endlessly interested in during the eighteenth and nineteenth centuries was protecting their shipping routes south from India, around the bottom of the Malay Peninsula by Singapore, and up northeast again and on to China. In thinking about those places loosely designated in English as the "East," the goal "repeatedly laid out by policy makers in London was not the acquisition of large amounts of territory—an idea repugnant to successive colonial secretaries—but the possession of strategically located and small naval stations and entrepôts which could command the sea routes through the Indian Ocean, the Straits of Malacca and the South China Sea."[1] Between Borneo and the mainland of the Malay Peninsula to the north of it were many small islands, some frequented by the Dutch and some the hiding places of Malayo-Muslim and non-Malay tribal raiders, constantly referred to in English as "pirates."[2] The mainland to the north was French-controlled Cochin-China. The Borneo coast itself also provided sanctuary for a fair number of the so-called pirates. There were thus a wide range of peoples interested in taking British cargoes and ships. The first few hundred miles heading northeast toward China after Singapore may well have felt to many British traders during the first half of the nineteenth century like running a gauntlet.

British commitments to a clear passage to China created a strategic importance not for Borneo itself but only for its northwest coast, almost all of which was in the first decades of the nineteenth century under the control of the kingdom of Brunei. British concern was spurred in part by increasing Dutch control of the southern part of Borneo, a control which might well extend to the whole island and thus end the possibility of a British safe port on the northwest side. During the 1840s Royal Navy boats did attack fairly aggressively various local tribes, which they referred to as "pirates," in the waters off the northwest coast of Borneo, with major encounters in 1843 and 1849. The willingness, even enthusiasm, of some of the naval officers and their men for this job was motivated a great deal by desire for profit. By the Act of 1825, initiated in response to "piracy" in the West Indies but applicable anywhere, the British government paid its seamen a bonus or "head-money" per pirate.[3] Members of the Royal Navy, particularly captains and officers, made a lot of money in the waters off Borneo. Designating local Malay and non-Malay tribes in the East Indies region as "pirates" turned out to be an expensive proposition for the British, and not just monetarily. Newspaper reports of the 1849 battles led to major criticism of the Royal Navy's activities in Borneo waters as constituting what one member of Parliament called naval "massacres"—given the superiority of British firepower—of these local groups.[4] The political results were a change in the head-money system, a sharp reaffirmation of British commitment to noninvolvement in the region, and an Admiralty order that naval ships from the 1850s on were not to engage in battles with the "pirates."

Reflecting their continuing imperial policy of antiterritorialism in the region, the British had signed a treaty with Brunei in 1847. The treaty did cede Brunei territory to the British, but only the tiny island of Labuan, just off the northwest coast. Labuan appeared to constitute a happy solution for the conflicting political needs of both England and Brunei. The British world now have a strategically located naval station and port just off the northwest coast of Borneo, while the sultan of Brunei, for his part, could presume that he had ended the threat of a British presence on the mainland. The sultan further agreed to cede no more of his territories to anyone without the permission of the British, thus protecting both Britain and Brunei from the threat of competition through territorial aggressions by other European imperial powers. By mid-century, with the

1847 treaty, Britain had gotten all it appeared to have wanted from the northwest coast of Borneo. And by 1850, though the Royal Navy had been strongly chastised for its aggressive attacks on indigenous tribes, the incidence of raids on British commercial ships appeared to have decreased. But with the familiar slippage between government and Colonial Office rhetoric in England and what happened in Southeast Asia, the English presence in Borneo continued to increase. By the end of the century, through a series of events related to what was happening on the Malay Peninsula (usually involving intervention in Malay affairs to "establish order"), north and northwest Borneo were completely under British control.

There were many significant differences between British colonial activities on the Malay Peninsula and in Borneo. My focus here is not on tracing these differences or providing some sort of revisionist history of British colonialism in the region but particularly on connecting a few of those activities with the rhetoric of some published memoirs about Sarawak written by Victorian women. Within that rather narrow focus, I will mention one notable difference between what was happening on the Peninsula and in northern Borneo. Because of the well-located free port of Singapore and also because of increasingly valuable leases on opium farms, on tin mines, and then on rubber plantations, British Malaya increasingly provided great riches for the empire. In spite of various attempts—such as trying to make the small off shore island of Labuan profitable by modeling it after Singapore, developing the coal mines at Muara, and chartering the top of Borneo as the North Borneo Company— northern Borneo was not to provide even adequate riches for the empire.[5] Hugh Low, afterward to be famous in British Malaya for the profits he made for England, could do nothing to develop Labuan while he was acting governor there.[6] The territorial drive needed for the English to take over so much of the island was simply not provided by economic forces, by the lure of profits. A common perception, reflected in frequent Colonial Office statements throughout the century, was that a British presence in Borneo would not make money, it would require money.

Why, then, in spite of declared colonial policy, did the British ultimately end up in the late nineteenth century taking over the huge territories which made up the northern part of Borneo? Economic hopes, though largely unrealized, did have a little something to do with it, and political hopes still more. The northernmost province of Sabah became unofficially British in the late 1870s when, after the sultan had leased it to that commercial invention, the North Borneo Company, the British government granted the Company a government charter, partly to engineer a buyout of its German partner.[7] This buyout is one of the many British actions in Southeast Asia taken for reasons which had to do not with perceptions of the value of the region itself but with competition between England and other European powers. In the case of Sabah and the North Borneo Company, the British government became involved in order to get Germany uninvolved. Precisely what the charter required was that the North Borneo Company get rid of its German element.[8]

One of those attempting, late in the century, to influence the government and the British public on the question of the economic value to England of Borneo was Ada Pryer. Wife of the first European Resident of British North Borneo, she wrote in 1893 an account of the ten years she spent building up hemp and coffee plantations there. The explicit political goal of her memoir was to persuade the British government of the great agricultural potential of the region.

The North Borneo Company may well have looked similar in conception to the East India Company. But even this apparently typical imperial combination of private enterprise intertwined with issues of public policy and rabid competitiveness with other European nations had another dimension. The North Borneo Company was created and then found official support from the Foreign Office partly because it was perceived as a possible rival, and therefore a much-desired check, to what was already the dominant British presence in Borneo, the state of Sarawak. Since by the 1870s Sarawak was supported by the Colonial Office, the creation of the North Borneo Company was partly a matter of interdepartmental competitiveness. Sarawak's dominant presence was itself driven not by economics but by what I might call a more immaterial imperial force, one which pervaded and animated the romanticized masculine rhetoric of many a British colonial enterprise: the sheer joy of taking over and running the world. In the case of Borneo this boyish imperial enthusiasm was almost entirely generated by and focused on a single family, the Brookes of Sarawak.

Sarawak was one of the southern states in the sultanate of Brunei, rather distant from the influence of the sultan and his court. In 1842 the sultan officially appointed an Englishman, James Brooke, to be the governor, or rajah, of the Brunei state of Sarawak. Inspired by the story of Raffles and Singapore, Brooke had been looking for a private venture with which to establish a British presence around Borneo. His appointment as governor of Sarawak fulfilled a pledge made to him by the sultan's second in command in Sarawak and only kept when Brooke turned his guns (including those from two British navy boats) on him. That pledge was to give Brooke the governorship of this small state if he could successfully end a rebellion (caused to a great extent by the injustices of the previous governor) by a coalition of tribes in Sarawak. In exchange for his appointment, the new governor agreed to pay the sultan an annual fee out of the tax revenue he could collect.

Then, in 1843, the sultan, almost certainly intimidated by the presence of what was now a flotilla of visiting British ships—Brooke having good friends in the Royal Navy—granted this British rajah the right to name his own heirs. James Brooke thus gained control of Sarawak in perpetuity. In fact, there would be only three White Rajahs, and only two of them were active rulers. Charles Brooke, younger son of James's sister, became rajah at James's death in 1868. James himself never married, though he appears to have had sexual relationships with Malay and tribal women and also acknowledged one illegitimate British son.[9] In the early 1860s James disinherited the declared heir to Sarawak, the older son of his sister, who had already been acting rajah, in favor of her second son, Charles. He ruled from 1863 on but only officially became rajah in 1868. During Charles's reign, in 1888, Sarawak became officially a British protectorate, but with independence internally. In 1917 Charles died, and his oldest son, Vyner Brooke, became the third and last rajah. But he did not actively rule, the way his two famous ancestors had.

The Japanese held Sarawak during World War II, and in 1946 Vyner gave it to England as a Crown Colony. Along with North Borneo, Sarawak became Britain's last colonial acquisition.

Sarawak is a rare, and perhaps unique, phenomenon in the nineteenth-century history of British imperial interventions. It was, in a continually contested sense, a British colony, but precisely not by any legal or public designation. It was a country as private property. But what, after all, is that? Throughout the second half of the nineteenth century Sarawak was a continual problem for England. The basic issue, in spite of all its complexities, was precisely the political location, the anomalous international legal status of Sarawak. What was its identity? Was it a nation, or a state within a nation? And if it were a nation, was it colonized by England or not? Rajah Brooke (James and then Charles) wanted Britain to recognize it officially as an independent country, a recognition which would, of course, have guaranteed the weight of British naval power behind their desires to make the state their very own.[10] The British government repeatedly refused to do so, in part because it was unacceptable to the sovereignty of England that a British subject should also be head of a foreign state. But at least as significant a reason was the British awareness that to recognize the sovereignty of Sarawak was to violate the sovereignty of Brunei, to which the state technically belonged, however much the Brookes preferred, and argued, otherwise.

As early as 1846 Lord Palmerston of the Foreign Office in his letter to the Admiralty was quite explicit in his reasons for trying to limit the extent to which the Royal Navy could help James Brooke sustain and expand his rule in Sarawak by fighting the coastal raiders. Brooke's cunning but dubious argument in asking for help was that the navy had to protect him and the other British in Sarawak as British subjects. Palmerston reminded the admiral that "Your Lordships are aware that it has not been the wish of Her Majesty's Government that British Subjects should possess territory on the mainland of Borneo."[11] The government was still making the same point in 1858, refusing to make Sarawak a protectorate on the clear grounds that "if every English subject were to be allowed to settle in any district he might think fit, and then afterwards to call upon the Government as a matter of right to give him military and civil protection, . . . it must lead the Government into endless difficulties and expenditure."[12]

Why this admirable governmental respect for the territorial rights of Brunei? After all, "the Existence of Sarawak, ruled as it was by a British subject, did serve Britain's interests in so far that it excluded other Powers from the area."[13] But in spite of the frequently asserted strategic usefulness of Sarawak, there was a specter even larger than competition with their Continental neighbors which haunted the correspondence of the Foreign Office and the Colonial Office during the mid- and late nineteenth century. An anxious parallel drawn again and again by British officials in their dispatches about British colonial pretensions in Southeast Asia was the undesirability of re-creating farther "east" the kind of involvement Britain had in India. I have discussed in the previous chapter the dilemma, clearly stated in British government discourses, of how to keep Malaya from becoming another India. But while in Malaya the British preferred to do things differently from how they had been done in India, in Borneo they preferred to do nothing at all. In the case of Sarawak, British anxiety may have been at least partially fed by the fact that James Brooke was Anglo-Indian: he had been born in India, where his father worked for the East India Company, and was only sent to England when he was twelve. Even before the "Mutiny" of 1857 Lord Wodehouse was quite explicit that "we have nothing to do with the domestic troubles of Brunei," . . . [for] we should hardly wish to make Borneo another India."[14]

The second, and related, problem the Brookes and Sarawak posed for British foreign policy was expansion. From the 1850s on, the first two Sarawak White Rajahs pursued what Wright has aptly dubbed an "absorption policy," annexing more and more of the river states of Brunei.[15] They did it in a variety of ways: by tricks in diplomacy, by magnifying minor incidents as threatening to either British lives or native rights or both, or simply by moving into a state and declaring it theirs. A measure of their success is that Sarawak increased from less than 5,000 square kilometers in 1841 to its present size of 125,000 square kilometers.[16] Obviously, one way to push back the political barriers to the sovereignty of Sarawak was to push them back literally, to take over, and become the sovereign of, Brunei. If Brunei ruled Sarawak, as the British government was given to insisting, then the Brookes could bring the government to recognize their claims to Sarawak by themselves ruling Brunei. The Brookes came very close to this stated goal, though they never totally succeeded.

Yet the limits of Britain's willingness to honor Brunei sovereignty above the claims of one of their own were marked in 1860. When James Brooke's two nephews, Charles and his brother, quite illegally invaded the Brunei province of Mukah, the British governor of Labuan, arguing that they, "as British subjects came under his consular jurisdiction," ordered them to lay down their arms and leave Brunei territory.[17] An outraged James Brooke applied to the British government, and the response was telling. The Foreign Office officially rebuked the governor of Labuan, and the Colonial Office not only removed him from his post but called him home in disgrace. "It was one thing to leave Rajah Brooke in a legal never-never land without official British support, but it was quite another matter to turn the full weight of British authority against an English gentleman."[18] The Brooke nephews were delighted and immediately traveled to Brunei, where they demanded and got the territory of Mukah. The now helpless sultan was forced to recognize that the British, when it came to one of their own, were not going to give the sultan the protection he had been promised by the treaty of 1847. He might well conclude that when aggressions against Brunei were made by an "English gentleman," the British implicitly gave their permission for him to cede his territories.

The British stayed involved in northwest Borneo in ways that tacitly supported the Brooke expansion, in part because of their continued policy of preventing other European powers from gaining power in northwest Borneo, a policy both the first and the second White Rajahs manipulated. Thus, in the 1860s James Brooke let it be known that he was negotiating with France, and then with Belgium for the sale of Sarawak. Brunei could be whittled away in part because of its own internal problems with rival groups, in part because it was a river kingdom and access to many of the states further from the city of Brunei was very difficult, and in part because, on the most direct level, the British and the Brookes had gunboats and they did not. Finally, Britain did move to declare the remaining territory of Brunei a British protectorate in 1888. They did so mainly because that seemed the only way the Sultan and the British government had left to keep Brunei in existence without the unacceptable option of the British actually fighting against "an English gentleman." Due to Sarawak's aggressions, by 1888 there was almost nothing left of Brunei—except, of course, some oil, discovered in 1903.

Writing Volumes on Sarawak

The imperial history of northern Borneo during most of the nineteenth century can be understood in terms of the history of the Brookes' efforts to relocate Sarawak, to transform the private into the public, to turn their family kingdom into a "real" country and themselves into "real" kings, with reality measured as formal international recognition of their national existence by Britain. Those efforts were enacted in the realm of discourse. It was all in a name, a linguistic argument, a matter of what the Brookes could call the place and, therefore, what they could call themselves. Charles Brooke was "very angry" when he was given a card of invitation to Queen Victoria's levee as Charles Brooke rather than as the Rajah of Sarawak.[19] There is a bizarre moment in the official Sarawak book, *Outlines of Sarawak History under the Brooke Rajahs*, when the significance of the 1888 Protectorate Treaty for Sarawak is summed up in just one sentence: "the Rajah was created a G.C.M.C., and later was entitled to a salute of 21 guns throughout the Empire, as the Ruler of an independent state."[20] In pursuit of the cause of recognition outside Sarawak, of being given their "real" name, James Brooke might well be accused of relentless ambition, and the methods of Charles Brooke have been explicitly described by a recent historian as "ruthless double-dealing and blackmail."[21]

Not surprisingly, such evaluations do not characterize the image of the White Rajahs sustained by most of the historians recording Brooke rule in Sarawak. The White Rajahs, and the country they claimed they owned, attained what I would call a mythic significance in Victorian imperial discourse. The myth was created in large part in the writing of people who were actual participants, the Brookes themselves and various people who were either related to them or worked for them or both; all committed to retelling what Sylvia called "the almost legendary story."[22] Sarawak was massively written about in the nineteenth century, and often enough in the twentieth. Along with extensive published papers arguing his cause, James Brooke had an extensive correspondence with Angela Burdett Coutts, the British millionaire who was his close friend and personal bank for loans to Sarawak in the early years.[23] In what was apparently a moment of particularly high affection, she bought him his first gunboat, that crucial instrument for threatening Malays into ceding power and territory. Charles Brooke also wrote three major published works on Sarawak and extensive short papers.

Charles's wife, Margaret Brooke, contributed two memoirs. In the twentieth century two of their daughters-in-law also wrote books about Sarawak. Bernard's wife offered a single work of "Recollections" and Vyner's wife, Sylvia, was not only the author of many novels and plays but also wrote three books involving Sarawak. In other words, there are six books by the Brooke women alone, and two more by the wife of a nineteenth-century bishop in Sarawak. In the nineteenth century there are innumerable accounts by travelers visiting Sarawak. Hugh Low, who would later charm Isabella Bird as the Resident of Perak, early in his phase as one of the most famous and economically successful administrators of British Malaya, wrote an entire book about his visit to Sarawak as a young naturalist.[24] His son would later be a Sarawak Resident in the administration of Rajah Charles. Then there were the frequent newspaper articles, the letters to editors, and, of course, the enormous Colonial Office and Foreign Office correspondence. There were, of course, admiring biographies, and the authorized *History of Sarawak under Its Two White Rajahs 1839–1908*.[25] All these writings tended to contribute to a vision of the Brookes and of Sarawak perceived through a "fog of semantic unreality."[26]

What accounts in part for the volume of this discourse is what Thomas Richards has analyzed in *The Imperial Archive* as the nineteenth-century British commitment to a "comprehensive knowledge upon which English hegemony" would rest.[27] Volumes were written about British Malaya and India as well. On the other hand, I am suggesting that what also accounts for this discourse is the unusual, even unique, imperial situation of Sarawak. Many Europeans connected with the state appear to have felt, at least frequently asserted, that they were participating in something special, something even magical, and something worth recording. More important, precisely because in public discourse in England Sarawak's political status was apparently unprecedented and difficult to locate, the political was in most thoroughgoing and often perfectly explicit ways to be located in the rhetorical. The problem of Sarawak was the problem of what to call it. The "semantic unreality" could become the "reality." This was, of course, only a British problem. The Dutch, for example, saw Sarawak as "no more than a somewhat unorthodox extension of the British empire."[28] But for the British, in a way that sets Sarawak's significance apart from that of other British colonial regions, the private aspect of Sarawak's takeover rendered the question of its identity—how to name it and thus to categorize it—a rhetorical issue within which were encompassed all the discourses on Sarawak.

Whatever Sarawak was, it could not easily be labeled. Its political identity was impressively unstable. Sarawak did not fit into any existing colonial categories, at least in the English language. Sarawak's meaning in the discourse of British imperialism can not, because it could not, be discerned simply by rounding up the usual imperial suspects, by looking for similarities to nearby colonial territories, or by invoking the seemingly omnipresent god of mammon. Its lack of economic identity may have been the most striking ideological problem in "naming" Sarawak. In opposition to British proceedings in the Malay Peninsula, the Brookes discouraged British commercial activities in Sarawak and actively blocked European investments which would take their profits at the expense of native interests. Nor was it clear that Sarawak really had many natural resources to "develop."

The line between economic and other motives is also a little blurred, as in the Brooke invasion of the Brunei state of Mukah which led to that key declaration of British government policy about not putting British military force against English gentlemen. The invasion was triggered by Mukah's refusal to give Sarawak traders access to its rich production of sago. But the Brooke invasion was even more driven by the fact that Mukah was the location of Malays resistant to Brooke rule. Generally, the Brookes were not motivated by material greed. Rajah Charles railed at "these times when eager speculators are always seeking for some new place to exploit, . . . when the white man comes to the fore and the dark coloured is thrust to the wall and when capital rules and justice ceases."[29] "The meaning" of Sarawak had to be located on a different ideological ground than the all-too-common one of some kind of intertwining of European superiority with the right to economic exploitation.

Unlike Malaya, Sarawak did produce, for the Brookes and for England, a kind of "wealth beyond the dreams of avarice," though in a sense that broke out of the material boundaries of meaning in the phrase. It was not territory, any more than commercial profits, which drove the Brookes, in spite of their almost ceaseless efforts to control more land. In their letters and speeches the Brookes continually discouraged any kind of British settlements and continually insisted that the state must exist to serve its own indigenous tribes. They set up a colonial administration which, under the level of the rajah, gave Malay administrators real power (unlike in British Malaya), though often as subordinates to English Residents. However, the ultimate power in Sarawak—economic, political, judicial, social—always as much as possible stayed with the rajah. What Sarawak was and would be, internally at least, was almost totally determined by the one-man rule of the Brookes. Their aim, of course, was totally to define its identity in the external world as well. Yet in the extensive materials that composed the imperial historiography about Sarawak, more was at stake than either the fulfillment of Brooke ambitions or the political fate in England of this one state in northern Borneo.

A Man's Adventure Tale

The argument about identity which informs many British imperial accounts of Sarawak is linked to another quality which is also a key element of the hermeneutic framework these writings construct and share. I have suggested that one reason so much was written about Sarawak was precisely because its meaning was open ended, a matter of debate. But openness was not emptiness. The very lack of definition which defined the British presence in Sarawak carried with it a distinctive cast. The writings of what Reece has aptly labeled "the court historians" share a perspective happily captured in a phrase by Harriette McDougall, wife of the first bishop of Sarawak, in the preface to her 1854 *Letters from Sarawak; Addressed to a Child.*[30] This was a book she had sent in sections to her son at school in England. Sarawak, she says, "has for the last seven years furnished a romance to the English public, which for a time made its Rajah a favourite hero."[31] How long that "romance" would last may be suggested by another account over a century later, by a would-be historian of Sarawak in 1960. "In all history only one man succeeded in coming from the West and making himself king over an Eastern race, and founding a dynasty which lasted for a hundred years. . . . He lived a life such as schoolboys dream of. . . . He looked like a romantic hero, and behaved like one."[32]

The romance that Sarawak "furnished" to fulfil the dreams of English schoolboys lay precisely in this matter of individual hero- ism, this "archetypal fantasy of isolated white men ruling over savages in a tropical setting."[33] What Sarawak and the ongoing debate about its identity represented was the possibility that an individual Englishman could go anywhere and become anything, could conquer pirates at sea and defeat jungle tribes on land, could get himself his very own country and become its king. He could do this not only in an eighteenth-century novel like *Robinson Crusoe* but in real life. An Englishman could have "a little kingdom carved out for himself."[34] In the words of Joseph Conrad's Marlow, narrator of the novel almost certainly inspired by the history of the White Rajahs, the romance-come-true of Sarawak represented the heroic fantasies of Lord Jim, who "had beheld the face of that opportunity which, like an Eastern bride, had come veiled to his side."[35]

The debate about imperial identity which informed most British writings about Sarawak in the nineteenth and early twentieth centu- ries was repeatedly cast in the language of the great boy's adventure tales. This particular legend was "at its best in boys' adventure stories of the early twentieth century when the European imperial system was at its zenith."[36] Brooke's Sarawak, that veiled "eastern

bride" of European dreams, was not only Jim's Patusan, in a novel
dazzling in its insights into and critique of the genre of imperial
adventure story, but also Kim's India and Peter Pan's Never-Never
Land. The ideological importance of Sarawak and the Brookes in
nineteenth- and twentieth-century England had everything to do
with the question of the "truth" value of the imperial fantasy.
Sarawak "proved" the truth of the claim made by so many colonial
apologists in British fiction, that the boy's dream of adventure could
be realized in the man's actual life in the big world, that a British
imperialist really could be a white knight as opposed to a greedy
tradesman.

The White Rajahs were a fantasy come to life, a dream come
true. Never-Never Land could be found on a chart, on the west
coast of Borneo; and so, quite literally, could Conrad's Patusan, an
actual village in a part of Brunei which the White Rajah took over,
thus making it a village in Sarawak. The Brookes' story becomes the
story of all "our" possibilities, of the individualist promise at the
heart of the imperial enterprise. Once the boy was cast as a man who
lit out for the territory, all that remained was to present the specifics
of what that dream consisted of and what its fulfillment was actually
like. The narratives had to fill in the details, send back the information from that fabulous reality. It is surely no coincidence that the
first book by the writer who described Sarawak as "furnish[ing] a
romance" to the British public was cast in the forms of letters to an
English schoolboy.

The fantasies of the Brookes and their admiring chroniclers
certainly differed. What their writings share in all the variety of
representations of Sarawak is the pervasive implication that in this
place, at least as it is created in their writings, the fantasies, which
inevitably consist of various European people being personally elevated to some regal and heroic state, have come true. Benedict
Anderson's evocative discussion of how a country is an imagined
community, with the imagined having real sovereignty in the sense
of national law, has a special resonance in the case of Sarawak.[37] For
the Brookes and many of the British people who worked in their
administrations and wrote about the experience, imagining the state
of Sarawak as a nation and having the power to make that picture

come true was a conscious preoccupation. Precisely at issue was what kind of country to imagine and thus to create. Giving Sarawak a national identity was intertwined with giving its various narrators heroic identities as well. What is marked about much of the rhetoric on Sarawak is that its specific, and often explicit, focus on establishing the political identity of the place is taken up in terms of establishing the subject identity of the Brookes and their apologists.

In a statement quoted with particular admiration by another imperial adventurer, Frank Swettenham, in the preface he wrote to Margaret Brooke's 1913 memoirs of her time in Sarawak, James Brooke asserted that "if it please God to permit me to give a stamp to this country which shall last after I am no more, I shall have lived a life which emperors might envy."[38] The rhetorical maneuver in a phrase like this rests in the claim that Brooke is some sort of pure soul, beyond the rewards of this world. But what there was to dream about and to envy about the Brooke life was precisely that it fulfilled the dreams of success in this world, that it literally was the life of an emperor, in an historical period when the role was almost impossible to come by, self-made emperors being virtually extinct.

Chris Bongie has defined Victorian exoticism as "the discursive practice intent on recovering 'elsewhere' values 'lost' with the modernization of European society."[39] Much of the discourse on Sarawak is a prime instance of this kind of exoticism. The Brooke narratives offered not only British superiority but relief from the anxieties of a time when the old absolute authority of a monarch had been replaced by the new authority of the nation. The story of the Brookes seemed to hold both together, uniting the discredited but reassuring ways of the past and the inevitable but frightening ways of the future. The result of this union was a dreamlike imperial present, which (and this was its unique contribution), though not quite in England, was, to steal Rupert Brooke's words at the beginning of World War I, at least in that "corner of a foreign field which is forever England."

Much of the discourse on Sarawak consists explicitly in articulating, which is to say, inventing, what kind of a "stamp" the first two Brookes gave to Sarawak, what kind of identity they created for themselves and for it. The repeated myth is that the Brooke "stamp" on Sarawak, with its invisible letters spelling "made in England," is to be measured not in such typical terms as cost of living or level of education or having one's own kingdom or any such concrete material measures. As Ulla Wagner put it, those "colonial subjects: missions, medicine and education; all these received scant support from the Brooke government."[40] In the place of such conventional colonial categories there were more purely ideological discussions of the character and motives of the White Rajahs. This can be seen in the clear emphasis in accounts of Sarawak on the legal and administrative systems created by the Brookes. They may not have brought schools to Sarawak, but they brought justice. The focus here is less on Malay well-being and more on Brooke character. Were they "really" honorable and selfless, did they "really" care about their Malay and tribal subjects, and, perhaps the question behind all the other questions, did they "really" transform British Victorian colonialism into something innocent and pure and good?

The most salient features of representations of the Brookes' identities are located in familiar enough conventions of boys' adventure tales. The Brookes are brave, pure, honorable, just, indifferent to wealth; they live to serve, et cetera, are sublimely selfless in the service of creating a sublime self. Also stressed, in a fascinating imperial inversion of Homi Bhabha's ideas on the mimicry of the colonized as it worked in British India, is the mimicry of the colonizers in Sarawak.[41] Part of the "selflessness" of the White Rajahs lay in their chameleon-like abilities to blend in with their subjects, to feel "an instinctive sympathy and affection," to rule successfully because they not only understood but could think like the natives.[42] Repeatedly, James and Charles Brooke are described as happier out with the tribes on the rivers than trapped in the royal residence. The requirement that the story of Sarawak have a British adventure hero balanced a corresponding requirement in representing the place itself, that the narrative "dwell on the exoticisms of Borneo and its inhabitants."[43] What is particularly interesting is the relations constructed between the hero and the place. Going even beyond Frank Swettenham's argument for rule of British Malaya by sympathy, the romance narratives of Sarawak image the Brookes's relations to their subjects as a matter of empathy. Uncomfortable with Europeans, Charles was "more at his ease when he entertained Malays or Dyaks."[44] One of Charles Brooke's British administrators assures the reader that for their part the Dyaks had "a great reverence for the Rajah; they summed it up by saying, 'He understands us Dyaks.'"[45] Moreover, "because his most formative years were spent among the Sea Dyaks, he came to acquire their manners, their ways of thought. . . . James felt closer to the Malays; Charles was happier in the company of the Dyaks and the Chinese. His mind worked in Oriental ways."[46] Even in 1970 Charles is still being represented as "a creature of his Eastern experiences; a child, in every sense, of Sarawak."[47]

If the Brookes were cast, and cast themselves, as the selfless chameleon heroes, the Victorian narrative creation of Sarawak required villains as well. This role could not be filled by the tribes (Sea Dyaks or Ibans, Land Dyaks, and Malays), because they were the people with whom James and then Charles professed such complete empathy. After all, the tribes, even including vanquished rebel leaders, were to become the rajah's subjects; they were generally represented as heroic and therefore salvageable. The villain role was filled in British narratives by the government from whom James and Charles were to take most of their territory, the nobles and ruling family of Brunei. Here is a small description of the sultan of Brunei from that arch colonialist-in-training, Hugh Low. "He is a man of fifty years of age, of dark complexion, and stupid features. On his right hand he has a malformation resembling a thumb. . . . His mind also is weak, approaching to idiotcy; he is, nevertheless, possessed of a wicked disposition."[48]

This theme of degeneracy, being deformed in body and mind, runs through the pro-Brooke British accounts. It is linked again and again with what might be ideologically the most important quality given the Brunei nobles: their extreme greed. It is this quality which must justify the private British presence there. In the metanarrative of the Brooke presence in Sarawak, greed has allowed the "pirates" to flourish, has resulted in the cruel excesses of taxation which drove the tribes to rebellion in the first place, and thus is the first cause for the Brookes needing to take over Sarawak. Moreover, the presumed willingness of the sultan and ruling family to turn over more and more of their states to the Brookes is once again easily accounted for by greed. The Brookes did not take territory, for that would have belied the representation of them as disinterested and heroic. The sultan, in acts of regal irresponsibility, turned his lands over to them for profit. This version continued strong in 1970, when we were assured about the ruling family of Brunei that "enriching themselves was their main motive in their role in the partition of their state."[49] The perverse claim, necessary to erase the specters of power-hungry Brookes and Royal Navy guns, is that the ruling family were so personally greedy that they were happy to sell off most of their country.

The sultan's greed conveniently replaces the direct aggressions and implicit threats of the British navy and the Brookes (selling Manhattan for beads—but the Indians really coveted those beads). Just as significant in terms of what is special about the conventions of the narratives of the British in Sarawak, greed functions in tidy opposition to the Brookes's indifference to the economic possibilities of the state, glossed here as evidence of their moral superiority. This particular dualism is quite distinct from the accounts of the difference between the British and the Malays in British imperial narratives about the Malay Peninsula. There, what tends to be emphasized about the natives is their internal squabbles, their inability to control their tempers or think beyond violence.[50] They stand in opposition to the Englishmen, who must restore and maintain order, providing rationality and civility. Not a great deal was said to establish the greed of the Malay princes. They could not effectively be glossed as greedy because the British could not persuasively be glossed as above such material concerns. It was, after all, the British who were economically driven in peninsular Malaya. The importance of the Peninsula and of the British presence there had to be justified to the British government and the British public precisely in terms of the profits to be made.

In British writings of the second half of the nineteenth century and on into the twentieth Sarawak had a special usefulness as a kind of model case, a microcosm of the ideological underpinnings of British imperial expansion. The morally problematic profit motive was not much operating in relation to Sarawak, so British hegemony could be much more innocently represented there. Give the right sort of Englishman a bit of land and authority over it and he'll do right by it. In James Brooke's own language of imperialism it consisted of "rights firmly maintained by power justly exerted."[51] Better than the case of Malaya, Sarawak by its very economic inadequacy, provided apt material for the narrative of British imperialism in Southeast Asia as uplifting and pure and good. James Brooke was in Sarawak, and was entitled to be in Sarawak, because he had arrived as a white knight to save the various peoples there from the wicked pirates and Malay overseers who had destroyed their prosperity and their family life.[52] Brooke was entitled to "own" Sarawak because he held it in trust for the people. He had restored prosperity and by the sheer force of his noble personality, with a little help from his friends in the British navy, kept in place and enforced a justice system which sustained that prosperity. He made life good for the people, and in return they were obedient and "rejoice[d] in his government."[53]

The Woman in a Man's Adventure Tale

Another quality of the boy's adventure tale rhetoric in which James and Charles Brooke and others wrote about the Brooke presence in Sarawak is that it did not invoke the domestic language and values of bourgeois ideology.[54] Both rajahs were often referred to as fathers of their childlike people. But it was very clear that this role did not function rhetorically as part of a more extensive representation of the British authorities as heads of a family, as it had in Isabella Bird's imperial narrative about British Malaya. On the contrary, a necessary quality of both rajahs, if they were to be represented as dashing heroes, was that they did not stay at home and were indifferent to family. Both were frequently and emphatically represented as bad family men, neglectful of their wives and quarrelsome with their children and relatives. James disowned his nephew, and Charles eagerly supplanted his brother. Moreover, Charles had virtually nothing to do with his sons, simply ignored them for years, until the oldest was ready to start training for becoming Rajah. As Margaret Brooke put it, "I soon realized how unreasonable it was to expect great rulers to be 'family-men' as well" (*Good Morning*, x). This trumpeted lack of domestic or family virtues is integrally connected to another typical feature of Victorian boys' adventure stories: they don't include girls.[55] Barrie's Peter Pan knew it, particularly when Wendy came to visit. Even Conrad's representations of characters who subvert the convention were true to it on this point. Marlow, speaking of Kurtz's "Intended," articulates the typical position in *The Heart of Darkness*: "It's queer how out of touch with truth women are. They live in a world of their own, and there has never been anything like it, and never can be."[56] Women represented the stay-at-homes, opposers of the roving adventurer, guardians of a bourgeois domesticity whose function, in Marlow's view, is to "stay in that beautiful world of their own, lest ours gets worse."

In terms of the writings establishing the heroic myths of James and Charles Brooke in Sarawak, European women are irrelevant for a specific reason: because they cannot participate in the intimate life of the European men who travel with their colonial subjects and live similarly to the indigenous enemies they labeled raiders and pirates. Women cannot "pass," which is to say they cannot adopt the customs and habits which emerge from having "instinctive sympathy" with the natives. The enactment of such sympathy is rendered as masculine: the ability to move through the jungles, to hunt, and most of all, to fight. The interesting rhetorical problem is, What happens to the gendered conventions of this quintessentially masculinized genre when the narrator claims a feminine identity? What can a woman represent herself as being or doing in Sarawak?

In his life and in his writing, James Brooke dispensed with the one reason a heroic ruler might have to deal with women—the need for an heir—by turning to his sister's life and selecting one of her children, then, displeased with him, selecting the other. Charles Brooke, not having appropriate nephews conveniently at hand, finally, when he reached forty, went to England to find a wife. Uncle James had suggested a cousin who was widowed and rich. But Charles quickly decided on her daughter, who was nineteen and, while not controlling the family fortune, was more appropriate for what was, after all, the only reason to have anything to do with her: child bearing. Charles married Margaret de Windt in October 1869 and was back in Sarawak with the bride, who was already pregnant, by the spring of 1870. Almost four years and three children later (a fourth was stillborn), the couple took passage for a trip back to England and all three children died on board in September 1873.[57] They stayed two years in England, where Margaret produced her fifth child, Vyner, in September 1874. In 1875 they went back to Sarawak, where her sixth child, and second son, was born in 1876. After this second four years for Margaret in Sarawak she was ill when pregnant, so the family went back again to England, where a third son was born in November 1879. Within ten years of marriage "to the cold indifferent man she did not love," the man who did not love her, appeared not even to like her, and was over twenty years her senior, Margaret had given birth to seven children.[58]

In 1880 Margaret and Charles went back to Sarawak without the three boys, leaving them safe in England in the care of Charles's widowed sister. Two years later, in 1882, the rajah arranged an allowance for Margaret and sent her back to England to live there permanently and raise the children. As Margaret would sardonically refer to her function, "the incubus of infant production" (105) was finally finished. Vyner's wife would later write that the ranee described her marriage as over when Charles killed her favorite doves and had them served to her for dinner.[59] After twelve years of marriage and three boys the rajah could be fairly certain he had provided an heir for the throne of Sarawak. His years of living with a wife, however occasionally he was home from his excursions, were finished, and he would never do so again. Nor was Margaret to find herself particularly welcome in Sarawak. In 1887 she and the three boys did visit Sarawak with the rajah's agreement. Charles wanted his sons, particularly Vyner, to become familiar with the country. Eight years later, in 1895, Margaret visited Sarawak for what would be the last time, bringing her second son, Bertram (who himself would not see it again for another seventeen years—when his father started considering disinheriting Vyner). Charles's desire to see Margaret was so slight that when she arrived he immediately left on an extended visit to England, returning only when she had gone, several months later.

Margaret Brooke, ranee of Sarawak, was a famous personage in

Victorian England, part of a social scene which included many other famous Victorians, from writers and painters to politicians and biologists. Brooke's particular claim to fame rested on the unusual circumstances of her life history, which was well known in England. Apart from *Impromptus,* a less-than-memorable collection of short stories set in England, she wrote just two travel autobiographies, one twenty years after the other. These books, the first completely and the second partly, are memoirs of what Brooke represented as the most exciting time of her life, her years as the ranee, or queen of Sarawak. The memoirs provide a dramatic view of the society of late Victorian England and of a woman's version of her role in what was one of the most bizarre instances of nineteenth-century British imperial enterprise. Brooke's writing needs to be read within the context of the dominant late nineteenth-century masculine narrative of the meaning of Sarawak.

"Where are the women?"[60] In Margaret Brooke's first book, *My Life in Sarawak,* when she arrives as a young girl, newly married, to the rajah's palace in the capital city of Kuching, this is the first question she asks him. Where, indeed, are the women of Sarawak? And by "women" Margaret means the indigenous women. "'What women?' he answered. 'The only English ladies staying in the place came to meet you" (11). In the narratives of the two White Rajahs and their appreciative biographers the indigenous women have been consistently, and notably, absent. The adventure tale premise, of course, is that these men were all boys, somehow prepubescent in their sexual purity, which had close rhetorical ties to their imperial purity. Like Kim, they are immaterial boys, uninterested in the world of physical consumption, economic or sexual, following instead a higher light. Therefore, of course, there can be no women in these adventure tales. We are to assume that the two Brookes and their European Residents spent literally years in Sarawak, often enough in out stations where they were the only Europeans, without female companions or heterosexual encounters (which, in the terms of these narratives, is the only kind). They were all officially celibate, priests in the noble and ennobling cause of Brooke rule. To be hired as cadets in the Sarawak civil service, young men actually were required to be unmarried and to commit themselves to years of service in

Sarawak, a policy designed both to enforce an image of purity and to encourage relations with the local people.

Women as sexual beings do lurk around the edges of these narratives about life in Sarawak. We catch glimpses of the hidden truth that these boys might actually be men, in such moments as Emily Hahn's remark that James Brooke "didn't argue the point when Reuben George [a man in his twenties, of limited education] claimed to be the result" of an early sexual encounter.[61] Reuben George was, perhaps, the child of a liaison with a British woman, but of a lower class. Female narrators have tended to mention the women, and thus the masculine sexuality, which the adventure tale versions of Sarawak have erased. Writing of Charles, Sylvia Brooke offers a momentary glimpse at family secrets and alternative narratives when she writes that "odd, disjointed love affairs were recorded in his Diaries."[62] Joan Lo comments with an overstrained discretion that "it was a widely accepted belief, both in Sarawak and in London, that Charles had fathered at least one child by a native mother."[63] Malay women can sometimes lurk quite literally, as in Margaret Brooke's account of visiting Fort Simanggang. When she is shown to her guest room, it normally being the quarters of Mr. Maxwell, the Resident of the fort, she sees "a pretty Dyak damsel standing by the wall" (*Good Morning*, 189). A "somewhat agitated" Mr. Maxwell (189) soon comes into the room and tells the damsel, clearly his mistress, to go away, then asks Margaret not to tell the rajah. Was that request for silence intended to hide the Dyak or to hide the fact that Margaret had seen her? Perhaps more to the rhetorical point, was the recording of Mr. Maxwell's request a convenient narrative detail put to service by Margaret to sustain the myth of a wife's testimonial to her husband's superior moral uprightness?

Sylvia Brooke, writing with some of the narrative sexual freedom of the second half of the twentieth century, mentions what had previously been unmentionable, that the policy of cadets being unmarried and requiring the rajah's permission to marry, "drove white men into the welcoming brown arms of the local girls, . . . and produced a harvest that remained long after they had gone."[64] The reference to that "harvest" brings up not only the question of where the women are but where the children are. Sylvia Brooke in the 1930s

would write a novel called *Lost Property*, on the fascinating subject of
a brother and sister who are the children of a Malay mother and a
British father, and move to London.[65] Representing Eurasians as
tragically fated, the author dedicated her novel to "those who walk
between two races, and never with either of them." The novel has
vanished from, or, rather, has never been acknowledged in, critical
writings and literary histories of twentieth-century British fiction.
Sylvia Brooke's own comment in *Queen of the Head-hunters* on the
reception of this novel focused precisely on its troubling subject
matter. As she so neutrally put it, the "problems of half-castes and
Eurasians and the tragedy of their lost and twilit world meant little"
(121) to her British audiences.

Officials in Sarawak did have sexual relations with, and even
lived with and had children with, Malay women. Concubinage and
even mixed marriages, along with miscegenation, was common in
Sarawak throughout the nineteenth century and the first few decades
of the twentieth.[66] This included Rajah Charles, who "had a series
of *gundek* or native concubines while he was stationed as Resident of
Simanggang, one of whom produced a son later baptized by the
local S.P.G. missionary as Isaka Brooke."[67] The point is not that
Europeans in Southeast Asia could not have sexual and familial
relations with Malays, even quite openly. "Concubinage was as
common at the nearby British colony of Labuan as it was in Sarawak,
although the official attitude was not so tolerant."[68] Hugh Low
married a Eurasian in Labuan. He had two children by her and at
least one child by a Malay woman. One of his Eurasian daughters
married the colonial governor of Labuan, John Pope Hennessey,
who went on to even more prestigious posts as a colonial governor,
and ended up a member of Parliament.

What was important for the Brooke purpose was that mixed
relations, in themselves highly desirable for the business of running
Sarawak, should not appear in, and thereby interfere with, the
Sarawak narrative for public consumption in England, the international site of the debate about Sarawak's national identity. This
policy, both political and rhetorical, may have been more sexist than
racist, more a matter of erasing women than of erasing Malays. In
his last published statement about Sarawak in 1907, *Queries, Past,*

Present and Future, Charles Brooke argued quite matter-of-factly for racial impurity, not explicitly in terms of its being greatly desirable but certainly in terms of its being inevitable and probably for the best. The book prophesies a future when European power is reduced and therefore the role of Europeans must necessarily be to become "fused into a mixed race and element, to become inhabitants of the Eastern hemisphere, better adapted than pure whites."[69] Some of that "race" fusing had already been happening through the convenient correspondence between the official policies and the unofficial practices of the Sarawak Civil Service.

Margaret Brooke had published *My Life in Sarawak* in 1913, just four years before Charles, who was rajah for almost fifty years, died. In that first book the moment with Resident Maxwell is narrated uneventfully, as "he cheerfully gave me his rooms, and disappeared" (111). The Dyak woman is unmentionable and erased (or perhaps not yet invented). It was already 1934 when Margaret published her second book, *Good Morning and Good Night*. This new and updated "story of my life" (ix), is only about half focused on the time in Sarawak. Its style is both more revelatory and it offers more outspoken criticisms than did the first book. Rajah Charles had been dead for close to twenty years, Margaret had lived in Paris and Italy and London, had been on friendly terms with William Morris and Joseph Conrad and Henry James, among many other well-known late Victorian figures. One of her sons was dead, and another had been rajah for close to twenty years. England had been through a world war and its literary conventions, along with almost everything else, were much changed. *Good Morning* constructs a self who is distinctly more outspoken and more given to taking verbal risks than the more careful narrator of the first book. In spite of this change, both books do offer a subject which, to a lesser and then to a greater degree, is constructed in ways that break out of a conventional feminine imperial narrative. Rather than focus on the differences between the two books, though these are significant, I want to look at how in some ways both of them, the second much more than the first, challenge an imperial rhetoric.

However tamely the subject of *My Life* represents herself and the Brooke enterprise, it is also important to see that the Margaret

Brooke of both these narratives is a long way from, for example, Anna Forbes and her feminine imperial perspective, her wifely version of "his" and "hers" accounts, as constructed in *Insulinde.* Part of that distance has to do with how each constructs the husband who is the reason for her presence in each particular place. Henry Forbes has several familiar identities in his wife's account, almost all of them positive. The husband of Margaret's books, first implicitly and then explicitly, was unresponsive, "silent" (*My Life,* 6), offered a home life that was "rather bleak," and had "a complete absence of a sense of humour" (*Good Morning,* x). Quite unlike Anna's location as the "dear companion" to Henry Forbes, Margaret's marital place is represented in her narratives as a deep and occasionally humiliating disappointment to her and a nuisance to her husband, a necessary and temporary evil for a man with an "extremely prosaic attitude towards matrimony" (*Good Morning,* x). There is no union, no harmony, no emotional connection between these two, only legal procreation, with Margaret as the baby machine. Therefore, Margaret would have to locate her place somewhere else than as the wife of Charles.

Margaret's willingness in 1934 to rewrite the scene by presenting the Dyak woman at the fort, clearly works to support the justifications for the Brooke presence in Sarawak by its implicit representation of Rajah Charles as a ruler of moral rectitude, alongside his representation as a cold and neglectful husband. The two qualities went together in the masculine adventure tale discourse on Sarawak. But Margaret's Brooke's presenting the Dyak woman in Mr. Maxwell's bedroom also, and simultaneously, works in quite an opposite way. To construct a vignette which put the "damsel" back into a picture she had presumably by policy been written out of is part of a general narrative strategy in the two books Margaret wrote about Sarawak: to represent herself as finding the women, as bringing them out from where British men and masculine adventure narratives have hidden them and into narrative view. That uncovering of the women which the Brooke men and their many apologists would hide included not only their Malay mistresses but also, and perhaps most centrally herself. The originary effect of the rhetorical move to rediscovery in both *My Life* and *Good Morning* is to reinscribe Margaret Brooke in her relations to Sarawak—the wife and the history Charles and the "court historians," both in their actions and their writings, would so consistently erase. Merely to say, "I was there! And I have something to say about being there!", was to contradict the dominant Brooke discourse.

What was female subjectivity as constructed in these two narratives? *My Life* begins with Margaret's journey to Sarawak, specifically with arriving in the region and visiting the port of Singapore. *Good Morning* begins much earlier, with Margaret's own lineage and childhood. This representation of life before the Brookes emphasizes a key feature of Margaret's identity as it is constructed by the second narrative: the fact that she was not, literally or emotionally, British. Descended on her mother's side from prerevolutionary French aristocrats, child of a half-French mother who was raised in France on the ancestral estate restored to the family after the Revolution, Margaret was also raised on that estate by her parents, her father having to take the French name of de Windt. The move to England was effectively an exile from a pastoral paradise. The account of childhood ends by asserting that "the country of one's birth, which one has lived in and loved in childhood's days, must always be closest to one's heart." France is "my most beloved land" (8).

The narrative function of locating herself as French is immediately put into operation in the rest of the paragraph and continues to operate throughout the narrative. It emphasizes that the feminine narrator's identity cannot be located in her marriage to an Englishman. And it provides an independent place to stand from which Margaret can criticize the English. Life, and discourse, did not begin for her at nineteen when Charles arrived. She had a previous identity which the narrative offers not only as prior but as taking precedence over the present Margaret in her public position in the world. Margaret quickly moves to reassure her British readers of her realizing that "England is the greatest country in the world," but greatness becomes an ambiguous quality when the emphasis falls on her next point, that the English do not have and do not care about a "sympathetic heart." Margaret both is, and is not, self-represented as a British wife. In other words, the whole question of the Brookes' private imperialist domain is narrated from the point of view of someone who considers herself (and is considered by them) not to be one of them (even as a wife), not a person with any power, not a man, and not even English.

Brooke's narrative, like Emily Innes's about British Malaya, stresses her financial powerlessness. But here the opposition who wields that power against her is not the British colonial administration but her own husband. Again and again in *Good Morning* we hear of Charles controlling all the money, including confiscating Margaret's own allowance check, and even refusing to buy her a dinner after a long trip on their wedding night or more than a few bakery biscuits as a honeymoon lunch. We also hear of Charles's refusal to acknowledge, perhaps even jealousy of, those moments when people in Sarawak publicly appreciated Margaret and his unwillingness himself to appreciate the moments when she made emotional connections with local peoples or showed physical bravery or intelligent diplomacy. Margaret received no support from her husband for her public role. We hear too of Margaret's dislike of the narrow interests and bickering of the "English society in Kuching" (49), including their reluctance to acknowledge her public position as ranee. And, of course, when she had produced enough sons for the succession to be assured, there "followed a period in which [she] felt helpless indeed" (208), for she was simply sent home to England, where she tried for the first time, and alone, to set up house for herself and her three children.

In terms of position, gender, and nationality, Margaret is self-identified throughout her narratives as an outsider, an "other" who does not belong with and is imaginatively as well as literally separated from the English in general and Charles in particular. Forever longing for a lost paradise, the narrator is freed from experiencing the advantages and the losses of the rest of the European community in Kuching. Her positioning, presented as simultaneously enforced and desired, enables the narrator to offer a critique of the ways of the British colonial community. That critique operated in a small way in *My Life*, in Margaret's account of arguing with Marianne North's imperial disdain for the locals. "'Don't talk to me of savages, . . . I hate them,'" was North's solid imperial position. But for Margaret, who goes on to defend the Dyak custom of head-hunting, "'they are not savages, . . . They are just like we are, only circumstances have made them different'" (154–155). The motif is extended in *Good Morning*, in Margaret's often-stated dislike of the society of the English women in Kuching, with in their bickering about status and their obsessions, in "the midst of the exquisite prodigality of the tropics" (52), with such overdetermined cultural objects as a half-ripe English strawberry.

The narrator's insistence on being born French and thus her justified refusal to identify with the English or occupy her own official place as an English wife function quite explicitly in *Good Morning* as the prerequisites for a different, and more desirable, adult location. As she says of the other ladies, "they all wanted to be oh, so English! whilst I hankered after being oh, so Malay!" (52). Margaret's desire to be Malay reappears in the long sections on adapting Malay dress and on making friends with the Malay women. With the rajah's frequent absences and her own distance from the "stilted conventional English" community (102), the narrator of *Good Morning* offers a vision of life in Kuching as déjà vu, a replay of her lost childhood. The vision is composed of "warm-hearted Malay women" who were capable of understanding, as the English were not, that "friendship is a most gentle thing." Space has replaced time in that place where, in L. P. Hartley's famous phrase, "the past is a foreign country." Even in *My Life*, Margaret's experience in Sarawak was that "every day that passed . . . I lost some of my European ideas, and became more of a mixture between a Dyak and a Malay" (61). What Margaret shares with the local groups, as with the French, is an open heart, the very organ she represents as so distinctly missing from Charles and the rest of the English community. It is the coldness of her husband, his embodiment of the masculine conventions of power and control, here nationally cast as English as well as masculine, which pushes Margaret outside the private sphere as English wife and outside the public sphere as a titled representative of the colonial community. Instead, she would locate her self-definition among the colonized.

This lonely young wife represents herself as finding her true place in Sarawak, choosing her appropriate identity there. Margaret locates that identity not in her imperial place as the ranee or queen, wife of the White Rajah, but in her separate place as a warm hearted young woman who was never really from England and was long ago displaced from France. Margaret is now part of a Malay woman's community and "happy to be among the women" (95). They cling to her "in a most affectionate manner," signifying that she is where she belongs. Margaret is home at last. This self-identification of the narrator as belonging to the Malay world of Sarawak and not to its European world also appears, in a particularly intense moment, in Brooke's first book. The narrator of *My Life* rejects her subject role as imperial author simultaneously with rejecting as a strange and foreign place the imperial geographic center. She finds it "sad to think that nearly everything we most look forward to in life does not come to pass," specifically that "I should be writing this book and wasting my life here in this city called London" (157). Opposed to this alienated stance is the life and the self she would have constructed if Charles in his coldness had not prevented it, "being with my sons, their wives, and their children, happily settled in Sarawak amongst the best friends we have in the world." That envisioned Sarawak self, culturally in harmony with her context, a part of an integrated familial and social world, is poignantly different from the subject as she represents herself in the later chapters of *Good Morning*, belonging nowhere and moving around to various houses in England, living alone though seeing many social acquaintances, and "very lonely" (273).

Sarawak is glossed as Margaret's true imaginative community, the only place since that long ago lost family estate of childhood where the subject belongs. If an ideology of Victorian imperialism can so often transform time into place, can recover the imagined past somewhere "over there," it can do so not simply for those who are at the center of the imperialist enterprise. It can also for those participants who are culturally and personally identified as on the fringe of it. These subjects, with their unstable locations, usually as the excluded, the outcasts, and the different, often find themselves participating as colonialists in a colonial society because of their own forms of powerlessness in relation to dominant others. The Margaret Brooke of the narratives locates herself as belonging to Sarawak not simply as a form of typical colonial exoticism, though that is certainly part of it, but also as a feminine gendered response to the oppressions, the exclusions, and the refusal to allow her to belong practiced upon her by her egotistical and authoritarian husband. Denied a place as a colonialist, existing only as a procreative function, she writes herself into a place where she can fit in, as a part of the female colonized where, "white or brown, we all belonged to one big family" (*Good Morning*, 96). Margaret's self-identification with Malay women in Sarawak has everything to do with representing both positions as sharing a single role in a culture where all women, white and brown, ranees as well as Malays, are required to walk four paces behind the men.

The female voice of *Good Morning* constructs a similarity, a virtual identity, between herself and the Malay women, built on the solid and shared basis of their inconsequence as Malay women in their own culture and as a powerless European woman in relation to her cold and indifferent husband. United without choice in their devaluation by men, Margaret and the Malay women in Kuching are also united by choice in their own valuation of their world of feelings. Margaret's valuation of the power and central importance of emotions leads her to define herself as originally French and now more Malay than British, culturally a citizen of Sarawak rather than of England. It also leads her to question one of the very foundations of a European imperialist ideology, the principle of racial superiority. She wonders "why white people should be so conceited and imagine themselves so inordinately superior to those whom they chose to class together as 'blacks!'" (101). When an Englishwoman asserts to her that "you would not like people to imagine that you were a *black* woman," Margaret offers a double response. First, she denies the reductive and racist classification, remarking that "Sarawak people are *not* black." Second, she places herself with the other group, claiming that "I should rather *like* being taken for a Malay" (*Good Morning*, 46). Margaret's expressed affection for the people and the place was so strong that she wished that when she died an angel would pass by "and inscribe 'Sarawak' in great golden letters right across my heart" (*Good Morning*, 267).

Inscribing Colonial Order

The warm hearted young woman who found herself in a cold English marriage in a faraway world she quickly came to love is the dominating self-portrait of Margaret Brooke's two narratives of her life in Sarawak. It would be hard to resist the charms of this amusing narrator who scorns the narrow colonial society, describes her end-less pregnancies as "my rabbit-like propensities" (*Good Morning*, 204), re-creates for us the felt delights of lying among a tangled pile of Malay women hanging suspended in a large mat when the floor of a Dyak house gave way, and tells of crouching behind a piano all night while an anxious resident afraid of possible Dyak attacks pushed plates of cold ham at her, "which I had to refuse, as I did not like ham and did not feel hungry" (*Good Morning*, 83). The point is not to take the heroic pose of keeping a sense of humor amid the vicissitudes of life but rather that the vicissitudes are most of the time a false alarm, and that is what is funny. Against the familiar masculine conventions of great dangers to be faced and great adventures to be had, Margaret's point is precisely that the men just made it up, that there is nothing more threatening in Sarawak than weak floorboards or the horrors of ham. The real adventure is to be one of the women.

But for all her self-representation as standing outside the British colonial community and rejecting its masculine myths of heroes and adventures without women, the Margaret of the two books is also self-defined as a special and premier member of that colonial com-munity. Her distance from the English social group in Kuching reflects her husband's as well, a stance which simultaneously con-tains the contradictory cultural positions of social superiority and exclusion from society. As the wife of the rajah, she is the ranee and, for that reason as much as because of her own tastes, she does not mingle freely with the lesser administrators and their wives. Does

Margaret place herself apart from the rest of the colonial women because she is not, and does not want to be, "pure" English and, therefore, does not belong, or because she is the arch-colonialist, the head of state, and they her inferior subjects? Both explanations, and both positions, are accurate. Finally, the framework of *My Life* and *Good Morning* is precisely that these are the accounts of a European woman who became a non-European queen, a Margaret de Windt who is also, and simultaneously, Ranee Margaret Brooke.

Conflicting with the representations of Margaret's antihegemonic friendships with certain Malay women, *My Life* and *Good Morning* offer several instances of that most ubiquitous of Victorian imperial tropes: the characterization of the Dyak tribes, who had opposed the Brooke takeover, as children. "What children they were, those darling Dyaks," says the narrator (*Good Morning*, 87), linking this representation with its inevitable ideological partner, the rightness of the colonial situation. But in the one-man-rule situation in Sarawak, that inevitably also means the rightness of Rajah Charles, who is transformed from coldhearted husband to warmhearted ruler, an imperial nurse who "had a large and scattered nursery to keep in order all over his country of Sarawak."

Margaret's claims to belong to the community of Malay women cannot be read as an unambiguous rejection of the imperialist stance. Within the hermeneutic framework of the narratives written by what Reece called the "court historians" about the Brooke presence in Sarawak, a key quality distinguishing the colonizer was empathy with the natives. In the light of this well-established convention about the colonizers, Margaret's representation of herself as connecting with the Malay women is in some ways, though not completely, a feminine variation of the very quality of empathy which characterized representations of James and Charles Brooke. Are her relations with the Malays to be read as a matter of a gendered bond created through mutual recognition of and sympathy with the inferior position to which both their cultures relegate women? Or are those relations a variation on imperial domination as a matter of emotional cooption?

The point, I think, is that we cannot privilege one or the other of these apparently contradictory readings. The constructed subject of

My Life and *Good Morning* occupies both these locations, a common enough phenomenon in Victorian women's accounts of being in Southeast Asia. But usually these narrative selves move around, as it were, defining themselves and their political place now one way, now the other, in different sections of their discourse. Much less common, and more fascinating, is that because of the specific colonizing methods touted in masculine narratives about the Brookes in Sarawak, in these two books Margaret can occupy both positions simultaneously. There is no definitive location for the female subject of Brooke's two books in some final resting place of imperial propaganda. Precisely because her friendship with local women, as opposed to the feelings of the Brookes for their native subjects, is based on a shared consciousness of a shared inequality, Margaret's gendered presentation of empathy captures the instability and the ambivalence of the situation of the imperial feminine.

There are, certainly, many moments in Margaret's two books which are not ambivalent about Brooke rule. The narrative repeatedly questions the rajah in terms of gender but not in terms of colonialism. Instead, this feminine voice sometimes explicitly joins the chorus of testimonials to the greatness of the Brooke reign over the peoples of Sarawak, as she "came to admire the way in which my husband governed his country" (*Good Morning*, 51). Moreover, in unspoken but structural ways, Margaret Brooke's writings clearly belong among the court histories of Sarawak. What the narratives conspicuously lack, in all their witty critiques, explicit and implicit of Margaret's life as Charles's baby machine, is any doubt as to the need to produce those babies. After the first four years, when the three children died and it was clear that Margaret's marriage was empty, she yet continued to produce children. The question here is not why she would do so but rather why, in these two narratives of her life, her doing so is not represented in any way as problematic. In the great adventure language of Sylvia Brooke, herself adopting the voice of court historian more often than she abandons it, we are assured that "Sarawak meant something more [to Margaret] than just a broken romance. This great heritage had been given to them," and thus, "whatever the Ranee's faults may have been, . . . I think these three sons prove beyond all question that Sarawak was in her heart."[70] The unquestioned premise of *My Life* and *Good Morning*, the basis not only of much of Margaret's adult life but also of much of her two books, is the imperial belief in the fundamental importance of providing Brooke heirs to the throne of Sarawak.

That these must be rightful heirs rather than illegitimate offspring of Charles's affairs with Malay women seems clear from another topic Margaret's narratives conspicuously lack. Not only did Margaret know of Charles's "mixed race" son, Isaka Brooke, a child about which both her books are completely silent. It was Margaret who, after her first sojourn in Sarawak, "took him back to England where he was fostered by the rector of Sheepstor in Devon."[71] Isaka was with the Brookes when Margaret's first three children died. He was the fourth child in her care on that ship, the one who lived. The framework of gender oppression which united Margaret with her Malay friends also, and inevitably, separated them. The procreative role placed the "white" woman in competitive opposition with the "brown" on the question of whose son should inherit Sarawak. Margaret's determination that it be hers may be seen from her taking Isaka away from Sarawak. In 1928, when Isaka made his claim, as the eldest living son, to the succession, Margaret's view was that he was "the half caste idiot."[72]

Finally, *My Life* and *Good Morning* have a public function. These are not private memoirs but memoirs of a public and political institution, participating in a stream of propaganda to shore up that institution. One published before World War I, the other before World War II, both argue for the larger-than-life drama, the greatness, even with its faults, of the Victorian imperial enterprise. In one sense, these books offer versions of the imperial nostalgia Renato Rosaldo has described so memorably in speaking of revivals of the British Raj in the 1970s and 1980s.[73] The Margaret of the second half of *Good Morning* has taken on her public identity as the ranee of Sarawak. Her presence and her book helped to create a climate of public opinion about Sarawak in the 1930s which would prove to be economically of real importance in deciding the fate of Sarawak and the Brookes. Should England take it over as a colony? And, at least as significant, what compensations should England and/or the Sarawak treasury provide to the family who had "created" Sarawak as a nation and ruled it for a century? The financial future of Margaret's family could well be influenced by her representations of the Brookes, including herself, in her books about Sarawak.[74]

The later part of *Good Morning* represents Margaret's royal identity as effectively creating the kind of life she has, a life narrated as a kind of ongoing series of vignettes about her encounters with other famous late nineteenth- and early twentieth-century personages. We hear, among many such moments, of Burne-Jones showing her his pictures, of a visit from the Divine Sarah, of Charles Swinburne visiting her sick son, and of falling off a ladder with Henry James. Margaret's is a life lived in public, lived amongst the rich, the talented, the famous. Literally excluded by her husband from taking up an identity, both cultural and physical, in Sarawak, Margaret takes up in England the very imperial status she found so publicly elusive, and so privately unfulfilling, in Sarawak. The space so wide in Sarawak between interior sense of self and exterior role is closed once Margaret is back in England. Her second book offers in its rather dull and conventional later pages an impersonal identity as the product of this narration of a European woman appropriated, by the masculine imperial demands of "obtaining a rightful successor" (*Good Morning*, ix), to inherit private property. The warm hearted young girl has been transformed by her own narratives into that most alien and self-alienating of British imperial subjects, an East Indian queen.

Housekeeping for God

I end this discussion of feminine discourses about Sarawak with a brief account of one other memoir of the place. Margaret's life in Sarawak in the 1870s began only a little over three years after another woman, after making a home there for close to twenty years, had left to return to England. Harriette McDougall, the only other woman to write an account of life in Sarawak in the nineteenth century, had sailed for England at the end of 1866 with her husband, the bishop of Sarawak. The new bishop, Dr. Chambers, and his wife, went out to their new post on the same ship which carried Margaret to Sarawak. In all accounts, including her own, Harriette McDougall was unambiguously a dedicated Christian missionary, a patriotic upper middle-class Englishwoman, loving mother, and loyal wife. She had already published her *Letters from Sarawak; Addressed to a Child* in 1854, put together as letters she sent to her son Charley, back in school in England. Charley had been left in England to protect him from the high mortality rate of English children in Sarawak. From 1848 to 1852 Harriette had lost five children in Sarawak and Singapore. In 1854 she lost the sixth. Charley "was killed at school playing cricket when he was eight years old, just a few weeks before the book was printed."[75] Harriette would go on to bear four more children, all of whom would live. It was not until 1882, almost fifteen years after returning to England, that she published her second and more extended account of life in Sarawak.

Sketches of Our Life in Sarawak included sections from *Letters from Sarawak* but covered many more years, and offered in particular a version of two events given central billing in the imperial histories of Brooke rule in Sarawak: the *kongsi*-Brooke conflict, always named in pro-Brooke narratives as the "Chinese Rebellion," of 1857 and the "Malay Plot" of 1859.[76] Originally hired by the Borneo Church Mission, which was founded in 1848 by "a little band of Sir James Brooke's friends" (*Sketches*, 80) but ran out of money in 1854, the McDougalls were paid from 1854 on by the Society for the Propagation of the Gospel in Foreign Parts. The 1882 *Sketches* was published by the Society for Promoting Christian Knowledge. Thus, the McDougalls' employers and publishers, those who paid for their "mission," were not simply Christians but Christian groups whose self-defined raison d'être was Propagation and Promotion, which is to say, proselytizing. This purpose carried an implicit (and, often enough, explicit) commitment to the familiar Victorian imperial premises of European Christian superiority and a representation of non-European peoples as not only inferior but also barbaric and savage. There could be no Brooke-like empathy for these peoples, no respect for their cultures as respectable cultures, only the pity which comes from defining them as without any real culture because without the light of true religion.

Sketches had a clear function as Christian and, by extension, imperial propaganda. Its mission, like its author's life as a missionary in Sarawak, was to be part of the effort to convert other peoples to Christianity. Within that hermeneutic framework, *Sketches* offers a predictable vision of the domestic virtues of the feminine imperial at work in Sarawak. Similar to Isabella Bird's writing on British Malaya, McDougall's book not only does not critique the colonial presence in Sarawak but functions as a virtual manual on the value and necessity of that presence. It is a classic instance of the historic function of Christianity, from at least the seventeenth century onward, as tool and weapon of European conquest. The Brooke claims to Sarawak, and their aggressive methods for ever expanding the boundaries of what was encompassed by the state of Sarawak, are represented as an unadulterated good. Colonialism is at the service of religion, functioning to provide the venue wherein the missionary purpose can be developed. In theory at least, the more land the Brookes took over, the easier it was to send missions to convert the peoples there. I would argue that during the last three hundred years (at least) of Christian missionary work in places outside Europe, imperial aggression is the always desirable, and almost always necessary, first step in the work of conversion. *Sketches* locates itself and its narrator solidly in the discursive tradition of British colonialism.

That might be all that need be said about *Sketches.* Christian missionary travel accounts are usually intolerable to read.[77] But the fascination of this book lies more in the charm of what it does not do than in the horror of what it does. Within the very specific hermeneutic framework of nineteenth- and twentieth-century books about Sarawak, *Sketches* is notable in being so unquestioningly colonialist without participating in the boys' adventure myth which would later become the favored nineteenth-century format for representing the history of the Brookes and Sarawak. Not only does *Sketches* rather directly refuse, in the language of its own author in her first book, to "furnish a romance" about Sarawak, but it mentions the Brookes very little. There were clear political reasons for this choice to "avoid alike all political questions, or, as much as possible, individual histories among the English community" (*Sketches*, 8). The frequently suggested, and quite plausible, explanation offered by commentators is that since the McDougalls were on the side of Brooke Brooke, the elder nephew, and felt that James Brooke and

Charles acted extremely badly in the 1850s and 1860s in disinheriting Brooke, Harriette chose to say nothing because she had nothing good to say. She could not tell the truth as she saw it because the injustice was irretrievable. Brooke Brooke was dead, and the second bishop, Dr. Chambers, had to get along with the second rajah, Charles, at whose pleasure the mission was allowed to operate in Sarawak.[78]

But Harriette's possible motives for writing Sketches as she did are not the point which interests me. More significant for this discussion is the sense in which McDougall's book is anti-imperial. For a nineteenth-century British narrative to avoid individual history in telling a history of colonial Sarawak is implicitly to speak against the role of Sarawak in the larger hermeneutic framework of British imperialism. It is to counter a basic premise in the representation of Sarawak to the British government and the public, that events there stood as thrilling evidence of the power of an heroic individual Englishman to create a brave new world. That there could even be another way to tell the story places the imperial promise that the fantasy/adventure story of Sarawak represented in British ideology at risk. In Sketches the discursive hymn to the glories of Christianity replaced the hymn to the glories of individualism. It would be simple enough to say that Sketches is devoted to the glorification of god rather than the glorification of man. But the rhetorical implications of that are what matter here. Certainly, no person, not even Harriette's husband, the bishop, receives a leading role in the narrative. Harriette is immersed so totally and uncritically in the feminine dependent role that the narrative undermines that position by its very extensiveness, representing a narrator devoted to God, to the rajah, to her husband, to her children, and to the missionary society supporting them, all at the same time.

Along with the absence of the single masculine hero, and perhaps rhetorically enabled by that absence, Sketches offers a new presence in British accounts of Sarawak: the children are here. Harriette starts a school soon after she arrives, and the first students she directly describes as "four little half-caste children" (20) of native mothers, clearly implying that they have European fathers. The myth of the heroic adventurer is replaced by a narrative which insists on at least one of the histories erased by the rhetoric of adventure: that of the existence of Eurasian children. *Sketches* focuses on the problems in feeding and educating these children, as well as on how McDougall's other major group of children came from the poor Chinese refugees driven into Sarawak from the Dutch attacks on them in Kalimantan in southern Borneo. There is nothing sentimentalized here, just children as the waste products of political and social aggressions and irresponsibility, explicitly Dutch and Chinese, but implicitly British and even Christian. Throughout *Sketches* the children appear, sometimes orphaned, sometimes stolen or sold, usually Chinese but sometimes of mixed races, always in need because of the aggressions of the various racial groups in Sarawak.

But the presence of the children in this narrative, while not sustaining the Brooke myth, in its own way does sustain British colonialism. The children most graphically presented in the narrative may be the two English children who had their heads cut off during the 1857 Chinese attack on Kuching, while their mother watched from her hiding place in one of the big water jars in her bathroom. But the two Cruikshank children stand in the narrative in the place of what may well have been hundreds of children who also were killed during the *kongsi*-Brooke war. "Some four hundred families of the slain Chinese miners were at the mercy of the Rajah's men," with an estimate that only four families survived.[79] The lack of mercy was apparent when several hundred women, children, and elderly took refuge in a cave. The rajah's men set fire to the entrance, suffocating and/or burning all of them. Harriette McDougall would unquestionably have known of the role of the rajah's forces in slaughtering the families of the rebellious miners. Yet she does not mention it; she mentions only the vengefulness of Malays and Dyaks. Even that pro-Brooke historian, Spenser St. John, put the number of Chinese killed or driven out at thirty-five hundred.[80] The Chinese rebellion in Sarawak, like the Indian "Mutiny," that other 1857 event which haunted the British and reappeared in proper imperial dress in subsequent narratives for the rest of the century, brought forward its tale of barbaric cruelty to a few British women and children to hide the much more extensive British cruelty to the innocent and the vulnerable of another race. It is likely that the

Indian "Mutiny" gathered some of its horror for audiences in England from its following so soon after the news of the Chinese rebellion in Sarawak.

Finally, the unification of Christian and imperial purpose in *Sketches* is perfectly and grotesquely captured in Harriette's account of Charles Brooke's 1862 raid on North Borneo against the Illanuns, a sea faring Malayo-Muslim tribe of raiders who took many prisoners. Bishop McDougall had been one of the attackers, had fought aggressively, and had written a long letter giving an account of the battle and of his own active fighting, for the London *Times*. There were many public objections expressed to this raid in England, including from other bishops, both to the moral appropriateness of the battle at all and, more particularly, to a bishop "shooting the poor heathen instead of converting them."[81]

That Brooke's group should itself be accurately, and perhaps negatively, defined as raiders who take prisoners seems not to be noticed in Harriette's account. Instead, we are told of how many of the captured Illanun were boys. One of them, about fourteen, Harriette kept "about me, and used to teach him; but he could not be tamed. He turned Mahometan" (213). In this odd juxtaposition of verbs what is buried is the point that the boy had not "turned" but already had a religion, was already a Muslim. Instead, the language equates being a Muslim with being virtually prereligious, a savage who cannot be "tamed." This little section of *Sketches* ends with a statement startlingly familiar in its similarity to one of the best-known and most horrifying lines in twentieth-century fiction, Kurtz's summary of how to handle difficult natives in Conrad's *Heart of Darkness*. Like her fictional counterpart, whose words were published more than fifteen years after *Sketches*, Harriette despairs of redeeming these "pests of the human race" (205). She concludes, quite in keeping with the Christian that she is, that "their extermination seems the only remedy" (214).

PART FOUR

An Uncolonized State

Women in "The Kingdom of the Free"

CHAPTER 7

Anna Leonowens

Women Talking in the Royal Harem of Siam

*"[The writer] is a great enough magician to tap our most
common nightmares, daydreams and twilight fancies, but he
never invented them either: he found them a place to live, a
green alternative to each day's madness here in a poisoned
world. We are raised to honor all the wrong explorers and
discoverers—thieves planting flags, murderers carrying
crosses. Let us at last praise the colonizers of dreams."*
—PETER BEAGLE, PREFACE TO
THE FELLOWSHIP OF THE RING

"There is a moment in each day that Satan cannot find."
—WILLIAM BLAKE

One country in what we now know as Southeast Asia has an
imperial history during the nineteenth century which is unique
in that it remained an imperial history and did not become a colonial
history. The Portuguese were quite active in Siam, as were the
French, those ubiquitous British, and also those representatives of a
younger imperialistic nation, the Americans. During the nineteenth
century (as well as before and after) Siam figured as a highly popular
and romanticized destination and was the subject of several travel
narratives. To twentieth-century readers, perhaps the most well
known of those narratives in English, or I should say the most well
known of those narrators, was Anna Leonowens, who wrote two
books about her years in Bangkok. Issues of gender, race, and European
and United States aggressions intersect in Leonowens's books in complex ways which I have found difficult to separate or clarify.

The complexities seem to me particularly knotty and particularly exciting in Leonowens's second book about her stay in Siam. A loose collection of stories about a few individual women in the royal harem and other places, it claims actually to transcribe the voices of those women. A critical approach to offering our own constructions of what we are hearing in these constructions of past voices needs to be placed within an historical and cultural context of United States and European discourse about Thailand, not only in the nineteenth century but continuing into the present. I suggest that we need to self-consciously read *The Romance of the Harem* and its women's voices from where readers, men and women, are presently placed: within the hermeneutic frame of late twentieth-century international economic and sexual politics.

The Sex Industry, Tourism, and Siamese Culture

A type of journalism piece about Thailand that appears regularly during the 1980s and 1990s in American and British newspapers and magazines and on television, is an exposé, usually with accompanying photographs or case histories of particular girls, of the Thai sex industry. The narrative typically covers the bars in the Patpong district of Bangkok, in the beach resort of Pattaya, and on the island of Phuket, along with the package sex tours run from Japan or western Europe, which include photograph albums for selecting who the customer wants to have waiting in his hotel room when he arrives. These stories often include the recruitment process, describing how scouts for the sex industry in Thailand go to the poor agricultural region of the northeast or to villages of the non-Thai tribes in the north, many of whom are addicted to heroin from their poppy crops. The scouts buy the children, usually the daughters, of these poor people, who sell them sometimes that the family may eat, sometimes that they may continue a drug habit. Prostitution in Thailand in this sense is represented as a family affair, with the daughters as a material resource, often the only one.[1] As the material for sexual exploitation, daughters have a crucial economic function for some poor families in Thailand that, for example, in certain parts of India they notably do not.

These details operate on other levels than as conventions in the reductive narratives of European and American discourse. It is easy enough to write the Thai sex industry as a matter of innocent female victims and male victimizers. To begin with, the cultural structures which enable daughters to be seen as a sexual resource operate for women as well as for men in Thailand, for the prostitutes as well as for those who make the profits. Yet complicity is not a simple matter. Prostitution in Thailand frequently does begin with the children, from eight to eleven or twelve being the choice years. Their relatives sell them and the industry recruiters buy them, often for a sum which the girls must work off. While many people become prostitutes in their mid- to late teens and on into their twenties, the business of sex in Thailand is sustained and continually rejuvenated by the extensive practice of purchasing children.

One of the most famous scandals in the last couple of decades was uncovered when ten buildings in a red-light district caught fire on the island of Phuket in January 1984. The corpses of five prostitutes eighteen and under (one testimony said they were aged from nine to twelve) were discovered locked in their rooms.[2] Many of the surviving prostitutes, including one "forced into prostitution" at thirteen, testified to a government committee of being routinely beaten, drugged, and tortured.[3] The wife of the owner of the brothel acknowledged that "the girls were held against their will."[4] Slavery is often the literally accurate term in describing the conditions of thousands of children in Thailand under the age of eighteen who are bought, sold, routinely locked up, frequently beaten, and occasionally chained.

Child prostitution is very big and profitable business. It is intertwined with the other big profitable business in Thailand in the last twenty years: tourism.[5] There are two intertwined issues here: the sex industry as it operates in Thailand and European and American media representations of the sex industry in Thailand, which are themselves of two sorts. Those vivid stories critical of the industry which are published outside Thailand compete with what can only be called vast public relations campaigns, occurring as much in foreign guidebooks as in information disseminated by the tourism industry in Thailand, touting the charms and—by implication—the availability of the Thais.[6] Exposes of the Thai sex industry in the foreign media tend to focus specifically on the connections between male foreign tourists and prostitution, often with the declared purpose of lessening the trade by educating European and American men in a graphic fashion about both its dangers to them and its cruelties to its young providers. There is no doubt that men from many countries, most saliently from Japan and Malaysia but also from various other European and Asian countries and the United States, go to Thailand and buy sex.[7] One simple reason is that they can get away with many activities there which, though illegal in Thailand as well as in their own country, are—and this is a key point—perceived by them as dangerously illegal at home. Also, in certain places in Thailand, virtually always mentioned in foreign guidebooks, sexual opportunities are highly visible, both easy to find and easy to arrange. The media exposés include de rigueur predictions in very high numbers about how many Thais will be HIV-positive by the year 2000.[8] Perversely, the threat of AIDS may well be a factor in the increased demand for child prostitution, as customers press for the relative security of virginal, or at least not overly worn, goods.

But whether the media stories take the form of advertising sex in Thailand or of condemning it, both approaches can be glossed as variations of an orientalizing perspective. Both are engaged, one approvingly and one disapprovingly, in representing Thailand as part of the exotic and feminized "east," a world of childlike women and highly visible, as well as highly available, sexuality, where a foreign man can go and get pretty much whatever he wants in the way of sex, without having to be concerned with those legal and social constraints which operate back home.[9] Of course, what does operate "back home" is itself an ideological matter. The idea that sex is readily available only in some far-off foreign land works to obscure the ways in which a similar kind of economically coerced sexuality is both available and ideologically erased in the United States. I would claim, for example, that even though I have never seen a media exposé of it, sexual exploitation of children—what amounts to child sexual slavery—is a huge business in the United States, possibly in sheer numbers larger than in Thailand.

Thai authorities who would stop sex crimes in their country face serious and often insurmountable difficulties prosecuting tourists. Major obstacles to prosecution are that the tourist industry is crucial to the present economy; that tourists are there briefly and, even if caught, can simply leave the country before formal charges are brought; that the charges do not stick because of claims of entrapment; that the children are justifiably afraid to testify; that building a case is expensive and the police budgets are low; that many police authorities are paid by or even participate in the business of sex; and that police authorities in the tourists' home countries do not and—given their own laws—usually cannot cooperate. Recognizing this dilemma has led groups in both Britain and Germany to try to pass laws which would make their citizens liable in their own country for sex crimes outside the country. Such a law passed in Germany, but a similar one was defeated in Britain, where the government held that the only crimes a British citizen can commit on foreign soil which are of legal interest at home are the time-honored ones of treason and murder. What Englishmen do to Thai children is not something anyone wants to know in any public way "back home."

If what foreigners do to Thai children does not seem significant to many foreigners or to their governments, it must be said that it has not seemed too significant to some Thais, either. While many members of the Thai government, including the present prime minister, have expressed their dedication to stopping or, more realistically, shrinking what is now the enormous business of sex in their country, many other Thais have not.[10] Prostitution is not some sort of secret side affair. It is big business in Thailand. Indeed, from the perspective of many Thais committed to their nation's "progress" into the twenty-first century, it is the key element in the tourist boom of the 1970s and 1980s. Tourism, which in 1982 overtook rice as the leading source of income for Thailand, is the golden cow which is leading the country into the future. For business leaders, for many in government, for airline companies, for hotel and restaurant owners and associations and even for busboys, prostitution is a necessary fuel in the drive to provide Thailand with a "modern" future. The material sources of that fuel are the hearts and minds of a whole class and more than one generation of children, made to sacrifice their own futures for the greater good of the nation. As a former vice-premier of Thailand, encouraging economic growth by reminding provincial governors that "we need money," put it in a public speech, "Consider the natural scenery of your provinces, together with some forms of entertainment that some of you might consider disgusting and shameful because we have to consider the jobs that will be created."[11]

The prostitution explosion of the last three decades in Thailand is inseparable from the tourism explosion.[12] The leap in numbers of tourists to Thailand happened, and is still happening, in part because so many European and American men are ideologically conditioned by tourist ads themselves to read Thailand as a safe and satisfying outlet for repressed sexual desires. Another reason is that since the 1960s sweeping conservative responses to women's liberation movements in Europe and the United States have led to a public relations bonanza of marketing images designed to make men hunger for the kind of feminine charms represented by "little slaves who give real Thai warmth" (Thanh-Dam Troung, 178). Yet another key factor was the Vietnam War: when the Americans started moving into Vietnam in the 1960s, they needed safe bases for "Rest and Recreation," for R and R, and Thailand was geographically the superior choice as the closest pro-American location.[13]

Although not since the early 1970s have Americans made up the major group of foreign men going to Thailand for sex, the American war presence in Vietnam was a leading cause of creating the Thai sex industry for tourists. It thus must also be credited as a major cause of the commitment to tourist development on the part of both the Thai government and the private sector. With the American pullout at the end of the war in the mid-seventies, Thai and foreign investors had to work hard to re-create a demand for the supply they already had, which meant generating new customers for the by then well-established sex trade. The tourism boom more than fulfilled their expectations. A great many of the specifics of the cultural and political history of the United States and the countries of Europe and Asia have been, and continue to be, factors in generating and shaping the recent history of prostitution in Thailand.

But in spite of the hoped-for political usefulness of some American and European media exposés in curbing the tourist demand, explanations of the mega-phenomenon of the Thai sex industry and its links with Thai tourism cannot be located solely within the realm of political and social events in other countries and their relations to Thailand. Apart from the orientalizing representations of the trade in English-language exposés and in English-language promotional materials for tourist-related businesses lies the fact that prostitution in Thailand has its origins and continuance in Thai culture. Large groups of people in a region do not simply move into the business practice of making their children into sex slaves as a way of generating income and raising the standard of living because they cannot resist the pressure of foreign desires that they provide such a service. This is not a phenomenon that just happens, or even that happens primarily, because of foreign political and ideological influences, however much a result of those influences the phenomenon is. For example, while many young female and male victims in this industry are Thai, a great many of them are recruited from among those non-Thai tribal groups (Akka, Karen, etc.) who live primarily in northern Thailand. The Thais themselves do not accept these tribes politically, have labeled them as foreign, and have denied them Thai citizenship. Sexual abuse of children is enabled partly through racist policies and attitudes among Thais.

Moreover, if the sexually exploited are often not Thai, the exploiters often are. By that I mean that while a great many customers of the sex industry are foreign men, it is also true that a great many customers are Thai men. One estimate is that "more than 75 percent of Thai males have been to prostitutes."[4] The almost universal use of prostitutes by Thai men of all classes as a socially acceptable phenomenon, along with the fact that many of the prostitutes they use are not Thai, eliminates reductive explanations of the sex industry. The Phuket fire happened in early 1984 when Phuket was just beginning its development as a major foreign-tourist destination and sex center and before many foreign tourists were visiting the island. Most of those who did get to Phuket were European student types, who went to backpack and camp or rent cheap bungalows on the beaches, quite a distance from the inland town where the young prostitutes were kept. The Phuket airport, that sine qua non for any major tourism, only opened to international flights in the early 1980s. Thus it is a fair guess that the customers of those coerced prostitutes found dead in 1984 were, for the most part not foreign tourists but local residents and traveling businessmen from other parts of Thailand. In spite of the pervasive and absolutely central links between foreign tourism and the sex industry, one cannot persuasively cast it in a straightforward imperialistic frame as only a matter of the imposition of foreign male desires on vulnerable Thai peoples.

Women and Independence in Siam

Certain forms of sexual slavery have a long history in Thailand. That history is entwined with, yet by no means a simple result of, aggressive designs by other countries, including imperialist pressures from Europe and the United States.[15] In other words, within the informing framework that a state's culture is always impacted by relations with other states, that a nation's "location" is always produced internationally, the current business of sex in Thailand has an indigenous historical base. What is sometimes referred to—almost always by its apologists—as the practice of "polygamy" was for centuries an aspect of Thai culture.

An extensive discussion of contexts for and functions of Thai versions of polygamy is beyond the scope of this chapter. I mention only two factors particularly relevant to my textual focus. First, the almost universal religion in Thailand is Buddhism, a system of belief which, as it has evolved in Thailand over the last three centuries has stressed qualities such as gentleness, kindness, the importance of accepting one's karma or fate, and the value of good deeds in improving one's karma so one will be reborn in a higher state in one's next incarnation. The goal is nirvana, when the soul will no longer need to be incarnated. Buddhism values all life but, as it so typically turns out in the actual historical practice of so many religions, not all life equally. In a dualism all-too-familiar to those of us raised in a Judeo-Christian culture, the phenomenal world is lower than the spiritual. And it is woman who, with her karma at a lower stage of development than man's, represents physical nature. In Thai Buddhism, monks are abjured from looking directly at or touching women. In Theravada Buddhism in the nineteenth century "women were regarded as lower beings, tied to the material, illusory world, and men capable of cutting through the illusion."[16] Only through rebirth as a man can a woman hope to reach nirvana.

Second, in the nineteenth century Thai Buddhist practices came to be were reflected in the legal position of women in Thailand. When the Rama dynasty began at the end of the eighteenth century, the new king moved the capital from Ayudhya, virtually ruined by attacks from their western neighbors, the Burmese, to Bangkok. Rama 1 also revised Siamese law, creating in 1805 what can be translated as the Three Seal Laws.[17] These increased already existing limits on women's sexual, domestic, and financial rights in what was seen as an effort to bring legislative practices into greater harmony with Buddhist religious practices.[18] Wives were "seen as items of commercial exchange—chattels, or in the stated legal term, *khwai* (water buffalo)."[19] Thus, at the beginning of the nineteenth century women in Siam (much as, for example, women in France) actually lost some of their legal rights.

Polygamy was a basic and pervasively practiced male legal right in nineteenth-century Siam. Men could keep as many women as they could afford, though usually only one had legal status as a wife.[20] The "second wife," a frequent phenomenon, had no legal status, but her children did, having the same rights of legitimacy in relation to their father as did the children of the main wife. Polygamy was typically linked to debt slavery, another pervasive nineteenth-century Siamese custom. Men could give and take women as payment for debts and could sell their wives, concubines, and children. Rich men routinely had what we in English call harems, composed of slave "wives" or concubines. The definition of women as sexual commodities, less spiritually valuable than men and needing literally to be contained, had a firm place in Thai culture quite apart from Thai relations with other Asian countries, with Europe, and with the United States, and well before the French or the Americans went to Vietnam.

The history of the devaluation and commodification of women

in Thailand, both in religious and in socio/legal practices, is intertwined during the nineteenth century with another aspect of Thai
history, often considered the most significant and illustrious of all:
Thailand's sustained status as the only country in Southeast Asia
which has never been colonized. Its territory has never been occupied for any length of time by a foreign government, the group who
tried the most often being Siam's long-term enemies, the Burmese. It
is difficult to exaggerate the significance of this political and cultural
fact in shaping the "imagined community" which constitutes twentieth-century Thailand. Indeed, the name of the country in its own
language, "Muong Thai," can be translated into English as the
"Kingdom of the Free," with Thai meaning "Free."

There are many ways in which the uncolonized condition of
Siam might be read as a legalistic fact, a technicality which must be
endlessly qualified. But that would be a distorting view. In spite of
many crucial qualifiers, Thailand's sustained national independence
is a substantive fact. Siam was not colonized in part, but only in
part, because more aggressive countries either did not want it or
forced Siam to concede the territories and the rights they did want.
During the nineteenth century the United States was simply not
interested in Siam to the extent that it was in, say, China or Japan.
Although the United States had an appointed consul in Bangkok by
the middle of the nineteenth century, the position was unpaid.
Congress only approved money for a consular salary in 1864.[21] The
major United States presence in Bangkok throughout most of the
century was religious, in the form of the various Protestant missions.
The Netherlands was occupied with the Indies, and Spain with the
Philippines.

The two dominant foreign government presences, defined literally as having consuls in Siam and politically as each occupying a
territory on either side of Siam around the middle of the century,
were the French and the British. France was focusing on Cochin-
China, on Siam's eastern border, and was also watching the British
in India and Burma, to Siam's west. Its interest in Siam had much to
do with its competitive relations with England.[22] Though England
might well have been willing to scoop up Siam from the mid-

nineteenth century on if given an opening, it showed no special eagerness to do so, assuming the French did not get it. The British government had no pressing political or economic reasons to decide that the effort would justify the cost. The lack of those pressing reasons was a result of the economic success of the various forms of French and British diplomatic involvement in Siam but also of Siam's strategic diplomacy, carefully choreographed by King Mongkut, and his son and heir, King Chulalongkorn.

Imperial concerns operated in a special way in the diplomatic relations between Britain and Siam. The British aggression was not a matter of literal force but of economic invasion. The major reason the British did not feel pressed to use their superior force to take Siam was that in 1855 the British had successfully arranged a treaty which gave them most of the rights and controls in Siam that they wanted anyway.[23] Sir John Bowring, the British governor of Hong Kong, negotiated an agreement which opened up Siam to "large-scale foreign commerce."[24] The terms of the Bowring Treaty were in a great many ways denigrating to the sovereignty of Siam. The treaty allowed Britain to trade freely in Siam with minimal taxes or duty, allowed British subjects to reside in and own land in Siam, and provided British consular jurisdiction over British nationals in all legal matters. Effectively, the British could now live in and do business in Siam wherever and however they liked, with their host country not being able to have much to say about it (though Siam's revenues did double as a result of the increase in trade).

The Thais had been pressured to give away most of their economic possibilities to the British primarily because of the ominous threat, recognized throughout the regions of Southeast Asia, of the British navy. Moreover, throughout the first half of the nineteenth century, the Thais had been watching the British take over Burma. The loss of state control under the Bowring Treaty was extensive. The king, and the Siamese legal system, had to relinquish civil and criminal jurisdiction not only over British nationals but over those, including Siamese, employed by British nationals.[25] What the British owned was considered British territory, and the Siamese government was liable for all damages to British property. Finally, Britain's most-favored-nation status in the treaty meant that whenever Siam signed any treaty with another nation, Britain would automatically receive at least the same concessions.

Unlike the Burmese, the Siamese did not lose all rights to govern themselves. Along with all its humiliations and loss of Siamese economic and legal rights, and even some loss of outlying territories, particularly along the Siam/Malaya border (like most borders in Southeast Asia in the first half of the nineteenth century, it was defined by influence rather than by land), the Bowring Treaty did ensure the national, if not the territorial, sovereignty of Siam.[26] Britain was in the process of taking over all of Burma on the western border of Siam and the Malay States on the southern border, while France was moving to make colonies out of the states on the east.[27] Geographically and politically, Siam was that small and continually threatened open space between the British and the French. It was no small feat, arguably even a great political and diplomatic feat, in spite of its heavy costs, for Siam to remain independent amidst the general colonial takeover of the states of Southeast Asia by the countries of Europe in the nineteenth century.

Credit for sustaining the sovereignty of Siam during a time of generally uncontrollable European aggression and in a region littered with collapsed states is generally given to Rama IV, King Mongkut, who ruled Siam from 1851 to 1868, and to his son, King Chulalongkorn, who ruled from 1868 to 1910. They were successful in what must have been the extraordinarily difficult task of directing Siam toward a strong national independence. King Mongkut was explicit and insightful about his country's difficult international position. He clearly recognized that the British and French viewed the Siamese as "wild and savage," even "as animals," and that British imperial policy consisted of "intimidation of us until we are afraid to go about our own business."[28]

Mongkut's impressive reputation among historians of Siam writing in English ranges from claims that he "towers intellectually and morally over his contemporaries, not only in Siam but throughout Southeast Asia" to a more restrained evaluation. In this version Mongkut "proceeded slowly" with his reforms while Chulalongkorn, with the aid of his numerous princely brothers, modernized Siam on the base their father had established.[29] Mongkut's working insight seems to have been that the primary goal of retaining Siam's independence required both an external policy of conciliation toward and balances with European aggressors and an internal policy of strong unity and centralized authority.[30]

Relations between nations, as Cynthia Enloe has reminded us about twentieth-century international politics, involve relations between genders.[31] Among many factors in Siam's nineteenth-century political defense of its independent status against the virtually all-consuming aggressions of the European countries through a policy of domestic unity, a crucial one was the royal "harem."[32] The harem was stocked (and that may be the most appropriate word) with girls and women given to the king by their noble and powerful families all over Siam. The royal harem helped to keep Siam independent because it helped in part to keep Siam united. Unlike the many states in India, when faced with the British threat the many fewer states making up what we could call nineteenth-century Siam did not present themselves as an uneasy grouping of disparate political regions ruled by often competing princes. Siam was composed of disparate states, and certainly "there was a vast difference between the absolute monarchy's ideal of centralization and the fact."[33] There were competing noble families in Siam. On the other hand, there was a recognized absolute monarch over all the states, even given the severe limitations of his real power. Working for that power and against the potential for divisiveness these separate groups represented was the institution of the royal harem. With its group of royal and nonroyal mothers coming from families all over Siam, the harem had a key political function as a unifying institution, existing in relation to one central paternal figure with the power to make state decisions for all the territories of Siam.

Through the harem, a kind of social substitute for a national infrastructure or a "Siam mapped," almost everyone else with any power in the country was a relative of the king. If we consider just King Mongkut and his eighty-two children, his relatives from those children constituted a staggering family group. The combination of monarch and harem from generation to accumulating generation helped to limit the internal disputes which could make civil decision making a struggle among conflicting powerful groups within the country and thus could weaken Siam's resistance to foreign take-over. The king was free to negotiate what he conceived as the best arrangement he could make for Siam. The harem was a crucial factor in ensuring his personal power, and thus the support for his particular choices and strategies throughout the rest of the country. The Bowring Treaty, with all its detailed inequities and grotesqueries, was observed in Siam because King Mongkut and his advisors said it must be. If the king had not had the personal or, rather, the family influence to enforce the treaty, the British might well have occupied Siam.

Yet the worth of Siam's successful struggle to protest its national independence from the forces of international imperialism must be measured against not only the cost of the royal harem women's independence in nineteenth-century Siam but also the cost in twentieth-century Thailand. Included in the heritage of freedom may well be the heritage of continuing sexual enslavement of many of Thailand's people. The institution of prostitution in twentieth-century Thailand needs to be read not only as one product of present-day imperial aggressions in the region (in the form of tourism) but also as one part of the inheritance of the institution of polygamy, which itself functioned as a weapon against imperialism in nineteenth-century Siam. One of the domestic hegemonic social mechanisms used in the past to defend against the foreigners has been transformed in the present into an international hegemonic economic mechanism at least partly imposed on the Thais by a range of foreigners.

One immediate problem with tracking, in terms of gender issues, the tangled relations in the past two hundred years between Thai cultural institutions, foreign pressures, and successful Thai resistance to European imperial aggressions is the lack of materials on nineteenth-century sexual practices in Siam. The most accessible eyewitness accounts, to Thais and to foreigners, indeed the only accounts known to exist in any language, about life inside the royal harem are the two historically implausible books written in English by Anna Leonowens. In the following discussion I will be focusing primarily on her second book, *The Romance of the Harem*. My efforts to approach Leonowens's writings bring up some of the most intrac-table and fascinating problems in the troubled critical confluence of issues of imperialism and of gender as they were constructed in British Victorian books about Southeast Asia. Leonowens was Brit-ish but perhaps might not have been and was a member of the gentry but perhaps might not have been. The situating of Siam, of its king, of its women, and of herself in her writings are all particularly problematic matters of place.

Who Was Anna Leonowens?

Siam's strategy for defending its sovereignty against European en-croachments included becoming knowledgeable about foreign ways. King Mongkut had learned English himself, and recognized the political necessity of having his heirs familiar with this language of imperial commerce.[34] Having been doing some teaching in Sin-gapore after her husband died, Anna Leonowens was offered the position of English tutor to the royal children of Siam. By the time she arrived in Siam seven years after the agreements with Bowring, Bangkok was in commercial terms an international city. Leonowens's appointment reflected the established policy of King Mongkut of ensuring that his country and its future leaders would be internally as well prepared as possible to undertake the dangerous business of successfully evading "the direct colonial control of the Western powers" and of providing for the "survival of an independent Siam."[35] Leonowens had five years and four months, from March 1862 to July 1867, of unique and almost unlimited access to the royal harem of Siam. She became fluent in Thai, got to know well many of the women in that harem, and wrote the only account in existence by any non-Thai (and possibly by any Thai) of life in the Siamese royal harem before the late nineteenth- and early twentieth-century reign of King Chulalongkorn.[36]

In March 1862, with her son, Louis, who was about seven years old, Leonowens sailed from British Singapore to Bangkok, a trip that took about five days, to take up her position as the English governess to the king's children. Her older child, a daughter named Avis, she had just sent to school in England. Among her royal pupils the most important, and the one most charged to develop a facility in English, was the king's eldest son, Crown Prince Chulalongkorn, then almost nine years old. Over the years in Bangkok Leonowens would also teach many other princes and princesses, along with many of their mothers and any of the other women in the king's harem who wished to take advantage of this opportunity to study English language, English knowledge, and English culture. Leonowens's schoolroom was the marble-floored grand hall of one of the many temples—evocatively named Wat Khoon Chom Manda Thai, Temple of the Mothers of the Free—within the harem. The name of the royal harem was Nang Harm, which can be translated as Veiled Women.

Harem is an impossible word in English, carrying an ideological meaning so overdetermined as to block any sense of how such a phenomenon actually functioned in particular cultural settings.[37] European images of harems are drawn from colonial portraits, verbal and pictorial, along with their twentieth-century celluloid variants, virtually all focusing on harems of the "middle east."[38] Nang Harm does not fit this image; nor, most likely, does any other so-called harem, including those in the "middle east." Nang Harm in the 1860s was a walled city. Wide avenues with graceful houses, parks, flower gardens, and small streets crowded with apartments and shops were all enclosed by an inner wall inside the Grand Palace area, with the whole enclosed by an outer wall. Leonowens estimated the population of Nang Harm to be about nine thousand people, all (with the exception of the priests, who were let in briefly every morning) women and children, and almost all captive there. Nang Harm functioned in many ways as its own city, with inhabitants in a range of classes, having a range of functions. The highest class consisted of members of the royal family. These women would never leave Nang Harm until, in Leonowens's own phrase, they had "by age and position attained to a certain degree of freedom."[39] The likelihood of a royal princess being allowed to marry was remote. Leonowens's employer, King Mongkut, had a vast number of sisters and aunts, as well as children in various kinds and degrees of relation to him, inherited as his responsibility on the death of previous kings. The women under his care included not only the relatives of his father but also the relatives of his immediate predecessor, his elder half-brother (not to mention their leftover concubines and all the ladies' slaves). The royal family also included King Mongkut's wives, his own children (eventually numbering eighty-two), and various other relatives.

Apart from the women and children of the royal family, Nang Harm contained perhaps thousands of women who performed the functions needed to maintain the harem. Many of the residents, including children, were slaves. Some of the women were or would be concubines (a title, complete with a decoration, gained by sharing the king's bed at least once) or had been concubines for a night or a week or longer. Some underwent the rigorous training needed to become dancers or performers in the royal theatre. A few of the women were or had been the king's "favorite." Even fewer were particularly blessed by having conceived during their time with him, thereby becoming concubine mothers. A fair estimate is that there were several hundreds of potential concubines, several scores of concubines, three dozen mothers, and several consorts. The rest of the women were all the varied kinds of people it takes to sustain a world. Given the crucial political function of the harem, the king's sexual attentions to women had to do not only with their personal charms but with which family they were from, children of royal mothers being particularly desirable. There were endless domestic slaves, cooks and tasters, seamstresses, teachers, soldiers (whom Leonowens named in English the Amazons), even doctors and judges. "This women's city is as self-supporting as any other in the world: it has its own laws, its judges, police, guards, prisons, and executioners, its markets, merchants, brokers, teachers, and mechanics of every kind and degree" (*Romance*, 13). In short, Nang Harm was an entire society of women and children.

Nang Harm was an elaborate and absolutely unique world, inaccessible to foreigners and, I stress, to virtually all Siamese as well. Although Anna Leonowens was not literally the first European woman to have access to the royal harem, she was the first really to do so. In 1851, eleven years before Anna's arrival in Bangkok, King Mongkut had acquired about thirty concubines in his initial five months as king and tried for the first time to provide the women of his harem with formal instruction in European cultural ways by inviting in the wives of three American Protestant missionaries residing in Siam.[40] Mrs. Mattoon, Mrs. Jones, and Mrs. Bradley took turns teaching English to some of the ladies of the harem during two weekday mornings on and off for almost three years, until one morning the palace gates were closed to them and the experiment was over. They had been abusing their mandate as language teachers in Nang Harm to distribute religious tracts from their mission and to proselytize for Christianity.

King Mongkut's next effort, probably reflecting his conclusion that he could not usefully recruit instructors from among the pool of European and American missionaries living in Bangkok and that other native English speakers in Bangkok would have had no teaching experience, was to bring in an outsider. Effectively, the king advertised in Singapore. Leonowens had been recommended "by his Chinese agent, Tam Kin Ching, in Singapore on the suggestion of John Adamson of the Borneo Company."[41] This time the plan worked. The king stipulated quite explicitly that the matter for study was to be cultural and intellectual rather than religious. In the king's own words in a letter to Leonowens, "you will do your best endeavour for knowledge of English language, science and literature, and not for conversion to Christianity."[42] For five years and four months Leonowens had virtually daily access to this special female world, though she lived outside its walls. She and her son walked into Nang Harm almost every morning and, just as uniquely, walked out of its gates again at night.

Leonowens's job did not remain solely being the governess to the king's children. During the decade when international business affairs, particularly British, were pressing on Siam as never before, Leonowens described the king as turning to this English teacher for secretarial help, at least in the matter of writing his letters in English, often rephrasing them with correct grammar. Leonowens, to the scoffing of her detractors among the "British experts" who reviewed her book, described this part of her job as occasionally including as well the task of providing a sounding board for the king's ponderings about how to deal with the European powers who were competing for trading rights in and, undoubtedly, for power over Siam. He would consult her not on policy matters but rather on European customs and attitudes, on possible British and French responses to positions he was planning to take. Having some sense of those responses could well help him in surmising European political motives and in choosing his own moves.

This Victorian woman in her early thirties found herself in the amazing and utterly unique position of daily moving between two normally inaccessible spheres: the female world of some of the most powerless people in Siam and the world of the one most powerful person in Siam, who in the 1860s still ruled by divine right. In certain limited ways she became the confidante, and the advisor, to each. Though a Christian, at least by the testimony of her writing, and declaredly sure her religion was the true one, there is no evidence to suggest that she thought it her Christian obligation to try to convert her Buddhist students. In fact, Dr. Bradley, the American missionary in Bangkok, is said to have wished that "she had appeared more frequently at church on Sunday."[43] Instead of what might be called a Christian or religious perspective, her books offer a self-created view of her own location as that of a spokesperson for the concerns of the women in Nang Harm, to the king while in Siam and to her British and American audiences afterward.

Who was Anna Leonowens? There are two conflicting discourses which narrate her history. Here is the story passed through Anna's own accounts and those of her family, immortalized in its bare outlines by all the standard dictionaries of biography and amplified in Margaret Landon's creative biography. Anna Harriette Crawford, growing up in Carnarvon, Wales until she finished school at fifteen, was the child of an uprooted couple. Born in Carnarvon on November 5, 1834, she was just six years old when her parents kissed her goodbye, left her to be raised by Mrs. Walpole (a relative who ran a school), and sailed to India. Captain Thomas Maxwell Crawford had been ordered to India with his regiment, and his wife went with him. Anna never saw her father again, for he was killed in a Sikh uprising when she was not quite seven. Her mother stayed on in India, and it would be almost ten years before Anna saw her again.

In 1849, when Anna Crawford was fifteen, she sailed to India. Her mother had remarried, and Anna now had a tyrannical stepfather (whose name has never been discovered). In Bombay this teenage girl met Major Thomas Louis Leonowens and, after an educational tour of the "middle east" with the Reverend Mr. Badger and his wife, Anna married Major Leonowens in 1851 (she would be around seventeen). Their first child died in India, their second in Australia. By 1853 they had gone back for a time to England, probably to have their children in what they perceived as a healthier climate. A daughter, Avis, was born in October 1853 and exactly a year later a son, Louis. In 1856 the family returned to Singapore, and in 1858 Thomas Leonowens died there, of heat prostration after a tiger hunt. Mrs. Leonowens started a school for the children of her husband's brother officers, but earning a living was a struggle. In 1862 she took a job as governess to the children of the king of Siam. Sending Avis, now seven, back to a boarding school in England, Anna Leonowens, along with Louis, now six, sailed to Bangkok in March 1862.

But there is another, more lurid, version of where to locate Anna's identity, of where she "came from." In 1976 W. S. Bristowe published what he titled "The True Story of Anna Leonowens," which he pieced together after checking birth and marriage records, army lists, and burial records in England, India, Wales, Singapore, and Penang.[44] He claims Anna Leonowens was born in India (not in Wales), on November 6, 1831 (not 1834), the second daughter of a poor army sergeant named Edwards (not a captain named Crawford), who died three months before she was born. Her mother, who may have been the child of a mixed marriage, married another soldier (a corporal, soon demoted to a private) when Anna was two months old. Anna and her sister, Eliza, were sent back to school in England. In 1845 they returned to India as teenagers. Eliza had just turned fifteen when she married a thirty-eight-year-old sergeant.

Anna met the thirty-year-old Reverend Mr. Badger upon her return to India at age fourteen and accompanied him to the "middle east" when his job as assistant chaplain transferred him there. He had no wife, and when he did marry a few years later, the girl was three years younger than Anna. Anna stayed with Mr. Badger in the "middle east" for a while, returned to India, and married Thomas Leon Owens—Mr. Owens—on Christmas Day, 1849, when she had just turned eighteen. Tom and Anna Owens seem to have moved a few times. No birth records have been found for their surviving children, Avis and Louis. A first daughter named Selina was born in India in 1851 and must have died. A second child may have been born in Australia and died, but no records have been found. Avis was probably born in 1854 and Louis in 1855. Tom Owens died in Malaya in May 1859. On the death record he is described as thirty-one years old. Most notably, in death his name has been changed. It is given as Thomas Leonowens on his impressive tomb in the Protestant Cemetery in Penang.[45]

What is at stake in the difference between these two versions of Anna Leonowens's life before becoming a governess in Siam is, most saliently, class, but also reputation, and possibly race. Was Anna Leonowens herself of mixed blood? Bristowe's suggestion that Anna's mother may have been the product of a union between an English soldier and an Indian woman is quite possible. It fits with what we know happened to a great many unmarried English soldiers below officer level while they were stationed in India and provides at least one motive for the discrepancies in Leonowens's own version. Nonetheless, however credible this suggestion is, we should not forget that it is also a complete invention. No one actually knows now who Anna's maternal grandmother was. No one has any facts about her except that her name was Anne and she married Anna's grandfather after he arrived in India.

What is not invention is that there definitely was "mixed blood" in Anna's family in the generation that came after hers. In Anna Leonowens's writings, including her book on her life in India long before moving to Singapore and then Siam, she never mentions her sister, Eliza.[46] That telling absence is only one aspect of the general absence of any mention of family in Leonowens's memoirs. Eliza's first child, Anna's niece, did marry around 1862 a man of "mixed" Indian and British blood, of "the class of Coloured Englishmen," as he called himself.[47] Their children were, therefore, what many British referred to as "Eurasian," and it is certain that the family felt the sting of discriminatory policies. One of the children of her niece's mixed marriage was Anna's great-nephew, William, known to us under his stage name of Boris Karloff.

We cannot responsibly speculate that Anna Leonowens rewrote some of her own history to hide the evidence of her "mixed blood," since we simply have no solid information about her ethnic ancestry. We can responsibly speculate that she rewrote her history to hide her class and, perhaps, some of the circumstances of her family history and birth. As Bristowe claims, the changes in her autobiography allowed her to present herself not as a lower-class working girl but "as a young gentlewoman whom ill-fate had forced to work for a living."[48] Bristowe's evidence suggests that Leonowens effectively took three years off her age, revised her father and husband into gentlemen of good family, and had herself born in Britain of good family as well. She changed names and places to hide the working-class origins of her family and her husband. In a world where good blood and good breeding mattered, Leonowens may well have rearranged the facts to provide herself with both.

And then there is Mr. Badger. Perhaps it was an educational tour. Nonetheless, as a young girl about fifteen years old Anna Edwards did go to the "middle east" unchaperoned with Mr. Badger, then an unmarried man of about thirty or thirty-one (her sister, at fifteen, had married a man of thirty-eight), and remained with him for an undetermined amount of time, between several months and two years. Whatever the degree of innocence this relationship may (or may not) have had in reality, its appearance must surely have been disreputable. What was Anna Edwards doing from age fourteen, when she arrived back in India, to age eighteen, when she married Tom Owens? If her relationship with Mr. Badger was as disreputable as it appears, part of her later lies may have been not so much a matter of social climbing as of escaping from that early loss of a much-needed respectability. Anna Crawford, widow of Major Leonowens, could not be that sinful Anna Edwards who had gone off to Egypt with Mr. Badger, then returned to India and married Tom Owens.

What, finally, might Bristowe have exposed? Was Leonowens an iconoclast or a social climber, a woman who rejected the socially and professionally limiting facts of her birth or a hustler with delusions of grandeur? Clearly, such judgments are a matter of which narrative we want to privilege. Moreover, the more a critic insists that

Leonowens "really" was lower-class, the less that critic can explain her high level of articulateness, and the more impressive it becomes. Nineteenth-century lower-class British women, children of army sergeants or privates, in England or in India, hardly completed early schooling, let alone studied at more advanced levels. Families of upper-class women sent their daughters to good boarding schools and/or hired private tutors to educate them at home. It is unlikely that either of these possibilities was open to Leonowens. Crawford or Edwards, gentlewoman or not, Anna was probably educated at some modest school until she returned to India at fourteen. One of many fascinating puzzles about Leonowens's books is where their author developed the writing skills which enabled her to express herself so powerfully.

Leonowens as Author

After her job as a governess in Siam ended when the king died, Leonowens became a professional lecturer and commercial writer. A large part of why she lectured and wrote about her experiences in Siam was to make money; it was how she earned her living. She left Siam in July 1867 for a long visit to Singapore and was still there in 1868 when Mongkut died. She then went briefly to England some time in the following months, left Louis at a school there, and picked up her daughter, Avis, from the school she had been in since just before Anna and Louis had sailed without her for Siam approximately six years earlier in 1862. Leonowens and Avis moved to the United States. Louis arrived some time after 1870 on his own and soon left for Australia. After a time in Australia Louis moved back to Siam, his real home, and spent the rest of his life there. He worked for his childhood friend, now King Chulalongkorn, who granted him a teak concession in Chiang Mai. It is one of the sad ironies frequent in family histories that while his mother is the single nineteenth-century voice outside Bangkok speaking of the evils of the Siamese harem, her son kept a harem in Chiang Mai for a few years before he was married.[49] Anna and Avis were to spend most of the rest of Leonowens's life together, Anna living with Avis a good deal of the time both before and after she was married. The two lived primarily in New York City during the first part of the seventies, summering in Newport, Rhode Island and the Adirondacks.[50] By 1878 Anna had moved with her daughter and new son-in-law to Halifax, Nova Scotia, and eventually died there.

Leonowens must have arrived in the United States some time in 1868 or early 1869. She had no income, no family, and herself and her daughter to support (as well as whatever money she may have needed to send to England for Louis). What Leonowens did have were her unique experiences in Siam, qualifications as a teacher, and talent as a writer. She lived first in New York City and Staten Island, started a little school with Avis, and wrote. The first book, *The English Governess at the Siamese Court: Being Recollections of Six Years in the Royal Palace in Bangkok,* came out in 1870, interest having been stimulated by three chapters first appearing in the *Atlantic Monthly.* Then came *The Romance of the Harem* in late December 1872. It was brought out in England in 1873, and already the orientalizing process of modifying the original title, thus obscuring (and, ultimately, erasing) the book's self-designation as fiction, had begun. The British title, with text unchanged, was *The Romance of Siamese Harem Life.*

The *Atlantic Monthly* continued its support of Leonowens's work by publishing a positive review of this second book. By the early 1870s Leonowens had become friends with Annie Fields, a published poet and the wife of James Fields, distinguished editor of the *Atlantic Monthly.* The two women also shared a mutual friend, Harriet Beecher Stowe, one of the most famous of the regular contributors to the *Atlantic Monthly* in the 1860s and 1870s. Stowe's articles, and the sheer association of her name, helped to give the magazine its antislavery reputation. A major link between Annie Fields, Harriet Beecher Stowe, and Anna Leonowens was pronounced opinions on the evils of slavery.[51] Leonowens's years in Siam coincided with the years of the American Civil War. In part because of that war but for other reasons as well, the issue of slavery was continually under public discussion, even among Europeans and Americans as far away as Southeast Asia.[52] Though it hardly became a bestseller, *The Romance of The Harem* received more reviews in the United States than it did in England, in part because of the author's friendship with Stowe and Annie and James Fields. Leonowens, and her work, probably had more visibility for an American audience than they had for a British.

In 1927 an American woman named Margaret Landon went to live in Siam with her husband, a minister, remaining there for ten years. Entranced by Leonowens's books about Siam, she pursued information about her life. In 1944 Landon combined that information (citing only that some of it came from Leonowens's grand-daughter, Avis Fyshe, and some from people who had known Leonowens in Bangkok) with the biographical information in Leonowens's books into a single fictionalized biography, *Anna and the King of Siam*. The book was a bestseller. Though in a culturally transmuted version, Anna Leonowens's unique adventure was to become famous at last. With Landon's book, Leonowens's story slipped into the place it still occupies, as the central representation of Siam in the twentieth-century ideology of American orientalism.

The next step in the exploding fame that began with Landon's book was that Hollywood noticed. First came a movie version, starring Rex Harrison and Irene Dunne. Then Broadway noticed, and the movie was followed by a play which would become a classic of American musicals, Rogers and Hammerstein's *The King and I*. It opened on Broadway on March 29, 1951, starring Gertrude Lawrence and Yul Brynner. Finally, Landon's revisionary history of Anna Leonowens and the king of Siam reached complete national exposure with *The King and I*, one of the classics of American musical cinema.[53] Deborah Kerr and Yul Brynner, as the decorous but firm-willed Anna and the despotic but sensitive King Mongkut, formed the unlikely couple who continue to dance together inescapably in the imaginations of us all. The orientalist images of this movie still influence the American ideology of Thailand.[54]

In 1952 *The Romance of the Harem* was reprinted at last, eighty years after it first appeared, with a new title: *Siamese Harem Life*. This new title eliminated completely the acknowledgment of the book's fictionality. It turned "Romance" (in Nathaniel Hawthorne's sense) into "Life," and thereby laid claim to being historical description rather than historical invention. In spite of this new edition, and the new title which attempted to advertise the ideological value of this fantastic book by denying its element of fantasy, the book has never entered the consciousnesses of American or British scholars, in startling opposition to the fame of Leonowens's experiences in twentieth-century American culture. If no one has heard of *The*

Romance of the Harem, everyone has heard of *The King and I*. I suspect that those facts are related.

Leonowens's work and its spin-offs have a negative reputation in Thailand, being considered insulting to the monarchy. When Prince Chula Chakrabongse, writing about the detrimental effect of *The King and I* on American and European ideas about Siam, remarks that "it is almost as fictional as *The Mikado* of Gilbert and Sullivan, but in its case it was advertised as a documentary," his critique is certainly accurate.[55] But *The Romance of the Harem* and *The English Governess* are not *The King and I*. Neither are they Landon's *Anna and the King of Siam*. Leonowens's books certainly participated in European and American people's biases about both the racial and the cultural inferiority of the Thais. I suggest that what the writings do not share is either culture's masculine bias about the inferiority of women.

Yet such a suggestion brings its own dilemmas. Looking primarily at *The Romance of the Harem*, because of its explicit and sustained focus on the plight of women in Siam's royal harem, I read Leonowens's work from a twentieth-century perspective which is appropriate to it in a way that seeing it as a kind of Ur-*The King and I* is not. Conveniently hidden by the bright stage lights and "romantic" narrative of the American musical is a powerful historical continuity between Leonowens's representation of a women's community and the updated version of that community in such accounts as Pasuk Phongpaichit's on the economically enforced sexual victimization of young women in twentieth-century Thailand. *The Romance* is precisely not a love story, at least not in the sense of being concerned with sexual love. In an effort to reinscribe what has been ideologically erased by American rewrites of Leonowens's narration, I would read *The Romance* in the light of twentieth-century perspectives on gender, on imperialism, and on what has been called "imperial feminism."[56]

Reading Leonowens's Romance

From its first publication in Boston in December 1872, Leonowens's fictionalized account of the lives of some of the women in the royal harem of Siam in the 1860s has had its warm admirers and its avid detractors—and no one in between. American reviewers who seemed to know nothing of Siam found the book both interestingly written and morally useful. The *New York Times* review on February 14, 1873 opened with what would be the quite mistaken prediction that "this tropical book disarms criticism" (9). The major American review, appearing in the May 15, 1873 issue of the *Nation*, was graciously upbeat, though pointing out that the tales in *The Romance of the Harem* "deserve the name of romances, so wild and strange are they in incident and atmosphere." In terms reminiscent of some of Nathaniel Hawthorne's introductions to his novels, the reviewer goes on to make his central point, that these tales are "all revealing the dark places of the earth, full of the habitations of cruelty, but revealing also some of the greatest and brightest qualities of human nature" (338). Another, much briefer, anonymous review for the *Atlantic Monthly* in May 1873 also implied that the tales in *The Romance of the Harem* are true. The writer went on to offer a useful summary of the traditional definition of the function of travel literature: "it is by the reading of such books as this, which intimately acquaint us with the remote life of other lands and religions, that we are to learn how true to one humanity are the traits of all the different peoples, and to feel the essential unity of the race" (625).

British responses were neither gracious nor upbeat. Those reviewers, again anonymous, who claimed to have some familiarity with Siam, were intensely critical. The major British reviewer, in the *Athenaeum*, began by reminding the reader that Leonowens's previous book, *The English Governess at the Siamese Court*, was full of errors (he may well have been the writer of the hostile review of that book in the *Athenaeum* of December 24, 1870).[57] The review went on to announce that "it is our duty to point to a few instances of manifest, we might almost say inexcusable error" (205) and spent the rest of a quite long discussion doing just that. Even in America, Leonowens must have received some substantial challenges to the truth of her writings. In a letter to the *New York Times*, March 3, 1875, she answers the reviewer of someone else's book who had charged that she never actually made the trip she had described to the newly discovered ruins of Angkhor Wat in Cambodia.[58] Leonowens cites the evidence of her passports, then more generally defends the accuracy of her methods by claiming that her written account is based on "several hundred pages of manuscript, notes, and translations made during the journey" (6).

In the twentieth century the responses to Leonowens's writing by those few European and American scholars of Siam who have deigned to pay any attention to it have also been resoundingly negative. They have labeled Leonowens's account of her experiences in the harem as at best a fantasy, at worst a fraud. Ian Grimble, who did a BBC (British Broadcasting Corporation) production on Leonowens on May 6, 1970, described her as "a mischief maker, a squalid little girl, . . . one of those awful little English governesses, a sex-starved widow."[59] Her two most thorough, and relentless, critics have been A. B. Griswold and W. S. Bristowe. Was Griswold right in his 1957 evaluation that Leonowens herself hovered "on the fringes of reality, often escaping into make-believe," or that "she had an acute sense of melodrama and absolutely no sense of proportion"?[60] What of the exposé Bristowe offered in 1976 in his biography of Louis Leonowens, Anna's son, that Anna Leonowens was a virtual con artist, who lied about everything in her background? Bristowe went so far as to surmise that Leonowens's revisions of her personal history become explicable as an attempt to cover the fact that she "may have had what was called 'a touch of the tar-brush' in her veins."[61]

Leonowens's own experiences in Siam formed the basis on which her books laid claim to some authority. British and American Thai "experts" have been emphatic in their insistence that her work does not have a right to make that claim. The opinion from all who present themselves, often through university appointments in England and the United States, as knowing anything about Thailand seems to be that she did not. They have denounced Leonowens as an amateur, an outsider, and a fake. The image of Leonowens that her critics have projected is that of a lower-class conniver of dubious respectability, ungrateful to her royal employer, crippled by ignorance, and blinded by narrow-minded religious prejudices. To steal an appropriate phrase from Joseph Conrad's Lord Jim, they have insisted that Leonowens is not "one of us." She has been disqualified from membership not only on the grounds of her lack of knowledge and her lack of rationality but also on that more fundamental ground of perhaps not being truly, which is to say, wholly, British. Leonowens is uninformed, irrational, a liar, and possibly not even "white."

Considering ideological rather than "aesthetic" or "factual" reasons for why *The Romance* and its author have produced such denunciations, I begin with the obvious point that the book, through offering an odd assortment of little tales, presents an eloquent indictment of the harem system in Siam, but hardly on the grounds of any sort of Victorian narrow-mindedness. Leonowens, certainly, did not appear to define it as an empowering social institution which strengthened Siam's resistance to British imperialism. There is no indication that such a crucial political function even occurred to the narrator of *The Romance*. What is clear is that the narrator believed that the harem should be abolished. Yet her distaste cannot be read as some sort of imperialist wish to weaken Siam by throwing her rhetorical weight on the side of British ambitions in the region.

Nor is the narrator's expressed distaste ever represented in terms of sexual prudishness or antieroticism. The sexual dimension of the harem is virtually nonexistent in *The Romance*. There is nothing like the comment offered by Malcolm Smith in his half-envious account of Siamese harems, that "sexual indulgence by the Siamese, as by many other tropical races, is carried to a degree that to most Europeans must seem incredible."[62] One of the common claims of Leonowens's critics is that she could not understand or evaluate properly the life she witnessed in Siam because she was blinded by her religious narrow-mindedness, possibly through being unduly influenced by her association with the American missionary community in Bangkok. The problem with this critique (apart from ignoring that its supposedly ultrapious subject is the very woman who toured with Mr. Badger and probably rewrote her autobiography) is that it does not fit the textual evidence.

The Romance of the Harem complains very little on religious grounds about the existence of the royal harem. The narrator does not energetically object to the harem as polygamous or promiscuous or even as an illicit offense against the principles of Christianity. Moreover, though the narrative does give occasional tributes to

Christianity, it frequently expresses profound admiration for the followers of Buddhism. Indeed, the structure of *The Romance* is of a series of tales each glorifying a woman from a different of religion and background, including Buddhist, Hindu, Muslim, and Christian. What the narrative explicitly and continually offers as the key objection to the harem arrangement is that, from the perspective of the women living in Nang Harm, their lives were not free.

Leonowens represented the world of Nang Harm in her writings as one in which numbers of women and children were being crushed, most of them spiritually and many of them physically. Many were born in the harem, or were brought there as young girls, victims of their family's political aspirations or the king's random and roving eye. She reports that it was the common practice for locally powerful families all over Siam to solidify or improve their relations with the king by giving him a young girl in their family. Once the girls were in the royal harem, they usually never saw their families again. But the tragedy of their fates was not simply that they were virtually imprisoned for life. In Mongkut's harem, with the exception of those thirty-five who were lucky enough to catch the king's favor and then to conceive and bear royal children, these women were doomed to virginity and/or childlessness, in a society where status for women (not to mention a practical occupation and a reason to look to the future) came through motherhood.

The Romance does not grant the political value of an integrating, even democratizing, social institution which continually fed the royal blood lines with new connections from other families, building a network of relations large enough to be a significant force in uniting a country and thus helping to preserve it from colonial takeover. *The Romance* does not even mention this particular political value, so certainly doesn't give it the kind of priority it seems to have had for King Mongkut, many other Thais, and many twentieth-century traditional political historians, all men. Perhaps this lack of interest in matters of national independence shows not so much a cultural ignorance and narrow-mindedness but simply different priorities from those of the book's detractors. The narrator objected to the harem, not because she supported British imperialism (which at many moments and in many ways the narrative does), not because she was a repressed Victorian prude (for which there is no textual evidence), not because she was under the sway of the rigid American Protestant missionaries in Bangkok (again, without textual evidence), not because she was blinded by her own cultural narrow mindedness, but because she was opposed to women's and children's slavery. As she explicitly maintained in *The English Governess*, "How I have pitied those ill-fated sisters of mine, imprisoned without a crime!"[63]

A continuing problem is that defending the social institution of the Siamese harem as a force against imperialism has also involved, however unwittingly, a defense of the social institution of slavery. Without slavery the harem could not exist. This involvement has long been recognized by various Thai, American, and European apologists for the institution of Siamese slavery. An early expression of what would become a familiar European attitude was Sir John Bowring's assertion in his 1857 account that "I saw few examples of harshness in the treatment of slaves, they are generally cheerful, amusing themselves with songs and jokes while engaged in their various toils."[64] Bowring goes on to cite the observations of a presumed authority, a "European gentleman living in Bangkok," who has assured Bowring that "in small families, the slaves are treated like the children of the masters."[65]

Quoting Bowring with some acceptance, and possibly even approval, Griswold articulates what is probably the standard European and American attitude in written accounts that do more than simply note the widespread existence of slavery in Siam. In his admiring book on King Mongkut Griswold claims that "slavery in Siam was not the terrible institution it was in some other lands."[66] The specific "other land" of terrible slavery that Bowring's account and Griswold's supportive summary invokes is, of course, the United States. Bowring's account of slavery in Siam is similar to contemporaneous accounts in America describing "darkies" singing happily on plantations and looked after by their benevolently paternal masters.

English-speaking readers now know enough about the grotesque inhumanity of slavery in nineteenth-century America, in the British colonies in the eighteenth century, and in various European colonies throughout the nineteenth century to be skeptical about lenient judgments of slavery, and thus of the harem as one form of slavery, in nineteenth-century Siam. Those lenient judgments have particularly emerged in studies of the character and achievement of King Mongkut. What many Thai scholars have found particularly offensive and deceitful about Leonowens's writing is its negative portrait of King Mongkut's rule over the harem. The narratives attribute atrocities which I read as probably fictional to an actual historic figure, one with arguable claims to being considered enlightened and progressive. As well as citing the distorting destructiveness of Leonowens's portrait for Mongkut's international reputation, Thai scholars have objected to the sheer ingratitude her writing shows. Some British critics have shared this view. That first 1873 review in the *Athenaeum* ended by questioning "the propriety of the writer's conduct in spending years in the service of the Siamese King, taking his pay, accepting his kindness, and afterwards publishing" such incidents. And in 1961 Griswold quoted the Siamese ambassador to London, who, in an attitude similar to that expressed by the British Colonial Office toward Emily Innes's work, reproached Leonowens for "slandering her employer."[67]

Male scholars just have not noticed that there might be a conflict of interest between gratitude to the king and gratitude to the women who may well have become Leonowens's friends. Moreover, there are many problems with the claim that Leonowens's accounts of incidents in the royal harem are "slander." In the first place, there is a lack of supporting evidence on either side. Leonowens's book is heavily fictionalized, maybe even all lies. Simultaneously, and conflictingly, it is the only existing eyewitness account accessible to non-Thai speakers (and to Thais) of the king's treatment of his harem. There simply is nothing else. Certainly, the royal court records of trials within Nang Harm would provide a superb source for discovering something of what went on in the harem. But they are not available. There is no easy way out of the problem of evaluating the perspective of *The Romance of the Harem.*

In the absence of substantial direct or corroborating evidence about Mongkut's treatment of the women in Nang Harm, writers who are engaged in what they see as restoring King Mongkut's unjustly slandered reputation tend to point out that Leonowens's harsh critiques are implausible by (re)constructing the particular character of the king. When Mongkut, the rightful heir to the throne, entered the Buddhist priesthood at age twenty to serve for a few weeks, as was Siamese custom, his father suddenly died, his elder brother took the throne, and Mongkut remained a monk for the next twenty-seven years. He became king in 1851 at age forty-seven. While a monk, Mongkut had become extremely learned, not only in Buddhism but in such areas as the sciences, French, and English. He kept the vows of strict poverty and traveled extensively in his country and among his people. Critics who reject Leonowens's book, with its intense attacks on slavery in the royal harem, and defend King Mongkut as an enlightened head of state rather than an occasional despot who would have his concubines whipped, imprisoned, and tortured, have recast the question of the significance of *The Romance of the Harem* in terms of a character debate.

And yet, after all the enumerations of Mongkut's personal virtues, after all the "historical" qualifications, after all the reminders that there were four categories of slavery in Siam and that people could buy themselves free, we are left with the fact that in nineteenth-century Siam some of the people had absolute control over many other people, usually for their entire lives, and often over their children as well. Leonowens's fictional instances of Mongkut's cruelty may well be slanderous, in attributing to him specific instances of cruelty that are perhaps untrue. On the other hand, what are we as critics doing and what kinds of interests are we serving by calling it a matter of mere religious or cultural narrow-mindedness for *The Romance* to characterize slavery as a fundamental evil? Even if we believe that the institution in Siam was both politically crucial in the successful Siamese resistance to imperial takeovers and was also benevolent relative to its counterpart in the United States, slavery is, by its very nature, violent, abusive, and cruel.

Nineteenth-century Siam was a sharply hierarchical society, with profound and unmistakable demarcations between classes. King Mongkut, as a deeply religious Buddhist with long experience as a monk, almost certainly would have valued life but would not have particularly valued women. Indeed, he was institutionally in the position of a man with absolute power who was instructed by both his religion and his culture to view women in terms of their functions rather than their selves. Mongkut was historically shaped by growing up in a time and place that found the evils of slavery customary. One can argue that he was less despotic a master than his more old-fashioned predecessors. Yet on the very grounds of plausibility, it seems likely that King Mongkut did abuse his slaves, including the women in the royal harem. Might Mongkut, on occasion, have ordered his slaves, including his women slaves, beaten or whipped or tortured? Was the mere fact of their being slaves, no matter what the particulars of their treatment, a form of spiritual torture that broke hearts and deadened joy, and that the King must in part be held accountable for? Were these women's own sexual desires, or lack of desires, irrelevant to their sexual usage? Were they ever killed? The religious justification for devaluing women as lesser humans; the mere fact that the women of the harem were kept, usually for life, inside the palace walls, many to be used as sexual pawns; the report in the 1860 *Bangkok Calendar* of an actual incident in 1859 in which a nobleman who had tried to win one of the king's concubines was executed, along with his wife—all suggest that the answer is yes.[68]

From the perspective that slavery in mid-nineteenth century Siam was a useful and not particularly cruel institution it is not far to Griswold's conviction that the women in the royal harem, with a few exceptions, liked it there and were "contented with their lot."[69] That argument has continued into this century. In his memoirs of being in Siam for many years during Chulalongkorn's reign, Malcolm Smith has many kind words to offer about the lives of the women in the royal harem, words directly related to his version of the women themselves. While acknowledging, just barely, that polygamy is "a state of affairs that has no strong defence," he assures his British readers that for the ladies of the harem, "a light-hearted, easy-going, pleasure-loving people, with an infinite capacity for enjoyment, it was an almost ideal existence."[70] They could play cards, watch dancers and shadow-plays, and, in season, fly kites. They were "housed, fed, clothed and entertained." In other words, they love their lifelong confinement, and the reason is not far to seek. "This contented state of the women of Siam must be attributed to their mental make-up, to their submissive nature, their lack of ambition, their lack of passion."[71]

Against such masculine representations of the nature and "mental make-up" of the women in the harem, against such narratives of their "almost ideal" existence in slavery, stands Leonowens's narrative. This account is from the only outsider who saw for several years the royal harem from inside and from the point of view of being a woman herself. Leonowens's narrative offers a radically different reading of the "mental make-up" of women in Siamese harems, and not only the royal harem. They

> have the appearance of being slightly blighted. Nobody is too much in earnest, or too much alive, or too happy. The general atmosphere is that of depression. They are bound to have no thought for the world they have quitted, however pleasant it may have been; to ignore all ties and affections; to have no care but for one individual alone, and that the master. But if you become acquainted with some of these very women . . . you might gather glimpses of recollections of the outer world, of earlier life and strong affections, of hearts scarred and disfigured and broken, of suppressed sighs and unuttered sobs. (107)

These are intense lines, emotional rather than rational, involved rather than detached, perhaps even melodramatic. The excessive and sentimental style of *The Romance of the Harem* is tied to the exaggerated and unbelievable quality of the particular events it narrates.

Did King Mongkut really build a scaffold outside Leonowens's window for Tuptim and her accused lover and there have the tortured and mutilated bodies burned alive? Only a gullible reader or an actively orientalizing reader (this includes the many people who view *The King and I* as informative about Thailand) would find such a narrative "true." On the other hand, only a hostile reader, appalled at the critique of a Siamese social institution designed to support male cultural and political power, would try to approach *The Romance* as factual history and then "demonstrate" the falseness of its "facts." The dramatic specifics of the group of tales which make up the book are clearly fiction. But what does that mean? For me the question of "truth," however tainted and dubious, does not quite dissolve in recognizing how much it is an artifact of the determining relations between a reader's ideological place and the narrative constructions of a place that was nineteenth-century Siam.

From the twentieth-century female tourist place where I stand and look at the big business of prostitution in Thailand, no matter how economically naive I am and no matter how little it is any of my presently American and somewhat "caucasian" affair, I see it as a business which most of the time financially benefits Thai and foreign men and only to a small extent financially benefits women. Moreover, the financial benefits to female prostitutes in Thailand are counteracted by the ways their practice of the profession deeply limits their possibilities for realizing, later in life, the cultural options open to other women in Thailand. From this perspective, I look at the stories in *The Romance* and, to borrow Wordsworth's language, "recognize" there a similar perspective, one which I half perceive and half create.

Women's Voices or a Woman's Voice

A Victorian book offering a sustained attack on a cultural phenomenon of a far-off country—particularly a phenomenon which helped that country resist European aggressions—is easily enough read as an example of imperialist jingoism. It slips into resembling another of what can seem an endless array of books exalting the superiority of British culture over the barbarous indigenous practices of peoples in the "east." Certainly, the issue of gender must complicate and ultimately critique any such reading. Yet gender alone is not enough. As Gayatri Spivak has pointed out, "white" women's books which construct foreign women and in the process construct themselves carry their own forms of imperialist appropriation, building a self on the lives of others, gaining a voice through other women's speechlessness.[72] I claim no anti-imperial innocence for Leonowens's book, because there is no way to leave out that this work, in speaking for the women of the royal harem, silences them. Readers, authors, and harem women are, indeed, always already constructed as cultural subjects, always past innocence. Moreover, among the many ways that "white women have benefitted fundamentally from the oppression" of other women, one is the simple economic fact that Leonowens had a job for over five years and got material to make money writing books and lecturing for several more years because there was a Siamese royal harem where women were enslaved.[73] In material as well as creative ways, Nang Harm's existence nourished her. Her career—both as teacher and writer—was built on the backs of the women in the harem. On the other hand, there would have been no moral high ground, no refusal to silence Siamese women, no escape from the place of exploiter, in Leonowens turning down the job as governess and/or in not having written *The Romance*.

The Romance is specifically structured as a self-defined British woman speaking for, and thus in the place of, Siamese women. It is also structured as a critique of a primary institution of another nation on the grounds that the institution oppresses its women. Such a self-positioning has contemporary parallels in American feminists in the 1990s objecting to such foreign cultural practices as Thai prostitution or arranged marriages or clitoridectomies or killing infant girls.[74] The political slipperiness of these kinds of critiques is fairly familiar. As Vron Ware has discussed in focusing on India, Victorian feminists tended to accept the "dominant ideology of imperialism: that it is only through contact with Western civilization that the 'natives' had any chance of being delivered from their own tyrannical customs."[75] Unlike what Ware has to say about Victorian feminists' rhetorics about British India, there is virtually no textual evidence in *The Romance* for concluding that it, or its author, considered the sexual customs of "Western civilization" as practiced by British men were superior to those of the Siamese. The British consul in Bangkok in the 1860s had a Thai "wife" and children, all of whom he would simply abandon when he retired to England. Anna's own son would set up a harem when he returned to Siam. Certainly, by English law both polygamy and slavery were illegal. But also by English law British soldiers were exempt from all legal and financial responsibility for their wives and legitimate children, a point Leonowens must have been quite familiar with.[76] There are ample biographical reasons to conclude that Leonowens might not have read the role of women in nineteenth-century British culture in progressive or universally rosy terms. If in *The Romance* Siam was a world of male hegemony, it hardly followed that England was not. Without detracting from the point of the generally imperializing quality of the rhetorical structure of *The Romance*, I want to point out how its imperial stance is so far from seamless as to be modified in some central ways.

Leonowens's narrative self-construction is not consistently that of an enlightened observer, herself liberated, who looks with pity on her unliberated sisters in another, less civilized, place and extends to them a helping hand (or helping pen). The subject of *The Romance* sometimes constructs herself through a notably close relation to the women about whom she speaks, as a woman among women, and a mother among mothers, as a member of a feminine community. At some moments it is her very membership in that community, albeit a partial membership, and not claims to cultural or racial superiority through her distance from it, which constitutes her right to speak. At some specific moments the narrative voice speaks not for the women around her but as one of them. That connection is created within the informing hegemonic framework of male domination, though Anna can leave the harem and they cannot.

A common occasion when the narrator's relations to women in the royal harem are represented as on the same level rather than hierarchical occurs when someone—Leonowens or another woman—wants something from the king. Often the representation is of co-conspirators, with the initiator and leader more often being someone other than Leonowens. Thus Lady Thieng, the head wife, is described as "always ready to sympathize with and help her suffering sisters" (155). It is Lady Thieng who arranges that when the king is angry at a woman and Lady Thieng wishes to deflect that anger, she will send for Anna to appear with a scholarly question of translation to distract him.

Perhaps the most salient relations these tales represent between the narrator and the women are when the narrator speaks not simply for them, a stereotypical imperial rhetorical stance, but actually as them. The book offers frequent testimonials to the rhetorical eloquence, the powerful voices, of the women in Siam. The book may inherently be an act of silencing those voices, in part because its colonizer/voice identifies herself as one of the "enlightened" imperialists. Yet, unlike any other European travel account about Southeast Asia I have read, the narrative consists to a significant extent of repeated and explicit claims of the value and the strength of the voices of the women of Siam. These claims are made in various ways. Not only is the narrative style in general one of dialogue, with the women in Siam represented as speaking for themselves. In at least two of the tales almost half the narrative is presented in the first-person voice of the woman represented as telling her story to Anna. Choy, the "favorite" of the harem, tells her own story. At the end of the chapter the narrator defines herself as no more than a copyist: "I hurried home and wrote down her narrative word for word, as nearly as I could" (144). L'Ore, the Mohammedan slave girl in chains, is her own narrator as well, as, "with wonderful power, combined with sweetness and delicacy, she repeated her sad tale" (47). Anna locates herself as just the transcriber of a meaning already understood by the two speakers, the mimetic recorder or literal transcriber rather than the overseeing interpreter of the Siamese women's world she experiences.

The plots of the various stories in *The Romance* function to reinforce the narrative depiction of the eloquence of the women of Nang Harm. Again and again the narrator represents herself as moved by, indeed, directed in how to act by, the power of the eloquence of these royal harem women in Siam. She takes what actions she does not only because women ask for her help and tell her what to do but almost because she cannot help herself, because she is so moved by them. The narrator often depicts herself as wanting to resist, as initially refusing to get involved, and then capitulating because of the power of their language. They speak "such words as women who have great and loving hearts only can" (117).

Nor is the narrator the only one who can hear such words. The moral touchstone of these tales for readers and characters alike is precisely the ability, or lack of it, to hear these women's voices. When Tuptim, who has disguised herself as a monk and run away from the palace, tells her tale, it is the priest and the male judges who are "unmoved," while the female judge seems touched by her youthful simplicity. Some kind of trial scene recurs regularly in all the stories, with Tuptim, with L'Ore, with Smayatee, with Boon and Chow, with Rungeah, and with May-Peah. Its function is in one sense always the same, as an occasion of eloquence, an opportunity for the woman to step forth as her own narrator, to tell her own tale.

The Romance, then, provides a kind of venue for the voices of the women, be they Siamese, Laotian, Mohammedan, Indian, who live within the oppressive political confines of the sexual system of Siam. One of the book's narrative techniques is to offer itself as a written record of their speech. In spite of the opinion of many of its detractors, and even though its focus is primarily on the women from various places and of various religions and classes and who find themselves caught in Nang Harm, The Romance can be read as a tribute to Siam. But it pays tribute to the women in Siam, represented by the very range of women in Nang Harm who are the subjects of the stories, rather than to Siamese men. Moreover, that the women in Nang Harm (and, by implication, in Siam) were opposed to the men is presented in the narrative not as a personal but as a structural truth. This opposition is inherent in the very institution of the harem—a political and domestic institution created not by the women but by the men. The book pays tribute to the women of Nang Harm through displaying the power of their characters as they respond to their state of oppression.

That the women's responses to male oppression are located in their eloquence can be read perhaps most luminously in the story of May-Peah. The persuasive power of speech of this Laotian girl from the north was such as to win the reluctant and fearful governess to her aid in taking secret messages to the princess of Chiang Mai, much as the song she sang to the prince of Chiang Mai wooed him to fall in love with and marry her mistress. The price May-Peah must pay to outwit the king and save her beloved princess is the ultimate one of silencing her own voice. This most eloquent of women cuts out her tongue so that she may never speak or sing again. For May-Peah as for Boon, the final sacrifice for a woman who would defy the masculine power is to silence herself.

One premise of Leonowens's book is that the oppression and

silencing of its women is the truth of the lives of the women in the harems of Siam. *The Romance*, in all its excess, insists on that consistently hidden, politically inconvenient truth. It also offers another, that the women subject to the harem system in Siam are not mere victims, any more than they are less fully human than men or that their lives and personal suffering are less important than the good of a unified Siam. In a rhetorical turn which works to counteract the powerful ways the narrative casts the women as innocent victims, *The Romance* presents these women as great heroines. They are represented as having great power, and precisely in terms of what they can say. The tales constitute a fantastic rhetorical gesture, in which the evils and the heroism are both painted larger than life. Against the cruel and apparently all-powerful masters are pitted the courage and purity of these outwardly powerless women: of Tuptim, the innocent sixteen-year-old Buddhist bricklayer who defies torture and death; of L'Ore, the Muslim slave and daughter of a slave who bore years of misery chained to a stake for the right to be free; of May-Peah, the stalwart Laotian whose loyalty to her friend outwits the forces of the whole Siamese penal and legal system; of Boon, whose generous love is stronger than the weakness of women and the fickleness of men.[77] The imperial impulse lurking in Leonowens's depiction of the women as innocent and victimized by wicked and barbaric men must be read against her representation of them as also powerful in courage and speech.

Judged from the realm of the actual, or from the conventions of narrative realism as laid out in Victorian novels, the tales in *The Romance of the Harem* are all preposterous. The narrative represents itself as speaking for, but also, I would claim, as being spoken by, the women of nineteenth-century Siam as no other writing about that place and time has. The book continually undermines a masculinized conclusion that these women were "contented." The irreducible narrative basis of these stories is one woman looking at other women's lives, frequently representing herself as listening to their own tales of how their lives are blighted, and being profoundly affected. For all its fantasy, the book insists on historical responsibility by actually naming the times, the place, and the man in charge of this blight.

The emphasis of the book falls not on the situation of these women's limited lives (which is all that so many male readers have noticed and disputed) but on how they narrate it and how they find their places by expressing themselves within it. Finally, *The Romance* is about the greatness, cast as the eloquence, of their response. As the dedication says, the book is written for "the noble and devoted women whom I learned to know, to esteem, and to love in the city of Nang Harm."

It is easy enough for a postcolonial critic to read the self-deceptions in the narrator's self-placement and in her placement of the women she constructs. The larger-than-life purity and childlike heroism of their tales, not to mention the basic fact that several of them die and it is the narrator who lives to tell their tales, points to the many ways the more experienced and worldly "British" governess is in charge of this representation of women in Siam. What may be less easy for a critic to read, but perhaps can be teased out by thinking about both the cultural history of male sexual control in Thailand and the complex critical question of voice, is the ways this narrative uses gender to depict places for the narrator and the characters which fall outside the usual imperial hierarchy.

The Romance is set in the realm of an imaginary Siam, as is Leonowens's previous book, *The English Governess*. The earlier book offers many more of the typical rhetorical conventions of travel narratives, what I think of as the "laws, customs, memorable sights, and practical difficulties" variety. Its opening section is a long account of the narrator's difficulties on first arriving in Siam, centering around finding a place to live. At issue was Anna's demand for her own house, separate from, which is to say, outside of, Nang Harm. One point of this section is the narrator's insistence on her distance from the women in the royal harem, but understood as her distance from having to exist within the hegemonic framework of the king's domestic sphere.

In *The English Governess* Anna and her young son and her two Indian servants finally do get a place of their own to live.[78] I would say that all of *The Romance* does the work of creating "a place to live," both for Leonowens and for the women in Siam. For a while they can all live together in its pages, in a life that might not be "actual" but that makes its claims, nonetheless, to being "real."[79] The real imagined community of these women may have its only existence in a book. But it is a place where women's voices—whether from Laos or England or India or Siam—are heard, a place shared, though with self-conscious qualifications and assertions of difference and ranges of privilege, among women of different cultures and nationalities.[80] It is a place, I suggest, which offers not a hierarchy but a vision, however flawed, however dimmed by the intrusions of male power and its own imperializing assumptions, of what a women's nation could be.

Listening

I want to close by quoting a piece from *The English Governess* which offers in a contained moment some of the irresolvably unstable locations I have been discussing in *The Romance*. This instability works, both at the level of the narrator's place and at the level of the place of the women in Siam, as some uneasy combination of speech and silence. Also intensely here is a narrative location I have not discussed, Anna and the women in the harem as mothers. The passage represents the community of mothers and children in Nang Harm as a community formed by male dominance and deeply damaged. The narrator, as outsider and visitor from a threatening imperial power, stands with her son while the other women and children kneel. But I suggest that these two move from observers to participants as Anna locates herself and her son as virtually, though not completely, members of this community. The two do not share the community's victimization or its power of eloquence (Anna's son can only give a "convulsive cry") but are represented in this passage as sharing its feelings and its literal silencing. The rhetorical force of this vignette, as with so many of the tales in *The Romance*, is precisely a matter of voice: its power and its repression.

The circumstances for the passage are that among the narrator's pupils was Wanne, a girl of eight, "with the low voice and subdued manner of one who had already had experience of sorrow." Wanne's mother, at one time the king's concubine, has become an obsessive gambler. She has abandoned her child, who is loved and cared for by one remaining slave attendant, Mai Noie. One day Mai Noie vanishes, and Wanne is left on her own. The following narrative tells how Wanne is then silenced. On the other hand, the represented force of the incident, its hermeneutic center, is precisely the power of this small girl's voice, emphasized as her own by her declaration being "quoted" in its original Thai.

Shortly afterward, as I entered the schoolroom one day, I perceived that something unusual was happening. I turned toward the princes' door, and stood still, fairly holding my breath. There was the king, furious, striding up and down. All the female judges of the palace were present, and a crowd of mothers and royal children. On all the steps around, innumerable slave-women, old and young, crouched and hid their faces.

But the object most conspicuous was little Wanne's mother, manacled, and prostrate on the polished marble pavement. There too was my poor little princess, her hands clasped helplessly, her eyes tearless but downcast, palpitating, trembling, shivering. Sorrow and horror had transformed the child.

As well as I could understand, where no one dared explain, the wretched woman had been gambling again, and had even staked and lost her daughter's slaves. At last I understood Wanne's silence when I asked her where Mai Noie was. By some means—spies probably—the whole matter had come to the king's ears, and his rage was wild, not because he loved the child, but that he hated the mother.

Promptly the order was given to lash the woman; and two Amazons advanced to execute it. The first stripe was delivered with savage skill; but before the thong could descend again, the child sprang forward and flung herself across the bare and quivering back of her mother.

Ti chan, Tha Moom! Poot-thoo ti chan, Tha Moom! ("Strike *me*, my father! Pray, strike me, O my father!")

The pause of fear that followed was only broken by

my boy, who, with a convulsive cry, buried his face desper-
ately in the folds of my skirt.

There indeed was a case for prayer, *any* prayer!—the
prostrate woman, the hesitating lash, the tearless anguish
of the Siamese child, the heart-rending cry of the English
child, all those mothers with grovelling brows, but hearts
uplifted among the stars, on the wings of the Angel of
Prayer. Who could behold so many women crouching,
shuddering, stupefied, dismayed, in silence and darkness,
animated, enlightened only by the deep whispering heart
of maternity, and not be moved with mournful yearning?

The child's prayer was vain. As demons tremble in the
presence of a god, so the king comprehended that he had
now to deal with a power of weakness, pity, beauty,
courage, and eloquence, "Strike *me*, O my father!" His
quick, clear sagacity measured instantly all the danger in
that challenge; and though his voice was thick and agitated
(for monster as he was at that moment, he could not but
shrink from striking at every mother's heart at his feet), he
nervously gave the word to remove the child, and bind her.
The united strength of several women was not more than
enough to loose the clasp of those loving arms from the
neck of an unworthy mother. The tender hands and feet
were bound, and the tender heart was broken. The lash
descended then, unforbidden by any cry. (114–115)

PART FIVE

Transit Lounge

CHAPTER 8

Looking Behind and Ahead

"The founder of Adelaide and son of Francis Light was a Siamese bastard."

—IAN MORSON

*F*rancis Light established an official British presence in the late eighteenth century on the island that would become during the nineteenth century the northernmost British "Straits Settlement" on the Straits of Malacca. Light is known in British imperial historiography as the "founder" of Penang. The illegitimate son of a Suffolk gentleman, who put him into the Royal Navy, Light has a solid and familiar place in that continuing historiography as a member of the Southeast Asian pantheon which also includes Frank Swettenham, Hugh Low, and Stamford Raffles. In his recent and admiring biography of Francis Light and his immediate family, Ian Morson focuses on describing the Lights in terms of their representing one of the most ubiquitous qualities appearing in imperial biographies of Southeast Asia: the mediations and/or violations of cultural, ethnic, and national boundaries.[1]

The artifice of speaking about a British imperialist, like that of speaking about the imperialized or about a Southeast Asian "region," as if either can have a coherent identity, becomes particularly piquant with Francis Light's son, William. As the illegitimate son of an English father and Siamese/Portuguese mother, William was a native of, was "from," the southern Siamese island of Phuket. This "Siamese bastard" spent some time in the Egyptian army and also "founded" the Australian city of Adelaide. His notably varied origins and locations, both familial, regional and professional, do not mitigate the point that William's political role, like his father's, was

269

that of British imperialist. Nor, I would also suggest, does his political role as British imperialist mitigate the significance of his varied nonimperialist origins and locations. The same point can be made about William's brother, Lanoon, who had an appointment under Raffles as the British Resident on the East Indian island of Banka. Their three sisters married, respectively, an officer in the Indian Army, a Bengal planter, and a doctor working for the East India Company. In other words, this single family, with all its unstable and even conflicting "racial" and national and class origins, served the British empire in Egypt, India, the Straits and the Malay Peninsula, Siam, the East Indies, and Australia.

The complexities of this particular generation of the Light family are exaggerated but hardly unique. Moreover, the identities of other "British" people in Southeast Asia sometimes carried quite different forms of complexities. Another exaggerated example, one outside the temporal boundaries of this study though surely in the direction it would go, is the writing of K'tut Tantri. She represents herself in her writings as being British in the special and marginalized sense of being born on the Isle of Man of Manx parents. K'tut Tantri's narrative recounts how, after school in Scotland and after World War I, she moved to the United States and wrote interviews with movie stars. In 1932 this Hollywood journalist saw an amazing foreign film on Hollywood Boulevard about "the Last Paradise," moved to the East Indies, and "became" Balinese. Through the training and guidance of Balinese friends, she dyed her red hair black, took her Balinese name, converted to being what she called a Brahman, lived in Bali for fifteen years, and spent the last of them as a freedom fighter for Indonesian independence against the Dutch, the Japanese, and the Dutch again after World War II. K'tut Tantri's narrative of her years as Balinese, *Revolt in Paradise*, was published in 1960.[2]

I offer the geographic and temporal sweep of the Lights and of K'tut Tantri, understood both as where they "came from" and where they "went to," to reaffirm the arbitrary boundaries of this study and the reductive distortions of the notions of a clearly defined "imperial" or "imperialized" identity and a coherent place called Southeast Asia. The place, the characters, including authors, peopling its discursive Victorian and early twentieth-century land-scapes and this present study of them, cannot claim any solid place, any more than can the simple notions of being British or Victorian. Nationality, historic period, region, gender, class: these are crude and deceptive boundaries. Finally, of course, Southeast Asia is just a geographic invention, a "cartographer's conspiracy," as Tom Stoppard called England. And yet, and yet. . . . Conspiracies, as those of us who came to political consciousness during the 1960s on American university campuses grew to understand, are political realities.

Leaving Home

There is an insular simplicity in basing political responsibility for the economic benefits a heritage of imperialism has brought to the United States and Europe on regional and racial identities. Just speaking critically of "white" men's or women's oppressions of indigenous (many of whom weren't so indigenous) peoples in South-east Asia is more blinding than illuminating. Sweeping and reductive labels such as "caucasian" or "Chinese," as much as "African Ameri-can" or "Hispanic" or "English" or "German" or "American," regardless of the politics of the labeler, carry a hegemonic value which serves the political right. Many a "white American" comes from heritages such as Russian Jewish, African, or Cherokee. Many a Thai or Singaporean has ancestors who are various sorts of Chinese.

On the other hand, somewhat tiredly, it is possible to wonder what doesn't serve the political right.[3] The alternative to reductive racist and ethnic categories may well not be some expansive recogni-tion of how many racial or ethnic or national categories an indi-vidual may be composed of. Lawrence Wright has offered a fascinating discussion of the political dangers lurking in the presum-ably antiracist concept of "multiracism." Wright asks the telling question, "Is it any accident that racial and ethnic categories should come under attack now, when being a member of a minority group brings certain advantages?"[4] This question echos one which many feminists asked ourselves during the early 1980s, as we wondered why male intellectuals' proclamations of the dissolution of the self and/or the death of the author coincided so neatly with the moment in cultural history when women through their own struggles were at last being recognized as having identities and being authors. In spite of all the theoretical and political difficulties, it is materially important to discuss both gender and "race," and the one along with the other, since gender is a racial and "race" a gendered cultural category. It is materially important to map the mappings of the gendered political geography of imperialism.[5]

The heritage of imperialism is as complex and resistant to tidy analyses or solutions as are the histories and heritage of racism and sexism. Nineteenth-century British imperial practices almost certainly have much to do with the poor economic condition of contemporary Britain, while the same heritage has played at least some part in the growing economic strength of many of the nations of the Pacific Rim. Yet women (and children) still work for oppressively low wages in Manila and Bangkok so that I and the millions of other women in the United States who are not in the top income brackets can go to chain stores and buy cotton shirts and children's clothes and cheap durable shoes. Those of us, boxed and labeled in a range of colors, who as consumers benefit from economic imperialism tend to be in the lower, middle, and upper-middle classes. Those who benefit through profits by owning and/or managing multinational companies tend to be upper-class, male, and, in the United States and Europe though not in Asia, culturally labeled as "white." The complexities and ambiguities of imperialism should not obscure the fact that its injustices, which Alatas succinctly defined as "the enslavement of nations," are alive and well.[6]

Does this study represent an "oppositional" critical practice, or a critical "intervention" in what are clearly continuing imperial practices? Of course not. The concepts of oppositional critical practice or intervention, with their faintly recollected aromas of revolutionary daring, invoke the stances of some professors of French or English or cultural studies in the United States and England in the 1970s, 1980s, and 1990s, who have cast themselves in the roles of a radical, new-wave, theoretical elite. As William Blake loved to remind his readers, the opposition sits in Parliament in full dignity, waiting its turn for power by balancing that which is the opposite of the opposition, which is to say the party officially in power. Yet that happy arrangement of political power sharing known as the two-party system, whether in nineteenth-century London or in twenti-eth-century Washington, D.C. or in United States universities (as assistant professors get tenure, and "we" become "they") or in any cultural text, is part of what this study hopes to be part of dissolving or fragmenting or perhaps no more than just trying not to invoke.

I would not claim much, though something, in the way of practical political usefulness for a critical book concerned with investigating how some instances of nineteenth-century British im-perialism operated.[7] My concern here has been the problematic, contradictory, sometimes collapsing qualities of a some British women's discourses in nineteenth- and early twentieth-century travel books about Southeast Asia. One fascination for me in these various representations of the female subject of British imperialism has rested precisely in those contradictions, those collapses. If this perspective seems unduly hopeful and unduly partial, I can only affirm that it is.

To say that I am a partial critic means that in my readings of these women's texts I am emotionally involved, both personally and collectively, in terms of private tastes and the public ideologies that made and are making those tastes. It also means, I would stress, that I write in fragments or pieces. I don't ask fragments or pieces of what. There is no rhetorical whole into which my discourse fits. This study is trapped by the totalizing villainies of an apparently endlessly dualistic English language. But I do here insist on limita-tions, the ways I don't understand, the ideas and patterns and ideologies which, because of my very specificities, I do not perceive or am not conscious of. Even this book which is partly focused on moments of outbreak and discursive freedom from the separations of imperialism in some Victorian women's writings cannot make a similar claim for itself.

It is close to impossible through academic discourse to offer material solutions to the injustices and continuing forms of profit which are the legacy of European and American imperialism. Rather, one useful political function of academic discourse has long been to uncover some duplicities of language. What this function means in the present is to discuss how terms like "white" and "heterosexual" and "feminine" are purely ideological categories, principles of exclusion which make suspect claims to inclusion or shared location, however difficult it is to erase their cultural power. One constructive implication of the dubiousness of notions of coherent identity is to recognize that greater and greater specificity doesn't help much, making its own totalizing claims, just little rather than big. To be an atom is still to assert wholeness, fullness, and completion.

Local knowledge and regionalism are critical concepts which can carry their own insidious implications of the truth of home and boundaries. It is important to be insistent about speaking piecemeal, to assert that sure grounds of experience are the sure grounds of saying very little, of saying wrong. Which are my only places to speak. Part of what I am suggesting here is that my own discourse not take up all the space, nationally as well as conceptually. Thai women have many places they are speaking from, though I cannot say much about how to locate those places, and can only read the few texts that are translated into my language. Said's apt warning in "Orientalism Reconsidered," that what haunts "local intellectual work" is how fragmentation and specialization can "impose their own parochial dominations and fussy defensiveness," points to an atomizing which can be somewhat addressed through the possibilities of the partial.[8] Ideologically, specialization remains a key form of intellectual and political domination.

Recognizing that it is close to impossible to see solutions or ways out of one's own culturally enforced blindnesses and visions, academic critics may be tempted by that traditional American political choice of isolationism, of just staying home, critically as well as literally, and leaving the whole problem alone. I think of this as a version of "knowing your place." That choice offers one explanation of why the extensive genre of Victorian women's travel books has been erased, has simply not existed in the institutions which have defined "Victorian literature" for European and North American culture. The choice to stay home has also helped to deflect the political impetus of the growing field of cultural studies, given what Paul Gilroy has called "its conspicuous problems with ethnocentricism and nationalism."[9] Yet, every time we go shopping we know that isolationism and nationalism are a mirage. A less ethnocentric choice is to accept one's own fragmentations and to leave "home," critically the same act, since accepting partiality means letting go of the notions of wholeness or centering or the integrity of subject location which continue to dominate the very meanings of the terms culture, nation, and home.

One positive implication of critically leaving home is affirming that a commitment to attending to difference is "an *ethical* imperative from which one is not excused by theoretical objections to the representation of culture."[10] Such objections include "those of translation, not merely in the literal sense but in the political sense as well: who is 'representative' of any non-Western culture? In what context can the speech of the Indian or African be made relevant to a Western understanding without betraying its origin?"[11] These are forceful objections to discussing and studying imperialized representations of other cultures, if only because of a history of criticism which has so visibly participated in the imperialism of those representations.

Yet there are even more compelling objections to not attending to difference. We must still look to and talk about other people and other cultures. Which is one reason why travel writing remains an important genre and why studying the conventions of its range of rhetorics is illuminating for critics who hope to challenge the rigid categories of identity within which we in the United States live. Finally, without the notion of fixed or rooted identity, there can be no place of critical innocence or of ethical purity in not taking up questions of difference. Purity, surely, is a false desire.

There is no "right" place to stand, staying "home" any more than traveling. Indeed, there is no "home," no local world carrying the stable, originary connotations of that term. There never was. So perhaps we need not mourn the loss of what was not there. The point, precisely, is that location itself, while occupying neither of the opposing poles of the solid or the ineffable, is yet unstable. And its very instability, "the mutability of identities which are always unfinished," is cause for celebration.[12] This is hardly to claim that the partial critical process leads to replacing nostalgia with some sort of idealized future. In spite of Spurr's eloquently expressed teleological hopes, I do not see much useful optimism in turning to a vision of a coming moment, in language or in life, "in which the play of difference could range free of the structures of inequality."[13]

The less grand, and for me more immediately hopeful, possibilities of the partial suggest that this study has frequently been ambushed by familiar ideologies masquerading as unfamiliar insights. But these possibilities also suggest that while critical writings may offer unresolvable inconsistencies, they at least can lower both claims and expectations and need not be focused on providing answers. These possibilities suggest that the value of other writers' analyses is also partial and contextual—and therefore cannot be rejected simply because their works may make totalizing claims. For with limitations, with fragmentations, can come the collapse of boundaries, what Caren Kaplan happily terms "deterritorializations."[14] After all, the rewards of partiality may well include partisanship. A move away from completion may also be a move away from isolation.

The discourse of the present study does have its preferences. Yet it claims no critical borders and marks out no fixed national or critical territories. Its incompleteness attempts to function as a kind of talisman against Said's "parochial dominations," which infuse academic work as well as nationalism and threaten to coopt a politics of specific locations. For without territory, without a stable meaning of such traditional institutional categories for grouping as "heterosexual" or "white" or "American" or "South African" or "female" (or even much smaller group categories of who "I" am), I establish no ground, no home base, and no nation from which to colonize others. Identity politics has too often been a failed route to liberation from the tyrannies of "race," of culturally defined gender and sexuality, and of nationality. It cannot be the critical route to illuminating colonialism. And if cultural studies has been ambushed by its own British nationalisms, it has also been ambushed by being predominately performed by men. Gender is not yet of central critical concern in the writings of most male academics, of whatever political and theoretical persuasion. I argue that attention to gender is central to the anti-imperialist commitments of postcolonial discourses.

Bringing the whole world home through her paintings and her writings, Marianne North served an empire which attempted to consume—and almost succeeded in consuming—everyone else. My distance from North cannot be marked by selecting a coherent self from her writing which I name imperial (creating a narrative self for my voice as postcolonial). *Recollections of a Happy Life* and the other "British" women's books I discuss offer narrative surfaces of mutating identities and shifting places, even as they present the solid conventions of rhetorics of domination as well. The subject voices in these narratives represent themselves and foreign locations and peoples in ways that, here and there, become so unstable, so dynamically fragmented, as to lose the definitions located by national and racial and individual boundaries. I have read that rare but happy loss as entwined with the instabilities of gender.

Some desirable aspects of critical and rhetorical partiality are not only that a voice claims no single or complete definition, no identifiable timbre, but also that its definitions do not serve to exclude or dominate relations to people or places positioned outside whatever at that rhetorical moment functions as the "self." As Donna Haraway puts it in her own style of language, "The moral is simple: only partial perspective promises objectivity."[15] What is lost, I hope, by partiality, by the fragmentation and flux as opposed to the multiplicity of a defined place, is the cursed dualistic demarcation which always already separates the "interior" location from whatever is outside it. Perhaps that is a hopeful feminist and anti-imperial task. To think in pieces. To turn the "inside" out. To lose the territorial imperative that lurks even in a politics of location.[16]

✣ *Notes* ✣

CHAPTER I

✣ *Place Matters*

1. The phrase is from Benedict Anderson, *Imagined Communities: Reflections on the Origin and Spread of Nationalism*, rev. ed. (London: Verso, 1991).

2. Edward Said, "Secular Interpretation, the Geographic Element, and the Methodology of Imperialism," *After Colonialism: Imperial Histories and Postcolonial Displacements*, ed. Gyan Prakash (Princeton: Princeton Univ. Press, 1995), 26.

3. There is a wonderful, and telling, photograph on the back cover of the paperback edition of *In Search of Southeast Asia: A Modern History*, rev. ed., David Joel Steinberg (Honolulu: Univ. of Hawaii Press, 1987). It features each of the contributors pointing to the particular section on a large wall map which represents the country he wrote about, pointing to his "area" of scholarship.

4. See Milton Osborne, "What Is Southeast Asia?" *Southeast Asia: An Illustrated Introductory History* (Sydney: Allen and Unwin, 1985), 1–15. A related point is made by Gerald Segal in *Rethinking the Pacific* (Oxford: Clarendon Press, 1990), an informative study which locates the Pacific in the minds of Europeans.

5. C. M. Turnbull, "The Concept of Southeast Asia," *The Cambridge History of Southeast Asia* Vol. 2, *The Nineteenth and Twentieth Centuries*, ed. Nicholas Tarling (Cambridge: Cambridge Univ. Press, 1992), 586–88.

6. *In Search of Southeast Asia*, 4.

7. J. D. Legge, Foreword to *A Short History of Malaysia, Singapore and Brunei* by C. Mary Turnbull (Singapore: Graham Brash, 1981), xi.

8. Ibid., xi.

9. Ann Laura Stoler, "Rethinking Colonial Categories: European Communities and the Boundaries of Rule," *Colonialism and Culture*, ed. Nicholas B. Dirks (Ann Arbor: Univ. of Michigan Press, 1992), 321.

10. Gauri Viswanathan, "The Beginnings of English Literary Study in British India," *Oxford Literary Review* 9(1987):1–26.

11. A useful example is offered in Rey Chow's discussion of what she labels the "Maoist," the foreign intellectual who in the 1970s admired the socialist revolution in China as "authentic" and now mourns for how that authenticity became tainted by "Western" desires. See her introduction, to *Writing Diaspora: Tactics of Intervention in Contemporary Cultural Studies* (Bloomington: Indiana Univ. Press, 1993), 1–26.

12. Sara Mills, *Discourses of Difference: An Analysis of Women's Travel Writing and Colonialism* (New York: Routledge, 1991), 198.

13. The phrase has been borrowed from anthropology with great effectiveness by Mary Louise Pratt, *Imperial Eyes: Travel Writing and Transculturation* (London: Routledge and Kegan Paul, 1992).

14. Mills's book is not just a United States publication, being published in London and simultaneously in the United States and Canada.

15. Billie Melman, *Women's Orients: English Women and the Middle East, 1718–1918: Sexuality, Religion and Work* (Ann Arbor: Univ. of Michigan Press, 1992).

16. Sara Mills, *Discourses of Difference*, 196.

17. Jenny Sharpe, *Allegories of Empire: The Figure of Woman in the Colonial Text* (Minneapolis: Univ. of Minnesota Press, 1993), 21. As Sharpe notes, her source here is Pierre Macherey, *A Theory of Literary Production*, trans. Geoffrey Wall (London: Routledge and Kegan Paul, 1978).

18. Sara Suleri, *The Rhetoric of British India* (Chicago: Univ. of Chicago Press, 1992).

19. See Gayatri Spivak's influential discussion, "Three Women's Texts and a Critique of Imperialism," *Critical Inquiry* 12(Autumn 1985):243–261.

20. Edward Said, *Orientalism* (1978; rpt. New York: Random House, 1979), and Patrick Brantlinger, *Rule of Darkness: British Literature and Imperialism, 1830–1914* (Ithaca: Cornell Univ. Press, 1988).

21. Quoted by Jenny Sharpe, *Allegories of Empire*, 165.

22. For an interesting discussion of how "orientalism" and romance function in two British fictions, see Gary R. Dyer's "The 'Vanity Fair' of Nineteenth-Century England: Commerce, Women, and the East in the Ladies' Bazaar," *Nineteenth-Century Literature* 46, 2 (Sept. 1991):196–222

23. Edward Said, *Orientalism*, 190.

24. Mary Louise Pratt, *Imperial Eyes*, pp. 38–85. Pratt's study uses primarily European works written before the mid-nineteenth century, when the imperialist role of explorer was more common than it was later.

25. A useful collection of essays is *Nationalisms and Sexualities*, ed. Andrew Parker, Mary Russo, Doris Sommer, and Patricia Yaeger (New York: Routledge, 1992).

26. Tropes of sexual conquest do appear in women's colonial writings, as Eva-Marie Kroller has pointed out about Isabella Bird's *Unbeaten Tracks in Japan*, in "First Impressions: Rhetorical Strategies in Travel Writing by Victorian Women," *Ariel: A Review of International English Literature* 21, 4 (Oct. 1990):89–91.

27. It is ideologically quite predictable that Margaret Landon's fictionalized rewrite of Anna Leonowens's account of life in the Siamese royal harem should make present what was so remarkably and delightfully absent from that account: some representation of Anna's having a heterosexual relation to the place, some suggestion of "romance."

28. Homi K. Bhabha, "Signs Taken for Wonders: Questions of Ambivalence and Authority under a Tree outside Delhi, May 1817," *Critical Inquiry* 12 (Autumn 1985):144–165.

29. Ada Pryer, Preface to *A Decade in Borneo* (London: Hutchinson and Co., 1893).

30. Though I suspect that one undesirable political effect has been conserva-

tive cooption of left imperial critique on the level of national politics. One haunting image is that George Bush's speech writers could do such a superb hatchet job on Saddam Hussein because Edward Said had provided such a lucid and handy list of "Oriental" qualities in *Orientalism*.

31. For what seems to me an exemplary moment, see Jyotsna Ramarathnam's quotation of Nicholas Dirk's list of critical influences on his methodology, in Ramarathnam's review of Dirk's *Colonialism and Culture, Nineteenth-Century Contexts: An Interdisciplinary Journal* 18, 1(1994):96.

32. Laurie Langbauer, "The Celebrity Economy of Cultural Studies," *Victorian Studies* 36, 4(Summer 1993):467. She applies this phrase to practices in a book, *Cultural Studies*, not to postcolonial theory. But her insights about one field, and specifically a particular text in it, are useful in looking at a different, but related, field.

33. Christopher L. Miller, *Theories of Africans: Francophone Literature and Anthropology in Africa* (Chicago: Univ. of Chicago Press, 1990), 65.

34. Laurie Langbauer, "The Celebrity Economy of Cultural Studies," 471.

35. For information on the British armies which were in the region, particularly in the three Straits Settlements (Singapore, Malacca and Penang) and Java, see Alan Harfield, *British and Indian Armies in the East Indies 1685–1935* (Chippenham: Picton, 1984).

36. For a detailed study of some of the inventions and places which represent the extent to which technology was a central enabling factor in nineteenth-century European imperialism, see Daniel R. Headrick's *The Tools of Empire: Technology and European Imperialism in the Nineteenth Century* (New York: Oxford Univ. Press, 1981).

37. The pressing importance of a workable stance on technology is a practical rather than simply a theoretical issue in many places in the world, as development organizations struggle with the imperialism involved in questions of where and what to do. One organization which is particularly explicit on the problematics of sharing technology is World Neighbors.

38. All the writers I mention in this section may be found in the Bibliography.

39. Three recent examples are Helen Tiffin, Julia Emberley, and Terry Goldie.

40. Nicholas Thomas, *Colonialism's Culture: Anthropology, Travel and Government* (Cambridge: Polity Press, 1994), 3.

CHAPTER 2

🦑 *Port of Entry*

1. One sign of this meaning production was that for months after the caning there were newspapers and magazines in the United States that would not run articles about the pleasures of tourism in Singapore.

2. See Geraldine Heng and Janadas Devan, "State Fatherhood: The Politics of Nationalism, Sexuality, and Race in Singapore," *Nationalisms and Sexualities*, ed. Andrew Parker, Mary Russo, Doris Sommer, and Patricia Yaeger (New York: Routledge, 1992), 343–364.

3. These discourses are sometimes collected. See Michael Wise and Mun Him Wise, eds., *Travellers' Tales of Old Singapore* (Singapore: Times Books International,

1985) and Charles Allen, ed., *Tales from the South China Seas: Images of the British in Southeast Asia in the Twentieth Century* (London: André Deutsch; British Broadcasting Corporation, 1983).

4. Paul Carter, *The Road to Botany Bay: An Essay in Spacial History* (London: Faber and Faber, 1987), xvi.

5. Ibid., xxiii.

6. Spatial history has also often been a form of imperial history, as imperial geography, particularly through the drawing of maps. There is a growing literature about mapping. See, for example, J. B. Harley, "Maps, Knowledge and Power," *The Iconography of Landscape*, ed. D. Cosgrove and S. Daniels (Cambridge: Cambridge Univ. Press, 1988), 277–312, and Graham Huggan, "Decolonizing the Map: Post-Colonialism, Post-Structuralism and the Cartographic Connection," *Ariel: A Review of International English Literature* 2, 4(1989):115–131. For a study of a particular place, see Thongchai Winichakul, *Siam Mapped: A History of the Geo-Body of a Nation* (Honolulu: Univ. of Hawaii Press, 1994).

7. E. R. Scidmore, *Java, The Garden of the East* (1899; rpt. Singapore: Oxford Univ. Press, 1984), 1.

8. The population of Singapore when Raffles and his group arrived has been a matter of some disagreement among historians, the number selected perhaps reflecting the political attitude of the writer to the British takeover. See Ernest C. W. Chew and Edwin Lee, eds. *A History of Singapore*, chap. 1–3. C. M. Turnbull has estimated the number of people on Singapore island in 1819 at up to one thousand. *A History of Singapore 1819–1988*, 2d ed. (Singapore: Oxford Univ. Press, 1989), 5. Alan Harfield, in *British and Indian Armies in the East Indies 1685–1935* (Chippenham: Picton, 1984), estimates the number at around one hundred and fifty (181). These books also discuss Singapore's population throughout the century.

9. European interest in writing the history of the region is indicated in part by the long publishing history of the *Journal of the Malaysian Branch of the Royal Asiatic Society* (known as *JMBRAS*), in existence under various titles since 1878. See *Singapore 150 Years*, ed. Tan Sri Dato' Mubin Sheppard (Singapore: Times Books International, 1982).

10. Quoted by Maya Jayapal, *Old Singapore* (Singapore: Oxford Univ. Press, 1992), 6.

11. The language of the treaty is quoted by Ernest C. T. Chew, "The Foundation of a British Settlement," *A History of Singapore*, ed. Ernest C. T. Chew and Edwin Lee (Singapore: Oxford Univ. Press, 1991), 39.

12. Singapore was not itself a separate colony until 1946. Until then it was one of the three Straits Settlements which together made up one colony. See M. Freedman, "Colonial Law and Chinese Society," *Journal of the Royal Anthropological Institute of Great Britain and Ireland* 80(1950):98.

13. Protecting the trade interests centered in Singapore was to become one of the major justifications for British encroachments (encouraged by strong voices in the British and Chinese business communities in Singapore) on the Malay Peninsula. Thus, as so often happened, what began as an alternative became a preamble.

14. Syed Hussein Alatas, *Thomas Stamford Raffles, 1781–1826: Schemer or Reformer?* (Sydney: Angus and Robertson), 39.

15. I will not be tracing the extensive discourse glorifying Raffles in this

discussion, but the materials are easily accessible. Perhaps the four most visible books devoted entirely to Raffles are C. E. Wurtzburg, *Raffles of the Eastern Isles* (1954; rpt. Singapore: Oxford Univ. Press, 1984); Maurice Collis, *Raffles* (1966; rpt. London: Century Hutchinson, 1988); Nigel Barley, *The Duke of Puddle Dock: Travels in the Footsteps of Stamford Raffles* (New York: Henry Holt and Co., 1991); and, last and most appreciative, that loving song of praise by his second wife, Lady Sophia Raffles, *Memoir of the Life and Public Services of Sir Thomas Stamford Raffles* (1830; rpt. Singapore: Oxford Univ. Press, 1991). The counterpoint to all this, and to the wealth of admiring discussions of Raffles in other books about both the history of Malaya and the history of Singapore, is that single slim volume by Syed Hussein Alatas, *Thomas Stamford Raffles, 1781–1826: Schemer or Reformer?*

16. For some of the details of Singapore's successful trade up through 1869 see Wong Lin Ken, "The Trade of Singapore, 1819–1869," *JMBRAS* 33, 4(Dec. 1960), 192.

17. For a compelling discussion of the role of the Singapore traders in Colonial Office policy, see D. R. SarDesai, *Trade and Empire in Malaya and Singapore, 1869–1874* (Athens, Ohio: Ohio Univ. Center for International Studies, 1970).

18. It has some similarities to another colonial island city, Hong Kong. See Rey Chow, "Things, Common/Places, Passages of the Port City: On Hong Kong and Hong Kong Author Leung Ping-kwan," *Differences: A Journal of Feminist Studies* 5.3(1993):179–204.

19. Wilfred Blythe, Introduction to the reprint of J. D. Vaughn's *The Manners and Customs of the Chinese of the Straits Settlements* (1879; rpt. Kuala Lumpur: Oxford Univ. Press, 1971), vi.

20. For useful discussions of the various Chinese communities in nineteenth-century Singapore, see C. F. Yong, *Chinese Leadership and Power in Colonial Singapore* (Singapore: Times Academic Press, 1991); Lee Poh Ping, *Chinese Society in Nineteenth Century Singapore* (Kuala Lumpur: Oxford Univ. Press, 1978); and Song Ong Siang, *One Hundred Years History of the Chinese in Singapore* (Singapore: Univ. of Malaya Press, 1967). A different and salutary view is provided by James Francis Warren, *Rickshaw Coolie: A People's History of Singapore (1880–1940)* (Singapore: Oxford Univ. Press, 1986).

21. See Myrna Braga-Blake, *Singapore Eurasians: Memories and Hopes* (Singapore: Eurasian Association, 1992). In nineteenth-century Singapore being Eurasian appears to have been culturally glossed as a perfectly honorable category of group identity.

22. The wealthiest members of this group have been influential in the twentieth-century history of mainland China.

23. The question of the language of Singapore has haunted it after colonial times. Its colonial language was English. During the time it was part of Malaysia the political impetus was to declare Malay the official language. After Singapore was ousted from Malaysia in 1965, its new prime minister defined the official language of the new nation as English and a "mother tongue." By the 1980s the government promoted a bilingualism of "two languages neither of which is native to Singapore." These were English and a "mother tongue" officially declared to be Mandarin, elevated to a language while other options are officially designated as mere dialects. See Jan B. Gordon, "The 'Second Tongue Myth': English Poetry in

Polylingual Singapore," *Ariel: A Review of International English Literature* 15, 4(1984):44. See also Kirpal Singh's earlier article, "An Approach to Singapore Writing in English," *Ariel: A Review of International English Literature* 15, 2(1984):5–24.

24. See Eze Nathan, *The History of Jews in Singapore 1830–1945* (Singapore: Herbilu Editorial and Marketing Services, 1986). C. M. Turnbull points out that "of 43 merchant houses in 1846, 20 were British, 6 Jewish, 5 Chinese, 5 Arab, 2 Armenian, 2 German, 1 Portuguese, 1 American, and 1 Parsi." See *A History of Singapore 1819–1988*, 39.

25. For a discussion of the transience of many of the Chinese who came to work in Singapore, see James Warren, *Rickshaw Coolie*, particularly chaps. 2 and 11–13.

26. An exception, and there were probably others, were the Indian convicts.

27. See Virginia Berridge and Griffith Edwards, "Part Seven: The Eastern Dimension and British Opium Use c. 1860–1900," *Opium and the People: Opiate Use in Nineteenth-Century England* (New York: St. Martin's Press, 1981), 173–205.

28. For a thorough and absorbing study of the complexities of the opium economy of Singapore, including discussions of the ways opium was the instrument measuring the effects of international capitalism in nineteenth-century Singapore, see Carl A. Trocki, *Opium and Empire: Chinese Society in Colonial Singapore, 1800–1910* (Ithaca: Cornell Univ. Press, 1990). I am indebted throughout my discussion to this book.

29. For an account of the British presence in Hong Kong which, among other qualities, erases the economic basis of that place in the opium trade, see Betty [pseud.], *Intercepted Letters: A Mild Satire on Hongkong Society* (Hong Kong: Kelly and Walsh, 1905).

30. These licenses were known as opium farms and the syndicate investors as farmers.

31. C. M. Turnbull, *A History of Singapore*, 15.

32. Cheng U Wen, "Opium in the Straits Settlements, 1867–1910," *Journal of Southeast Asian History* 2, 1(Mar. 1961):52.

33. Eng Lai Ah points out that in 1884 in Singapore "there were 60,000 Chinese men compared with 6,600 women of whom at least 2,000 were prostitutes." See *Peasants, Proletarians and Prostitutes: A Preliminary Investigation into the Work of Chinese Women in Colonial Malaya* (Singapore: Institute of Southeast Asian Studies, 1986), 33.

34. Syndicates who lost the bid for leases sometimes smuggled in opium, which would be sold at lower than the official price. See Edwin Lee, "The Opium Conspiracy," *The British as Rulers Governing Multiracial Singapore 1867–1914* (Singapore: Singapore Univ. Press, 1991), 103–116.

35. Carl Trocki, *Opium and Empire*, 70. See his discussion, 70–81.

36. Ibid., 2.

37. The shared interests and values among the ruling-class Europeans and the merchant-class Chinese are particularly vivid in an early twentieth-century work which remains the most informative and well-known Chinese history of Singapore, Song Ong Siang's *One Hundred Years History of the Chinese in Singapore* (1923; rpt. Singapore: Univ. of Malaya Press, 1967). Song was a Christian convert who

admired the British government as enlightened and benevolent. His avowed purpose in writing this fascinating and detailed decade-by-decade account was that future generations of Chinese would get "stimulus to serve the colony" (xi). For a more critical perspective, see C. F. Yong, "British Attitudes toward the Chinese Community Leaders in Singapore, 1819–1941," *Journal of the South Seas Society* 40, 1 and 2(1985):73–82.

38. Edwin Lee, *The British as Rulers*, 47.

39. As one step in the effort to control its residents in response to the riots, the colonial government in 1877 established the office, to be held by a European, of "Protector of Chinese."

40. Many books discuss the Chinese secret societies in Singapore. See note 20. See also Donald and Joanna Moore, *The First 150 Years of Singapore* (Singapore: Donald Moore Press, 1969), 391–430.

41. Carl Trocki, *Opium and Empire*, 63.

42. James Warren, *Rickshaw Coolie*, 213. Except for the inconsiderate visibility of the street people, these words might describe Hong Kong today, along with New York and Los Angeles.

43. It was not always the first destination, as can be seen in Annabella Keith Forbes's narrative, *Insulinde*. She went to and from Europe through the port of Batavia.

44. There were exceptions, particularly accounts written by British who had lived in India. Singapore was scorned in Charles Kinloch's account on the precise grounds that it was inferior as a colony to that greatest of British holdings, India. The food, the hotels, the public amusements, are all a poor second to those known to the British in India, and "the Indian [referring to an Englishman residing in India] visitor will soon get tired of Singapore." *Rambles in Java and the Straits in 1852*, by a "Bengal Civilian" (1853; rpt. Singapore: Oxford Univ. Press, 1987), 16.

45. Quoted by Maya Jayapal, *Old Singapore*, 33.

46. F. W. Burbidge, *The Gardens of the Sun: A Naturalist's Journal of Borneo and the Sulu Archipelago* (1880; rpt. Singapore: Oxford Univ. Press, 1991), 16–17.

47. Throughout the 1970s and 1980s Singapore, along with Hong Kong, was touted as a desirable tourist destination for Americans and Europeans on the very grounds that it was a bargain place to shop for all manner of American and European, as well as Asian, goods.

48. Isabella Bird, *The Golden Chersonese and the Way Thither* (1883; rpt. London: Century Publishing, 1983), 118.

CHAPTER 3

The Holy Land of Victorian Science

1. The significant exceptions would be parts of the island of Borneo.

2. For some histories of European colonizing of the islands east of Singapore, see Holden Furber, *Rival Empires of Trade in the Orient, 1600–1800* (Minneapolis: Univ. of Minnesota Press, 1976); John S. Furnivall, *Netherlands India: A Study of Plural Economy* (Cambridge: Cambridge Univ. Press, 1944); and M. C. Ricklefs, *A History of Modern Indonesia, c. 1300 to the Present* (Bloomington: Indiana Univ. Press, 1981).

3. See Daniel Chew, *Chinese Pioneers on the Sarawak Frontier 1841–1941* (Singapore: Oxford Univ. Press, 1990); and Leonard Blusse, "Batavia, 1619–1740: The Rise and Fall of a Chinese Colonial Town," *Journal of Southeast Asian Studies* 12, 1(Mar. 1981):159–178.

4. See Clive Day, *The Policy and Administration of the Dutch in Java* (London: Macmillan, 1904) and J. S. Furnivall's *Netherlands India*.

5. For a fascinating discussion of the Eurasian as "not merely a biological but a socio-economic and cultural concept," see Paul W. van der Veur's "The Eurasians of Indonesia: A Problem and Challenge in Colonial History," *Journal of Southeast Asian History* 9, 2(Sept. 1968):191–207.

6. Compare Jean Gelman Taylor's discussion of mixed races in Batavia in *The Social World of Batavia: European and Eurasian in Dutch Asia* (Madison: Univ. of Wisconsin Press, 1983) with the situation in Singapore, in *Singapore Eurasians: Memories and Hopes*, ed. Myrna Braga-Blake (Singapore: Eurasian Association, 1992).

7. Jean Gelman Taylor, *The Social World of Batavia*, 142. I am indebted throughout this chapter to Taylor's informative book. See also Paul W. Van der Veur, *Education and Social Change in Colonial Indonesia* (Athens, Ohio: Ohio Univ. Center for International Studies, 1969); and "The Eurasians of Indonesia," 191–207.

8. The British imperial imperative not to "mix" was perhaps most vividly contained in the advice Roland Braddell's father offered about living in Singapore. "If you want to be happy, remember that the country is just round the corner waiting to black-jack you. Don't admit that you are living in an Oriental country. . . . Above all, never wear a sarong and buja; that's the beginning of the end!" Quoted by Roland Braddell, *The Lights of Singapore* (London: Metheun, 1934), 21.

9. John Crawfurd, *History of the Indian Archipelago: Containing an Account of the Manners, Arts, Languages, Religions, Institutions, and Commerce of its Inhabitants* (Edinburgh: Archibald Constable, 1820), 1:142.

10. See Nicholas Tarling's two studies, *Anglo-Dutch Rivalry in the Malay World, 1780–1824* (Cambridge: Cambridge Univ. Press, 1962); and *British Policy in the Malay Peninsula and Archipelago, 1824–1871* (Kuala Lumpur: Oxford Univ. Press, 1969).

11. John Bastin, "Raffles and British Policy in the Indian Archipelago, 1811–1816," *Journal of the Malayan Branch of the Royal Asiatic Society* 27, 1(1954):84–119.

12. See the attitudes of Stamford Raffles to the Dutch in Thomas Stamford Raffles, *The History of Java*, 2 vols. (1817; rpt. London: John Murray, 1830).

13. John Crawfurd, *History of the Indian Archipelago*, 3:264.

14. Rob Nieuwenhuys, *Mirror of the Indies: A History of Dutch Colonial Literature*, trans. Frans van Rosevelt (1972; rpt. Amherst: Univ. of Massachusetts Press, 1982), xi.

15. James William B. Money, *Java, or, How to Manage a Colony; Showing a Practical Solution to the Questions Now Affecting British India* (London: Hurst and Blackett, 1861), quoted in *In Search of Southeast Asia: A Modern History*, rev. ed., ed. David Joel Steinberg (Honolulu: Univ. of Hawaii Press, 1987), 157.

16. For a thorough discussion of the Culture System, including an analysis of its eventual stagnation, see J. S. Furnivall's *Netherlands India*.

17. Part of the Dutch profits came from their opium farms in Java, which were run on a system, similar to the British system in Singapore, of selling very expensive government leases to enterprising "farmers," usually Chinese business-

men. For a detailed study of the Dutch version of the business which brought huge incomes to European colonizers throughout Southeast Asia, see James R. Rush, *Opium to Java: Revenue Farming and Chinese Enterprise in Colonial Indonesia, 1860–1910* (Ithaca: Cornell Univ. Press, 1990).

18. Condescending British attitudes toward the Dutch in the Netherlands East Indies are represented with the ease of long familiarity throughout Violet Clifton's account of her 1912 journey, *Islands of Queen Wilhelmina*, published in 1927 and reprinted as *Islands of Indonesia* (Singapore: Oxford Univ. Press, 1991). For a Dutch perspective from about the same time, see Augusta De Wit, *Java: Facts and Fancies* (1912; rpt. Singapore: Oxford Univ. Press, 1987).

19. Mary Louise Pratt, *Imperial Eyes: Travel Writing and Transculturation* (London: Routledge, 1992).

20. A vivid exception, which I will discuss in chapter 4, is Emily Innes's account of her experiences in British Malaya, *The Chersonese with the Gilding Off* (1885; rpt. Kuala Lumpur: Oxford Univ. Press, 1993).

21. Henry Ogg Forbes, *A Naturalist's Wanderings in the Eastern Archipelago: A Narrative of Travel and Exploration from 1878 to 1883* (1885; rpt. Singapore: Oxford Univ. Press, 1989).

22. Annabella Forbes, *Insulinde: Experiences of a Naturalist's Wife in the Eastern Archipelago* (London: William Blackwood and Sons, 1887); rpt. as *Unbeaten Tracks in Islands of the Far East: Experiences of a Naturalist's Wife in the 1880s* (Singapore: Oxford Univ. Press, 1987).

23. Multatuli [Eduard Douwes Dekker], *Max Havelaar; or, The Coffee Auctions of the Netherlands Trading Company*, trans. Roy Edwards (1860; rpt. Amherst: Univ. of Massachusetts Press, 1982).

24. This was observed with some disparagement by Alfred Russel Wallace, who argued that there was widespread colonial corruption, and thus nothing special about Dutch practices in the East Indies. See *The Malay Archipelago, the Land of the Orang-Utan and the Bird of Paradise; a Narrative of Travel, with Studies of Man and Nature* (1869; rpt. Singapore: Oxford Univ. Press, 1986, with an introduction by John Bastin), 104.

25. "A Dutch Political Novel," *North British Review*, n.s. 42, 7(1867):323.

26. That such an erasure is not the only choice is clear from the 1991 Oxford University Press reissue in Singapore of Violet Clifton's 1927 *Islands of Queen Wilhelmina* with a new, and distinctly postcolonial, title: *Islands of Indonesia*.

27. Benedict Anderson, *Java in a Time of Revolution* (Ithaca: Cornell Univ. Press, 1972).

28. See the essays in *Nation and Narration*, ed. Homi K Bhabha (London: Routledge, 1990).

29. For an analysis of the intricate psychological costs of being colonized, see Frantz Fanon's classic 1952 study, translated as *Black Skin, White Masks* by Charles Lam Markmann (New York: Grove Press, 1967). A superb study which focuses particularly on Southeast Asia is Syed Hussein Alatas, *The Myth of the Lazy Native: A Study of the Image of the Malays, Filipinos and Javanese from the 16th to the 20th Century and its Function in the Ideology of Colonial Capitalism* (London: Frank Cass, 1977).

30. *In Search of Southeast Asia*, 308.

31. See, for example, Lee Ting Hui's article, "Singapore Under the Japanese 1942–45," extracted as "Japanese Racial Policies in Singapore, *Malaysia: Selected Historical Readings*, comp. John Bastin and Robin W. Winks (Kuala Lumpur: Oxford Univ. Press, 1966), 320–325.

32. The language and the insight are Benedict Anderson's. *Imagined Communities: Reflections on the Origin and Spread of Nationalism* (1983; rev. ed. London: Verso, 1991).

33. For a history of this resistance, see John G. Taylor's *Indonesia's Forgotten War: The Hidden History of East Timor* (Leichhardt, NSW: Pluto Press Australia, 1991).

34. Benedict Anderson, *Imagined Communities*, and Gauri Viswanathan, "Raymond Williams and British Colonialism," *Yale Journal of Criticism* 4, 2(1991):47–66.

35. *Unbeaten Tracks in Islands of the Far East*, vii. All further references are to this edition.

36. John Bastin, introduction to Alfred Russel Wallace, *The Malay Archipelago*, vii.

37. I am indebted to John Bastin's introduction (ix–xi) for this discussion of the written sources of *The Malay Archipelago*.

38. Mary Louise Pratt, *Imperial Eyes*, 27, 28.

39. Ibid. 30.

40. The presumably apolitical quality of the discourse of natural history also applied to Americans. Albert Bickmore, who was to found the American Museum of Natural History in New York, also made a scientific collecting trip to the East Indies and wrote about it. His *Travels in the East Indian Archipelago* came out in December 1868, four months earlier than Wallace's *The Malay Archipelago*, and was considered more up-to-date by some reviewers. See John Bastin introduction, to *The Malay Archipelago* and Albert Bickmore, *Travels in the East Indian Archipelago* (1868; rpt. Singapore: Oxford Univ. Press, 1991), vii.

41. Alfred Russel Wallace, *The Malay Archipelago*, 29.

42. John Bastin, introduction to Alfred Russel Wallace, *The Malay Archipelago*, xvii.

43. Ronald Clark, *The Survival of Charles Darwin* (New York: Random House, 1984), 95.

44. "Wallace's Malay Archipelago," *Anthropological Review* 7(1869):315.

45. William M. Hornaday, *Two Years in the Jungle: The Experiences of a Hunter and Naturalist in India, Ceylon, the Malay Peninsula and Borneo* (New York: Charles Scribner's Sons, 1885).

46. Odoardo Beccari, *Wanderings in the Great Forests of Borneo* (1904; rpt. Singapore: Oxford Univ. Press, 1986).

47. Carl Bock, *The Head-Hunters of Borneo: A Narrative of Travel up the Mahakkam and down the Barito; also, Journeyings in Sumatra* (1881; rpt. Singapore: Oxford Univ. Press, 1985).

48. Charles Hose, *The Field-Book of a Jungle-Wallah: Being a Description of Shore, River and Forest Life in Sarawak* (1929; rpt. Singapore: Oxford Univ. Press, 1985).

49. Charles Hose, *Natural Man: A Record from Borneo* (1926; rpt. Singapore: Oxford Univ. Press, 1988).

50. Redmond O'Hanlon, *Into the Heart of Borneo* (1984; rpt. New York: Random House, Vintage, 1987).

51. Henry Forbes, *A Naturalist's Wanderings*, 11.

52. Ibid., 300.

53. Ibid., 53.

54. This is a different variety of colonial positioning to the one analyzed in Mary Louise Pratt's useful discussion of the monarch-of-all-I-survey scene in *Imperial Eyes*. The point, I think, is that there is a range of imperial positioning.

55. Peter Allen Dale, *In Pursuit of a Scientific Culture* (Madison: Univ. of Wisconsin Press, 1989), 219.

56. James Krasner, in his chapter on "The Geometric Jungle: Imperialistic Vision in the Writings of Alfred Russel Wallace, H. M. Tomlinson, and Joseph Conrad" in *The Entangled Eye: Visual Perception and the Representation of Nature in Post-Darwinian Narrative* (New York: Oxford Univ. Press, 1992), offers a more uniform view of what he calls Wallace's "transformative vision . . . as the perceptual colonization and industrialization of the new world" (117).

57. James A. Boon, *Affinities and Extremes: Crisscrossing the Bittersweet Ethnology of East Indies History, Hindu-Balinese Culture, and Indo-European Allure* (Chicago: Univ. of Chicago Press, 1990), 23.

58. Mary Louise Pratt, *Imperial Eyes*, 105.

59. Alfred Russel Wallace, *The Malay Archipelago*, 598.

60. Ibid., 596.

61. Ibid., 597.

62. Ibid., 599.

63. Patrick Brantlinger, *Rule of Darkness: British Literature and Imperialism, 1830–1914* (Ithaca: Cornell Univ. Press, 1988), 32–35.

64. Gayatri Spivak, "Three Women's Texts and a Critique of Imperialism," *Critical Inquiry* 12(Autumn 1985):243–61.

65. Laura Donaldson, "The Miranda Complex: Colonialism and the Question of Feminist Reading," *Diacritics* (Fall 1988):65–77.

66. Ibid., 71.

67. "Two Women Wanderers," *Spectator*, Sept. 1, 1888, 1195.

68. Henry Ogg Forbes, *A Naturalist's Wanderings*, 283.

69. Ibid., 427.

70. Elaine Scarry, *The Body in Pain: The Making and Unmaking of the World* (New York: Oxford Univ. Press, 1985), 11. Throughout the following discussion I am indebted to Scarry's insights and to those of Mary Jean Corbett, who first suggested that I read Scarry's book in relation to *Insulinde*.

71. For a brief but fascinating discussion of some discourses on the politics of cultural identity between the Maori and the Europeans in New Zealand, see Simon During, "Waiting for the Post: Some Relations between Modernity, Colonization, and Writing," *Ariel: A Review of International English Literature* 20, 4(Oct. 1989):31–61.

72. Terry Goldie has published an impressive study which includes looking at images of the Maori: *Fear and Temptation: The Image of the Indigene in Canadian, Australian, and New Zealand Literatures* (Kingston: McGill-Queens Univ. Press, 1989).

73. Mrs. H. O. Forbes, *Helena: A Novel* (Edinburgh: William Blackwood and Sons, 1905), 328, 321.

74. For a fascinating analysis of novels written by Dutch women about late colonial society, and particularly about miscegenation, in the Netherlands East Indies, see Jean Gelman Taylor, *The Social World of Batavia*, 145–158.

CHAPTER 4

❦ *Botany and Marianne North*

1. Suzanne Zeller, review of *Scientist of Empire: Sir Roderick Murchison, Scientific Exploration and Victorian Imperialism, Victorian Studies* by Robert Stafford, 36, 1(Fall 1992):96.

2. Peter Morton, *The Vital Science: Biology and the Literary Imagination, 1860–1900* (London: George Allen and Unwin, 1984), 3, 13.

3. For a detailed account of the role of newspapers in British expansion in the nineteenth century, see Beau Riffenburgh, *The Myth of the Explorer: The Press, Sensationalism, and Geographical Discovery* (London: Belhaven Press, 1993).

4. Beau Riffenburgh, *The Myth of the Explorer*, 55–56.

5. A compelling older study of a range of causes of Victorian imperial intervention in Africa is Ronald Robinson and John Gallagher with Alice Denny, *Africa and the Victorians: The Official Mind of Imperialism* (New York: St Martin's Press, 1967).

6. Mary Louise Pratt, *Imperial Eyes: Travel Writing and Transculturation* (London: Routledge, 1992), 51.

7. Patrick Brantlinger, *Rule of Darkness: British Literature and Imperialism, 1830–1914* (Ithaca: Cornell Univ. Press, 1988), 173–197.

8. Patrick Brantlinger, *The Rule of Darkness*, 180–181.

9. Edward W. Said, *Orientalism* (New York: Vintage Books, 1979), 7.

10. Robert Stafford, *Scientist of Empire: Sir Roderick Murchison, Scientific Exploration and Victorian Imperialism* (Cambridge: Cambridge Univ. Press, 1989), 221.

11. I am indebted throughout this discussion to Beau Riffenburgh's *The Myth of the Explorer*, particularly its examination of the relations between nineteenth-century newspapers, both American and British, and Victorian images of Africa and of the people who wrote memoirs about their travels there.

12. Beau Riffenburgh, *The Myth of the Explorer*, 68.

13. For informative analyses of the extent and characteristics of Victorian interest in the natural sciences, see Lynn Barber, *The Heyday of Natural History: 1820–1870* (Garden City, N. Y.: Doubleday and Co., 1980); and Lynn L. Merrill, *The Romance of Victorian Natural History* (New York: Oxford Univ. Press, 1989).

14. Susan Faye Cannon, *Science in Culture: The Early Victorian Period* (New York: Dawson and Science History Publications, 1978), 1, passim.

15. Lynn L. Merrill, *The Romance of Victorian Natural History*, 11, ix.

16. Morris Berman, "'Hegemony' and the Amateur Tradition in British Science," *Journal of Social History* 8(1975):34. This article is a fascinating discussion of why "the evolution of the English scientific community becomes understandable only when seen within the framework of the cultural imprint of the ruling class."

17. The next step was probably tourism, travel as a leisure activity, "sightseeing." But the fun Henry Forbes and Marianne North wrote about was inextricable from hard work.

18. Henry Walter Bates, *The Naturalist on the River Amazons: A Record of Adventures, Habits of Animals, Sketches of Brazilian and Indian Life, and Aspects of Nature under the Equator, during Eleven Years of Travel* (1863; rpt. New York: Penguin Books, 1989), 306.

19. Marianne North, *Recollections of a Happy Life: Being the Autobiography of Marianne North*, ed. by her sister, Mrs. John Addington Symonds (London: Macmillan, 1892), 2:99.

20. Quoted by Dea Birkett, "A Victorian Painter of Exotic Flora," *New York Times*, Nov. 22, 1992, 30.

21. Laura Ponsonby, *Marianne North at Kew Gardens* (Exeter: Webb and Bower, 1990), 9.

22. The phrase is quoted in W. Botting Hemsley's own review of "The Marianne North Gallery of Paintings of 'Plants and Their Homes,'" *Nature: A Weekly Illustrated Journal of Science* 26(June 15, 1882):155.

23. Sir Joseph Hooker, "The North Gallery, Kew," *Journal of Horticulture and Home Farmer. A Chronicle of Country Pursuits and Country Life*, 3d ser., 51(Oct. 19, 1905):364.

24. Dea Birkett, "A Victorian Painter of Exotic Flora," 30.

25. Laura Ponsonby, *Marianne North at Kew Gardens*, 7.

26. The North family was long distinguished among English country gentry. Its most famous ancestor was the seventeenth-century Roger North, a lawyer, historian, and musician. Roger is best remembered as a writer. He wrote an autobiography and the biographies of his three distinguished brothers: Sir Francis North, successful politician who became attorney general of England; John North, distinguished Cambridge professor, master of Trinity College, and friend of Sir Isaac Newton; and Dudley North, successful businessman and merchant in the Middle East, returning to become a member of Parliament.

27. Laura Ponsonby, *Marianne North at Kew Gardens*, 11.

28. Marcia Myers Bonta, in her fascinating account of *Women in the Field: America's Pioneering Women Naturalists* (College Station: Texas A & M Univ. Press, 1991), points out that these women "nearly all had male mentors early in their careers" (xiii).

29. Marianne North, *Recollections of a Happy Life: Being the Autobiography of Marianne North*, vol. 1, ed. and intro. Susan Morgan (Charlottesville: Univ. Press of Virginia, 1993), 35. All further references to Vol. 1 are to this edition.

30. Somerville College, Oxford University, Marianne North Letters to Amelia Edwards, no. 236.

31. Quoted by Brenda E. Moon, "Marianne North 1830–1890," in Marianne North, *A Vision of Eden: The Life and Work of Marianne North*, ed. Graham Bateman (Exeter: Webb and Bower, 1980), 235.

32. Royal Botanic Gardens, Kew, Marianne North Letters to Dr. Burnell, no. 12 (Feb. 5, 1878).

33. For a thorough discussion of this subject see Brenda E. Moon's excellent article "Marianne North's *Recollections of a happy life*: How They Came to Be Written and Published," *Journal of the Society for the Bibliography of Natural History* 8, 4(1978):497–505.

34. Royal Botanic Gardens, Kew, Marianne North Letters to Dr. Burnell, no. 31 (Jan. 17). I agree with Brenda Moon's assumption that this letter, dated only January 17, was in fact January 17, 1880.

35. Brenda Moon, "Marianne North's *Recollections of a Happy Life*," 500.

36. Ibid., 501.

37. Ibid., 502; quoted by Moon from the Marianne North papers at Rougham Hall.

38. Marianne North, *Some Further Recollections of a Happy Life: Selected From the Journals of Marianne North Chiefly between the Years 1859 and 1869*, ed. by her sister, Mrs. John Addington Symonds (London: MacMillan, 1893), 315.

39. Brenda Moon, "Marianne North's *Recollections of a Happy Life*," 503.

40. Sara Suleri, *The Rhetoric of English India* (Chicago; Univ. of Chicago Press, 1992), 75.

41. See Dea Birkett's discussion of the image of "the intrepid woman botanist" *Spinsters Abroad: Victorian Lady Explorers* (London: Basil Blackwell, 1989), 101, and passim.

42. Royal Botanic Gardens, Kew, Marianne North Letters to A. R. Wallace.

43. Royal Botanic Gardens, Kew, Marianne North Letters to Dr. Burnell, no. 15 (Feb. 26, 1878); no. 35 (Feb. 21, 1878 [but probably 1879]).

44. Margaret Brooke, ranee of Sarawak, *Good Morning and Good Night* (1934; rpt. London: Century Publishing, 1984), 171, 173.

45. A. G. Morton, *History of Botanical Science: An Account of the Development of Botany from Ancient Times to the Present Day* (London: Academic Press, 1981), 288.

46. A. G. Morton, *History of Botanical Science*, 294.

47. Lucile Brockway, *Science and Colonial Expansion: The Role of the British Royal Gardens* (New York; Academic Press, 1979), 80. I am indebted throughout my discussion of nineteenth-century botany to this compelling and marvelously detailed book.

48. I am indebted throughout the following discussion of American botany to Marcie Myers Bonta's excellent book *Women in the Field*.

49. See the introduction to Edward Said's *Orientalism* (New York: Vintage Books, 1979) for a discussion of different sorts of European imperialism.

50. Lucile H. Brockway, *Science and Colonial Expansion*, 80.

51. Ibid.

52. Ibid., 85.

53. Ibid., 92.

54. Ibid., 96.

55. Ibid., 101.

56. "Kew and Cinchona," *Science and Colonial Expansion*, 103–140.

57. British doctors advised against quinine as a help for malaria from 1804 to 1840, when the policy changed.

58. Donovan Williams, "Clements Robert Markham and the Introduction of the Cinchona Tree into British India, 1861," *Geographical Journal*, Dec. 1962.

59. The history of British relations to quinine in the nineteenth century is one element of the connections between British imperialism, botany, and another emerging "science," medicine. For an excellent discussion of British medicine in the service of imperialism in colonial India, see David Arnold, *Colonizing the Body: State Medicine and Epidemic Disease in Nineteenth-Century India* (Berkeley: Univ. of California Press, 1993).

60. For a discussion of the history of quinine, cast as a hymn to progress, see

Henry Hobhouse, *Seeds of Change: Five Plants That Transformed Mankind* (New York: Harper and Row, 1986), 3–40.

61. Mary Louise Pratt, *Imperial Eyes*, 57, 56.

62. Somerville College, Oxford University, Marianne North Letters to Amelia Edwards, no. 258.

63. Royal Botanic Gardens, Kew, Marianne North Letters to Dr. Burnell, no. 27 (July 27, 1878).

64. Royal Botanic Gardens, Kew, Letters to W. B. Hemsley, vol. II, no. 44 (June 27, 1882).

65. Royal Botanic Gardens, Kew, Letters to W. B. Hemsley, vol. II, no. 68 (Nov. 5, 1882).

66. Royal Botanic Gardens, Kew, Letters to the Shaen Family, 1875–1884, no. 3 (probably early 1876).

67. Royal Botanic Gardens, Kew, Letters to the Shaen Family, 1875–1884, no. 2.

68. Royal Botanic Gardens, Kew, Marianne North Letters to Dr. Burnell, no. 37 (Mar. 20, 1878 but must actually be 1879).

69. Royal Botanic Gardens, Kew, Marianne North Letters to Dr. Burnell, no. 5, (1878).

70. Royal Botanic Gardens, Kew, Marianne North Letters to Dr. Burnell, no. 9 (Jan. 20, 1878).

71. "Wallace's Malay Archipelago," *Anthropological Review* 7 (1869): 315.

72. The United States also had scientific and ideological interests in Brazil, which I have not explored. Louis Agassiz was a professor of natural history at Harvard and one of the best-known naturalists in the United States. His fame rested in part on an expedition he made to the Amazon in 1865. William James went along, as did Agassiz's American wife, Elizabeth Cabot Agassiz. With Louis, Elizabeth Agassiz published a memoir of the trip, *A Journey in Brazil* (1868; rpt. New York: Praeger, 1969), which stimulated North's own interest in going to Brazil.

73. For a range of useful perspectives on Brazil's special colonial history, see *From Colony to Nation: Essays on the Independence of Brazil*, ed. A.J.R. Russell-Wood (Baltimore: The Johns Hopkins Univ. Press, 1975).

74. I cannot see what difference this unusual, and apparently anticolonial, colonial history made in the lives of the indigenous peoples and imported workers and slaves in Brazil. To paraphrase a line W. B. Yeats claimed Parnell had said to a roadworker cheering for home rule, "Ireland shall have her freedom, and you shall still break stones."

75. See, for example, Dale Tomich's compelling analysis of the economy of sugar in *Slavery in the Circuit of Sugar: Martinique and the World Economy, 1830–1848* (Baltimore: Johns Hopkins Univ. Press, 1990); or Thomas Holt's *The Problem of Freedom: Race, Labor, and Politics in Jamaica and Britain, 1832–1938* (Baltimore: Johns Hopkins Univ. Press, 1992).

76. Mary Louise Pratt, *Imperial Eyes*, 146.

77. Lynn L. Merrill, *The Romance of Victorian Natural History*, 55.

78. This is now known as "Batesian mimicry," and other types have since been identified. I am indebted to Michael Rubingh, one of my graduate students at

Miami University, for first pointing out to me, in an unpublished paper entitled "Darwin and the Question of Colonialism" (Fall 1992), the connections between this and Homi Bhabha's theory in "Signs Taken for Wonders: Questions of Ambivalence and Authority under a Tree outside Delhi, May 1817," *Critical Inquiry* 12(Autumn 1985):144–165. In discussing the complexities of mimicry, Rubingh suggested that "Bhabha's theory might benefit from some science" (11).

79. Quoted by Alex Shoumatoff introduction to Henry Walter Bates, *The Naturalist on the River Amazons*, xiii.

80. See, for example, Nicholas Canny's *Kingdom and Colony: Ireland in the Atlantic World, 1560–1800* (Baltimore: Johns Hopkins Univ. Press, 1988).

81. Royal Botanic Gardens, Kew, Marianne North Letters to Dr. Burnell, no. 7 (Jan. 12, 1878).

CHAPTER 5

❧ *The Company as the Country*

1. For an impressive, if sketchy, overview of several European countries' colonial activities in terms of their technological, economic, and aesthetic manifestations in South Asia and the Philippines, see Susantha Goonatilake, *Crippled Minds: An Exploration into Colonial Culture* (New Delhi: Vikas Publishing House, 1982).

2. For a clear, though generalized, account of the basic phases of European aggressions in the regions of Southeast Asia from the sixteenth to the nineteenth centuries, see *In Search of Southeast Asia: A Modern History*, rev. ed., ed. David Joel Steinberg (Honolulu: Univ. of Hawaii Press, 1987). See in particular the useful sketch of French Indochina, pp. 187–192.

3. R. K. Webb, *Modern England From the Eighteenth Century to the Present* (New York: Dodd, Mead, and Co., 1972), 167.

4. Charles Cowan, *Nineteenth-Century Malaya: The Origins of British Political Control* (London: Oxford Univ. Press, 1960), 2.

5. Cyril Northcote Parkinson, *British Intervention in Malaya 1867–1877* (Kuala Lumpur: Univ. of Malaya Press, 1964), xx.

6. Nicholas Tarling, "British Policy in Malayan Waters in the Nineteenth-Century," *Papers on Malayan History*, ed. K. G. Tregonning (Singapore: Univ. of Malaya Press, 1962), 75.

7. Quoted by Francis Watson, *A Concise History of India* (1974; rpt. New York: Thames and Hudson, 1987), 131.

8. Eunice Thio, *British Policy in the Malay Peninsula, 1880–1910*, vol. 1 (Kuala Lumpur: Univ. of Malaya Press, 1969), xvii.

9. Nicholas Tarling, *The Fall of Imperial Britain in South-East Asia* (Singapore: Oxford Univ. Press, 1993), 2.

10. There have been many analyses of the circumstances and events leading to the British takeover of the Malay States. See, for example, Khoo Kay Kim, *The Western Malay States, 1850–1873* (Kuala Lumpur: Oxford Univ. Press, 1974); L. A. Mills, *British Malaya 1834–67* (Kuala Lumpur: Oxford Univ. Press, 1966); and Nicholas Tarling, *British Policy in the Malay Peninsula and Archipelago, 1824–1871* (Kuala Lumpur: Oxford Univ. Press, 1969).

11. *In Search of Southeast Asia*, 143.

12. Nicholas Tarling, "British Policy in Malayan Waters in the Nineteenth Century," 88.

13. William Roff, Introduction to *Stories and Sketches by Sir Frank Swettenham* (Kuala Lumpur: Oxford Univ. Press, 1967), xiv.

14. Cyril Northcote Parkinson, *British Intervention in Malaya*, 269.

15. Robert Heussler, *British Rule in Malaya: The Malayan Civil Service and Its Predecessors, 1867–1942* (Westport, Conn.: Greenwood Press, 1981), 35, 82–83.

16. Frank Swettenham, *Footprints in Malaya* (London: Hutchinson and Co., 1942), 101. Downing Street is not number 10 but number 14, which was the location of the Colonial Office.

17. Frank Swettenham, *British Malaya: An Account of the Origin and Progress of British Influence in Malaya* (1908; rpt. New York: SMS Press, 1975), 221.

18. Frank Swettenham, "British Rule in Malaya," *Honourable Intentions: Talks on the British Empire in South-East Asia Delivered at the Royal Colonial Institute, 1874–1928*, ed. Paul Kratoska (Singapore: Oxford Univ. Press, 1983), 194.

19. "The Malay," *Saturday Review* 80 (Oct. 19, 1895):513.

20. For recent discussions of the particular conventions of the discourse of tourism, see James Buzard, *The Beaten Track: European Tourism, Literature, and the Ways to Culture, 1800–1918* (Oxford: Oxford Univ. Press, 1993) and John Urry, *The Tourist Gaze: Leisure and Travel in Contemporary Societies* (London: Sage Publications, 1990).

21. Sir Frank Athelstane Swettenham, "With a Casting Net," *Malay Sketches* (London: John Lane The Bodley Head), 226.

22. For an impressive study, see Sara Suleri, *The Rhetoric of British India* (Chicago: Univ. of Chicago Press, 1992).

23. Kernial Singh Sandhu, *Indians in Malaya: Some Aspects of Their Immigration and Settlement (1786–1957)* (Cambridge: Cambridge Univ. Press, 1969), 47.

24. A good example of the prevailing attitude up through the 1860s is John Cameron's 1865 book with its telling title *Our Tropical Possessions in Malayan India* (Rpt. Kuala Lumpur: Oxford Univ. Press, 1965).

25. John Turnbull Thomson, *Glimpses into Life in Malayan Lands* (Singapore: Oxford Univ. Press, 1984) first published in 1864 as *Some Glimpses into Life in the Far East*.

26. Swettenham, "British Rule in Malaya," *Honourable Intentions*, 183.

27. Lucile H. Brockway, *Science and Colonial Expansion: The Role of the British Botanical Gardens* (New York: Academic Press, 1979), 101.

28. Isabella Bird, *The Golden Chersonese and the Way Thither* (1883; rpt. London: Century Publishing Co., 1983). All further references are to this edition.

29. The new title Oxford University Press gave its reprint of Anna Forbes's *Insulinde* clearly echos Bird's *Unbeaten Tracks in Japan*.

30. Pat Barr, *A Curious Life for A Lady: The Story of Isabella Bird* (London: Macmillan, 1970), 15.

31. Interview with Roy Lichtenstein, *National Public Radio*, Nov. 10, 1993.

32. Syed Hussein Alatas, *The Myth of the Lazy Native: A Study of the Image of the Malays, Filipinos and Javanese From the 16th to the 20th Century and its Function in the Ideology of Colonial Capitalism* (London: Frank Cass, 1977), 77.

33. There was, of course, a problem in translation. Using the ideology of the British bourgeois nuclear family was ineffectual to motivate Malay people into a docile work force, since for then the "family" signified an entire village living in a longhouse.

34. Quoted by Pat Barr, *A Curious Life for a Lady*, 140.

35. Quoted by Chai Hon-Chan, *The Development of British Malaya, 1896–1909* (Kuala Lumpur: Oxford Univ. Press, 1964), 14. He also notes the similarities between this view and the British perspective on Egypt.

36. Review of *The Golden Chersonese, Spectator*, July 14, 1883, 897.

37. Quoted by Pat Barr, *A Curious Life for a Lady*, 191.

38. Pat Barr, *A Curious Life for a Lady*, 184.

39. *Nation*, June 1883, 516.

40. *Spectator*, July 14 1883, 898; *Athenaeum*, May 12, 1883, 598.

41. This quality was not confined to Bird's writing about the Malay Peninsula. Of her book on traveling in the Rocky Mountains the reviewer in the *Spectator* commented that "although she vouchsafes us no self-drawn portrait, . . . we insensibly derive an idea of her appearance and traits from the impress which these make upon the circumstances of her position." Reading the book, we have "made a charming acquaintance." *Spectator*, Nov. 8, 1879, 1414.

42. Anna M. Stoddart, in *The Life of Isabella Bird (Mrs. Bishop), Hon. Member of the Oriental Society of Pekin, F.R.G.S., F.R.S.G.S.* (London: John Murray, 1907), continually plays with the possible double character of her subject. Pat Barr, in a book the title of which reflects this apparently inexplicable opposition between the two personalities of Bird, begins *A Curious Life for a Lady* with a play on her subject's two names: the Bird who flies and the stolid Bishop.

43. Bird finished the book in February 1883, according to Anna Stoddart (*The Life of Isabella Bird*, 160).

44. Emily Innes, *The Chersonese with the Gilding Off*, 2 vols. (1885; rpt. Kuala Lumpur: Oxford Univ. Press, 1974). All further references are to this edition.

45. John G. Butcher, *The British in Malaya 1880–1941: The Social History of a European Community in Colonial South-East Asia* (Kuala Lumpur: Oxford Univ. Press, 1979), 57.

46. John M. Gullick, "Captain Speedy of Larut," *Journal of the Malaysian Branch of the Royal Asiatic Society* 26 (1953):1–103.

47. *Athenaeum*, Dec. 12, 1885, 764.

48. *Asiatic Quarterly Review* 1 (Jan.–Apr. 1886):253.

49. Mrs. Douglas Cator's "Some Experiences of Colonial Life" is reproduced in *Honourable Intentions*, 288–299.

50. Pat Barr, *A Curious Life for a Lady*, 136–137.

51. Robert Heussler, *British Rule in Malaya: The Malayan Civil Service and Its Predecessors, 1867–1942*, 55, 9.

52. Ibid., 67.

53. Referred to in a compelling article by Lim Teck Ghee, "The Two Faces of the Chersonese," *Peninjau Sejarah: Journal of the History Teachers' Association of Malaya* 2, 1(Apr. 1967):32.

54. Khoo Kay Kim, Introduction to *The Chersonese With the Gilding Off*, by Emily Innes (Kuala Lumpur: Oxford Univ. Press, 1974), v.

55. For a modern representation of what it might be like to be a government servant's wife, see the chapter on "Diplomatic Wives" in Cynthia Enloe's *Bananas, Beaches and Bases: Making Feminist Sense of International Politics* (Berkeley: Univ. of California Press, 1990), 93–123.

CHAPTER 6

⚹ *"One's Own State"*

1. L. R. Wright, *The Origins of British Borneo* (Hong Kong: Hong Kong Univ. Press, 1970), 1.

2. For a thorough discussion of the problematics of this term, see Robert Pringle's *Rajahs and Rebels: The Ibans of Sarawak under Brooke Rule, 1841–1941* (Ithaca: Cornell Univ. Press, 1970).

3. Nicholas Tarling, *The Burthen, the Risk, and the Glory: A Biography of Sir James Brooke* (Kuala Lumpur: Oxford Univ. Press, 1982), 57–58.

4. Ibid., 125.

5. I am indebted throughout my discussion of British relations to the northwest part of Borneo to D. S. Ranjit Singh, *Brunei 1839–1983: The Problems of Political Survival* (Singapore: Oxford Univ. Press, 1984); Nicholas Tarling, *Britain, the Brookes and Brunei* (Kuala Lumpur: Oxford Univ. Press, 1971); and L. R. Wright, *The Origins of British Borneo.*

6. See James Pope-Hennessey, *Verandah: Some Episodes in the Crown Colonies, 1867–1889* (1964; rpt. London: Century Publishing, 1984), 57–109.

7. See the chapter on "Britain and North Borneo" in L. R. Wright, *The Origins of British Borneo*, 126–173.

8. The process of establishing the North Borneo Company indicates how smart businessmen could get an initially uninterested British (or other European) government to become interested in backing the establishment of businesses in regions of Southeast Asia by the process of negotiating with other governments to back the business or by taking on private investor/partners of another nationality.

9. Nicholas Tarling, *The Burthen, the Risk, and the Glory*, 125–131.

10. See particularly Nicholas Tarling's detailed analysis of the history of relations between the Brookes and the British government on the subject of the status of Sarawak, in *Britain, the Brookes and Brunei.*

11. Quoted by Nicholas Tarling, *Britain, the Brookes and Brunei*, 56. Naval ships did help Brooke—sometimes simply by their presence and sometimes in actual battles—much more extensively than their orders allowed.

12. Quoted from Lord Derby by Emily Hahn, *James Brooke of Sarawak: A Biography of Sir James Brooke* (London: Arthur Barker, 1953), 231–232.

13. Colin N. Crisswell, *Rajah Charles Brooke: Monarch of All He Surveyed* (Kuala Lumpur: Oxford Univ. Press, 1978), 57.

14. Quoted by Nicholas Tarling, *Britain, the Brookes and Brunei*, 101.

15. L. R. Wright, *The Origins of British Borneo*, 202.

16. This information is provided by Ulla Wagner in her excellent account of Brooke rule, *Colonialism and Iban Warfare* (Stockholm: OBE-Tryck, 1972), 36.

17. Robert Pringle, *Rajahs and Rebels*, 120. I am indebted to Pringle's discussion of this incident (97–134).

18. Ibid., 123.

19. See the discussion by Margaret Brooke, the ranee of Sarawak, *Good Morning and Good Night* (1934; rpt. London: Century Publishing, 1984), 243. All further references are to this edition.

20. *Outlines of Sarawak History under the Brooke Rajahs 1839–1946*, com. A. B. Ward and D. C. White (Kuching: Sarawak Government Printing Office, 1957), 14.

21. Nicholas Tarling, *Britain, the Brookes and Brunei*, 181.

22. Sylvia Brooke, *Queen of the Head-hunters: the Autobiography of H.H. the Hon. Sylvia, Lady Brooke, the Ranee of Sarawak* (1970; rpt. Singapore: Oxford Univ. Press, 1990), 171.

23. See *Rajah Brooke and Baroness Burdett Coutts, Consisting of the Letters from Sir James Brooke, First White Rajah of Sarawak, to Miss Angela (afterwards Baroness) Burdett Coutts*, ed. Owen Rutter (London: Hutchinson and Co., 1935).

24. Hugh Low, *Sarawak, Its Inhabitants and Productions: Being Notes during a Residence in That Country with His Excellency Mr. Brooke* (1848; rpt. London: Frank Cass, 1968).

25. S. Baring-Gould and C. A. Bampfylde, *A History of Sarawak under Its Two White Rajahs 1839–1908* (London: Henry Sotheran and Co., 1909).

26. Robert Pringle, *Rajahs and Rebels*, 66. Daniel Chew, in *Chinese Pioneers on the Sarawak Frontier 1841–1941* (Singapore: Oxford Univ. Press, 1991), has pointed out that Pringle in *Rajahs and Rebels*, along with Craig Lockard in *From Kampung to City: A Social History of Kuching, Malaysia, 1820–1970*, Monographs in International Studies, Southeast Asia Series, no. 75 (Athens, Ohio: Ohio Univ. Center for International Studies, 1987), "were among the first historians to write historiographically on Sarawak from 'Asiancentric' standpoints" (ix).

27. Thomas Richards, *The Imperial Archive: Knowledge and the Fantasy of Empire* (London: Verso, 1993), 29.

28. Robert Pringle, *Rajahs and Rebels*, 97.

29. Quoted by R.H.W. Reece, *The Name of Brooke: The End of White Rajah Rule in Sarawak* (Kuala Lumpur: Oxford Univ. Press, 1982), 7.

30. R.H.W. Reece, *The Name of Brooke*, xxv. The "court historians" would include C. A. Bampfylde, S. Baring-Gould, and Colin Crisswell. Also there is Spenser St. John, *The Life of Sir James Brooke, Rajah of Sarawak, from His Personal Papers and Correspondence* (Edinburgh: W. Blackwood and Sons, 1879). Two recent versions of this enduring and always increasing group are Robert Payne, *The White Rajahs of Sarawak* (1960; rpt Singapore: Oxford Univ. Press, 1986), and Joan Lo, *Glimpses from Sarawak's Past* (Kuching, Sarawak: AGAS (S) SDN BHD, 1986).

31. Harriette McDougall, *Letters from Sarawak; Addressed to a Child* (Norwich: Thomas Priest, 1854), v. Further references are to this edition.

32. Robert Payne, *The White Rajahs of Sarawak*, 14–15.

33. R.H.W. Reece, *The Name of Brooke*, xxv.

34. Review of *Memoirs of Francis Thomas McDougall, D.C.L., F.R.C.S., Sometime Bishop of Labuan and Sarawak, and of Harriette His Wife, Athenaeum*, Dec. 28, 1889, 886.

35. Joseph Conrad, *Lord Jim* (1899; rpt. New York: New American Library, 1961), 307.

36. R.H.W. Reece, *The Name of Brooke*, xxv.

37. Benedict Anderson, *Imagined Communities: Reflections on the Origin and Spread of Nationalism* (London: Verso, 1991).

38. Frank Swettenham, Preface to *My Life in Sarawak* by Margaret Brooke, (1913; rpt. Singapore: Oxford Univ. Press, 1986), xi. All further references to this text are to this edition.

39. Chris Bongie, *Exotic Memories: Literature, Colonialism and the Fin de Siècle* (Stanford: Stanford Univ. Press, 1991), 5.

40. Ulla Wagner, *Colonialism and Iban Warfare*, 42.

41. Homi Bhabha, "Signs Taken for Wonders: Questions of Ambivalence and Authority under a Tree outside Delhi, May 1817," *Critical Inquiry* 12(Autumn 1985):144–165.

42. Steven Runciman, *The White Rajahs: A History of Sarawak From 1842 to 1946* (Cambridge: Cambridge Univ. Press, 1960), 156.

43. R.H.W. Reece, "Colin N. Crisswell, *Rajah Charles Brooke: Monarch of All He Surveyed*," *Borneo Research Bulletin* 13, 1(Apr. 1981):60.

44. Steven Runciman, *The White Rajahs*, 220.

45. A. B. Ward, *Rajah's Servant* (Ithaca: Data Paper no. 61, Southeast Asia Program, Cornell Univ., 1966), 41.

46. Robert Payne, *The White Rajahs of Sarawak*, 119.

47. Robert Pringle, *Rajahs and Rebels*, 101.

48. Hugh Low, *Sarawak, Its Inhabitants and Productions*, 107–108.

49. L. R. Wright, *The Origins of British Borneo*, 202.

50. For a fascinating discussion of how specific negative qualities of Malays were constructed to fit specific colonial needs, see Syed Hussein Alatas, *The Myth of the Lazy Native; A Study of the Image of the Malays, Filipinos and Javanese from the 16th to the 20th Century and Its Function in the Ideology of Colonial Capitalism* (London: Frank Cass, 1977).

51. Brooke uses the phrase in a letter discussing how to deal with the king of Siam, which is quoted by Nicholas Tarling, *The Burthen, the Risk, and the Glory*, 132.

52. A modern version of this rhetoric appeared during the Gulf War in the extensive newspaper accounts self-described as background biography which were actually elaborate propaganda: extraordinarily sentimental hymns to the brave and heroic character of the leader of the American forces, General Schwartzkopf.

53. Hugh Low, *Sarawak, Its Inhabitants and Productions*, 111.

54. Yet James Brooke, I was sad to learn, deeply admired Austen's novels. See Ann Tagge, "Jane Austen and the Rajah of Sarawak," *Persuasions* 15(Dec. 1993):30–31.

55. Given James Brooke's bachelor status, speculations about his sexuality abound in the commentaries on Brooke rule. A good example is Robert H. W. Reece's surmise: "the circumstantial evidence points to the possibility that Brooke was homosexual, at least latently so." "European-Indigenous Miscegenation and Social Status in Nineteenth-Century Borneo," *Female and Male in Borneo: Contributions and Challenges to Gender Studies*, ed. Vinson H. Sutlive, Borneo Research Council Monograph Series, vol. 1 (Williamsburg, Va.: Borneo Research Council, College of William and Mary, 1991), 457.

56. Joseph Conrad, *Heart of Darkness, Three Novels by Joseph Conrad* (New York: Washington Square Press, 1970), 158.

57. It is plausible to guess that the decision to make this trip reflected Charles's

sense that since he had gotten an heir (one of the twins being a boy), he could now get rid of Margaret.

58. Sylvia Brooke, *Queen of the Head-hunters*, 28.

59. Ibid.

60. Margaret Brooke, *My Life in Sarawak*, 11.

61. Emily Hahn, *James Brooke of Sarawak: A Biography of Sir James Brooke* (London: Arthur Barker, 1953), 224.

62. Sylvia Brooke, *Queen of the Head-hunters*, 85.

63. Joan Lo, *Glimpses of Sarawak's Past*, 73.

64. Sylvia Brooke, *Queen of the Head-hunters*, 81.

65. Sylvia Brooke, *Lost Property* (London: E. Nash and Grayson, 1930).

66. For the details of this widespread phenomenon, see R.H.W. Reece, "A 'Suitable Population': Charles Brooke and Race-Mixing in Sarawak," *Itinerario* 9, 1(1985):67–112.

67. R.H.W. Reece, "Colin N. Crisswell, *Rajah Charles Brooke: Monarch of All He Surveyed*," 61.

68. R.H.W. Reece, "A 'Suitable Population,'" 83.

69. Quoted by Robert Payne, *The White Rajahs of Sarawak*, 138.

70. Sylvia Brooke, *The Three White Rajahs* (London: Cassell and Company, 1939), 73–74.

. 71. R.H.W. Reece, "Colin N. Crisswell, *Rajah Charles Brooke: Monarch of All He Surveyed*," 61. Isaka Brooke moved as an adult to Canada. It is plausible that part of Sylvia Brooke's inspiration for writing *Lost Property* was the biographic history of Isaka.

72. R.H.W. Reece, "A 'Suitable Population,'" 101.

73. Renato Rosaldo, "Imperialist Nostalgia," *Representations* 26 (Spring 1989):107–122.

74. For an extensive discussion of the fate of Sarawak as a private colony during the twentieth century and of the complex and evolving financial arrangements made for the Brooke family, see R.H.W. Reece, *The Name of Brooke*.

75. R.H.W. Reece and A.J.M. Saint, Introduction to *Sketches of Our Life at Sarawak*, by Harriette McDougall (Singapore: Oxford University Press, 1992), vi–vii. All further references to *Sketches* are to this edition.

76. Both of these events have been the material for revised histories told from Malay and Chinese perspectives. See Robert Pringle's *Rajahs and Rebels*, 97–134. Daniel Chew, *Chinese Pioneers on the Sarawak Frontier*, 18–49; John M. Chin, *The Sarawak Chinese* (Kuala Lumpur: Oxford Univ. Press, 1981), 22–39; and Paul Yong, *A Dream of Freedom: The Early Sarawak Chinese* (Petaling Jaya: Pelanduk Publications, 1991).

77. A rare exception for me is at least some of an account by the daughter of missionaries, Olive Jennie Bixby's *My Child-Life in Burmah; or, Recollections and Incidents* (Boston: W. G. Corthell, 1880).

78. See R.H.W. Reece and A.J.M. Saint, Introduction to *Sketches of Our Life at Sarawak*, by Harriette McDougall.

79. Paul Yong, *A Dream of Freedom*, 100.

80. Quoted by Daniel Chew, *Chinese Pioneers*, 38.

81. Charles John Bunyon, *Memoirs of Francis Thomas McDougall, D.C.L., F.R.S.,*

Sometime Bishop of Labuan and Sarawak, and of Harriette His Wife (London: Longmans, Green, and Co., 1889), 228.

CHAPTER 7

🜳 *Anna Leonowens*

1. See the case histories recounted by Pasuk Phongpaichit in *From Peasant Girls to Bangkok Masseuses* (Geneva: International Labour Office,1982).

2. *Bangkok Post*, Feb. 1, 1984, 1. For some details of the fire and the sex industry, see the fifth chapter of Yayori Matsui, *Women's Asia*, trans. Mizuko Matsuda (London: Zed Books, 1987).

3. *Bangkok Post*, Feb. 9, 1984, 3.

4. *Bangkok Post*, Feb. 3, 1984, 5.

5. For an extended look at the connections between the sex trade and tourism see Thanh-Dam Truong, *Sex, Money and Morality: Prostitution and Tourism in Southeast Asia* (London: Zed Books, 1990), particularly the sections focusing on Thailand, 131–191.

6. See Pasuk Phongpaichit, "Bangkok Masseuses: Tourism—Selling Southeast Asia," *Southeast Asian Chronicle* 78(Apr. 1981):15–16.

7. According to Linda K. Richter, "the country's two largest sources of traffic [are] Japan and Malaysia, totalling a 29 percent share in 1981." "Thailand: Where Tourism and Politics Make Strange Bedfellows," *The Politics of Tourism in Asia* (Honolulu: Univ. of Hawaii Press, 1989), 86.

8. See Steven Erlanger, "A Plague Awaits," *New York Times*, July 14, 1991, sec. 6, 24–26, 49, 53.

9. Edward W. Said offers an analysis of this sexual component of the "Orient" as it is conceived of in European orientalism, in *Orientalism* (1978; New York: Random House, 1979), 186–190 and throughout.

10. See Santi Mingmongkol, "Official Blessings for the 'Brothel of Asia,'" *Southeast Asia Chronicle* 78(1981):24–25.

11. Thanh-Dam Truong, *Sex, Money and Morality*, 179.

12. See, for example, Erik Cohen, "Thai Girls and Farang Men: The Edge of Ambiguity," *Annals of Tourism Research* 9(1982):403–428.

13. Thanh-Dam Truong, *Sex, Money and Morality*, 178.

14. Steven Erlanger, "A Plague Awaits," 26.

15. Pasuk Phongpaichit made a similar point in "Bangkok Masseuses: Tourism—Selling Southeast Asia," 17.

16. Khin Thitsa, *Providence and Prostitution: Image and Reality for Women in Buddhist Thailand* (London: International Reports: Women and Society, n.d.), 16.

17. I am indebted throughout this discussion to David K. Wyatt's now-classic study, *Thailand: A Short History* (New Haven: Yale Univ. Press, 1982).

18. For a more detailed discussion of the legal curtailment of women's rights in 1805, see Thanh-Dam Truong, *Sex, Money and Morality*, 141–149.

19. Khin Thitsa, *Providence and Prostitution*, 5.

20. There was a "minor" wife, a second wife who did not herself have the legal status of a first wife but who was distinguished in that her children did have full legal status as their father's children.

21. *Records of the United States Consul in Bangkok, 1856–1865*, (Washington: National Archives and Records Service, 1960).

22. There were, certainly, forces in France which pushed for the takeover of more territory in the South Seas region. Ludovic Hébert, Marquis of Beauvoir, offered a brief plea for the French takeover of Siam in his highly popular *A Week in Siam 1867*. This was an extract from the English translation of *Voyage Autour du Monde* (1870; rpt. Bangkok: Siam Society, 1986).

23. Among many accounts of this treaty, see Nicholas Tarling, "The Independence of Siam," *The Cambridge History of Southeast Asia*, vol. 2, *The Nineteenth and Twentieth Centuries*, ed. Nicholas Tarling (Cambridge: Cambridge Univ. Press, 1992), 46–53.

24. David Wyatt, *Thailand: A Short History*, 185.

25. For many details of the legal position of the British in Siam, see W.A.R. Wood, *Consul in Paradise: Sixty-Nine Years in Siam* (1965; rpt. Bangkok: Trasvin Publications, 1991).

26. For a superbly detailed analysis of the historical process of Siam's developing definitions of its territories and, therefore, of its nationhood, see Thongchai Winichakul, *Siam Mapped: A History of the Geo-Body of a Nation* (Honolulu: Univ. of Hawaii Press, 1994). Yet even this outstanding study does not consider the role of women in the territorial shaping of Thailand as a nation.

27. Britain did not take Upper Burma until 1885, when the French also completed their conquest of northern Vietnam. The French took over what had been Siamese Laos in the 1890s.

28. These are some lines from Mongkut's letter of March 4, 1867 to the head of his embassy to Paris, analyzing Siam's position. Abbot Low Moffat, *Mongkut, the King of Siam* (Ithaca, Cronell Univ. Press, 1961), 119, 121.

29. Abbot Low Moffat, *Mongkut, the King of Siam*, ix; and David Wyatt, *Thailand: A Short History*, 188.

30. For a fascinating Siamese account of a Siamese embassy to England in 1857, see M. L. Manich Jumsai, *King Mongkut of Thailand and the British (The Model of a Great Friendship)* (Bangkok: Chalermit, 1991).

31. Cynthia Enloe, *Bananas, Beaches and Bases: Making Feminist Sense of International Politics* (1989; rpt. Berkeley: Univ. of California Press, 1990).

32. Among the many reasons apart from the harem that helped Siam keep its independence, I would number the kind of extensive ethnic and business connections among a partly assimilated (and thus partly Thai) overseas Chinese family in Siam traced by Jennifer Cushman in her fascinating study, *Family and State: The Formation of a Sino-Thai Tin-Mining Dynasty 1797–1932* (Singapore: Oxford Univ. Press, 1991). It is important to remember what a dubious term the word "harem" is in the English language.

33. Walter F. Vella, *The Impact of the West on Government in Thailand* (Berkeley: Univ. of California Press, 1955), 330.

34. The king understood English aggressions in part because he could read their newspapers in Singapore and Hong Kong. Since the English, of course, spoke no Thai, without knowing their language he could not even have read documents, such as the Bowring Treaty, that he had to sign.

35. David Wyatt, *Thailand: A Short History*, 181.

36. An account of the gradual breakup of the royal harem after Chulalongkorn's death is offered by Ruth Adams Knight in *The Treasured One: The Story of Rudivoravan, Princess of Siam*, as told to Ruth Adams Knight (New York: E. P. Dutton, 1957). According to the princess, when Chulalongkorn's son became king, "it became known" that those of his "father's feminine household" who "had relatives would be allowed to leave and go home to them, if they made formal request to do so" (41). An important implication of this account is that before and during Chulalongkorn's reign the "feminine household" was not "allowed to leave."

37. See Leila Ahmed's critique in "Western Ethnocentrism and Perceptions of the Harem," *Feminist Studies* 8, 3(Fall 1982):521—534. See also Billie Melman's *Women's Orients: English Women and the Middle East, 1718—1918: Sexuality, Religion and Work* (Ann Arbor: Univ. of Michigan Press, 1992), particularly part 2, 59—162.

38. See the visual representations collected in Malek Alloula's *The Colonial Harem*, trans. Myrna Godzich and Wlad Godzich (Minneapolis: Univ. of Minnesota Press, 1986). See also Irvin Cemil Schick, "Representing Middle Eastern Women: Feminism and Colonial Discourse," *Feminist Studies* 16, 2(Summer 1990):345—380; and Emily Apter, "Female Trouble in the Colonial Harem," *Differences: A Journal of Feminist Cultural Studies* 4, 1(1992):205—224.

39. Anna Leonowens, *The Romance of the Harem*, ed. Susan Morgan (Charlottesville: Univ. Press of Virginia, 1991), 13. All further references are to this edition.

40. See William L. Bradley's account in *Siam Then: The Foreign Colony in Bangkok before and after Anna* (Pasadena: William Carey Library, 1981), 101—104.

41. W. S. Bristowe, *Louis and the King of Siam* (New York: Thai-American Publishers, 1976), 22.

42. Ibid.

43. William Bradley, *Siam Then*, 103.

44. "Anna Unveiled," *Louis and the King of Siam*, 23—31.

45. The full inscription reads: "Sacred to the Memory of Thomas Leonowens, Who Departed This Life on the 8th of May, 1859, Aged 31 years and 5 days, Lord Have Mercy."

46. Anna Leonowens, *Life and Travel in India: Being Recollections of a Journey before the Days of Railroads* (Philadelphia: Porter and Coates, 1884).

47. This is from a letter to the India Office, protesting their discriminatory policies. It is quoted by Bristowe in *Louis and the King of Siam*, 29.

48. W. S. Bristowe, *Louis and the King of Siam*, 30.

49. The American missionaries in Bangkok certainly opposed polygamy and harems on religious grounds.

50. Leonowens's whereabouts during the 1870s can be partially tracked by her correspondence with Annie Fields, which is now part of the Fields Collection in the Huntington Library, San Marino, California.

51. Both of Leonowens's books on her time in Siam denounce slavery. The second book, with its focus on the women in the royal harem rather than on many aspects of Siamese life, denounces their slavery in detail.

52. Slavery was a frequent topic in the English-language newspapers in Singapore and Bangkok in the 1860s, the *Singapore Straits Times* and *Bangkok Recorder*.

53. Jill Castleman points out that Yul Brynner even went on to re-create the role of King Mongkut in a short-lived television series, *Anna and the King*, in 1972, and at least once more on Broadway. "For most people, Yul Brynner *is* the King of Siam." "The Making of a Myth: Anna Leonowens and Thailand" (Undergraduate paper, Cornell University, 1985).

54. For a fascinating discussion of "Western cinema's geographical and historical constructs as symptomatic of the colonialist imaginary generally but also more specifically as a product of a gendered Western gaze," see Ella Shohat, "Gender and the Culture of Empire: Toward a Feminist Ethnography of the Cinema," *Quarterly Review of Film & Video* 13, 1–3(1991):45–84.

55. Chula Chakrabongse, prince of Thailand, *Lords of Life: The Paternal Monarchy of Bangkok, 1872–1932*, (London: Alvin Redman, 1960), 209.

56. The phrase is from Valerie Amos and Pratibha Parmar, "Challenging Imperial Feminism," *Feminist Review* 17 (July 1984):3–19.

57. Trubner responded by a notice in the March 15, 1873 issue of the *Athenaeum* that the publishing company had received the two photographers' permission to reproduce their work as the illustrations.

58. As David Wyatt pointed out to me in conversation, the ruins were hardly "lost." The Thais and Cambodians knew all about them. But "westerners" had not heard of them.

59. Reported in the *New York Times*, Aug. 8, 1970, 25.

60. A. B. Griswold, *King Mongkut of Siam* (New York: Asia Society, 1961), 3.

61. W. S. Bristowe, *Louis and the King of Siam*, 27.

62. This remark appears in Malcolm Smith's memoirs of his time in Siam during Chulalongkorn's reign, *A Physician at the Court of Siam* (1957; rpt. Kuala Lumpur: Oxford Univ. Press, 1982), 142. Smith's next sentence assures his possibly envious readers, clearly male, that sex for Siamese men "between the ages of 18 and 40 . . . is the overmastering passion of their lives, with the result that many of them, by the time they have reached the middle forties, if not already impotent, are well on the road to being so." Mongkut, of course, fathered his eighty-two children well after his "middle forties."

63. *The English Governess at the Siamese Court: Being Recollections of Six Years at the Royal Palace in Bangkok* (Boston: 1870; rpt. Singapore: Oxford Univ. Press, 1988), 103. Further references are to this edition.

64. Quoted by A. B. Griswold, *King Mongkut of Siam*, 35.

65. Marianne North would probably have agreed.

66. A. B. Griswold, *King Mongkut of Siam*, 35.

67. Ibid., 49.

68. The report, cryptic and tantalizing, was that on June 29 "a young Siamese Nobleman was executed for the crime of seeking to win one of the 1st King's Concubines for a wife. The wife of the man was also executed for having abetted him in his designs." *Bangkok Calendar* (Bangkok: American Missionary Association, 1860), 50.

69. A. B. Griswold, *King Mongkut of Siam*, 45.

70. Malcolm Smith, *A Physician at the Court of Siam*, 145, 143.

71. Ibid., 145.

72. Gayatri Spivak's classic essays on this topic are "Three Women's Texts and a Critique of Imperialism," *Critical Inquiry* 12 (Autumn 1985):243–261; and "Can the Subaltern Speak? Speculations on Widow Sacrifice," *Marxism and the Interpretation of Culture*, ed. Cary Nelson and Lawrence Grossberg (Urbana: Univ. of Illinois Press, 1988), 271–313.

73. Valerie Amos and Pratibha Parmar, "Challenging Imperial Feminism," 8.

74. See the discussion of Valerie Amos and Pratibha Parmar, in "Challenging Imperial Feminism," p. 15. Their point is that "it is not up to them to accept or reject . . . but up to us to challenge, accept, or reform, depending on our various perspectives, on our own terms and in our own culturally specific ways."

75. Vron Ware, *Beyond the Pale: White Women, Racism and History* (London: Verso, 1992), 147.

76. For a detailed study, see Myna Trustram's excellent *Women of the Regiment: Marriage and the Victorian Army* (Cambridge: Cambridge Univ. Press, 1984).

77. The tale of Boon may well have been inspired by the incident recorded in the 1860 *Bangkok Calendar*. Like much of the rest of the book, it is probably grounded in actual events—but does not stay on the ground.

78. It is notable that Anna's servants are a couple and the man soon leaves Bangkok, but the woman stays. Thus, Anna's household, like the harem, is composed only of women and children (in this case only one). On the one hand, there is no question of the hegemonic structure of this three-member household. On the other, it is represented as a loving family (a familiar enough dynamic).

79. The primary function of the preface is to assert that the "occurrences related in the following pages" are true.

80. As Leonowens has Lady Thieng explicitly remark to Anna in the narrative, "You are a foreigner, he has not the same power over you, and you can go away whenever you like" (159).

CHAPTER 8

⚘ *Looking Behind and Ahead*

1. Ian Morson, *The Connection Phuket, Penang and Adelaide: A Short Account of Francis Light* (Bangkok: Siam Society, 1993).

2. K'tut Tantri, *Revolt in Paradise* (1960; rpt. New York: Clarkson N. Potter, 1960).

3. See the article by David Rieff, "Multiculturalism's Silent Partner: It's the Newly Globalized Consumer Economy, Stupid," *Harper's*, Aug. 1993, 62–72.

4. See Lawrence Wright, "One Drop of Blood," *New Yorker* (Aug. 25, 1994), 55. I am indebted to Heidi Slatkin for bringing this article to my attention.

5. I am indebted for the phrase "map the mappings" to my colleague, Laura Mandell.

6. Syed Hussein Alatas, *Thomas Stamford Raffles 1781–1826: Schemer or Reformer?* (Sydney: Angus and Robertson, 1971), 43.

7. Ketu Katrak has stressed the social responsibility of critics/theorists and asked the key question, "How can we, within a dominant Eurocentric discourse, make our study of postcolonial texts itself a mode of resistance?" "Decolonizing

Culture: Toward a Theory for Postcolonial Women's Texts," *Modern Fiction Studies* 35, 1(Spring 1989):158. Katrak's insights are not immediately portable, because the materials she considers are postcolonial rather than colonial texts.

8. Edward Said, "Orientalism Reconsidered," *Cultural Critique* 1 (Fall 1985):107.

9. Paul Gilroy, *The Black Atlantic: Modernity and Double Consciousness* (Cambridge: Harvard Univ. Press, 1993), 5.

10. David Spurr, *The Rhetoric of Empire: Colonial Discourse in Journalism, Travel Writing, and Imperial Administration* (Durham, N. C.: Duke Univ. Press, 1993), 189.

11. Ibid., 193.

12. Paul Gilroy, *The Black Atlantic*, xi.

13. David Spurr, *The Rhetoric of Empire*, 201.

14. See Caren Kaplan's thoughtful essay, "Deterritorializations: The Rewriting of Home and Exile in Western Feminist Discourse," *Cultural Critique* 6(Spring 1987):187–198.

15. Donna Haraway, "Situated Knowledges: The Scientific Question in Feminism and the Privilege of Partial Perspective," *Feminist Studies* 14, 3(Fall 1988):583. I am indebted to Mary Jean Corbett for telling me about this article.

16. This wonderful phrase is, of course, from Adrienne Rich's "Notes toward a Politics of Location (1984)," *Blood, Bread, and Poetry: Selected Prose 1979–1985* (New York: Norton, 1986).

✺ Selected Bibliography ✺

Abdullah Bin Abdul Kadir. *The Hikayat Abdullah.* 1849. Trans. A. H. Hill. Kuala Lumpur: Oxford Univ. Press, 1970.

Acts and Ordinances of the Legislative Council of the Straits Settlements, from the 1st April 1867 to the 7th March 1898. 2 vols. London: Eyre and Spottiswoode, 1898.

Adam, Ian, and Helen Tiffin, eds. *Past the Last Post: Theorizing Post-Colonialism and Post-Modernism.* Calgary: Univ. of Calgary Press, 1990.

Agassiz, Elizabeth Cabot, and Louis Agassiz. *A Journey in Brazil.* 1868. Rpt. New York: Praeger, 1969.

Ahmed, Leila. "Western Ethnocentrism and Perceptions of the Harem." *Feminist Studies* 8, 3(Fall 1982):521–534.

Alatas, Syed Hussein. *The Myth of the Lazy Native: A Study of the Image of the Malays, Filipinos and Javanese from the 16th to the 20th Century and Its Function in the Ideology of Colonial Capitalism.* London: Frank Cass, 1977.

———. *Thomas Stamford Raffles, 1781–1826: Schemer or Reformer?* Sydney: Angus and Robertson, 1971.

Alavi, Hamza, P. L. Burns, G. R. Knight, P. B. Mayer, and Doug McEachern. *Capitalism and Colonial Production.* London: Croon Helm, 1982.

Allan, Mea. *The Hookers of Kew, 1785–1911.* London: Michael Joseph, 1967.

Allen, Charles, ed. *Tales from the South China Seas: Images of the British in South-east Asia in the Twentieth Century.* London: André Deutsch, British Broadcasting Corporation, 1983.

Alloula, Malek. *The Colonial Harem.* Trans. Myrna Godzich and Wlad Godzich. Minneapolis: Univ. of Minnesota Press, 1986.

Althusser, Louis. "Ideology and Ideological State Apparatuses (Notes towards an Investigation)." *Lenin and Philosophy and Other Essays.* Trans. Ben Brewster. New York: Monthly Review Press, 1971. 127–186.

Amherst, the Hon. Alicia. *A History of Gardening in England.* London: Bernard Quaritch, 1895.

Amin, Mohamed, and Malcolm Caldwell, eds. *Malaya: The Making of a Neo-Colony.* Nottingham: Bertrand Russell Peace Foundation, 1977.

Amos, Valerie, and Parmar Pratibha. "Challenging Imperial Feminism." *Feminist Review* 17(July 1984):3–19.

Andaya, Barbara Watson, and Leonard Y. Andaya. *A History of Malaysia.* New York: St. Martin's Press, 1982.

Anderson, Benedict. *Imagined Communities: Reflections on the Origin and Spread of Nationalism.* Rev. ed. London: Verso, 1991.

————. *Java in a Time of Revolution: Occupation and Resistance, 1944–46*. Ithaca: Cornell Univ. Press, 1972.

————. *Language and Power: Exploring Political Cultures in Indonesia*. Ithaca: Cornell Univ. Press, 1990.

Anderson, Benedict, and Ruchira Mendiones, eds. and trans. *In the Mirror: Literature and Politics in Siam in the American Era*. Bangkok: Editions Duang Kamoi, Suk Soongsawang, 1985.

Anthropological Review. Review of *The Malay Archipelago*, by Alfred Russel Wallace. 7(1869):310–320.

Apter, Emily. "Female Trouble in the Colonial Harem." *Differences: A Journal of Feminist Cultural Studies* 4,1(1992):205–224.

Arac, Jonathan, and Harriet Ritvo, eds. *Macropolitics of Nineteenth-Century Literature: Nationalism, Exoticism, Imperialism*. Philadelphia: Univ. of Pennsylvania Press, 1991.

Armstrong, Nancy. *Desire and Domestic Fiction: A Political History of the Novel*. New York: Oxford Univ. Press, 1987.

Arnold, David. *Colonizing the Body: State Medicine and Epidemic Disease in Nineteenth-Century India*. Berkeley: Univ. of California Press, 1993.

Asiatic Quarterly Review. Review of *The Chersonese with the Gilding Off*, by Emily Innes. 1(1886):252–253.

————. Review of *Journeys in Persia and Kurdistan*, by Isabella Bird. 3(1892):500–501.

Athenaeum. Review of *The English Governess at the Siamese Court*, by Anna Leonowens. Dec. 24, 1870,236.

————. Review of *The Romance of Siamese Harem Life*, by Anna Leonowens. Feb. 15, 1873,205–207.

————. Notice about *The Romance of Siamese Harem Life*, Anna Leonowens. Mar. 15, 1873,344.

————. Review of *The Golden Chersonese and the Way Thither*, by Isabella Bird. May 12, 1883,597–599.

————. Review of *The Chersonese with the Gilding Off*, by Emily Innes. Dec. 12, 1885,763–764.

————. Review of *Memoirs of Francis Thomas McDougall, D.C.L., F.R.C.S., Sometime Bishop of Labuan and Sarawak, and of Harriette His Wife*, by Charles John Bunyon. Dec. 28, 1889,886–887.

————. Obituary of Marianne North. Sept. 6, 1890,319.

————. Review of *Recollections of a Happy Life: Being the Autobiography of Marianne North*. Feb. 27, 1892,269–270.

————. Review of *Some Further Recollections of a Happy Life*, by Marianne North. June 17, 1893,755–756.

Atkins, Anna. *Sun Gardens: Victorian Photographs*. Text by Larry J. Schaaf. New York: Aperture, 1985.

Atkinson, Jane Monnig, and Shelly Errington, eds. *Power and Difference: Gender in Island Southeast Asia*. Stanford: Stanford Univ. Press, 1990.

Atlantic Monthly. Review of *The English Governess at the Siamese Court*, by Anna Leonowens. 25(Apr., May, June 1870) 396, 554, 730.

————. Review of *The Romance of the Harem*, by Anna Leonowens. 26(1873):144.

"Back to Bali." *Times Literary Supplement*, Dec. 30, 1960,839.

Bailey, Susan F. *Women and the British Empire: An Annotated Guide to Sources*. New York: Garland, 1983.

Ballhatchet, C. *Race, Sex and Class under the Raj: Imperial Attitudes and Policies and Their Critics, 1793–1905.* New York: St. Martin's Press, 1980.

Barber, Lynn. *The Heyday of Natural History: 1820–1870.* Garden City, N. Y.: Doubleday and Co., 1980.

Barber, Noel. *Sinister Twilight: The Fall and Rise Again of Singapore.* London: W. Collins, 1968.

Baring-Gould, S., and C. A. Bampfylde. *A History of Sarawak under Its Two White Rajahs, 1839–1908.* 1909. Rpt. Singapore: Oxford Univ. Press, 1989.

Barker, Lady. *Station Life in New Zealand.* 1883. Rpt. Boston: Beacon Press, 1987.

Barley, Nigel. *The Duke of Puddle Dock: Travels in the Footsteps of Stamford Raffles.* New York: Henry Holt, 1991.

Barr, Pat. *A Curious Life for a Lady: The Story of Isabella Bird.* London: John Murray, 1970.

————. *Taming the Jungle: The Men Who Made British Malaya.* London: Secker and Warburg, 1977.

Bastin, John. *Essays on Indonesian and Malayan History.* Singapore: Eastern Universities Press, 1961.

————. "Raffles and British Policy in the Indian Archipelago, 1811–1816." *Journal of the Malayan Branch of the Royal Asiatic Society* 27, 1(1954):84–119.

Bastin, John, and Robin W. Winks, eds. *Malaysia: Selected Historical Readings.* Kuala Lumpur: Oxford Univ. Press, 1966.

Basu, Dilip K., ed. *The Rise and Growth of the Colonial Port Cities in Asia.* Santa Cruz: Center for South Pacific Studies, Univ. of California, 1979.

Bates, Henry Walter. *The Naturalist on the River Amazons: A Record of Adventures, Habits of Animals, Sketches of Brazilian and Indian Life, and Aspects of Nature under the Equator, during Eleven Years of Travel.* 1863. Rpt. New York: Viking, Penguin, 1989.

Bayly, C. A. *The New Cambridge History of India.* Vol. 2, *Indian Society and the Making of the British Empire.* Cambridge: Cambridge Univ. Press, 1988.

Bean, William Jackson. *The Royal Botanic Gardens, Kew: Historical and Descriptive.* London: Cassell, 1908.

Beccari, Odoardo. *Wanderings in the Great Forests of Borneo.* 1902. English trans. 1904. Rpt. Singapore: Oxford Univ. Press, 1986.

Begbie, P. J. *The Malayan Peninsula.* 1834. Rpt. Kuala Lumpur: Oxford Univ. Press, 1967.

Behdad, Ali. *Belated Travelers: Orientalism in the Age of Colonial Dissolution.* Durham, N.C.: Duke Univ. Press, 1994.

Berman, Morris. "'Hegemony' and the Amateur Tradition in British Science." *Journal of Social History* 8(1975):30–50.

Berridge, Virginia, and Griffith Edwards. *Opium and the People: Opiate Use in Nineteenth-Century England.* New York: St. Martin's Press, 1981.

Betty [pseud.]." *Intercepted Letters: A Mild Satire on Hong Kong Society.* Hong Kong: Kelly and Walsh, 1905.

Bhabha, Homi. K. "Signs Taken for Wonders: Questions of Ambivalence and Authority under a Tree outside Delhi, May 1817." *Critical Inquiry* 12(Autumn 1985):144–65.

————, ed. *Nation and Narration.* London: Routledge, 1990.

Bickmore, Albert S. *Travels in the East Indian Archipelago.* 1868. Rpt. Singapore: Oxford Univ. Press, 1991.

Bingham, Madeleine, Baroness Clanmorris. *The Making of Kew*. London: Michael Joseph, 1975.

Bird, Isabella. *The Golden Chersonese and the Way Thither*. 1883. Rpt. London: Century Publishing Co., 1983.

———. "Sketches in the Malay Peninsula." *Leisure Hour* 32(1883):17–23.

———. *This Grand Beyond: The Travels of Isabella Bird Bishop*. Selected by Cicely Palser Havely. London: Century Publishing Co., 1984.

———. *Unbeaten Tracks in Japan*. 1880. Rpt. London: Virago, 1984.

Birkett, Dea. *Spinsters Abroad: Victorian Lady Travellers*. London: Basil Blackwell, 1988.

———. "A Victorian Painter of Exotic Flora." *New York Times*, Nov. 22, 1992,30.

Bivona, Daniel. *Desire and Contradiction: Imperial Visions and Domestic Debates in Victorian Literature*. Manchester: Manchester Univ. Press, 1990.

Bixby, Olive Jennie. *My Child-Life in Burmah; or, Recollections and Incidents*. Boston: W. G. Corthell, 1880.

Blakely, Brian L. *The Colonial Office 1868–1892*. Durham, N.C.: Duke Univ. Press, 1972.

Blunt, Wilfred. *In for a Penny: A Prospect of Kew Gardens: Their Flora, Fauna and Falballas*. London: Hamish Hamilton, 1978.

Blusse, Leonard. "Batavia, 1619–1740: The Rise and Fall of a Chinese Colonial Town." *Journal of Southeast Asian Studies* 12, 1(Mar. 1981):159–178.

Bock, Carl. *The Head-Hunters of Borneo: A Narrative of Travel up the Mahakkam and down the Barito; also, Journeyings in Sumatra*. 1881. Rpt. Singapore: Oxford Univ. Press, 1985.

———. *Temples and Elephants: Travels in Siam in 1881–1882*. 1884. Rpt. Singapore: Oxford Univ. Press, 1986.

Bongie, Chris. *Exotic Memories: Literature, Colonialism and the Fin de Siècle*. Stanford: Stanford Univ. Press, 1991.

Bonta, Marcia Myers. *Women in the Field: America's Pioneering Women Naturalists*. College Station: Texas A & M Univ. Press, 1991.

Books about Singapore. Singapore: National Library, 1993.

Boon, James A. *Affinities and Extremes: Crisscrossing the Bittersweet Ethnology of East Indies History, Hindu-Balinese Culture, and Indo-European Allure*. Chicago: Univ. of Chicago Press, 1990.

Booth, Anne W. J. O'Malley, and Anna Weidemann. *Indonesian Economic History in the Dutch Colonial Era*. Southeast Asia Monograph Series, no. 35. New Haven: Yale Center for International and Area Studies, 1990.

Bowring, Sir John. *The Kingdom and People of Siam*. 2 vols. 1857. Rpt. Kuala Lumpur: Oxford Univ. Press, 1969.

Braddell, Roland St. J. *The Lights of Singapore*. 1934. Rpt. Kuala Lumpur: Oxford Univ. Press, 1982.

Bradley, William L. *Siam Then: The Foreign Colony in Bangkok before and after Anna*. Pasadena, Calif.: William Carey Library, 1981.

Braga-Blake, Myrna, ed. *Singapore Eurasians: Memories and Hopes*. Singapore: Times Editions, 1992.

Brailey, Nigel J. *Thailand and the Fall of Singapore: A Frustrated Asian Revolution*. Boulder, Colo.: Westview Press, 1986.

Brantlinger, Patrick. *Crusoe's Footprints: Cultural Studies in Britain and America*. New York: Routledge, 1990.

―――. *Rule of Darkness: British Literature and Imperialism, 1830–1914.* Ithaca: Cornell Univ. Press, 1988.

Brassey, Annie. *In the Trades, the Tropics, and the Roaring Forties.* London: Longmans, Green and Co., 1880.

―――. *The Last Voyage, to India and Australia in the "Sunbeam."* London: Longmans, Green and Co., 1889.

―――. *Sunshine and Storm in the East; or, Cruises to Cyprus and Constantinople.* London: Longmans, Green and Co., 1880.

―――. *Tahiti.* London: Sampson, Law, Marston, Searle and Rivington, 1882.

―――. *A Voyage in the "Sunbeam," Our Home on the Ocean for Eleven Months.* 4th ed. London: Longmans, Green and Co., 1878.

Bristowe, W. S. *Louis and the King of Siam.* New York: Thai- American Publishers, 1976.

Britten, James, and George S. Boulger. *A Biographical Index of Deceased British and Irish Botanists.* London: Taylor and Francis, 1931.

Brockway, Lucile H. *Science and Colonial Expansion: The Role of the British Royal Botanic Gardens.* New York: Academic Press, 1979.

Broeze, Frank, ed. *Brides of the Sea: Port Cities of Asia from the Sixteenth to the Twentieth Centuries.* Honolulu: Univ. of Hawaii Press, 1989.

Brooke, Charles. *Ten Years in Sarawak.* 2 vols. 1866. Rpt. Singapore: Oxford Univ. Press, 1990.

Brooke, Sir Charles. *Queries, Past, Present and Future.* London: Planet Press, 1907.

Brooke, Gladys, H.H. the Dayang Muda of Sarawak. *Relations and Complications: Being the Recollections of H.H. the Dayang Muda of Sarawak.* London: John Lane, 1929.

Brooke, James. "Brazil Seeks to Return Ancestral Lands to Descendants of Runaway Slaves." *New York Times,* Aug. 15, 1993, International Sec., 12.

Brooke, Sir James. *Rajah Brooke and Baroness Burdett Coutts, Consisting of the Letters from Sir James Brooke, First White Rajah of Sarawak, to Miss Angela (Afterwards Baroness) Burdett Coutts.* Ed. by Owen Rutter. London: Hutchinson and Co., 1935.

Brooke, Margaret, the Ranee of Sarawak. *Good Morning and Good Night.* 1934. Rpt. London: Century Publishing Co., 1984.

―――. *My Life in Sarawak.* 1913. Rpt. Oxford: Oxford Univ. Press, 1986.

Brooke, Sylvia. *Lost Property.* London: E. Nash and Grayson, 1930.

―――. *Queen of the Head-hunters: The Autobiography of H. H. the Hon. Sylvia, Lady Brooke, the Ranee of Sarawak.* 1970. Rpt. Singapore: Oxford Univ. Press, 1990.

―――. *A Star Fell.* London: Harrison-Hilton, 1940.

―――. *Sylvia of Sarawak: An Autobiography.* London: Hutchinson and Co., 1936.

―――. *The Three White Rajas.* London: Cassell, 1939.

Buckley, Arabella. *Life and Her Children: Glimpses of Animal Life from the Amoeba to the Insects.* 1880. Rpt. London: MacMillan, 1957.

Buckley, Charles Burton. *An Anecdotal History of Old Times in Singapore from the Foundation of the Settlement under the Honourable The East India Company on February 6th 1819 to the Transfer to the Colonial Office as Part of the Colonial Possessions of the Crown on April 1st 1867.* 1902. Rpt. Singapore: Oxford Univ. Press, 1984.

Bunyon, Charles John. *Memoirs of Francis Thomas McDougall, Sometime Bishop of Labuan and Sarawak, and of Harriette His Wife.* London: Longmans, Green, 1889.

Burbidge, F. W. *The Gardens of the Sun; or, A Naturalist's Journal on the Mountains and in the*

Forests and Swamps of Borneo and the Sulu Archipelago. 1880. Rpt. Singapore: Oxford Univ. Press, 1989.

Butcher, John G. *The British in Malaya, 1880–1941: The Social History of a European Community in Colonial South-East Asia.* Oxford: Oxford Univ. Press, 1979.

Buzard, James. *The Beaten Track: European Tourism, Literature, and the Ways to Culture, 1800–1918.* New York: Oxford Univ. Press, 1993.

Caddy, Florence. *To Siam and Malaya in The Duke of Sutherland's Yacht "Sans Peur."* 1889. Rpt. Singapore: Oxford Univ. Press, 1992.

Cain, P. J., and A. G. Hopkins. *British Imperialism: Innovation and Expansion 1688–1914.* London: Longmans, 1993.

Caldwell, Malcolm. *Thailand: Towards the Revolution.* London: Ad Hoc Group for Democracy in Thailand, 1976.

Cameron, Charlotte. *Wanderings in South-Eastern Seas.* London: T. Fisher Unwin, 1924.

Cameron, John. *Our Tropical Possessions in Malayan India.* 1865. Rpt. Kuala Lumpur: Oxford Univ. Press, 1965.

Campbell, Mary B. *The Witness and the Other World: Exotic European Travel Writing, 400–1600.* Ithaca: Cornell Univ. Press, 1988.

Cannon, Susan Faye. *Science in Culture: The Early Victorian Period.* New York: Science History Publications, 1978.

Canny, Nicholas. *Kingdom and Colony: Ireland in the Atlantic World, 1560-1800.* Baltimore: Johns Hopkins Univ. Press, 1988.

Carter, Paul. *The Road to Botany Bay: An Essay in Spacial History.* London: Faber and Faber, 1987.

Cassell's Magazine of Art. London, H. V. Barnett. 5:430.

Catalogue of the Books, Manuscripts, Maps and Drawings in the British Museum (Natural History). London, 1933.

Cell, John W. *British Colonial Administration in the Mid-Nineteenth Century: The Policy-Making Process.* New Haven: Yale Univ. Press, 1970.

Chai, Hon-Chan. *The Development of British Malaya, 1896–1909.* Kuala Lumpur: Oxford Univ. Press, 1964.

Chambers, Iain. *Border Dialogues: Journeys in Postmodernity.* London: Routledge, 1990.

Chapple, J.A.V. *Science and Literature in the Nineteenth Century.* London: Macmillan Education, 1986.

Chaudhuri, Nupur, and Margaret Strobel, eds. *Western Women and Imperialism: Complicity and Resistance.* Bloomington: Indiana Univ. Press, 1992.

Cheah, Boon Kheng. "Chiefs, Rajas and Rebels: Malay Resistance to British Rule in the 19th Century and Early Twentieth Century." Paper delivered at the British Institute in Southeast Asia Symposium, Jan. 1981.

Cheng U Wen. "Opium in the Straits Settlements." *Journal of Southeast Asian History* 2(Mar. 1961):52–74.

Chew, Daniel. *Chinese Pioneers on the Sarawak Frontier, 1841–1941.* Singapore: Oxford Univ. Press, 1990.

Chew, Ernest C. T., and Edwin Lee, eds. *A History of Singapore.* Singapore: Oxford Univ. Press, 1991.

Chew Sock Foon. *Ethnicity and Nationality in Singapore.* Southeast Asia Series, no. 78. Athens, Ohio: Ohio Univ. Press, 1987.

Chiang, Hai Ding. *A History of Straits Settlements Foreign Trade, 1870–1915*. Singapore: National Museum, 1978.

Chin, John. *The Sarawak Chinese*. Kuala Lumpur: Oxford Univ. Press, 1981.

Chomchai, Prachoom. *Chulalongkorn the Great*. Tokyo: The Centre for East Asian Cultural Studies, 1965.

Chow, Rey. *Writing Diaspora: Tactics of Intervention in Contemporary Cultural Studies*. Bloomington: Indiana Univ. Press, 1993.

———. "Things, Common/Places, Passages of the Port City: On Hong Kong and Hong Kong Author Leung Ping-kwan." *Differences: A Journal of Feminist Studies* 5.3(1993):179–204.

"Christian Cemeteries of Penang and Perak." Private papers of Khoo Su Nin, Penang.

Chula Chakrabongse, Prince of Thailand. *Lords of Life: The Paternal Monarchy of Bangkok, 1782–1932*. London: Alvin Redman, 1960.

Clark, Ronald. *The Survival of Charles Darwin*. New York: Random House, 1984.

Clarke, Patricia. *The Governesses: Letters from the Colonies, 1862–1882*. London: Hutchinson and Co., 1985.

Clements, H. *Alfred Russel Wallace, Biologist and Social Reformer*. London: Hutchinson and Co., 1983.

Clifford, James. "Traveling Cultures." *Cultural Studies*. Ed. Lawrence Grossberg, Cary Nelson, Paula Treichler. New York: Routledge, 1991. 96–116.

Clifton, Violet. *Islands of Indonesia*. Singapore: Oxford Univ. Press, 1991. Rpt. of *Islands of Queen Wilhelmina*. London: Constable and Co., 1927.

Clodd, H. P. *Malaya's First British Pioneer: The Life of Francis Light*. London: Luzac and Co., 1948.

Coates, Austin. *City of Broken Promises*. 1967. Rpt. Hong Kong: Oxford Univ. Press, 1987.

———. *The Commerce in Rubber, the First 250 Years*. Singapore: Oxford Univ. Press, 1987.

Cohen, Erik. "Thai Girls and Farang Men: The Edge of Ambiguity." *Annals of Tourism Research* 9, 3(1982):403–428.

Colonial Directory of the Straits Settlements, Including Sarawak, Labuan, Bangkok, and Saigon, 1875. Singapore: Mission Press, 1875.

Cooper, A. M. *Men of Sarawak*. Singapore: Oxford Univ. Press, 1968.

Conrad, Joseph. *Lord Jim*. 1900. Rpt. New York: New American Library, 1961.

———. *Three Novels*. New York: Washington Square Press, 1970.

Conrad, Robert Edgar. *Children of God's Fire: A Documentary History of Black Slavery in Brazil*. Princeton: Princeton Univ. Press, 1983.

———. *The Destruction of Brazilian Slavery, 1850–1888*. Berkeley: Univ. of California Press, 1972.

———. *World of Sorrow: The African Slave Trade to Brazil*. Baton Rouge: Louisiana State Univ. Press, 1986.

Cort, Mary Lovina. *Siam, or The Heart of Farther India*. New York: Anson D. F. Randolph and Co., 1886.

Cortazzi, Sir Hugh, and Gordon Daniels, eds. *Britain and Japan 1859–1991, Themes and Personalities*. London: Routledge, 1991.

Costumes through Time, Singapore. Singapore: National Heritage Board, 1993.

Cottom, Daniel. "Discipline and Publish." *Victorian Studies* 36, 4(Summer 1993):461–465.

Cowan, Charles. *Nineteenth-Century Malaya: The Origins of British Political Control.* London: Oxford Univ. Press, 1961.

————. Review of *Revolt in Paradise*, by Ktut Tantru. *Pacific Affairs* 34(1961):211.

Crawfurd, John. *History of the Indian Archipelago. Containing an Account of the Manners, Arts, Languages, Religions, Institutions, and Commerce of Its Inhabitants.* 3 vols. Edinburgh: Archibald Constable and Co., 1820.

————. *Journal of an Embassy from the Governor-General of India to the Courts of Siam and Cochin-China; Exhibiting a View of the Actual State of Those Kingdoms.* 1828. Rpt. Kuala Lumpur: Oxford Univ. Press, 1967.

Crawfurd Papers: A Collection of Official Records Relating to the Mission of Dr. John Crawfurd, Sent to Siam by the Government of India in the Year 1821. 1915. Rpt. Westmead, England: Gregg International Publishers Ltd., 1971.

Crisswell, Colin. *Rajah Charles Brooke, Monarch of All He Surveyed.* Kuala Lumpur: Oxford Univ. Press, 1978.

Crosby, Alfred. *Ecological Imperialism: The Biological Expansion of Europe, 900–1900.* Cambridge: Cambridge Univ. Press, 1986.

Cushman, Jennifer Wayne. *Family and State: The Formation of a Sino-Thai Tin-Mining Dynasty, 1797–1932.* Ed. Craig J. Reynolds. Singapore: Oxford Univ. Press, 1991.

Dale, Peter Allen. *In Pursuit of a Scientific Culture.* Madison: Univ. of Wisconsin Press, 1989.

Damrong, H.R.H. Prince. "The Introduction of Western Culture in Siam." *The Siam Society.* Vol. 7, *Relationship with Portugal, Holland, and the Vatican.* Bangkok: Siam Society, 1959. 1–12.

Darwin, Charles. *The Correspondence of Charles Darwin.* 6 Vols. Cambridge: Cambridge Univ. Press, 1985–1990.

————. *Journal of Researches into the Geology and Natural History of the Various Countries Visited during the Voyage of H.M.S. Beagle, Under the Command of Captain Fitzroy, R.N., from 1832 to 1836.* London: Henry Colburn, 1839.

Daud, Fatimah. *"Minah Karan": The Truth about Malaysian Factory Girls.* Kuala Lumpur: Berita Publishing, 1985.

Day, Clive. *The Policy and Administration of the Dutch in Java.* New York, London: Macmillan, 1904.

De Wit, Augusta. *Java: Facts and Fancies.* 1912. Rpt. Singapore: Oxford Univ. Press, 1987.

Desmond, Ray. *Dictionary of British and Irish Botanists and Horticulturists, Including Plant Collectors and Botanical Artists.* London: Taylor and Francis, 1977.

Dial. Review of *Further Recollections of a Happy Life*, by Marianne North. 15(Aug. 1893):64–66.

Dickens, Molly. "Marianne North (Illustrated)." *Cornhill Magazine.* 1031 (Spring 1962):319–329.

Dirks, Nicholas B., ed. *Colonialism and Culture.* Ann Arbor: The Univ. of Michigan Press, 1992.

Dodge, Ernest. *Islands and Empires: Western Impact on the Pacific and East Asia.* Minneapolis: Univ. of Minnesota Press, 1976.

Donaldson, Laura. "The Miranda Complex: Colonialism and the Question of Feminist Reading." *Diacritics* (Fall 1988):65–77.

Drabble, J. H. *Rubber in Malaya 1876–1922: The Genesis of the Industry.* Kuala Lumpur: Oxford Univ. Press, 1973.

Duff Gordon, Lady Lucie. *Lady Duff Gordon's Letters from Egypt.* 1865. Rpt. New York: Praeger, 1969.

During, Simon. "Waiting for the Post: Some Relations between Modernity, Colonization, and Writing." *Ariel: A Review of International English Literature* 20, 4(Oct. 1989):31–61.

"A Dutch Political Novel." *North British Review* 4, 2(1867):319–342.

Dyer, Gary R. "The 'Vanity Fair' of Nineteenth-Century England: Commerce, Women, and the East in the Ladies' Bazaar." *Nineteenth-Century Literature* 46, 2(Sept. 1991):196–222.

Ellegard, Alvar. *Darwin and the General Reader: The Reception of Darwin's Theory of Evolution in the British Periodical Press, 1859–1872.* 1958. Rpt. Chicago: Univ. of Chicago Press, 1990.

Ellis, Beth. *An English Girl's First Impression of Burmah.* 3d ed. London: Simpkin, Marshall, Hamilton, Kent and Co., 1899.

Emberley, Julia. *Thresholds of Difference: Feminist Critique, Native Women's Writings, Postcolonial Theory.* Toronto: Univ. of Toronto Press, 1993.

Enloe, Cynthia. *Bananas, Beaches and Bases: Making Feminist Sense of International Politics.* 1989. Rpt. Berkeley: Univ. of California Press, 1990.

Erlanger, Steven. "A Plague Awaits." *New York Times*, July 14, 1991, sec. 6, 24–28, 53.

Fanon, Frantz. *Black Skin, White Masks.* Trans. Charles Lam Markmann. New York: Grove Press, 1964.

———. *The Wretched of the Earth.* Trans. Constance Farrington. New York: Grove Press, 1966.

Feltus, George Haws, ed. *Abstract of The Journal of Rev. Dan Beach Bradley, M.D.* Ed. Rev. Dan F. Bradley. Cleveland, Ohio: Pilgrim Church, 1936.

Ferguson, Moira. *Colonialism and Gender Relations from Mary Wollstonecraft to Jamaica Kincaid: East Caribbean Connections.* New York: Columbia Univ. Press, 1993.

———. *Subject to Others: British Women Writers and Colonial Slavery, 1670–1834.* New York: Routledge, Chapman and Hall, 1992.

Field, J. W., and others. *The Institute for Medical Research, 1900–1950.* Kuala Lumpur: Government Press, 1951. 127–77.

Fisch, Audrey A. "'Exhibiting Uncle Tom in Some Shape or Other': The Commodification and Reception of *Uncle Tom's Cabin* in England." *Nineteenth-Century Contexts* 17, 2(1993):145–158.

Fletcher, Nancy McHenry. *The Separation of Singapore from Malaysia.* Southeast Asia Program, Data paper 73. Ithaca: Cornell Univ., 1969.

Forbes, Annabella (Mrs. H. O.). *Helena, a Novel.* Edinburgh: William Blackwood and Sons, 1905.

———. *Insulinde: Experiences of a Naturalist's Wife in the Eastern Archipelago.* London: William Blackwood and Sons, 1887. Rpt. as *Unbeaten Tracks in Islands of the Far East: Experiences of a Naturalist's Wife in the 1880s.* Singapore: Oxford Univ. Press, 1987.

Forbes, Henry Ogg. *A Narrative of the Expedition of the Australian Squadron to the South-East Coast of New Guinea, October to December, 1884. With Illustrations.* Sydney: Thomas Richards, 1885. Facsimile ed., Bathurst, NSW: Robert Brown and Associates, 1984.

————. *A Naturalist's Wanderings in the Eastern Archipelago: A Narrative of Travel and Exploration from 1878 to 1883.* 1885. Rpt. Singapore: Oxford Univ. Press, 1989.

Forbes, Henry Ogg, with William Robert Ogilvie-Grant. *The Natural History of Sokotra and Abd-El-Kuri.* Liverpool: Henry Young and Sons, 1903.

Foucault, Michel. *The History of Sexuality.* Vol. 1. Trans Robert Hurley. 1978. Rpt. New York: Vintage, 1990.

Fountaine, Margaret. *Love among the Butterflies: The Travels and Adventures of a Victorian Lady.* Ed. W. F. Cater. 1980. Rpt. Harmondsworth, Middlesex: Penguin, 1982.

Frankfurter, Dr. O. "King Mongkut." *Journal of the Siam Society* 1(1904):191–206.

Freedman, M. "Colonial Law and Chinese Society." *Journal of the Royal Anthropological Institute of Great Britain and Ireland* 80(1950):97–126.

————. "Family Life in Early Singapore." *Journal of Southeast Asian History* 3, 2(1962):65–73.

Furber, Holden. *Rival Empires of Trade in the Orient, 1600–1800.* Minneapolis: Univ. of Minnesota Press, 1976.

Furnivall, J. S. *Netherlands India: A Study of Plural Economy.* 1939. Rpt. Cambridge: Cambridge Univ. Press, 1967.

Garden: An Illustrated Weekly Journal of Horticulture in All Its Branches. Obituary of Marianne North. 58(Oct. 29, 1900):300–301.

Gardner, George. *Travels in the Interior of Brazil: Principally through the Northern Provinces, and the Gold and Diamond Districts, during the Years 1836–1841.* London: Reeve Brothers, 1846.

Gascoigne, Gwendolen Trench. *Among Pagodas and Fair Ladies: An Account of a Tour through Burma.* London: A. D. Innes, 1896.

Geikie, Sir Archibald. *Annals of the Royal Society Club: The Record of a London Dining-Club in the Eighteenth and Nineteenth Centuries.* London: Macmillan, 1917.

Gendron, Charisse. "Images of Middle Eastern Women in Victorian Travel Books." *Victorian Newsletter* 79(Spring 1991):18–23.

————. "Lucie Duff Gordon's 'Letters from Egypt.'" *Ariel: A Review of International English Literature* 17, 2(1986):49–61.

Gidley, Mick, ed. *Representing Others: White Views of Indigenous Peoples.* Exeter: Univ. of Exeter Press, 1992.

Gilroy, Paul. *The Black Atlantic: Modernity and Double Consciousness.* Cambridge: Harvard Univ. Press, 1993.

Girling, J.L.S. *Thailand: Society and Politics.* Ithaca: Cornell Univ. Press, 1981.

"A Glimpse of Sarawak." *Chambers's Journal of Popular Literature, Science and Arts* 7, 181(June 20, 1857):390–392.

Goldie, Terry. *Fear and Temptation: The Image of the Indigene in Canadian, Australian and New Zealand Literatures.* Kingston: McGill-Queens Univ. Press, 1989.

Goonatilake, Susantha. *Crippled Minds: An Exploration into Colonial Culture.* New Delhi: Vikas Publishing House Pvt Ltd., 1982.

Gordon, Jan B. "The 'Second Tongue' Myth: English Poetry in Polylingual Singapore." *Ariel: A Review of International English Literature* 15, 4(1984):41–65.

Gordon-Cumming, Constance. *At Home in Fiji.* 2 vols. Edinburgh: William Blackwood and Sons, 1881.

————. *Two Happy years in Ceylon.* Edinburgh: William Blackwood and Sons, 1892.

————. *Wanderings in China.* Edinburgh: William Blackwood and Sons, 1886.

Great Britain, Foreign Office in Siam. Correspondence 1867-1948. Kew, Richmond, Surrey: Public Record Office, 1984. Microfilm.

Green, Daniel. *A Plantation Family.* Ipswich: Boydell Press, 1979.

Green, Eda. *Borneo: The Land of River and Palm.* London: Borneo Mission Association, 1901.

Green, J. Reynolds. *A History of Botany 1860–1900.* 1909. Rpt. New York: Russell and Russell, 1967.

Green, Martin. *Dreams of Adventure, Deeds of Empire.* New York: Basic Books, 1979.

Green, William A. *British Slave Emancipation: The Sugar Colonies and the Great Experiment, 1830–1865.* Oxford: Clarendon Press, 1976.

Griswold, A. B. *King Mongkut of Siam.* New York: Asia Society, 1961.

Grosskurth, Phyllis. *John Addington Symonds: A Biography.* London: Longmans, Green and Co., 1964.

Guha, Ranajit. "On Some Aspects of the Historiography of Colonial India." *Subaltern Studies.* Vol. 1: *Writings on South Asian History and Society.* Ed. Ranajit Guha. Delhi: Oxford Univ. Press, 1982.

Gullick, J. M. "Captain Speedy of Larut." *Journal of the Malaysian Branch of the Royal Asiatic Society* 26(1953):1–103.

———. "Emily Innes, 1843–1927." *Journal of the Malaysian Branch of the Royal Asiatic Society* 55(1982):87–113.

———. *Malay Society in the Late Nineteenth Century: The Beginnings of Change.* Singapore: Oxford Univ. Press, 1987.

Hahn, Emily. *James Brooke of Sarawak: A Biography of James Brooke.* London: Arthur Barker, 1953.

Hammerton, A. James. *Emigrant Gentlewomen: Genteel Poverty and Female Emigration, 1830–1914.* London: Croon Helm, 1979.

Haraway, Donna. "Situated Knowledges: The Science Question in Feminism and the Privilege of Partial Perspective." *Feminist Studies* 14, 3(Fall 1988):575–599.

Hardstone, Peter. *The Role of the Straits Steamship Company in the Political Development of Malaysia.* Singapore: Institute of Humanities and Social Sciences, Nanyang Univ., 1976.

Harfield, Alan. *British and Indian Armies in the East Indies, 1685–1935.* Chippenham: Picton, 1984.

———. *Fort Canning Cemetery, Singapore.* London: British Association for Cemeteries in South Asia, 1981.

Hassam, Andrew. "'As I Write': Narrative Occasions and the Quest for Self-Presence in the Travel Diary." *Ariel: International Review of English Literature* 21, 4(Oct. 1990):33–47.

Headrick, Daniel. *The Tools of Empire: Technology and European Imperialism in the Nineteenth Century.* London: Oxford Univ. Press, 1981.

Hébert, Ludovic, Marquis of Beauvoir. *A Week in Siam January 1867.* An extract from the original English transl. (1870) of *Voyage autour du monde.* Rpt. Bangkok: Siam Society, 1986.

Hemsley, W. B. "Earlier Recollections of Marianne North." *Nature: A Weekly Illustrated Journal of Science* 48(July 27, 1893):291–292.

———. "In Memory of Marianne North." *The Journal of Botany, British and Foreign* 28(1898):329–335.

————. "The Marianne North Gallery at Kew." *Gardener's Chronicle*, Sept. 5, 1885,296.

————. "The Marianne North Gallery of Paintings of 'Plants and Their Homes,' Royal Gardens, Kew." *Nature: A Weekly Illustrated Journal of Science* 26(June 15, 1882):155–156.

————. "The Travels of a Painter of Flowers." *Nature: A Weekly Illustrated Journal of Science* (Apr. 28, 1892):602–603.

Heussler, Robert. *British Malaya: A Bibliographical and Biographical Compendium.* New York: Garland, 1981.

————. *British Rule in Malaya: The Malayan Civil Service and Its Predecessors, 1867–1942.* Westport, Conn.: Greenwood Press, 1981.

Higginson, Sarah Jane. *Java: The Pearl of the East.* New York: Houghton Mifflin, 1890.

Hillier, Mrs. Charles B. "A Pair of Siamese Kings." *Household Words*, Apr. 24, 1853,447–451.

————. "At Home in Siam." *Household Words*, Nov. 21, 1857,481–488.

————. "Siamese Women and Children." *Household Words*, Dec. 11, 1853,40–42.

Hobhouse, Henry. *Seeds of Change: Five Plants that Transformed Mankind.* New York: Harper and Row, 1986.

Hodges, Nan Powell, ed. *The Voyage of the Peacock: A Journal by Benajah Ticknor, Naval Surgeon.* Ann Arbor: Univ. of Michigan Press, 1991.

Holt, Thomas. *The Problem of Freedom: Race, Labor and Politics in Jamaica and Britain, 1832–1938.* Baltimore: Johns Hopkins Univ. Press, 1992.

Hooker, Sir Joseph Dalton, ed. *Hooker's Icones Plantarum; or, Figures, with Descriptive Characters and Remarks, of New and Rare Plants, Selected from the Kew Herbarium.* 3d ser. Vol. 5. London: Williams and Norgate, 1883–1885.

Hopkinson, Amanda. *Julia Margaret Cameron.* London: Virago Press, 1986.

Hornaday, William T. *The Experiences of a Hunter and Naturalist in the Malay Peninsula and Borneo.* Kuala Lumpur: Oxford Univ. Press, 1993. Rpt. of the second half of his *Two Years in the Jungle: The Experiences of a Hunter and Naturalist in India, Ceylon, the Malay Peninsula and Borneo.* New York: Charles Scribner's Sons, 1896.

Hose, Charles. *The Field-Book of a Jungle-Wallah: Being a Description of Shore, River and Forest Life in Sarawak.* 1929. Rpt. Singapore: Oxford Univ. Press, 1985.

————. *Natural Man: A Record from Borneo.* 1926. Rpt. Singapore: Oxford Univ. Press, 1988.

Hose, Charles, and William McDougall. *The Pagan Tribes of Borneo: A Description of Their Physical, Moral and Intellectual Condition with Some Discussion of Their Ethnic Relations, with an Appendix on the Physical Characters of the Races of Borneo by A. C. Haddon.* 2 vols. 1912. Rpt. Singapore: Oxford Univ. Press, 1993.

Howarth, David. *Tahiti: A Paradise Lost.* New York: Viking Press, 1984.

Hoynck van Papendrecht, P. C. "Some Old Private Letters from the Cape, Batavia and Malacca (1778–1788)." *Journal of the Malayan Branch of the Royal Asiatic Society* 2, 1(June 1924):9–24.

Huggan, Graham. "Decolonizing the Map: Post-Colonialism, Post-Structuralism and the Cartographic Connection." *Ariel: A Review of International English Literature* 2, 4(1989):115–131.

Huntington Library, San Marina, Calif. Anna Leonowens Letters. James and Annie Fields Collection.

Huttenback, Robert A. *Race and Empire: White Settlers and Colored Immigrants in the British Self-Governing Colonies 1830–1910.* Ithaca: Cornell Univ. Press, 1976.

Hyma, Albert. *A History of the Dutch in the Far East.* Ann Arbor, Mich.: George Wahr Publishing Co., 1953.

Ingleson, John. *Expanding the Empire: James Brooke and the Sarawak Lobby, 1839–1868.* Nedlands: Centre for South and Southeast Asian Studies, Univ. of Western Australia, 1979.

Innes, Emily. *The Chersonese with the Gilding Off.* 2 vols. 1885. Rpt. Kuala Lumpur: Oxford Univ. Press, 1974.

Jameson, Fredric. "Third World Literature in the Era of Multinational Capitalism." *Pretexts: Studies in Writing and Culture* 3, 1–2(1991):82–104.

Jayapal, Maya. *Old Singapore.* Singapore: Oxford Univ. Press, 1992.

Joaquin, Nick. *Culture and History: Occasional Notes on the Process of Philippine Becoming.* Manila: Solar Publishing, 1988.

Journal of Horticulture, Cottage Gardener, and Home Farmer. A Chronicle of Country Pursuits and Country Life. 3d ser. 21 (July–Dec. 1890), 271–272. 51 (July–Dec. 1905),364–365.

Jumsai, M. L. Manich. *King Mongkut of Thailand and the British (The Model of a Great Friendship).* Bangkok: Chalermit, 1991.

Kabilsingh, C. "Buddhism and the Status of Women." *Buddhism and Society in Thailand.* Ed. B. J. Terwiel and S. Sahai. Gaya: Centre for South Asian Studies, 1984.

Kaplan, Caren. "Deterritorializations: The Rewriting of Home and Exile in Western Feminist Discourse." *Cultural Critique* 6(Spring 1987):187–198.

Kartini, Raden Adjeng. *Letters of a Javanese Princess.* 1911. Rpt. Kuala Lumpur: Oxford Univ. Press, 1976.

Katrak, Ketu H. "Decolonizing Culture: Toward a Theory for Postcolonial Women's Texts." *Modern Fiction Studies* 35, 1(Spring 1989):157–179.

Kennedy, J. *A History of Malaya, A.D. 1400–1959.* London: Macmillan, 1962.

Keppel, Henry. *The Expedition to Borneo of HMS Dido for the Suppression of Piracy, with Extracts from the Journal of James Brooke, Esq.* 1846. Rpt. Singapore: Oxford Univ. Press, 1991.

Khoo Kay Kim. *The Western Malay States, 1850–1873.* Kuala Lumpur: Oxford Univ. Press, 1972.

Khoo Su Nin. *Streets of Georgetown Penang: An Illustrated Guide to Penang's City Streets and Historic Attractions.* Penang: Janus Prints and Resources, 1993.

Kingsley, Mary. *Travels in West Africa: Congo Français, Corisco and Cameroons.* 1897. Rpt. Boston: Beacon Press, 1982.

Kinloch, Charles. *Rambles in Java and the Straits in 1852, by a Bengal Civilian.* 1853. Rpt. Singapore: Oxford Univ. Press, 1987.

Knapman, Claudia. *White Women in Fiji, 1835–1930: The Ruin of Empire?* Sydney: Allen and Unwin, 1986.

Knight, Ruth Adams. *The Treasured One: The Story of Rudivoravan, Princess of Siam.* New York: E. P. Dutton, 1957.

Koompirochana, Vikrom. "Siam in British Foreign Policy 1855–1938: The Acquisition and Relinquishment of British Extraterritorial Rights." Ph.D. diss., Michigan State Univ., 1972.

Koop, John Clement. *The Eurasian Population in Burma.* Cultural Report Series, no. 6. New Haven: Yale Univ. Press, 1960.

Krasner, James. *The Entangled Eye: Visual Perception and the Representation of Nature in Post-Darwinian Narrative.* New York: Oxford Univ. Press, 1992.

Kratoska, Paul. *Index to British Colonial Files Pertaining to British Malaya, 1838–1946.* Kuala Lumpur: Arkib Negera Malaysia, 1990.

————, ed. *Honourable Intentions: Talks on the British Empire in South-East Asia Delivered at the Royal Colonial Institute, 1874–1928.* Singapore: Oxford Univ. Press, 1983.

Kroch Library, Cornell University. *Bangkok Post,* Feb. 1984.

————. *Bangkok Recorder. A Semi-Monthly Journal.* Bangkok: American Missionary Association, 1865–1866.

————. Bradley, Dan Beach. *The Bangkok Calendar.* Bangkok: American Missionary Association, 1859–1869.

————. Hart, Donn Vorhis. "Preliminary Check List of Novels With a Malayan Background." Pamphlet, [1959–1960?]. Wason Collection, Cornell Univ.

————. *Untitled Photograph Album.* John M. Echols Collection, Lock Press, n.d.

Kroef, Justus M. van der. "The Colonial Novel in Indonesia," *Comparative Literature* 10, 3(Summer 1958):215–231.

Kroller, Eva-Marie. "First Impressions: Rhetorical Strategies in Travel Writing by Victorian Women." *Ariel: A Review of International English Literature* 21, 4(Oct. 1990):87–99.

Lach, Donald. *Asia in the Making of Europe.* 2 vols. Chicago: Univ. of Chicago Press, 1965–1977.

Lai Ah Eng. *Peasants, Proletarians and Prostitutes: A Preliminary Investigation into the Work of Chinese Women in Colonial Malaya.* Singapore: Institute of Southeast Asian Studies, 1986.

Landon, Margaret. *Anna and the King of Siam.* New York: The John Day Co., 1943.

Langbauer, Laurie. "The Celebrity Economy of Cultural Studies." *Victorian Studies* 36, 4(Summer 1993):466–472.

Leask, Nigel. *British Romantic Writers and the East: Anxieties of Empire.* Cambridge: Cambridge Univ. Press, 1992.

Lee, Edwin. *The British as Rulers: Governing Multiracial Singapore 1867–1914.* Singapore: Singapore Univ. Press, 1991.

Lee Poh Ping. *Chinese Society in Nineteenth Century Singapore.* Kuala Lumpur: Oxford Univ. Press, 1978.

Lees-Milne, Alvilde. "Marianne North." *Journal of the Royal Horticultural Society* 89, 5(May 1964):231–251.

Leonowens, Anna Harriette. *The English Governess at the Siamese Court: Being Recollections of Six Years at the Royal Palace in Bangkok.* 1870. Rpt. Singapore: Oxford Univ. Press, 1988.

————. *Life and Travel in India: Being Recollections of a Journey before the Days of Railroads.* Philadelphia: Porter and Coates, 1884.

————. *Our Asiatic Cousins.* Boston: D. Lothrop, 1889.

————. *The Romance of the Harem.* 1873. Rpt. Ed. Susan Morgan. Charlottesville: Univ. Press of Virginia, 1991.

Library of Congress. Division of Bibliography. *British Malaya and British North Borneo: A Bibliographical List.* Comp. Florence S. Hellman. Washington, D.C. 1943.

Lim Teck Ghee. "Two Faces of the Chersonese." *Peninjau Sejarah, Journal of the History Teachers' Association of Malaya* 2, 1(Apr., 1967):30–35.

Lindley, John. *Ladies' Botany: or, A Familiar Introduction to the Study of the Natural System of Botany*. London: H. G. Bohn, 1865.

Lo, Joan. *Glimpses from Sarawak's Past*. Kuching, Sarawak: AGAS (S) SDN BHD, 1986.

Lockard, Craig. *From Kampung to City: A Social History of Kuching, Malaysia, 1820–1970*. Monographs in International Studies, Southeast Asia Series, no. 75. Athens, Ohio: Center for International Studies, Ohio Univ., 1987.

―――. *Old Sarawak: A Pictorial Study*. Kuching: Borneo Literature Bureau, 1972.

Lott, Emmeline. *The English Governess in Egypt: Harem Life in Egypt and Constantinople*. London: Bentley, 1865.

Loudon, Jane Webb. *The Ladies' Companion to the Flower Garden*. 3d. ed. London: W. Smith, 1844.

―――. *The Ladies' Flower-Garden of Ornamental Annuals*. London: W. Smith, 1840.

―――. *The Young Naturalist's Journey; or, The Travels of Agnes Merton and Her Mama*. London: William Smith, 1840.

Low, Hugh. *Sarawak, Its Inhabitants and Productions: Being Notes during a Residence in That Country with His Excellency Mr. Brooke*. 1848. Rpt. London: Frank Cass, 1968.

Lulofs, Madelon H. *Coolie*. 1932. Trans. G. J. Renier and Irene Clephane. 1936. Rpt. Singapore: Oxford Univ. Press, 1987.

―――. *Rubber*. 1931. Trans. G. J. Renier and Irene Clephane. 1933. Rpt. Singapore: Oxford Univ. Press, 1987.

McCracken, Donal. *Natal: The Garden Colony: Victorian Natal and the Royal Botanic Gardens, Kew*. Sandton, South Africa: Frandsen Publishers, 1990.

McDougall, Harriette. *Letters from Sarawak; Addressed to a Child*. London: Grant and Griffith, 1854.

―――. *Sketches of Our Life at Sarawak*. 1882. Rpt. Singapore: Oxford Univ. Press, 1992.

Macgregor, Sir W. "Journey to the Summit of the Owen Stanley Range, New Guinea." *Proceedings of the Royal Geographic Society and Monthly Record of Geography* 12(1890):193–222.

Macherey, Pierre. *The Theory of Literary Production*. Boston: Routledge and Kegan Paul, 1978.

McMahan, Anna B. "A Botanist's Journeyings." *Dial*, May 1892,15–17.

McNair, J.F.A., et al. *Report of the Census Officers for the Straits Settlements of Singapore 1871*. Singapore: Straits Settlements Government Press, 1872.

Makepeace, Walter, Gilbert E. Brooke, and Roland St. J. Braddell. *One Hundred Years of Singapore*. 2 vols. 1921. Rpt. Singapore: Oxford Univ. Press, 1991.

Marks, Harry. *The First Contest For Singapore, 1819–1824*. 'S-Gravenhage, Holland: Martinus Nijhoff, 1959.

Masani, Zareer. *Indian Tales of the Raj*. London: BBC Books, 1987.

Masselman, George. *The Cradle of Colonialism*. New Haven: Yale Univ. Press, 1963.

Matsui, Yayori. *Women's Asia*. Trans. Mizuko Matsuda. London: Zed Books, 1987.

Melman, Billie. *Women's Orients: English Women and the Middle East, 1718–1918: Sexuality, Religion and Work*. Ann Arbor: Univ. of Michigan Press, 1992.

"Memoirs of Bishop McDougall and Harriette His Wife." *Church Quarterly Review* 30(July 1990):379–389.

Meredith, George. *The Works of George Meredith*. New York: Charles Scribner's Sons, 1910.

Merrill, Lynn. *The Romance of Victorian Natural History.* New York: Oxford Univ. Press, 1989.

Mershon, Elizabeth. *With the Wild Men of Borneo.* Mountain View, Calif.: Pacific Press Publishing Assoc., 1922.

Middleton, Dorothy. "Flowers in a Landscape." *The Geographical Magazine* 35, 8(Dec. 1962):445–462.

———. *Victorian Lady Travellers.* London: Routledge and Kegan Paul, 1965.

Miller, Christopher. *Theories of Africans: Francophone Literature and Anthropology in Africa.* Chicago: Univ. of Chicago Press, 1990.

Mills, L. A. *British Malaya 1824–67.* 1925. Rpt. Kuala Lumpur: Oxford Univ. Press, 1966.

Mills, Sara. *Discourses of Difference: An Analysis of Women's Travel Writing and Colonialism.* London: Routledge and Kegan Paul, 1991.

Milne, Mary Lewis (Harper). *Shans at Home: With Two Chapters on Shan History and Literature by the Rev. Wilbur Willis Cochrane.* 1910. Rpt. New York: Paragon Book Reprint Corp., 1970.

Mingmongkol, Santi. "Official Blessings for the 'Brothel of Asia.'" *Southeast Asia Chronicle* 78(1981):24–25.

Minney, R. J. *Fanny and the Regent of Siam.* London: Collins, 1962.

Moffat, Abbot Low. *Mongkut, the King of Siam.* Ithaca: Cornell Univ. Press, 1961.

Mohanty, Chandra Talpade, Ann Russo, and Lourdes Torres, eds. *Third World Women and the Politics of Feminism.* Bloomington: Indiana Univ. Press, 1991.

Money, James William B. *Java; or, How to Manage a Colony, Showing a Practical Solution of the Questions Now Affecting British India.* 2 vols. London: Hurst and Blackett, 1861.

Moon, Brenda E. "Marianne North's *Recollections of a Happy Life:* How They Came to Be Written and Published." *Journal of the Society for the Bibliography of Natural History* 8, 4(1978):497–505.

Moore, Cornelia Niekus, ed. *Insulinde: Selected Translations from Dutch Writers of Three Centuries on the Indonesian Archipelago.* Honolulu: Univ. of Hawaii Press, 1978.

Moore, Donald, ed. *Where Monsoons Meet: The Story of Malaya in the Form of an Anthology.* London: George G. Harrap and Company, 1956.

Moore, Donald, and Joanna Moore. *The First 150 Years of Singapore.* Singapore: Donald Moore Press, in association with the Singapore Chamber of Commerce, 1969.

Morson, Ian. *The Connection Phuket Penang and Adelaide: A Short Account of Francis Light.* Bangkok: Siam Society, 1993.

Morton, A. G. *History of Botanical Science: An Account of the Development of Botany from Ancient Times to the Present Day.* London: Academic Press, 1981.

Morton, Peter. *The Vital Science: Biology and the Literary Imagination. 1860–1900.* London: Allen and Unwin, 1984.

Motherlands: Black Women's Writing from Africa, the Caribbean, and South Asia. New Brunswick, N.J.: Rutgers University Press, 1992.

Mouhot, Henri. *Travels in Siam, Cambodia, and Laos, 1858–1860.* Singapore: Oxford Univ. Press, 1989. Rpt. from *Travels in the Central Parts of Indo-China (Siam), Cambodia, and Laos, during the Years 1858, 1859, and 1860.* London: John Murray, 1864.

Mukherjee, Aparna. *British Colonial Policy in Burma: An Aspect of Colonialism in South East Asia, 1840–1885.* New Delhi: Abhinau Publications, 1988.

Multatuli (Edouard Douwes [Dekker]). *Max Havelaar; or, The Coffee Auctions of the Dutch Trading Company.* 1860. Trans. Roy Edwards. Amherst: Univ. of Massachusetts Press, 1982.

Nandy, Ashis. *The Intimate Enemy: Loss and Recovery of Self under Colonialism.* Delhi: Oxford Univ. Press, 1983.

Nathan, Eze. *The History of Jews in Singapore 1830–1945.* Singapore: Herbilu Editorial and Marketing Services, 1986.

Nation. Review of *The English Governess at the Siamese Court,* by Anna Leonowens. Mar. 9, 1871,161–162.

———. Review of *The Romance of the Harem,* Anna Leonowens. May 15, 1873,337–338.

———. Review of Recollections of a Happy Life: Being the *Autobiography of Marianne North.* June 2, 1892,417–418.

———. Review of *Some Further Recollections of a Happy Life,* by Marianne North. Aug. 31, 1893,162.

———. Review of *The Golden Chersonese and the Way Thither,* by Isabella Bird. June 1883,516.

National Archives, Hill Street, Singapore. Despatches to Secretary of State from Straits Settlements, 1867.

———. Government House Guestbook.

National Library, Singapore. *Sarawak Gazette,* 1874–1912.

———. *Straits Settlements Government Gazette.*

———. *Straits Times,* 1860–80.

Neale, Frederick Arthur. *Narrative of a Residence at the Capitol of the Kingdom of Siam; with a Description of the Manners, Customs, and Laws of the Modern Siamese.* London: National Illustrated Library, 1852.

Neill, Desmond. *Elegant Flower: Recollections of a Cadet in Cathay.* 1956. Rpt. Hong Kong: Oxford Univ. Press, 1987.

Nemenzo, Francisco. *Revolution and Counter-Revolution: A Study of British Colonial Policy as a Factor in the Growth and Disintegration of National-Liberation Movements in Burma and Malaya.* Ph.D. diss., Univ. of Manchester, 1964.

New York Times. Review of *The English Governess at the Siamese Court,* by Anna Leonowens. Dec. 10, 1870, sec. 2, 1.

———. Review of *The Romance of the Harem,* by Anna Leonowens. Feb. 14, 1873, sed. 9, 2.

———. Review of *Revolt in Paradise,* by Ktut Tantri. Oct. 9, 1960, Book Review sec., 38.

(See also Oct. 20, 1874, sec. 4,7; Mar. 3, 1875, sec. 6,7; Aug. 2, 1953, Book Review sec.,3; and Aug. 8, 1970, sec. 1,25.)

Newbold, T. J. *Political and Statistical Account of the British Settlements in the Straits of Malacca.* 2 vols. 1832. Rpt. Singapore: Oxford Univ. Press, 1971.

Nieuwenhuys, Rob. *Mirror of the Indies: A History of Dutch Colonial Literature.* 1972. Trans. Frans van Rosevelt. Amherst: Univ. of Massachusetts Press, 1982.

Nish, Ian. *Britain and Japan 1600–1975.* Vol. 1. *Historical Perspective.* London: Information Centre, Embassy of Japan, 1975.

North, Marianne. *Recollections of a Happy Life: Being the Autobiography of Marianne North.* Ed. by her sister, Mrs. John Addington Symonds. 2 vols. London and New York: Macmillan, 1892.

————. *Recollections of a Happy Life: Being the Autobiography of Marianne North.* Vol. 1. Ed. Susan Morgan. Charlottesville: Univ. Press of Virginia, 1993.

————. *Some Further Recollections of a Happy Life: Selected from the Journals of Marianne North Chiefly between the Years 1859 and 1869.* Ed. by her sister, Mrs. John Addington Symonds. London: Macmillan, 1893.

————. *A Vision of Eden: The Life and Work of Marianne North.* Ed. Graham Bateman. Exeter: Webb and Bower, 1980.

O'Hanlon, Redmond. *Into the Heart of Borneo.* 1984. Rpt. New York: Random House, 1985.

Oldenburg, Veena Talwar. "Lifestyle as Resistance: The Case of the Courtesans of Lucknow, India." *Feminist Studies* 16, 2(Summer 1990):259–287.

Ong Choo Suat, ed. *Guide to the Sources of History in Singapore.* Singapore: National Archives, 1989–1991.

Osborne, Milton. *Southeast Asia: An Illustrated Introductory History.* Sydney: Allen and Unwin, 1985.

Owen, Norman G., ed. *Death and Disease in Southeast Asia: Explorations in Social, Medical and Demographic History.* Singapore: Oxford Univ. Press, 1987.

Parker, Andrew, Mary Russo, Doris Sommer, and Patricia Yaeger, eds. *Nationalisms and Sexualities.* New York: Routledge, 1992.

Parkinson, Cyril Northcote. *British Intervention in Malaya, 1867–1877.* Kuala Lumpur: Univ. of Malaya Press, 1964.

Payne, Robert. *The White Rajahs of Sarawak.* 1960. Rpt. Singapore: Oxford Univ. Press, 1986.

Pfeiffer, Ida. *A Lady's Second Journey around the World.* 2 vols. London: Longmans, Brown, Green and Longmans, 1855.

Phongpaichit, Pasuk. "Bangkok Masseuses: Holding Up the Family Sky." *Southeast Asia Chronicle* 78(Apr. 1981):15–23.

————. *From Peasant Girls to Bangkok Masseuses.* Geneva: International Labor Office, 1981.

Ponsonby, Laura. *Marianne North at Kew Gardens.* Exeter: Webb and Bower, 1990.

Pope-Hennessy, James. *Verandah: Some Episodes in the Crown Colonies 1867–1889.* 1964. Rpt. London: Century Publishing Co., 1984.

Prakash, Gyan, ed. *After Colonialism: Imperial Histories and Postcolonial Displacements.* Princeton: Princeton Univ. Press, 1995.

Pramoj, M. R. Kukrit. *Si Phaendin, Four Reigns.* Trans. Tulachandra. 2 vols. Bangkok: Duang Kamol, 1981.

Pramoj, M. R. Kukrit, and M. R. Seni Pramoj. *A King of Siam Speaks.* Bangkok: Siam Society, 1987.

Pratt, Anne. *The Flowering Plants, Grasses, Sedges, and Ferns of Great Britain, and Their Allies, the Club Mosses, Pepperworts and Horsetails.* London: F. Warne and Co., 1873.

————. *The Poisonous, Noxious and Suspected Plants of Our Fields and Woods.* London: Society for Promoting Christian Knowledge, 1857.

————. *Wild Flowers.* London: Society for Promoting Christian Knowledge, 1852.

Pratt, Mary Louise. *Imperial Eyes: Travel Writing and Transculturation.* London: Routledge and Kegan Paul, 1992.

Pringle, Robert. *Rajahs and Rebels: The Ibans of Sarawak under Brooke Rule, 1841–1941.* Ithaca: Cornell Univ. Press, 1970.

Pritchard, George. *The Aggressions of the French at Tahiti and Other Islands in the Pacific.* Auckland: Auckland Univ. Press, 1983.

Pryer, Ada (Mrs. W. B.). *A Decade in Borneo.* London: Hutchinson and Co., 1893.

Quarterly Review. Review of *The Golden Chersonese and the Way Thither,* by Isabella Bird. 157(1884):325–357.

Raffles, Lady Sophia. *Memoir of the Life and Public Services of Sir Thomas Stamford Raffles.* Singapore: Oxford Univ. Press, 1991. Rpt. of *Memoir of the Life and Public Services of Sir Thomas Stamford Raffles, F.R.S. etc., Particularly in the Government of Java, 1811–1816, and of Bencoolen and Its Dependencies, 1817–1824; with Details of the Commerce and Resources of the Eastern Archipelago and Selections from His Correspondence.* London: John Murray, 1830.

Raffles, Sir Thomas Stamford. *The History of Java.* 1817. 2d ed. 2 vols. London: John Murray, 1830.

Records of the United States Consulate in Bangkok. 1856–1912. Washington: National Archives and Records Service.

Reece, R. H. W. "Colin N. Crisswell, *Rajah Charles Brooke: Monarch of All He Surveyed.*" *Borneo Research Bulletin* 13, 1(Apr. 1981):59–62.

———. "European-Indigenous Miscegenation and Social Status in Nineteenth-Century Borneo." *Female and Male in Borneo: Contributions and Challenges in Gender Studies.* Ed. V. Sutlive. Borneo Research Council Monograph Series, vol. 1. Williamsburg: College of William and Mary, 1991. 455–488.

———. *The Name of Brooke: The End of White Rajah Rule in Sarawak.* Kuala Lumpur: Oxford Univ. Press, 1982.

———. "A 'Suitable Population': Charles Brooke and Race-Mixing in Sarawak." *Itinerario* 9, 1(1985):67–112.

Rich, Adrienne. *Blood, Bread, and Poetry: Selected Prose 1979–1985.* New York: Norton, 1986.

Richards, Thomas. *The Imperial Archive: Knowledge and the Fantasy of Empire.* London: Verso, 1993.

Richings, Emily. *Through the Malay Archipelago.* London: H. Drane, 1909.

Richon, Olivier. "Representation, the Despot and the Harem: Some Questions around an Academic Orientalist Painting by Lecomte-Du-Nouy (1885)." *Europe and Its Others.* Vol 1. Colchester: Univ. of Essex, 1985. 1–13.

Richter, Linda. *The Politics of Tourism in Asia.* Honolulu: Univ. of Hawaii Press, 1989.

Ricklefs, M. C. *A History of Modern Indonesia, c. 1300 to the Present.* Bloomington: Indiana Univ. Press, 1981.

Rieff, David. "Multiculturalism's Silent Partner: It's the Newly Globalized Consumer Economy, Stupid." *Harper's Magazine,* Aug. 1993,62–72.

Riffenburgh, Beau. *The Myth of the Explorer: The Press, Sensationalism, and Geographical Discovery.* London: Belhaven Press, 1993.

Robbins, Bruce. "Colonial Discourse: A Paradigm and its Discontents." *Victorian Studies* 35, 2(Winter 1992):209–214.

Robinson, Jane, ed. *An Anthology of Women Travelers.* New York: Oxford Univ. Press, 1994.

Robinson, Ronald and John Gallagher, with Alice Denny. *Africa and the Victorians: The Official Mind of Imperialism.* New York: St. Martin's Press, 1967.

Roff, William R., ed. *Stories and Sketches by Sir Frank Swettenham.* Kuala Lumpur: Oxford Univ. Press, 1967.

Romero, Patricia W., ed. *Women's Voices on Africa: A Century of Travel Writings.* Princeton, N. J.: Marcus Wiener, 1992.

Rosaldo, Renato. "Imperialist Nostalgia." *Representations* 26 (Spring 1989):107–122.

Royal Botanic Gardens, Kew. Catalogue of the Library. London: Darling and Son, Ltd., 1899.

Royal Botanic Gardens, Kew. Director's Correspondence. Chinese and Japanese Letters, 1865–1900.

———. Director's Correspondence. English Letters, 1854, 1857, 1859–1900.

———. Director's Correspondence. Mascarene Islands Letters, 1866–1900.

———. Kew: North Gallery 1879–1896.

———. Letters to J. D. Duthie. Vol. 2.

———. Letters to W. B. Hemsley. Vol. 2.

———. Letters to J. D. Hooker. Vol. 16.

———. Letters to the Shaen Family, 1875–1884.

———. Marianne North Letters to Dr. Burnell, 1878.

———. Marianne North's Letters to A. R. Wallace.

Runciman, Sir Steven. *The White Rajahs; A History of Sarawak from 1841 to 1946.* Cambridge: Cambridge Univ. Press, 1960.

Rush, James. *Opium to Java: Revenue Farming and Chinese Enterprise in Colonial Indonesia, 1860–1910.* Ithaca: Cornell Univ. Press, 1990.

Russell-Wood, J. R., ed. *From Colony to Nation: Essays on the Independence of Brazil.* Baltimore: Johns Hopkins Univ. Press, 1975.

Rutnin, Mattani Mojdara. "The Role of Thai Women in Dramatic Arts and Social Development Problems Concerning Child Prostitution in Thailand: A Case Study, Accompanied by a Video-tape on the Lives of Child Prostitutes." Paper delivered at International Conference on Thai Studies. Aug. 22–24, 1984, Bangkok, sponsored by Thai Studies Program, Chulalongkorn Univ.

Said, Edward. *Culture and Imperialism.* New York: Alfred A. Knopf, 1993.

———. *Orientalism.* 1978. Rpt. New York: Random House, 1979.

———. "Orientalism Reconsidered." *Cultural Critique* 1 (Fall 1985):89–107.

Saint, Max. *A Flourish for the Bishop and Brooke's Friend Grant: Two Studies in Sarawak History 1848–68.* Braunton, Devon: Merlin Books, 1985.

Sandhu, Kernial Singh. *Early Malaysia: Some Observations on the Nature of Indian Contacts with Pre-British Malaya.* Singapore: Univ. Education Press, 1973.

———. *Indians in Malaya: Some Aspects of Their Immigration and Settlement (1786–1957).* Cambridge: Cambridge Univ. Press, 1969.

Sandison, Alan. *The Wheel of Empire: A Study of the Imperial Idea in Some Late Nineteenth and Early Twentieth-Century Fiction.* New York: St. Martin's Press, 1967.

Sangster, Ian. *Sugar and Jamaica.* London: Nelson, 1973.

SarDesai, D. R. *Trade and Empire in Malaya and Singapore 1869–1874.* Athens, Ohio: Ohio Univ. Center for International Studies, 1970.

Saunders, Graham. *Bishops and Brookes: The Anglican Mission and the Brooke Raj in Sarawak 1848–1941.* Singapore: Oxford Univ. Press, 1992.

Saturday Review. Review of *Recollections of a Happy Life,* by Marianne North. 73(Mar. 5, 1892):282–283.

Savage, Victor. *Western Impressions of Nature and Landscape in Southeast Asia*. Singapore: Singapore Univ. Press, 1984.

Scarry, Elaine. *The Body in Pain: The Making and Unmaking of the World*. New York: Oxford Univ. Press, 1985.

Schick, Irvin Cemil. "Representing Middle Eastern Women: Feminism and Colonial Discourse." *Feminist Studies* 16, 2(Summer 1990):345–380.

Schuler, Monica. *"Alas, Alas, Kongo": A Social History of Indentured African Immigration into Jamaica, 1841–1865*. Baltimore: Johns Hopkins Univ. Press, 1980.

Schwab, Raymond. *The Oriental Renaissance: Europe's Rediscovery of India and the East, 1680–1880*. Trans. Gene Patterson-Black and Victor Reinking. New York: Columbia Univ. Press, 1984.

Schweinitz, Karl de, Jr. *The Rise and Fall of British India: Imperialism as Inequality*. London: Methuen, 1983.

Scidmore, Elizabeth Ruhamah. *Java: The Garden of the East*. 1899. Rpt. Singapore: Oxford Univ. Press, 1984.

Scientific American 63(Oct. 18, 1890):245.

Scourse, Nicolette. *The Victorians and Their Flowers*. London: Croon Helm, 1983.

Segal, Gerald. *Rethinking the Pacific*. Oxford: Clarendon Press, 1990.

Sereewat, S. *Prostitution: Thai-European Connection*. Geneva: World Council of Churches, 1983.

Seton, Grace Thompson. *Poison Arrows: Strange Journey with an Opium Dreamer, Annam, Cambodia, Siam, and the Lotos Isle of Bali*. London: John Gifford, 1938.

Shanley, Mary Lyndon. *Feminism, Marriage, and the Law in Victorian England, 1850–1895*. Princeton: Princeton Univ. Press, 1989.

Sharpe, Jenny. *Allegories of Empire: The Figure of Woman in the Colonial Text*. Minneapolis: Univ. of Minnesota Press, 1993.

Shattock, Joanne. "Travel Writing Victorian and Modern: A Review of Recent Research." *The Art of Travel: Essays on Travel Writing*. Ed. Philip Dodd. London: Frank Cass and Company, 1982.

Shaw, J. C. *The Seal of Tammatari*. Chiang Mai: Craftsman Press, 1985.

Shenon, Philip. "Fear and Repression Still Rule War-Torn Indonesian Island." *New York Times*, Apr. 21, 1993, sec. 1,1, 4.

Sheppard, Tan Sri Dato' Mubin. *Singapore 150 Years*. Singapore: Malaysian Branch of the Royal Asiatic Society, 1982.

Shohat, Ella. "Gender and the Culture of Empire: Toward a Feminist Ethnography of the Cinema." *Quarterly Review of Film and Video* 13(1991):45–84.

Sinclair, James Patrick. *Papua New Guinea: The First Hundred Years*. Bathurst, NSW: Robert Brown and Associates, 1985.

Singh, D. S. Ranjit. *Brunei 1839–1983: The Problems of Political Survival*. Singapore: Oxford Univ. Press, 1984.

Singh, Kirpal. "An Approach to Singapore Writing in English." *Ariel: A Review of International English Literature* 15, 2(1984):5–24.

Skinner, G. W. "Change and Persistence in Chinese Culture Overseas: A Comparison of Thailand and Java." Parts 1 and 2. *Journal of the South Seas Society* 16(1960):86–100.

Smith, Bernard. "European Vision and the South Pacific." *Journal of the Warburg and Courtauld Institutes* 13:65–100.

Smith, Malcolm. *A Physician at the Court of Siam.* 1957. Rpt. Singapore: Oxford Univ. Press, 1982.

Social Text Collective, ed. *Third World and Post-Colonial Issues.* Intro. John McClure and Aamir Mufti. *Social Text.* Vol. 10, nos. 2 and 3. Durham, N.C.: Duke Univ. Press, 1993.

Somerville College, Oxford. Marianne North Letters to Amelia Edwards. Amelia Edwards Collection.

Song Ong Siang. *One Hundred Years' History of the Chinese in Singapore.* 1967. Rpt. Singapore: Oxford Univ. Press, 1984.

Spear, Percival. *The Nabobs: A Study of the Social Life of the English in Eighteenth-Century India.* London: Oxford Univ. Press, 1963.

Spectator. Review of *An Englishwoman in America* by Isabella Bird. Nov. 8, 1879,1414–1415.

———. Review of *The Golden Chersonese and the Way Thither,* by Isabella Bird. July 14, 1883,897–899.

———. Review of *Recollections of a Happy Life* by Marianne North. Feb. 27, 1892,306.

Spivak, Gayatri Chakravorty. "Can the Subaltern Speak? Speculations on Widow Sacrifice." *Marxism and the Interpretation of Culture.* Ed. Cary Nelson and Lawrence Grossberg. Urbana: Univ. of Illinois Press, 1988. 271–313.

———. "Neocolonialism and the Secret Agent of Knowledge." *Oxford Literary Review* 13, 1–2(1991):220–251.

———. "Three Women's Texts and a Critique of Imperialism." *Critical Inquiry* 12(Autumn 1985):243–261.

Spurr, David. *The Rhetoric of Empire: Colonial Discourse in Journalism, Travel Writing, and Imperial Administration.* Durham, N.C.: Duke Univ. Press, 1993.

St. John, Sir Spenser. *The Life of Sir James Brooke, Rajah of Sarawak, from his Personal Papers and Correspondence.* Edinburgh: W. Blackwood and Sons, 1879.

———. "Piracy in the Indian Archipelago." *Journal of the Indian Archipelago and Eastern Asia* 3,4:251–260.

———. *Rajah Brooke: The Englishman as Ruler of an Eastern State.* London: Unwin, 1899.

Stafford, Robert. *Scientist of Empire: Sir Roderick Murchison, Scientific Exploration, and Victorian Imperialism.* Cambridge: Cambridge Univ. Press, 1989.

Stafleu, F. A. *Linnaeus and the Linnaeans: The Spreading of Their Ideas in Systematic Botany, 1735–1789.* Utrecht: International Assoc. for Plant Taxonomy, 1971.

Steinberg, David Joel, ed. *In Search of Southeast Asia: A Modern History.* Rev. Ed. Honolulu: Univ. of Hawaii Press, 1987.

Stenson, Michael. *Class, Race and Colonialism in West Malaysia: The Indian Case.* Vancouver: Univ. of British Columbia Press, 1980.

Stevenson, Catherine Barnes. *Victorian Women Travel Writers in Africa.* Boston: G. K. Hall, 1982.

Stimson, Dorothy. *Scientist and Amateurs: A History of the Royal Society.* New York: Harry Schuman, 1948.

Stoddart, Anna M. *The Life of Isabella Bird (Mrs. Bishop) Hon. Member of the Oriental Society of Pekin, F.R.G.S., F.R.S.G.S.* London: John Murray, 1907.

Stoler, Ann Laura. "'In Cold Blood': Hierarchies of Credibility and the Politics of Colonial Narratives." *Representations* 37(Winter 1992):151–189.

———. "Making Empire Respectable: The Politics of Race and Sexual Morality in 20th-Century Colonial Cultures." *American Ethnologist* 16,4(Nov. 1989):634–660.

Strobel, Margaret. *European Women and the Second British Empire.* Bloomington: Indiana Univ. Press, 1991.

Suleri, Sara. *The Rhetoric of English India.* Chicago: Univ. of Chicago Press, 1992.

Swettenham, Sir Frank. *British Malaya: An Account of the Origin and Progress of British Influence in Malaya.* 1908. Rpt. New York: AMS Press, 1975.

———. *Footprints in Malaya.* London: Hutchinson and Co., 1942.

———. "From Perak to Slim, and down the Slim and Bernam Rivers." *Journal of the Straits Branch of the Royal Asiatic Society,* no. 5:51–68.

———. *Malay Sketches.* Singapore: G. Brash, 1984.

———. *Sir Frank Swettenham's Malayan Journals, 1874–1876.* Kuala Lumpur: Oxford Univ. Press, 1975.

———. *Stories and Sketches by Sir Frank Swettenham.* Kuala Lumpur: Oxford Univ. Press, 1967.

———. *Watercolours and Sketches of Malaya, 1880–1894.* Kuala Lumpur: Malaysian-British Society, 1988.

Symonds, Margaret. *Out of the Past.* London: John Murray, 1925.

Tabor, Margaret. *Pioneer Women. Third Series: Mrs. Sherwood, Isabella Bird, Mary Kingsley, Gertrude Bell.* London: Sheldon Press, 1930.

Tagge, Anne. "Jane Austen and the Rajah of Sarawak." *Persuasions* 15(Dec. 1993):30–31.

Tantri, K'tut. *Revolt in Paradise.* 1960. Rpt. New York: Clarkson N. Potter, 1989.

Tarling, Nicholas. *Anglo-Dutch Rivalry in the Malay World, 1780–1824.* Cambridge: Cambridge Univ. Press, 1962.

———. *Britain, the Brookes, and Brunei.* Kuala Lumpur: Oxford Univ. Press, 1971.

———. *British Policy in the Malay Peninsula and Archipelago, 1824–1871.* Kuala Lumpur: Oxford Univ. Press, 1969.

———. *The Burthen, the Risk, and the Glory: A Biography of Sir James Brooke.* Kuala Lumpur: Oxford Univ. Press, 1982.

———. *The Fall of Imperial Britain In South-East Asia.* New York: Oxford Univ. Press, 1993.

———. *Imperial Britain in South-East Asia.* Kuala Lumpur: Oxford Univ. Press, 1975.

———, ed. *The Cambridge History of Southeast Asia.* Vol. 2, *The Nineteenth and Twentieth Centuries.* Cambridge: Cambridge Univ. Press, 1992.

Taussig, Michael. *Shamanism, Colonialism, and the Wild Man: A Study in Terror and Healing.* Chicago: Univ. of Chicago Press, 1987.

Taylor, Jean Gelman. "Raden Adjeng Kartini." *Signs: Journal of Women in Culture and Society* 1, 3(Spring 1976):639–661.

———. *The Social World of Batavia: European and Eurasian in Dutch Asia.* Madison: Univ. of Wisconsin Press, 1983.

Taylor, John G. *Indonesia's Forgotten War: The Hidden History of East Timor.* Leichhardt, NSW: Pluto Press Australia, 1991.

Templer, John C., ed. *The Private Letters of Sir James Brooke, KCB, Rajah of Sarawak, Narrating the Events of His Life, from 1838 to the Present Time.* 3 vols. London: Bentley, 1853.

Thio, Eunice. *British Policy in the Malay Peninsula 1880–1910.* Vol. 1, *The Southern and Central States.* Kuala Lumpur: Univ. of Malaya Press, 1969.

Thitsa, Khin. *Providence and Prostitution: Image and Reality for Women in Buddhist Thailand.* London: International Reports: Women and Society, 1980.

Thomas, Nicholas. *Colonialism's Culture: Anthropology, Travel and Government.* Cambridge: Polity Press, 1994.

Thomson, James Claude. *Sentimental Imperialists: The American Experience in East Asia.* New York: Harper and Row, 1981.

Thomson, John Turnbull. *Glimpses into Life in Malayan Lands.* 1864. Rpt. London: Oxford Univ. Press, 1984.

———. *Sequel to Glimpses into Life in the Far East.* London: Richardson and Co., 1865.

Thorn, William. *Memoir of the Conquest of Java, with the Subsequent Operations of the British Forces in the Oriental Archipelago.* London: T. Egerton, 1815.

Tinling, Marion, ed. *Women into the Unknown: A Source Book on Women Explorers and Travelers.* Westport, Conn.: Greenwood Press, 1982.

Tomich, Dale. *Slavery in the Circuit of Sugar: Martinique and the World Economy, 1830–1848.* Baltimore: Johns Hopkins Univ. Press, 1990.

Toplin, Robert Brent. *The Abolition of Slavery in Brazil.* New York: Atheneum, 1972.

Torgovnick, Marianna. *Gone Primitive: Savage Intellects, Modern Lives.* Chicago: Univ. of Chicago Press, 1990.

Toussaint, J. R. "Dutch Ladies Who Lived in Ceylon." *Journal of the Dutch Burgher Union of Ceylon* 29, 2(Oct. 1939):31–43.

Trager, Helen. *Burma through Alien Eyes: Missionary Views of the Burmese in the Nineteenth Century.* Bombay: Asia Publishing House, 1966.

Tregonning, K. C. *The British in Malaya: The First Forty Years, 1786–1826.* Tuscon: Univ. of Arizona Press, 1965.

———, ed. *Malaysian Historical Sources: A Series of Essays on Historical Material Mainly in Malaysia on Malaysia.* Singapore: Dept. of History, Univ. of Singapore, 1962.

———, ed. *Papers on Malayan History.* Singapore: Journal of South-East Asian History, 1962.

Trocki, Carl A. *Opium and Empire: Chinese Society in Colonial Singapore, 1800–1910.* Ithaca: Cornell Univ. Press, 1990.

———. *Prince of Pirates: The Temenggongs and the Development of Johor and Singapore, 1784–1885.* Singapore: Singapore Univ. Press, 1979.

Truong, Thanh-Dam. *Sex, Money and Morality: Prostitution and Tourism in Southeast Asia.* London: Zed Books, 1990.

Trustram, Myna. *Women of the Regiment: Marriage and the Victorian Army.* Cambridge: Cambridge Univ. Press, 1984.

Turnbull, C. M. *A History of Malaysia, Singapore, and Brunei.* Sydney: Allen and Unwin, 1989.

———. *A History of Singapore, 1819–1988.* 2d.ed. Singapore: Oxford Univ. Press, 1989.

———. *The Straits Settlements 1826–67; Indian Presidency to Crown Colony.* London: Athlone Press, 1972.

Turrill, William Bertram. *The Royal Botanic Gardens Kew, Past and Present.* London: Herbert Jenkins, 1959.

Turton, A. "Thai Institutions of Slavery." *Asian and African Systems of Slavery.* Ed. J. L. Watson. Berkeley: Univ. of California Press, 1980.

Twining, Elizabeth. *Illustrations of the Natural Orders of Plants with Groups and Descriptions.* London: S. Low, Son, and Marston, 1868.

———. *The Plant World.* London: T. Nelson and Sons, 1866.

"Two Women Wanderers." *Spectator,* Sept. 1, 1888,1194–1195.

Urry, John. *The Tourist Gaze: Leisure and Travel in Contemporary Societies.* London: Sage Publications, 1990.

Van der Veur, Paul. *Education and Social Change in Colonial Indonesia.* Athens, Ohio: Ohio Univ. Center for International Studies, 1969.

———. "The Eurasions of Indonesia: A Problem and Challenge in Colonial History." *Journal of Southeast Asian History* 9, 2(Sept. 1968):191–207.

Vaughan, J. D. *The Manners and Customs of the Chinese of the Straits Settlements.* 1879. Rpt. Singapore: Oxford Univ. Press, 1971.

Vella, Walter F. *The Impact of the West on Government in Thailand.* Berkeley: Univ. of California Press, 1955.

———. *Siam under Rama III, 1824–1851.* Locust Valley, N.Y.: J. J. Augustin, 1957.

Vichit-Vadakan, Juree. "Thai Women in Politics: An Uneasy and Half-Hearted Intrusion into a 'Male Domain.'" *Asia Pacific Women's Studies Journal* 2(1992):39–44.

Vincent, Frank. *The Land of the White Elephant: Sights and Scenes in Burma, Siam, Cambodia, and Cochin-China (1871–2).* 1873. Rpt. Bangkok: White Lotus, 1988.

Viswanathan, Gauri. "The Beginnings of English Literary Study in British India." *Oxford Literary Review* 9(1987):2–26.

———. *Masks of Conquest: Literary Study and British Rule in India.* New York: Columbia Univ. Press, 1989.

———. "Raymond Williams and British Colonialism." *Yale Journal of Criticism* 4, 2(1991):47–66.

Voon, Phin Keong. *Western Rubber Planting Enterprises in Southeast Asia, 1876–1921.* Kuala Lumpur: Penerbit Univ. Malaya, 1976.

Wagner, Ulla. *Colonialism and Urban Warfare.* Stockholm: OBE-Tryck, 1972.

Wahid, Datuk Zainal Abidin Bin Abdul, ed. *Glimpses of Malaysian History.* Kuala Lumpur: Dewan Bahasa Dan Pustaka, 1980.

Walker, Mrs. E. A. *Sophia Cooke; or, Forty Two Years Work in Singapore.* London: E. Steck, 1899.

Wallace, Alfred Russel. *The Malay Archipelago; the Land of the Orang-Utan, and the Bird of Paradise, a Narrative of Travel, with Studies of Man and Nature.* London: Macmillan and Co., 1869. Rpt. Singapore: Oxford Univ. Press, 1986.

———. *My Life: A Record of Events and Opinions.* 2 vols. New York: Dodd, Mead and Co., 1906.

———. *A Narrative of Travels on the Amazon and Rio Negor, with an Account of the Native Tribes, and Observations on the Climate, Geology, and Natural History of the Amazon Valley.* 1895. Rpt. New York: Greenwood Press, 1969.

Walsh, Judith. *Growing Up in British India: Indian Autobiographies on Childhood and Education under the Raj.* New York: Holmes and Meier, 1983.

Ward, A. B. *Rajah's Servant.* Southeast Asia Program, Data paper 61. Ithaca: Cornell Univ., 1966.

Ward, A. B., and D. C. White. *Outlines of Sarawak History Under the Brooke Rajahs 1839–1946.* Kuching: Sarawak Govt. Printing Office, 1957.

Ware, Vron. *Beyond the Pale: White Women, Racism and History.* London: Verso, 1992.

Warren, James Francis. *Rickshaw Coolie: A People's History of Singapore (1880–1940).* Singapore: Oxford Univ. Press, 1986.

Watson, Francis. *A Concise History of India.* 1974. Rpt. New York: Thames and Hudson, 1987.

Webb, R. K. *Modern England from the Eighteenth Century to the Present.* New York: Dodd, Mead, and Co., 1972.

Weld, Charles Richard. *A History of the Royal Society, With Memoirs of the Presidents.* 2 vols. London: John W. Parker, 1848.

Williams, Donovan. "Clements Robert Markham and the Introduction of the Cinchona Tree into British India, 1861." *Geographical Journal* 78(1962):431–442.

Williams, Lea E. "Chinese Leadership in Early British Singapore." *Asian Studies* 2, 2(1964):170–179.

Winichakul, Thongchai. *Siam Mapped: A History of the Geo-Body of a Nation.* Honolulu: Univ. of Hawaii Press, 1994.

Wise, Michael, and Mun Him Wise, eds. *Traveller's Tales of Old Singapore.* Singapore: Times Books International, 1985.

Wolff, Janet. "On the Road Again: Metaphors of Travel in Cultural Criticism." *Cultural Studies* 7, 2(May 1993):224–239.

Wong Lin Ken. *The Trade of Singapore, 1819–69. Malayan Branch of the Royal Asiatic Society* 33, 4 (Dec. 1960).

Wood, W.A.R. *Consul in Paradise: Sixty-Nine Years in Siam.* 1965. Rpt. Bangkok: Trasvin Publications, 1991.

Wright, L. R. *The Origins of British Borneo.* Hong Kong: Hong Kong Univ. Press, 1970.

Wright, Lawrence. "One Drop of Blood." *New Yorker,* July 25, 1994,46–55.

Wurtzburg, C. E. *Raffles of the Eastern Isles.* 1954. Rpt. Singapore: Oxford Univ. Press, 1984.

Wyatt, David K. *The Politics of Reform in Thailand: Education in the Reign of King Chulalongkorn.* New Haven: Yale Univ. Press, 1969.

———. *Thailand: A Short History.* New Haven: Yale Univ. Press, 1982.

Yen Ching-hwang. *A Social History of the Chinese in Singapore and Malaya 1800–1911.* Singapore: Oxford Univ. Press, 1986.

Yong Ching Fatt. "British Attitudes Towards the Chinese Community Leaders in Singapore, 1819–1941." *Journal of the South Seas Society* 40, 1 and 2(1985):73–82.

———. *Chinese Leadership and Power in Colonial Singapore.* Singapore: Times Academic Press, 1992.

Yong, Paul. *A Dream of Freedom: The Early Sarawak Chinese.* Petaling Jaya: Pelanduk Publications, 1991.

Young, Ernest. *The Kingdom of the Yellow Robe: Being Sketches of the Domestic and Religious Rites and Ceremonies of the Siamese.* 1898. Rpt. Singapore: Oxford Univ. Press, 1986.

Young, Robert. *White Mythologies: Writing History and the West.* London: Routledge, 1990.

Zeller, Suzanne. Review of *Scientist of Empire: Sir Roderick Murchison, Scientific Exploration and Victorian Imperialism,* by Robert A. Stafford. *Victorian Studies* 36, 1(Fall 1992):95–97.

Index

Adamson, John, 238
Adelaide (Australia), 269
adventurism, 94–95, 96, 97, 209. *See also*
   explorer-hero
Africa, 23, 57; imperial intervention in,
   290n5; travel narratives of, 94, 97
Agassiz, Elizabeth Cabot, 293n72
Agassiz, Louis, 293n72
AIDS, and Thai prostitution, 224
Akka (Thai tribe), 227
Alatas, Syed, 24, 37, 151–152, 272, 287n29,
   299n50
Alexander, Annie Montague, 112
American imperialism, 230; acquisition
   of Philippines, 6; and Siam, 221
American Museum of Natural History,
   288n40
Anderson, Benedict, 61, 63, 191, 279n1
Anderson, Sir John, 43
Angkhor Wat, 247, 304n58
Anglo-Dutch Treaty of 1824, 137
Anglo-Indian women, 107–108
Anna and the King of Siam (Landon), 245,
   246, 280n27
Anthropological Review, review of Wallace's
   Malay Archipelago in, 66
Appiah, Kwame, 21
archaeology, British, in Egypt, 68
aristocracy, 120
Armenians, in Singapore, 39
army, British, in Straits Settlements,
   281n35
Arnold, Matthew, 126
arranged marriages, 257
Asiatic Quarterly Review, reviews *Chersonese
   with the Gilding Off*, 165
Association of Southeast Asia (ASA), 5
Association of South-East Asian
   Nations (ASEAN), 5

Atheneum: reviews *Chersonese with the Gilding
   Off*, 165; reviews *The English Governess at
   the Siamese Court*, 247; reviews North's
   Recollections, 107; reviews *The Romance of
   the Harem*, 247, 252
Atkins, Anna, 117
Atlantic Monthly: publishes first chapters
   of *The English Governess at the Siamese
   Court*, 244; reviews *The Romance of the
   Harem*, 247
Austen, Jane, 169, 299n54
Ayudhya (former Thai capital), 229

Badger, Rev. Mr., 240, 242, 249
Bali, 270
Bampfylde, C. A., 298n30
Bangkok, 23; sex industry at, 222
Bangkok Calendar of 1860, reports double
   execution, 254, 304n68, 305n77
Banks, Sir Joseph, 111, 114
barbarism, of colonizers, 73
Baring-Gould, S., 298n30
Barr, Pat, 166, 296n42
Barrow, John, 94
Batavia, 24, 34, 42, 53–54, 59, 285n43. *See
   also* Jakarta
Bates, Henry Walter, 99, 125–126
Batesian mimicry, 293–294n78
Beauvoir, Ludovic Hébert, Marquis de,
   302n22
Beccari, Odoardo, 67
Begbie, P. J., 45–48
Berman, Morris, 290n16
Bernhardt, Sarah, 213
Bhabha, Homi, 19, 21, 22, 62, 193, 294n78
Bickmore, Albert, 288n40
biology, Victorian, and botany, 92
Birch (Resident of Perak), murder of, 155
Bird, Henrietta, 149, 161

333

Bird, Isabella, 3–4, 11, 17, 18, 19, 28, 46, 47, 135, 149–154, 166–174 passim, 187, 196, 215, 280n26, 296n41, 296n42, 296n43

Birkett, Dea, 101

Bixby, Olive Jennie, 300n77

Blake, William, 121, 272

Bock, Carl, 67

Bolivia, restricts botanical exports, 116

Bongie, Chris, 192

Bonta, Marcia Myers, 291n28

Boon, in *The Romance of the Harem*, 260, 261, 305n77

Boon, James, 71

Borneo, 8, 20, 28, 51, 52, 164, 177, 285n1; imperial history, 178–186; travel and naturalist literature on, 66–67

Borneo Church Mission, 214

botany, 63, 64, 65, 66; American, 112; and imperialism, 91–92, 95–96, 97–99, 109–117; North's introduction to, 103

Bowring, Sir John, 231, 251

Bowring Treaty (Britain-Siam), 231–232, 302n34

Braddell, Roland, 286n8

Bradley, Dr.and Mrs. (missionary couple), 238, 239

Brandegee, Kate, 112

Brantlinger, Patrick, 13, 74, 94

Brazil: American interests in, 293n72; and botanical imperialism, 92, 98, 123, 124–126; slavery in, 125, 128–131; visited by North, 109

Bristowe, W. S., 240, 241, 242, 248

Britain, 6; army of in Straits Settlements, 281n35; as "cartographer's conspiracy," 271; invades Dutch colonies, 54–55, 136; makes alliance with Brazil, 124; navy of, 22, 179, 180, 182, 183, 297n12; rejects overseas sexual offenses act, 225. See also British imperialism

British Association for the Advancement of Science, 89

British East India Company, 35, 36, 40, 41–42, 44, 53, 136, 138, 145, 146, 147

British imperialism, 7–8, 27–28, 302n27, 302n34; botany in service of, 113–117; and founding of Singapore, 35–38; and rhetoric of superiority, 12–13; and Siam, 221, 230–232

British Malaya, *see* Malaya

British North Borneo, 177

"British Rule in Malaya" (Swettenham lecture), 142

British Rule in Malaya: The Malayan Civil Service and Its Predecessors (Heussler), 166

Britton, Elizabeth, 112

Brockway, Lucile, 24, 115

Brontë, Charlotte, 169

Brooke, Bertram, 198

Brooke, Brooke, 215, 216

Brooke, Charles, 182–205 passim, 210, 215–216, 218, 299–300n57

Brooke, Isaka, 201, 212, 300n71

Brooke, James, 182, 183, 184, 187, 193, 194, 196, 197, 200, 210, 215–216, 299n51, 299n54, 299n55

Brooke, Margaret, 3, 12, 14, 17, 18, 26, 29, 46, 67, 110, 187, 193–213, 300n57; as ranee of Sarawak, 209–213

Brooke, Mrs. Bernard, 187

Brooke, Sylvia, 187, 200–201, 211, 300n71

Brooke, Vyner, 182, 183, 197

Brown, Robert, 111

Brunei, 177, 178–179, 182, 183, 184–186, 194

Brynner, Yul, 245, 304n53

Buddhism, in Thailand, 228–229, 253

Bugis (Sumatrans), and trade along Malay Peninsula, 137

Burma, 4, 51, 145, 229, 230, 232, 302n27

Burne-Jones, Sir Edward, 213

Burnell, Dr., 104, 105, 120, 121, 129

Burton, Richard, 94

Bush, George, speechwriters for, 281n30

Calcutta, 136; opium auctions at, 42

Cambodia, 5, 51

Cameron, John, 295n24

Canning, George, 136

Canterbury Museum (New Zealand), 89

Canton (China), 150

Cape Colony, South Africa, 57

Carnarvon, Lord (Earl Henry Howard Molyneux Herbert), 140

Carter, Paul, 33

Castleman, Jill, 304n53

Castlereagh, Lord (Viscount Robert Stewart), 137

Cator, Mrs. Douglas, 166

Cawnpore (Kanpur, India), 1857 massacre at, 147
Cesaire, Aime, 21
Ceylon (Sri Lanka), 136
Chambers, Dr. (bishop of Sarawak), 213, 216
chattel, Siamese wives as, 229
Chersonese with the Gilding Off, The (Innes), 18, 163–175
Chew, Daniel, 24, 298n26, 300n76
Chew, Ernest C. T., 282n11
children; in McDougall's Sketches, 217; Thai prostitution of, 223–224
Chin, John M., 300n76
China trade, 6, 40, 136, 139, 145, 146, 151; and "piracy," 178
Chinese: in Borneo, 194; and kongsi-Brooke conflict, 213, 217–218; in Malay Archipelago, 52, 58; in Malay States, 138–139, 146; and opium, 42, 43, 44, 47; refugees, in Sarawak, 217; in Siam, 302n32; in Singapore, 35, 36, 38–39, 139, 146, 282n13, 283n22, 284n25, 284n33, 284–285n37, 285n39, 285n40
Chinese Rebellion, see kongsi-Brooke conflict
Chow, Rey, 279n11
Choy, "favorite" of Siamese royal harem, 259, 260
Christianity and European imperialism, 215, 218
Chula Chakrabongse, prince of Thailand, 246
Chulalongkorn, king of Siam, 231, 232, 234, 235, 243, 254, 303n36, 304n62
cinchona, 115–17, 130
"civilizing," colonial presence as, and metropolitan space, 34, 37–38
Civil War, American, 244
Clarke, Sir Andrew, 139, 151
class, socioeconomic: and colonial hierarchy, 209; and gender, 17–18, 120–121, 122, 158; gentry, 101–102, 120; in Leonowens biographical myths, 241, 242–243; and the natural sciences, 93, 98, 290n16
Clifton, Violet, 287n18
coal, on Borneo, 180
Cochin-China, 5, 51, 178, 230

coffee, forced cultivation of, 52–53. See also Cultivation System
Collection of Voyages, A (Dampier), 65
collectors: of Egyptian antiquities, 68; of scientific specimens, 66, 81
colonialism, as prerequisite for travel narrative, 118
Colonial Office, British, 6, 18, 27, 36, 93, 138, 139, 140, 141, 142, 163, 166, 167, 180, 181, 185, 252, 295n16
colonial origins, author's, 1–3
colonies, formal and informal, 27
colonizer/colonized dichotomy, 7–8
Commonwealth of Nations, British, 2–3
concubinage: in Sarawak, 201, 300n66; in Siam, 229
Conrad, Joseph, 81, 98, 190, 202, 218, 248
conservatism and the construct "Singapore," 31–32
consumer: and imperialism, 272, 274–275; tourist, Singapore as marketplace for, 285n47; woman as, in east, 46, 48
contact zones, colonies as, 57
convict labor, Indian, in Singapore, 36
Cook, Capt. James, 111
Corbett, Mary Jean, 289n70, 306n15
Coutts, Angela Burdett, 187
Crawford, Anna Harriette, see Leonowens, Anna
Crawford, Eliza, 240, 241
Crawford, Capt. Thomas Maxwell, 239
Crawfurd, John, 54, 55, 65, 118
Crisswell, Colin, 298n30
Crown Colonies, 33, 36; Sarawak, 183; Singapore, 44
Cruikshank children, beheading of, 217
Cultivation System, Dutch colonial, 55
Cushman, Jennifer, 302n32

Dampier, William, 65
"Dark Continent" rhetoric, 97
Darwin, Charles, 66, 68, 100, 107, 108, 109, 114, 118, 131
Dawson, William, 115
debt slavery, 148, 163, 170, 229
decadence, 123
decorum, 158
Defence of Poetry (Shelley), 72
Dekker, Eduard Douwes ("Multatuli"), 60

"deterritorialization," 276
De Windt, Margaret, *see* Brooke,
    Margaret
Dial, The, reviews North's *Recollections*,
    107
Dilly (Timor), disease at, 78, 82
Dirk, Nicholas, 281n31
Discourses of Difference (Mills), 11
domesticity, 18, 158; absent from Sarawak
    myth, 196–197; ethic lost in
    translation, 296n33; foreign, in
    Forbes's *Insulinde*, 72; in *The Golden
    Chersonese*, 152–153; ideology of,
    transformed, 13; versus professional-
    ism, 127; rejected in *The Chersonese with
    the Gilding Off*, 174; without men,
    305n78
Donaldson, Laura, 77
Douglas, Bloomfield, 152–153, 163, 164,
    165, 166, 171
Drake, Sir Francis, 65
During, Simon, 289n71
Dutch East India Company, 52–53
Dutch East Indies, 4, 12, 61; as scientific
    space, 68
Dutch imperialism, 27, 54–55, 136–137,
    178, 179, 217; and founding of
    Singapore, 35, 36, 37; in the Malay
    Archipelago, 52–57; and the opium
    trade, 286–287n17, 287n18
Dutrochet, R.-J.-H., 111
Dyaks (tribe in Sarawak), 194, 206; as
    children, 210; in McDougall's *Sketches*,
    217
dying, in service to imperial enterprise,
    80–81

east: as consumer product, in Singapore,
    46–48; and erasure of place, 23;
    feminized, and Thai prostitution,
    224; as way to invent "west," 8
Eastern Archipelago, 6, 52, 61. *See also*
    Indonesia; Malay Archipelago
East Indies, 6; as botanical paradise, 92.
    See also Dutch East Indies; Malay
    Archipelago
East Timor, 52; annexed by Indonesia, 63
Eastwood, Alice, 112
Ecuador, restricts botanical exports, 116
Edwards, Amelia, 103, 106
Edwards, Anna, *see* Leonowens, Anna

Edwards, putative father of Anna
    Leonowens, 240
Egypt, 8, 68, 296n35
emancipation rhetoric, in North's
    Recollections, 119, 121, 122
empathy, 210–211. *See also* sympathy
Eng Lai Ah, 24, 284n33
England, *see* Britain
English Governess at the Siamese Court, The
    (Leonowens), 244, 247, 251, 262
Englishwoman in America, An (Bird), 149
Enloe, Cynthia, 233, 297n55
"Ethical Policy," Dutch East Indies, 63
Eurasians, 286n5; of Batavia, 286n6; in
    Leonowens family, 241, 248; in
    Malaya, 168; of Sarawak, 201, 216; of
    Singapore, 39, 286n6
evolution, 66, 67, 68, 74. *See also* social
    Darwinism
expertise, postcolonial, 20–25
explorer-hero: botanist as, 119; and
    Eurasian children, 216–217;
    masculine, 118; in popular press, 94–
    95, 96; scientist as, 117

false alarms, male adventures as, 209
famines, Indian, of 1880s, 145–146
Fanon, Frantz, 15, 21, 287n29
Farquhar, Col., 36, 43
Fay, Michael, punished in Singapore, 31,
    281n1
Federated States, Malay, 140, 141. *See also*
    Protected States
feeling, lack of, in North's *Recollections*,
    130–132
feminine domination, rhetorics of, 17
feminine picturesque, 107–108
femininity: and class, 157, 158; of
    Malayan colonial administration,
    155–159
Field-Book of a Jungle-Wallah, The (Hose),
    67
Fields, Annie, 244, 303n50
Forbes, Anna, 3, 17, 18–19, 27, 59, 60, 63,
    64, 92, 118, 119, 169, 203, 285n43;
    describes her malaria, 85–86;
    poisoned, 80–81; as ratifier of
    Wallace, 69–70; writes *Helena*, 90
Forbes, Henry Ogg, 59–69 passim, 80,
    82–83, 88–89, 95, 99, 114–119 passim,
    131, 203, 290n17

Foreign Office, British, 183, 184, 185
France: imperialism of, 6, 58, 136, 221,
    230, 302n22, 302n27; invades
    Portugal, 124; and Margaret Brooke's
    identity, 204, 206, 207
free trade, at Singapore, 42, 44
funding of Victorian science, 92–93
Funnell, William, 65
Furbish, Kate, 112

Galton, Francis, 103
gaze: of colonized and fellow colonizer,
    78, 83; confirmation of previous
    traveler's, 69–70; Western gendered,
    304n54
gender: and class, in *The Chersonese with the
    Gilding Off*, 168; femininity of
    Malayan colonial policy, 155–159; in
    imperial narratives, 10–20; and
    international relations, 233; and
    narrative voice, 3; in North's
    Recollections, 119–121; and politics of
    identity, 276, 277; and race, 271, 272;
    and self-definition, in *The Chersonese
    with the Gilding Off*, 168; in the service
    of imperialism, 75–78
genital mutilation, 257
geography, physical versus political, 143,
    144, 146
Geological Society (Britain), 95
George III, king of England, 111
George, Reuben, 200
Germany: botany in, 111, 112–113;
    imperialism of, 112, 136; passes
    overseas sexual offenses act, 225
Gilbert, Sir Davie, 103
Gilroy, Paul, 274
"going native," 75, 286n8
Golden Chersonese and the Way Thither, The
    (Bird), 11, 28, 149–154, 165, 167, 172,
    296n43; domesticity and joy in, 159–
    164; feminine cast of, 155
Golden Chersonese with the Gilding Off, The
    (Innes), 18, 28
Goldie, Terry, 289n72
Good Morning and Good Night (Brooke),
    202–204, 206, 208–209, 210, 212, 213
Gramsci, Antonio, 22
Great Britain, *see* Britain
greed, attributed to sultans of Brunei,
    194–195

Grimble, Ian, 248
Griswold, A. B., 248, 251, 252, 254
Gulf War, 299n51. *See also* Hussein,
    Saddam

Hahn, Emily, 200
Haraway, Donna, 277
Hardy, Thomas, 125
harem: of Louis Leonowens, at Chiang
    Mai, 243; politics of, in Siam, 233–
    234; as term, 302n32
Harfield, Alan, 281n35, 282n8
Harrison, Frederic, 69–70
Hartley, L. P., 206
Hawthorne, Nathaniel, 245, 247
Headhunters of Borneo, The (Bock), 67
head-hunting, 206
Headrick, Daniel R., 281n36
Heart of Darkness, The (Conrad), 81, 98,
    197, 218
Hébert, Lodovic, Marquis of Beauvoir,
    302n22
Helena (Forbes), 90
Hemsley, W. Botting, 101, 109, 120
Hennessey, John Pope, 201
hero: explorer as (*see* explorer-hero);
    White Rajah as, 190–191
Heussler, Robert, 166
hierarchy: in *The Chersonese with the Gilding
    Off*, 168; civil service, in Malaya, 168,
    170; in Siamese society, 253
history: imperial, 33, 58–59; literary, as
    cultural history, 8–9; spatial, 282n6
History of Java, The (Raffles), 65
*History of Sarawak under Its Two White Rajahs
    1839–1908*, 187
History of the Indian Archipelago (Crawfurd),
    65
HIV, and Thai prostitution, 224
Hofmeister, Wilhelm, 110
Holy Land, middle east as, 74, 97
Hong Kong, 42, 146, 149–150, 231,
    283n18, 285n47
Hooker, Jason, 95
Hooker, Sir Joseph, 95, 100, 103, 109, 115
Hooker, Sir William, 103, 109, 111, 113–
    114, 115
Hornaday, William, 67
Hose, Charles, 67
Hussein, Saddam, 281n30
Huxley, Thomas, 114

identity: alternative, Margaret Brooke's, 204, 206, 207–208; of British in Southeast Asia, 270; Eurasian, of Singapore, 283n21; female, in Forbes's *Insulinde*, 78–84; and location, 2–3; national, of Sarawak, 186, 188, 192, 201; politics of, and gender, 276, 277; unstable, 275
Illanuns, Brooke raid on, 218
Imperial Archive, The (Richards), 187
"imperial eye," 75; female, 88. *See also* gaze
Imperial Eyes (Pratt), 11
imperial histories, 33; conflicting, 58–59
imperialism, 292n49, 294n1, 294n2; as adventure, 29 (*see also* adventurism); American, 6, 221, 230, 293n72; British, 7–8, 12–13, 27–28, 29, 35–38, 221; Christianity in service of, 215, 218; and the consumer, 272, 274–275; Dutch, 27, 35, 36, 37, 52–57, 58, 136–137, 178, 179, 217, 286–287n17, 287n18; French, 221, 230, 302n22, 302n27; German, 112, 136; and metaphors of sexuality, 15–16; and the natural sciences, 64, 65–67, 91–99, 109–117; Portuguese, 27, 52, 58, 63, 124–125, 136, 221; and race/progress ideologies, 71; Sarawak as fantasy of, 190–196; Spanish, 136; and subjectivity, 10
Impromptus (Brooke), 199
In Darkest Africa (Stanley), 94
India, 7, 12, 22, 23, 51, 230, 233; British intervention in, 138, 140; colonial, and founding of Singapore, 36; versus Malaya, in British colonial rhetoric, 144–148; and nonintervention, 184; and the opium trade, 42; rebellion of 1857, 56, 115, 147; and the Straits Settlements, 40; supplies workers for Malaya, 145; tea industry in, 115; and trade route to China, 136
India Act of 1784, 138
Indian Archipelago, 3
Indian Civil Service, 148
Indochina, 136
Indonesia, 6, 26, 27, 28, 53, 177; identity of, 62–63. *See also* Java
infanticide, female, 257
Innes, Emily, 4, 12, 14, 17, 18, 25, 28, 46, 135, 162, 163–175, 205, 287n20

Innes, James, 162, 163, 169
Insulinde, 53, 54, 61. *See also* Dutch East Indies
Insulinde (Dutch translation of Wallace's *Malay Archipelago*), 65
Insulinde (Forbes), 60, 64, 77, 118, 119, 285n43; precursors to, 64–68; as social text, 69–74
Into the Heart of Borneo (O'Hanlon), 67
Iran, state control through opium in, 44
Ireland, travel narratives about, 127
isolation, 87
isolationism, 275

Jakarta, 23, 53. *See also* Batavia
James, Henry, 202, 213
James, William, 293n72
Jane Eyre (Brontë), 76
JanMohamed, Abdul, 21
Japan, 8, 23, 62, 183; Bird's travels to, 149, 150
Jardin du Roi (France), 110. *See also* Musée d'histoire naturelle
Java, 7, 42, 51, 53, 55, 58, 63, 136
Java, or How to Manage a Colony (Money), 55
Jews, in Singapore, 39
Johnson, Samuel, on female divines, 19
Johore (Malay State), 35, 36, 140
Jones, Mrs. (missionary's wife), 238
Journal of the Malaysian Branch of the Royal Asiatic Society, 282n9
Joy, in Bird's *Golden Chersonese*, 159–164

Kalimantan (Borneo), 177, 217. *See also* Borneo
Kaplan, Caren, 276
Karen (Thai tribe), 227
Karloff, Boris, 241
Katrak, Ketu, 305–306n7
Keats, John, 69
Keith, Annabella, 59. *See also* Forbes, Anna
Kerr, Deborah, 245
Kew (England), Royal Botanic Gardens at, 95, 108, 109, 111–117, 148; North Gallery, 100–101, 117
Kim (Kipling), 191
King and I, The (Rodgers and Hammerstein), 245, 255
Kingsley, Mary, 97–98, 122

Kinloch, Charles, 285n44
kongsi-Brooke conflict (1857), 214, 217–218
Krasner, James, 289n56
Kroller, Marie, 280n26
Kuala Lumpur, 23, 34, 140

Labuan, 177, 179; concubinage at, 201
Lady's Life in the Rocky Mountains, A (Bird), 158, 296n41
Lake Victoria, 94
Landon, Margaret, 239, 245, 280n27
Langbauer, Laurie, 21, 281n32
language: diversity of, within postcolonial nation-state, 62; ideological categories within, 273–274; place-names, 60–61; of Singapore, 283–284n23
Laos, 4, 5, 302n27
Lawrence, Gertrude, 245
Ledger, Charles, 116
Leonowens, Anna, 4, 12, 14–15, 17, 18, 25, 29, 46, 221–222; as author, in 1870s, 243–246, 303n51; biography and legend, 234–235; denounces slavery, 303n51; as sexual ethnographer, 233; on the Siamese royal harem, 246–256
Leonowens, Avis, 234, 240, 241, 243
Leonowens, Louis, 234, 240, 241, 243, 248, 257, 263, 264–265
Leonowens, Maj. Thomas Louis, 240, 303n45. See also Owens, Thomas Leon
Leonowens, Selina, 241
Letters from Sarawak; Addressed to a Child (McDougall), 190, 214
licenses, opium, at Singapore, 42, 43–44
Lichtenstein, Roy, 150
Light, Francis, 145, 269
Light, Lanoon, 270
Light, William, 269–270
Lindley Report, 111
Linnaean Society (England), 111
Linnaeus (Carl von Linné), 65
Linschoten His Discours into ye Easte & West Indies (Linschoten), 65
Livingstone, David, 94
Lloyd (Superintendant at Pangkor), 162–163
Lo, Joan, 200, 298n30
location, 6. See also place
Lockard, Craig, 298n26

London Daily Telegraph, and Stanley's expedition, 96
London Times, reviews Bird's Lady's Life in the Rocky Mountains, 158
Lord Jim (Conrad), 190, 191, 248
L'Ore, Siamese slave girl, 259, 261
Lost Property (Brooke), 201
Loudon, Jane Webb, 117
Low, Hugh, 149, 153, 156, 157, 163–171 passim, 180, 187, 194, 201, 269
Lyell, Charles, 114

McDougall, Bishop, 218
McDougall, Charley, 214
McDougall, Harriette, 3, 17, 18, 29, 190, 213
Madras (India), 136
Mai Noie, Siamese palace slave, 264
Malacca, 37, 38, 39, 137, 145, 152
malaria, 85, 116, 292n57
Malaya, 3–4, 12, 24, 27–28, 37, 46, 51; as construct, 137; imperial history of, 135–141; versus India, in British colonial rhetoric, 144–148; justice system, 19; rubber industry, 115
Malayan Civil Service, 141, 142, 148, 162–169
Malay Archipelago: as contact zone, 57–58; Dutch imperialism in, 52–57, 137; as name, 61; as naturalist's paradise, 74, 98, 114, 118, 123–124, 125; visited by North, 109
Malay Archipelago, the Land of the Orang-Utan and the Bird of Paradise, The (Wallace), 64–67, 68–74 passim, 124, 125, 126
Malay Peninsula, 5, 6, 11, 22, 28, 51; imperial history of, 135–141
"Malay Plot" of 1859, 214
Malays: Bird's view of, 151–152; in Brunei, 188; in The Chersonese with the Gilding Off, 172, 174; and the Civil Service, 148; construed to fit colonial needs, 299n50; and identity of Margaret Brooke, 206–209 (see also sympathy); of Indonesia, 55; in McDougall's Sketches, 217; and mining, 138; in Sarawak, 194; in Singapore, 35, 36, 38, 39; in Swettenham's accounts, 147; women, Brooke identifies with, 210
Malaysia, 5, 177, 283n23. See also Malay States

Malay Sketches (Swettenham), 143, 149
Malay States, 14, 36, 51, 137, 138, 232;
    British takeover of, 139–140, 294n10
male hegemony and imperial presence, 16
Mandell, Laura, 305n5
Mansfield, Lord Chief Justice, 128
Mansfield Park (Austen), 169
Maoists, Western, 279n11
Maoris, 90, 289n71, 289n72
mapping, 282n6; natural science as, 65;
    rhetorical, 26
Marianne North at Kew Gardens
    (Ponsonby), 101
Markham, Clements, 116
marriage: arranged, 257; in North's
    Recollections, 120, 121
masculinity, as power and control, 206.
    See also explorer-hero; femininity
maternal care and slavery, North on,
    129–131
Mattoon, Mrs. (missionary's wife), 238
*Max Havelaar; or, The Coffee Auctions of the
    Dutch Trading-Company* (Dekker), 60
Maxwell (Perak colonial), 155, 157
Maxwell (Resident of Fort Simanggang,
    Sarawak), 200, 202, 203
May-Peah, in *The Romance of the Harem*,
    260, 261
Melman, Billie, 11
Memmi, Albert, 21
Merrill, Lynn, 98
metropolis, 32; versus periphery,
    discursive perils of, 22–23
Mexia, Ynes, 112
middle east as Holy Land, 74, 97
Mikado, The (Gilbert and Sullivan), 246
Miller, Christopher, 21
Mills, Sara, 10, 11
Milton (Blake), 121
mimicry, 19, 22, 126, 193; Batesian, 293–
    294n78
mining, 138, 146
"Miranda complex, The" (Donaldson),
    77
miscegenation, 90, 201, 289n74
missionaries, 97, 214–215, 230, 238,
    300n77, 303n49
Missionary Travels (Livingstone), 94
"mixed-race" children, 90. *See also*
    Eurasians
Mohanty, Chandra and Satya, 21

Mohl, Hugo von, 110
Money, James W. B., 55
Mongkut, king of Siam, 15, 231–243
    passim, 252, 253–254, 257, 302n28,
    304n62; Yul Brynner enacts role of,
    304n53 (*see also King and I, The*)
monkeys, 129
Moon, Brenda, 291n34
moral development, and the feminine
    sphere, 72
Morgan, Susan, 1–3, 273
Morris, William, 202
Morson, Ian, 269
Morton, Peter, 92
Mountbatten, Lord Louis, 4
Muara (Borneo), coal mines at, 180
Mukah (Brunei), annexed by Sarawak,
    185, 187–188
Multatuli, *see* Dekker, Eduard Douwes
Murchison, Sir Roderick, 95
Murray, Capt. (Resident in Sungei
    Ujong), 152, 157
Murray, John, 152, 158
Musée d'histoire naturelle (France), 110
"Mutiny" of 1857 (India), 56, 115, 147,
    184, 217
My Life in Sarawak (Brooke), 199, 202–
    204, 205–208, 210, 212

Nageli, Carl W., 110
naming of places, 60–61
Nang Harm, *see* Siamese royal harem
Nanyang (Southeast Asia), 4
Napoleonic Wars, 55, 124, 136
"Narrating the Anti-Conquest" (Pratt),
    94
*Narrative of Travels on the Amazon and Rio
    Negro, A* (Wallace), 125
narrator, female, 3
Nation: reviews Bird's *Golden Chersonese*,
    150; reviews North's *Recollections*, 107;
    reviews *The Romance of the Harem*, 247
nationalism, 275
"native trade" in opium, 42
natural history, American discourse of,
    288n40. *See also* botany
Naturalist on the River Amazon, The (Bates),
    125–126
*Naturalist's Wanderings in the Eastern
    Archipelago, A* (Forbes), 60, 64, 67–68,
    72, 73, 82, 116

Natural Man: A Record from Borneo, A (Hose), 67

natural sciences, imperialism and, 64, 65–67, 91–99, 109–117

natural selection, 66, 126. *See also* evolution; social Darwinism

navy, British, 22, 179, 180, 182, 183, 297n12

Netherlands East Indies, *see* Dutch East Indies

newspapers, 290n3, 290n11; of Singapore and Hong Kong, intelligible to King Mongkut, 302n34; and Singapore tourism, 281n1; and travel narratives, 94–95, 96–97

Newton, Sir Isaac, 291n26

New York Herald, and Stanley's expedition, 96

New York Times, reviews *The Romance of the Harem*, 247

New Zealand, 89–90

nonintervention, rhetoric of, 138, 140, 141, 174

North, Catherine, *see* Symonds, Catherine (North)

North, Dudley, 291n26

North, Sir Francis, 291n26

North, Frederick, 102–103, 105, 113, 119

North, John, 291n26

North, Marianne, 3, 14, 17, 18, 27, 92, 99, 158, 205–206, 277, 290n17, 293n72; biography, 100–109; and the "happy life," 127–132; and network of botanists, 114; writes *Recollections*, 117, 118–123

North, Roger, 291n26

North Borneo Company, 180, 181, 238, 297n8

objectivity, masculinized, 132

O'Hanlon, Redmond, 67

"On Cinchona" (Dawson), 115

"On the Tendency of Varieties to Depart from the Original Type" (Wallace), 66

opium, 26, 139, 145, 180, 284n30, 284n34, 284n28, 284n29; and imperialist policy, 41–45; in Java, 286–287n17; Singapore's dependence on, 47

Ord, Governor (Singapore), 46

Orientalism, 15; of *The King and I*, 245; and sexuality, 301n9

Orientalism (Said), 13, 15, 25, 281n30

"Orientalism Reconsidered" (Said), 274

Origin of Species, The (Darwin), 66, 114

Other, primitive, 129. *See also* outsider

Outlines of Sarawak History under the Brooke Rajahs, 186

outsider, 208; Margaret Brooke as, 205; Emily Innes as, 168–169; Anna Leonowens as, 248, 305n80. *See also* Other

Owens, Thomas Leon, 240–241, 242. *See also* Leonowens, Maj. Thomas Louis

Oxford University Press, 24; Singapore branch, 60

pain and subjectivity, in Forbes's *Insulinde*, 84–88

Pall Mall Gazette, reviews North's paintings, 100

Palmerston, Lord (Viscount Henry John Temple), 183

Pangkor Engagement, 139, 141

Parliament, on the purpose of empire, 138

Parnell, Charles S., 293n74

Paterson, William, 94

patriarchal culture, 76, 77

Pattaya (Thailand), sex industry at, 222

Payne, Robert, 298n30

Pedro, Dom, ruler of Brazil, 124

Penang, 38, 39, 40, 54, 139, 145, 155

Perak (Malay State), 139, 140, 141, 149, 151, 153, 162, 164; debt slavery banned at, 163

Peru, restricts botanical exports, 116

Peter Pan (Barrie), 191, 197

Philippines, 4, 6, 26, 136, 294n1

Phongpaichit, Pasuk, 24, 246, 301n15

Phuket (Thailand), 269–270; prostitution at, 222, 223, 227, 228

"pirates," 178, 183, 194–195, 297n2; head-bounty for, 178, 179

place, 3, 7, 8; contact zones, 57; feminized "east," 224; knowing one's, versus "leaving home," 274–275; metropolitan, 22–23, 32; naming of, 60–61; past as elsewhere, 207; and presumed expertise of critics from former colonies, 20–25; scientific,

place *(continued)*
  Malay Archipelago as, 68, 74, 123–
  124, 125; Swettenham's representation
  of Malaya, 143–144; in Victorian
  natural sciences, 92–93
polygamy, in Siam, 228, 229, 233, 254,
  257, 301n18, 301n20, 303n49
Ponsonby, Laura, 101
Portuguese imperialism, 27, 52, 58, 63,
  124–125, 136, 221
postcolonial studies, canon of, 21
Potsdam Conference of 1945, 4
Pratt, Anne, 117
Pratt, Mary Louise, 11, 15, 57, 65, 94, 117–
  118, 125, 280n24, 289n54
primitivism, 124–125, 126, 129, 130–131,
  144, 210
Principles of Scientific Botany (Schleiden), 110
Pringle, Robert, 298n26, 300n76
profit, 148, 195, 273
progress: of human race, confirmed by
  primitivism, 70; myths of, 20, 21, 23;
  and prostitution, in Thailand, 225–
  226; and race, 71
prostitution, in Thailand, 222–228, 246,
  256, 257
Protected States (Malaya), 148, 151. *See
  also* Federated States
"Protector of Chinese" at Singapore,
  285n39
Pryer, Ada, 20, 181
purity, as false desire, 275

Quebec Conference of 1943, 4
Queen of the Head-Hunters (Brooke), 201
Queries, Past, Present and Future (Brooke),
  201–202
quiet, 159–160
Quillin, Ellen, 112
quinine, 116, 292n57, 292n59, 292–293n60

racial impurity, 201–202. *See also*
  miscegenation
racism, 9, 208; among Thais, 227; used
  to discredit colonialism, 173
Raffles, Sir Stamford, 35–36, 37, 54, 56–
  57, 65, 269; praise for, 282–283n15
Rama I, king of Siam, 230
Rama IV, *see* Mongkut, king of Siam
Ramarathnam, Jyotsna, 281n31

Rebellion of 1857 (India), 56, 115, 147,
  184, 217
"Recollections" (Brooke), 187
*Recollections of a Happy Life: Being the
  Autobiography of Marianne North*
  (North), 103, 106, 109, 117, 118–123,
  128, 277
Reece, Robert H. W., 190, 210, 299n55
religion and science, in travel narratives
  of Africa, 97
repetition, visual, as confirmation, 69–70
research funding, Victorian, 92–93
Resident system, British, in Malay
  States, 139–141, 142, 155, 156, 164
Revolt in Paradise (Tantri), 270
rhetorical mapping, 26
rhododendrons, Himalayan, 115
rice, replaced by tourism, in Thailand,
  225
Rich, Adrienne, 306n16
Richards, Thomas, 187
riding dress, Bird's, 158–159
Ridley, Henry, 115
Riffenburgh, Beau, 290n3, 290n11
Robinson Crusoe (Defoe), 190
Romance of the Harem, The (Leonowens),
  29–30, 222, 233; accuracy of, 249–252;
  critical responses to, 246–249, 252;
  publication history, 244–246
Rosaldo, Renato, 212
Royal Botanic Gardens, Kew (England),
  95, 108, 109, 111–117, 148; North
  Gallery, 100–101, 117
Royal Colonial Institute, 142, 148, 166
Royal Geographical Society, 89, 95
Royal Navy, British, 22, 179, 180, 182,
  183, 297n12
rubber, 27, 115, 148, 180
Rubingh, Michael, 293–294n78
Rule of Darkness, The (Brantlinger), 13, 74
Rungeah, in *The Romance of the Harem*, 260

Sabah (Borneo), 177, 181. *See also* British
  North Borneo
Sabine, Sir Edward, 103
sacrifice, 86, 87
Said, Edward, 4, 13, 15, 17, 21, 25, 95, 274,
  276, 281n30, 292n49, 301n9
Saigon, visited by Bird, 150
St. Andrew's Cathedral, Singapore, 46
St. John, Spenser, 217

Sarawak, 3, 6, 12, 14, 24, 28–29, 46, 164, 177, 181–186; as Brooke's imaginative community, 207–208; court histories of, 298n30; and imperial fantasy, 190–196; in the 20th century, 300n74

Sarawak Civil Service, 201–202

Sarawak Protectorate Treay of 1888, 186

sarong, wearing of, by colonizers, 75, 286n8

satellite gardens, 114, 130

Saturday Review, reviews Swettenham's Malay Sketches, 143

Scarry, Elaine, 84, 87, 289n70

Schleiden, M. J., 110

Schwartzkopf, Gen. Norman, paeans to, 299n51

Scidmore, Elizabeth, 34, 44

science, and imperialism, 91–99

Scotland, travel narratives about, 127

secret societies, Chinese, at Singapore, 285n40

Selangor (Malay State), 140, 141, 151, 162; James Innes magistrate at, 164

Sepoy "Mutiny" of 1857 (India), 56, 115, 147, 184, 217

sex industry, Thai, 222–228, 246, 256, 257, 301n5, 301n7

sexuality: as imperialist metaphor, 15–16, 280n26; travel narratives as discourse of desire, 118, 119

sexual slavery, 15, 228; and imperialism, 301n15

Shaw, Capt. (lieutenant governor of Malacca), 152, 156, 157

Shelley, Percy Bysshe, 72

Shohat, Ella, 304n54

Siam, 4, 5, 6, 12, 15, 24, 26, 29–30, 46, 51, 137; French interest in, 302n22

Siamese royal harem, 236–237, 238; breakup of, 303n36

"sidekick" model of imperial narratives, 17–18

Sikhs, as British police in Malaya, 146

Singapore, 6, 12, 22, 23, 24, 26, 31–48, 51, 137, 139, 155, 169, 180; Bird visits, 150; business lobby at, 146; Chinese at, 283n22, 284n25, 284n33, 284–285n37, 285n39, 285n40; colonial depictions of, 32–35; as consumer marketplace, 285n47; demography of, 38–41; economic history of, 45–48; as

Eurasian, 283n21; founding and imperial history of, 34, 35–38, 282n8; and Hong Kong, 283n18; language of, 283–284n23; Leonowens recruited from, 238; as Straits Settlement, 282n12; trade interests at, and British policy, 282n13; Victorian detractors, 285n44

Singh, D. S. Ranjit, 297n5

Sketches of Our Life in Sarawak (McDougall), 214–218

sketching, gender, and class, 107–108

Skinner, Mrs., 105

Slatkin, Heidi, 305n4

slavery, 128–131, 244, 253, 303n51, 303n52; in Brazil, 125; and colonial wives, 81; debt, 148, 163, 170, 229; illegal under English law, 257; sexual, 15, 228, 301n15; and the Siamese royal harem, 251–252, 253, 254–255; and the sugar trade, 293n75; of Thai prostitutes, 223

Smayatee, in The Romance of the Harem, 260

Smith, Malcolm, 249, 254, 304n62

social Darwinism, 71, 73, 74, 97, 129; in Forbes's Insulinde, 76

Society for Promoting Christian Knowledge, 214

"Some Experiences of Colonial Life" (Cator lecture), 166

Some Glimpses of Life in the Far East (Thomson), 147

Somerset, James, 128

Song Ong Siang, 284–285n37

Southeast Asia, 3–5, 294n1, 294n2; versus Africa, in rhetoric of travel, 95, 97; definition and identity in, 269–271; and the Napoleonic Wars, 136; Singapore as hub of, 45–48

South East Asia Command (SEAC), 4

Soviet Union, 31

Spanish-American War, 6

Spanish imperialism, 136

Sparrman, Anders, 94

spatial history, 33, 282n6

specimens, scientific, 66, 81

Spectator: reviews Bird's Golden Chersonese, 150; reviews Bird's A Lady's Life in the Rocky Mountains, 296n41; reviews Forbes's Insulinde, 78, 84

Speke, John Hanning, 94

spheres of influence, colonial, 136, 137
spinsterhood, Victorian, 100
Spivak, Gayatri, 21, 22, 76, 256, 305n72
Spurr, David, 275–276
stabilization, social, through scientific taxonomy, 98
Stafford, Robert, 95–96
Stanley, Sir Henry Morton, 94, 96
Stevens, Wallace, 38, 126
Stoddart, Anna M., 296n42, 296n43
Stoler, Ann, 7–8
Stoppard, Tom, 271
Stowe, Harriet Beecher, 244
Straits of Malacca, 136, 178, 269
Straits Settlements, 6, 40, 47, 138, 139, 141, 145, 269, 282n12; removed from Indian administration, 146–147. See also Malacca; Malay States; Penang; Singapore
subaltern, 22
subjectivity: in Bird's Golden Chersonese, 157; in Brooke narratives, 202–209; in Forbes's Insulinde, 78–84; gendered, and the "happy life," 127–132; and pain, 84–88; Victorian constructions of, 12; women's, and regional histories, 13
Suez Canal, 139, 141
sugar, and slavery, 293n75
Suleri, Sara, 12, 21, 107
Sumatra, 4, 51, 137
Sungei Ujong (Malay State), 151, 152, 157
Swettenham, Frank, 37, 135, 141–143, 149, 151, 152, 155, 161, 166, 172, 174, 192, 193, 269
Swinburne, Algernon Charles, 213
Swinburne, Maj. Paul, 157
Symonds, Catherine (North), 102, 106
Symonds, John Addington, 102
sympathy, 147–148, 152, 155, 157, 172, 173–174, 193, 197, 210–211; disinterested, 174–175

Tam Kin Ching (King Mongkut's agent), 238
Tantri, K'tut, 270
Tarling, Nicholas, 297n5, 297n10
taste, good, 157–158
Taylor, Jean Gelman, 24, 286n6, 289n74
tea: Chinese exports of, 145; Indian industry in, 115

technology, 23; and colonial activities, 294n1; and imperialism, 281n36, 281n37; versus moral development, 72
telegraph, extended to Singapore, 141
Tess of the d'Urbervilles (Hardy), 125
Thailand, 4, 5; sex industry in, 222–228, 246, 256, 257, 301n5, 301n7; shaping of, as nation, 302n26; unconquered, 230. See also Siam
Thieng, Lady (head wife of King Mungkot), 258, 305n80
Thiselton-Dyer, W. T., 115
Thomas, Nicholas, 30
Thomson, John, 147
Three Seal Laws (Siam), 229
Timor, 58, 63; edenic, 78–80. See also East Timor
tin mining, 27, 138–139, 146, 180
tourism, 290n17; discourse of, 295n20; and sex industry, 222, 301n5; Singapore's, after Fay punishment, 281n1. See also travel narratives
travel narratives, 11; and discourse of sexuality, 118, 119; as gendered discourses, 15; as quest romances, 93–95; "scientific," 69–70, 93; universalist argument for, 247
Travels into Muscovy . . . and Part of the East-Indies (Bruyn), 65
Travels in West Africa (Kingsley), 97–98
Treaty of Nanking, 42
Treaty of Vienna, 136
Trocki, Carl, 24, 44
"True Story of Anna Leonowens, The" (Bristowe), 240
Tunku Chi, 174–175
Tuptim, Siamese bricklayer, 259–260
Turnbull, C. M., 282n8, 284n24
Turnbull, Mary, 4
Twining, Elizabeth, 117

Unbeaten Tracks in Islands of the Far East (modern edition of Forbes's Insulinde), 60
Unbeaten Tracks in Japan (Bird), 149, 150, 280n26, 295n29
Unfederated States (Malaya), 140
United States, see American imperialism

Van der Veur, Paul, 286n7
Victoria, queen of England, 149, 186

Vietnam, 4, 5, 6, 51, 302n27
Vietnam War, 4, 226
Villette (Brontë), 169
vision as revision, trope of, 69–70
Viswanathan, Gauri, 8–9, 21
VOC, *see* Dutch East India Company
voices, Siamese women's, articulated
    through Leonowens, 256–265. *See also*
    subjectivity
vote, women's right to, 90
Voyage Round the World, A (Funnell), 65
vulnerability, 87

Wagner, Ulla, 193, 297n16
Wales, travel narratives about, 127
Walker, Capt., 157
Wallace, Alfred Russel, 64–67, 68, 73,
    95, 108, 109, 114, 118, 125, 131, 287n24,
    289n56
Walpole, Mrs., raises Leonowens, 239
Wanderings in the Great Forests of Borneo
    (Beccari), 67
Wanne, daughter of concubine punished
    for gambling, 263–265
Ware, Vron, 257
West Indies, 23
"white," 271, 272
Winichakul, Thongchai, 24
Wodehouse, Lord, 184
women: Anglo-Indian, 107–108; as
    audience for Forbes's *Insulinde*, 71–72;
backlash against liberation of, and
    prostitution, 226; as consumers of
    the east, 46, 48; European, in North's
    Recollections, 120; Malay, in Brooke's
    narratives, 206–209, 210; naturalists,
    99, 291n28; peripheral in Sarawak's
    official myth, 197, 198, 199, 201–202;
    rights curtailed under King Rama I
    of Siam, 229, 301n18; of science, and
    North's "happy life," 127–132;
    Siamese royal harem as community
    of, 246, 256–263; slave mothers,
    North on, 129–131; susceptibility to
    malaria, 116; in Thai culture, 222–
    229; as travelers, 78, 83, 105, 161–162
*Women's Orients: English Women and the
    Middle East, 1818-1918* (Melman), 11
World Encompassed, The (Drake), 65
World Neighbors, 281n37
Wright, L. R., 184, 297n5
Wright, Lawrence, 271
writing as political action, in Bird, 159–
    160
Wyatt, David K., 301n17, 304n58

Yeats, W. B., 293n74
Yong, C. F., 285n37
Yong, Paul, 24, 300n76

Zed Press, 23
Zeller, Suzanne, 91

About the Author

Susan Morgan is a faculty affiliate of the Women's Studies Program and a professor of English at Miami University in Oxford, Ohio. She is the author of *Sisters in Time: Imagining Gender in Nineteenth-Century Fiction* and *In the Meantime: Character and Perception in Jane Austen's Fiction*. She is the editor of Anna Leonowens's *The Romance of the Harem* and Marianne North's *Recollections of a Happy Life*, vol. 1.